Law, Governance and Technology Series

Volume 76

The *Law, Governance and Technology Series* is intended to attract manuscripts arising from an interdisciplinary approach in law, artificial intelligence and information technologies. The idea is to bridge the gap between research in IT law and IT-applications for lawyers developing a unifying techno-legal perspective. The series will welcome proposals that have a fairly specific focus on problems or projects that will lead to innovative research charting the course for new interdisciplinary developments in law, legal theory, and law and society research as well as in computer technologies, artificial intelligence and cognitive sciences. In broad strokes, manuscripts for this series may be mainly located in the fields of the Internet law (data protection, intellectual property, Internet rights, etc.), Computational models of the legal contents and legal reasoning, Legal Information Retrieval, Electronic Data Discovery, Collaborative Tools (e.g. Online Dispute Resolution platforms), Metadata and XML Technologies (for Semantic Web Services), Technologies in Courtrooms and Judicial Offices (E-Court), Technologies for Governments and Administrations (E-Government), Legal Multimedia, and Legal Electronic Institutions (Multi-Agent Systems and Artificial Societies).

Nadia Pocher

Crypto-Asset Ecosystems and the EU Anti-Money Laundering Framework

Law and Technology Perspectives

Springer

Nadia Pocher
SnT - Interdisciplinary Centre
for Security, Reliability and Trust
University of Luxembourg
Luxembourg, Luxembourg

ISSN 2352-1902 ISSN 2352-1910 (electronic)
Law, Governance and Technology Series
ISBN 978-3-031-94697-4 ISBN 978-3-031-94698-1 (eBook)
https://doi.org/10.1007/978-3-031-94698-1

This Springer imprint is published by the registered company Springer Nature Switzerland AG
The registered company address is: Gewerbestrasse 11, 6330 Cham, Switzerland

Curiosity will conquer fear
even more than bravery will.

—James Stephens

Acknowledgements

This book is largely based on the outcomes of my PhD research conducted between 2019 and 2023 at the Autonomous University of Barcelona, the Alma Mater Studiorum University of Bologna, and KU Leuven, within the Law, Science and Technology Joint Doctorate—Rights of the Internet of Everything.[1]

I could not have completed my doctoral journey without the unwavering support of my main supervisor, Prof. Carles Górriz—I am deeply grateful for his kindness, guidance, and warm encouragement in pursuing this publication. I am also thankful to Prof. Monica Palmirani, for her passion and resilience in coordinating the doctoral program, and for believing in the value of my work. To my PhD colleagues and friends goes a huge thank you for sharing this unforgettable experience with me.

As I was taking my first steps as an interdisciplinary researcher, I was blessed with the opportunity of collaborating with brilliant experts. Working with them helped me discover what can be achieved at the crossroads between Law and Technology—and, perhaps most importantly, how incredibly fulfilling it can be. My gratitude goes to my co-authors Prof. Stefano Ferretti (University of Bologna and University of Urbino Carlo Bo), Prof. Andreas Veneris (University of Toronto), and my friend and colleague Dr. Mirko Zichichi.

I am also truly grateful to the reviewers and the committee members of my doctoral defence, held at the University of Bologna on 31 March 2023. Their constructive feedback helped me improve my work tremendously. The suggestions I could not integrate in this publication will definitely guide my work in the upcoming years. In particular, my heartfelt thanks go to Prof. Louis de Koker (La Trobe University) for his support and our insightful conversations.

[1] The LAST-JD-RIoE was funded under the Marie Skłodowska-Curie Actions, Innovative Training Networks, European Joint Doctorates, Grant Agreement No 814177 EU Horizon 2020. My doctoral dissertation is available as Pocher, N. (2023). *Distributed ledger technologies between anonymity and transparency: AML/CFT regulation of cryptocurrency ecosystems in the EU*. PhD thesis, Alma Mater Studiorum Università di Bologna, KU Leuven, Universitat Autònoma de Barcelona. https://doi.org/10.48676/unibo/amsdottorato/10659.

Since May 2023, my exploration of the Law and Technology research field continues as postdoctoral researcher at the Finatrax (Digital Financial Services and Cross-Organisational Digital Transformations) research group at the Interdisciplinary Centre for Security, Reliability and Trust (SnT) of the University of Luxembourg.[2] For his mentorship and exemplary openness to cutting-edge interdisciplinary research, I would like to warmly thank my supervisor Prof. Gilbert Fridgen. Being part of Finatrax is a constant reminder to look for research inspiration also beyond the more straightforward and beaten paths.

I am also more than grateful to my fantastic Finatrax colleagues and co-authors. In particular, I would like to mention Martin Brennecke, Dr. Muriel Frank, Dr. Alexandra Höß, and Dr. Johannes Sedlmeir. Thank you—not only for sharing with me your extraordinary skills and expertise, but above all for letting me witness your passion for such diverse and fascinating research topics and methods.

Completing my doctoral journey and planning the following steps required considerable resilience, determination, and perseverance. But nothing would have been, nor would be, the same without the warm affection and encouragement of a few amazing people. As usual in life, some of them come and go. My special thanks go to those who stayed—and to those who, though our paths crossed much more recently, make it feel like they have always been there.

Words simply cannot express my gratitude to my parents and my brother, to the rest of my family, to my friends and loved ones—you know who you are, but I will make sure to remind you. Last but not least, to my wonderful partner, the best companion I could ever wish for, and my greatest source of laughter, joy, and endless inspiration. Thank you all—for never ceasing to evolve with me through the roads of life. You are and always will be the brightest part of my days.

Ville de Luxembourg, Luxembourg Nadia Pocher
March 2025

---

[2] The work to update and finalise this book for publication was supported by the Luxembourg National Research Fund (FNR) and PayPal, PEARL grant reference 13342933/Gilbert Fridgen, as well as by grant reference NCER22/IS/16570468/NCER-FT (CryptoReg).

Contents

1 Introduction and Methodology 1
1.1 Introduction 1
1.2 Research Objectives and Methods 3
1.3 Methodological Building Blocks 6
1.4 Structure of the Book 10
References 12

2 Phenomenology of Crypto-Asset Ecosystems 17
2.1 Introduction 17
2.1.1 From Distributed Consensus to the Internet of Value 18
2.1.2 What Is the Internet of Money? 20
2.2 On a Hunt for Definitions Between Tokens and Crypto-Assets 21
2.2.1 Terminological Notes from an EU and FATF Perspective 22
2.2.2 Tokens: Bridging Techno-Legal Definitional Gaps 25
2.2.3 Taxonomy Initiatives 27
2.2.4 The Regulatory Role of Tokens 30
2.2.5 Cryptocurrencies and Qualification as Legal Tender 31
2.3 The Accountability Conundrum: Architectures and Transactions 34
2.3.1 Crypto-Asset Ecosystems: Stakeholders and Socio-Technical Traits 34
2.3.2 Multi-Layered Dynamics: Remarks on Access Control and Governance 36
2.3.3 Decentralisation and Non-Centralisation: A Matter of Degree 37
2.4 Theory and Practice at Ever-Changing Crossroads 40
2.4.1 Disintermediation Riddles 40
2.4.2 The (R)evolution of (Global) Stablecoins and Digital Fiat Money 42
2.5 Backing Phenomenology with Conceptual Frameworks 44
2.5.1 Regulation and Crypto-Asset Ecosystems: Reaching Beyond the Complexity 44

2.5.2 The Crypto-Asset Sphere as an Ecosystem of Socio-Technical (Eco)systems 45
2.6 Conclusions 47
References 48

3 Disintermediation and Anonymity 53
3.1 Introduction 53
3.1.1 Encryption, Cyberspace Anonymity and Crypto-Assets 55
3.1.2 Defining the Scope of the Conundrum 57
3.2 Making Sense of Anonymity and Transparency: Two Sides of the Same (Crypto)Coin 59
3.2.1 Conceptual Granularity of Anonymity 61
3.2.2 Context-Specificity of Anonymity: Identifiability and Identification 62
3.2.3 User Anonymity and Ledger Transparency 64
3.2.4 Transparency of Operations and Financial Transparency 66
3.2.5 Pseudonymity and Monetary Fungibility 67
3.2.6 Observer-Dependency and Broadness of the Notion of Anonymity 72
3.2.7 Contextualisation: Privacy and Anonymity 74
3.2.8 Anonymity and Transparency: A Paradox or a Combination? 76
3.3 The Uptake of Enhanced Disintermediation, Atomicity and Impacts on Accountability 77
3.3.1 Atomic Cross-Chain Swaps and Multi-Layered Protocols 78
3.3.2 Peer-to-Peer Transactions and the FATF 80
3.3.3 Self-hosted Wallets and Decentralised Custody 81
3.3.4 Decentralised Exchanges and Decentralised Finance 83
3.4 Conclusions 86
References 87

4 Obfuscation and Traceability 95
4.1 Introduction 95
4.1.1 Transaction Obfuscation and the Money Laundering Process 96
4.1.2 Anonymity as a Red Flag Indicator 99
4.2 Methods to Obfuscate Financial Flows and the Role of Traceability 102
4.2.1 Anonymity Enhanced Currencies 105
4.2.2 Four AEC Use Cases 107
4.2.3 Crypto-Mixing: The First Type of Crypto-Cleansing 110
4.2.4 Users and a Diversified Bundle of 'Best' Practices 112
4.2.5 Network-Level Anonymity-Enhancements: On-Chain and Off-Chain Layers 112

4.3 Intelligence Strategies: Following Funds Across the Ecosystems 114
4.3.1 Blockchain Forensics: The Unfolding of Different Techniques 115
4.3.2 Analysis of the Transaction Network and the Role of Clustering 116
4.3.3 Machine Learning-Based Approaches to Anomaly Detection 119
4.4 An Accountability-Based Approach to a Socio-Technical Conundrum 122
4.4.1 Obfuscation Red Flags and Crypto-Asset Forensics 123
4.4.2 The Multi-Layered Nature of Accountability in the Crypto-Asset Sphere 125
4.5 Conclusions 127
References 128

5 AML/CFT and Crypto-Assets: EU Law and Global Standards 135
5.1 Introduction 135
5.1.1 Ratio and Evolution of AML/CFT Regimes 136
5.1.2 What About Crypto-Assets? The Dark Web and the Silk Road 138
5.1.3 The Rise and Fall of Darknet Markets and the Present Day 140
5.1.4 Multi-Layered Efforts and Global Financial Standards 143
5.2 International Standards and the Financial Action Task Force 145
5.2.1 The FATF and Virtual Assets: Definitions and Timeline 147
5.2.2 The Risk-Based Approach and Crypto Regulated Entities: The FATF and the EU 149
5.2.3 An Extensive Array of Obligations: The FATF and the EU 152
5.2.4 From the FATF Standards to Regulatory and Technical Standardisation 155
5.3 The EU AML/CFT Regime for Crypto-Asset Transactions 158
5.3.1 The Involvement of EU Law: From Harmonisation to the 2021 AML Package 159
5.3.2 The EU-Wide Rulebook Under Regulation (EU) 2024/1624 162
5.3.3 Regulation (EU) 2024/1620 and the New AML Authority 163
5.3.4 EU Law, International Standards, and AMLA's RTSs 165
5.4 The Crypto Travel Rule and Active Cooperation 168
5.4.1 The Travel Rule: FATF Recommendation 16 and Regulation (EU) 2015/847 168
5.4.2 The Advent of the Crypto Travel Rule: Recent Evolutions 170
5.4.3 Regulation (EU) 2023/1113: Self-Hosted Addresses and Other Debates 173

5.4.4 Active Cooperation and the Challenge of Attribution vis-à-vis Disintermediation ... 175
5.5 Conclusions ... 178
References ... 179

6 Trade-Offs in Central Bank Digital Currencies ... 187
6.1 Introduction ... 187
6.2 Overview on Central Bank Digital Currencies ... 189
6.2.1 CBDC Typology and Drivers ... 190
6.2.2 History of Domestic and Cross-Border CBDC Projects ... 191
6.3 The Impacts of CBDC Design Choices ... 196
6.3.1 What Type of Ledger and What Distribution Model? ... 196
6.3.2 What Type of Wallet? ... 199
6.3.3 How Can End-User Identity Be Managed? ... 200
6.3.4 Can the CBDC Be Transferred Offline? ... 201
6.3.5 Are Transactions and/or Accounts Tiered? ... 202
6.3.6 The Public-Private Interplay ... 203
6.4 AML/CFT Considerations in the CBDC Domain ... 205
6.4.1 CBDCs and Limits to the Flow of Cash ... 206
6.4.2 The Privacy and Data Protection Conundrum ... 209
6.4.3 The Competence for AML/CFT Compliance ... 211
6.5 Privacy vs. Transparency: The Topical Role of Trade-Offs ... 212
6.5.1 The Role of Privacy-Enhancing Technologies ... 213
6.5.2 Classifying Embedded Trade-Offs ... 215
6.6 Conclusions ... 220
References ... 221

7 Techno-Regulatory Standards and 'Through Design' Approaches ... 231
7.1 Introduction ... 231
7.1.1 Technology- vs. Individual Case-Based AML/CFT Regulation ... 232
7.1.2 Categorising Impacts and the Sandbox Model ... 233
7.2 A Regulatory Methodology for the Crypto-Asset Space ... 236
7.2.1 (Lack of) Accountability and the Teleological Approach ... 237
7.2.2 Managing the Risk of Overfitting: Rules- and Principles- Based Approaches ... 239
7.2.3 The Impacts of Disintermediation on Regulatory Methodology ... 241
7.2.4 Identifying the Risks: Rules-Based Indicators ... 244
7.2.5 Ranking the Risks: The Value of Taxonomies ... 247
7.3 From 'Code is Law' to 'Through Design' Approaches ... 248
7.3.1 When the 'Law' Meets 'Code', Perhaps on a Blockchain ... 249
7.3.2 Placing the Debate Within the Crypto-Asset Domain ... 251
7.3.3 Toward a Flexible Understanding of 'Code Is/As Law' ... 252
7.3.4 Regulation-Enabled Compliance Through Design ... 255

7.4 'Through Design' Techno-Regulatory Standards 257
7.4.1 'Embedded Compliance' Between (Dis)intermediation and Institutional Adoption 258
7.4.2 From 'Regulated Self-Regulation' to 'Polycentric Co-Regulation' 260
7.4.3 From 'Law + Technology' to Techno-Regulatory Standards 264
7.5 Use Case: CBCD-Based Machine-to-Machine Payments 265
7.5.1 Applying 'Trade-Offs Through Design' 266
7.5.2 A Preliminary Model of Techno-Regulatory Integration 269
7.6 The Intervention of EU Law: Notes on Legitimacy and Effectiveness 270
7.6.1 Legitimacy and the Need for Uniformity 271
7.6.2 Effectiveness: Standards and Flexibility 'Through Design' 273
7.6.3 The Role of the EU in Setting Techno-Regulatory Standards 274
7.7 Conclusions 275
References 277

8 Concluding Remarks 285
8.1 Anonymity and an Unwarranted Double Standard 285
8.2 Anonymity-Transparency Trade-Offs in Crypto-Asset Socio-Technical Ecosystems 287
8.3 A Holistic Approach to a Risk-Based Taxonomy Effort 290
8.4 Polycentric Techno-Regulatory Standardisation in the EU 292
8.5 A 'Regulation-Enabled Compliance Through Design' Regime 294
8.6 Final Remarks 296
Reference 297

List of Abbreviations

AEC	Anonymity Enhanced Currency
AI	Artificial Intelligence
AML	Anti-Money Laundering
AMLA	Anti-Money Laundering Authority
AMLD	Anti-Money Laundering Directive
BCBS	Basel Committee on Banking Supervision
BIS	Bank for International Settlements
BSA	Bank Secrecy Act
CASP	Crypto-Asset Service Provider
CBDC	Central Bank Digital Currency
CDD	Customer Due Diligence
CEX	Centralised Exchange
CFT	Countering the Financing of Terrorism
CIoT	Consumer Internet of Things
CJEU	Court of Justice of the European Union
CPF	Countering the Financing of Proliferation
CPMI	Committee on Payments and Markets Infrastructure
CT	Confidential Transactions
DAG	Directed Acyclic Graph
DeFi	Decentralised Finance
DEX	Decentralised Exchange
DLT	Distributed Ledger Technology
DNFBP	Designated Non-Financial Businesses and Professions
EBA	European Banking Authority
EC	European Commission
ECB	European Central Bank
EMD	Electronic Money Directive
EMD2	Electronic Money Directive 2
ESAs	European Supervisory Authorities
ESMA	European Securities and Markets Authority
FATF	Financial Action Task Force

FIU	Financial Intelligence Unit
FSB	Financial Stability Board
FTR	Fund Transfers Regulation
GAT	Graph Attention Network
GCN	Graph Convolutional Network
GDPR	General Data Protection Regulation
HKMA	Hong Kong Monetary Authority
I2P	Invisible Internet Project
IASB	International Accounting Standards Board
ICO	Initial Coin Offering
IMF	International Monetary Fund
IoM	Internet of Money
IOSCO	International Organisation of Securities Commissions
IoT	Internet of Things
IoV	Internet of Value
IP	Internet Protocol
IS	Information Systems
ISO	International Standardisation Organisation
ITIN	International Token Identification Number
ITS	Implementing Technical Standard
ITSA	International Token Standardisation Association
ITU	International Telecommunication Union
KYC	Know Your Customer
LEI	Legal Entity Identifier
M2M	Machine to Machine
MiCAR	Markets in Crypto-Assets Regulation
MSB	Money Service Business
NFT	Non-Fungible Tokens
OFAC	Office of Foreign Assets Control
OSINT	Open-Source Intelligence
OSP	Online Service Provider
P2P	Peer to Peer
PCN	Payment Channel Network
PET	Privacy Enhancing Technology
PF	Proliferation Financing
PoC	Proof of Concept
PoS	Proof of Stake
PoW	Proof of Work
PPP	Public-Private Partnership
PSD	Payment Services Directive
PSD2	Payment Services Directive 2
PSP	Payment Services Provider
RBA	Risk-Based Approach
RTS	Regulatory Technical Standard
SAR	Suspicious Activity Report

SE	Secure Element
SRA	Supranational Risk Assessment
SSM	Single Supervisory Mechanism
STR	Suspicious Transaction Report
STS	Socio-Technical System
TEE	Trusted Execution Environment
TEU	Treaty on the European Union
TFEU	Treaty on the Functioning of the European Union
TOR	The Onion Router
TT	Trustworthy Technologies
TTF	Token Taxonomy Framework
TTI	Token Taxonomy Initiative
TXID	Transaction ID
UN	United Nations
UTXO	Unspent Transaction Output
VA	Virtual Assets
VASP	Virtual Asset Service Provider
VC	Virtual Currency
VPN	Virtual Private Network
WMD	Weapons of Mass Destruction
XML	Extensible Markup Language
ZKP	Zero-Knowledge Proof
ZK-SNARK	Zero Knowledge Succinct Non-Interactive Argument

Chapter 1
Introduction and Methodology

1.1 Introduction

The genesis block of the Bitcoin blockchain was mined in January 2009 and marked a decisive change in the way monetary transactions are envisioned. Building on years of research in distributed systems and cryptography, the Bitcoin whitepaper suggested not only new mechanisms to handle the drawbacks of traditional payment means, but also seemingly safe alternatives to intermediation.[1] The consequent blockchain hype inspired the idea of an alternative global economy in which Internet users can take part directly through an economic layer embedded into the web.[2] This disintermediated exchange of value on distributed ledgers was made possible by peer-to-peer (P2P) transfers and by the creation of digital representations of (physical or non-physical) assets or rights, the so-called tokenisation.[3]

When compared to the level of intermediation within the traditional financial system, this setup shows a conceptual disruption. Hence, it is not surprising that the advent of blockchain and distributed ledger technologies (DLTs) had global repercussions that are challenging to grasp in their entirety. Although blockchain-based solutions are now deployed in a vast range of industries, their first roots were in the financial world, where the term Internet of Money (IoM) was coined to label the interplay between individuals and disintermediated monetary transactions.[4] Meanwhile, the concept of ledger transparency as implemented in Bitcoin generated

[1] Nakamoto (2008).

[2] Swan (2015); Antonopoulos (2017b).

[3] Herian (2019); Werbach (2019).

[4] Antonopoulos (2016, 2017a).

N. Pocher, *Crypto-Asset Ecosystems and the EU Anti-Money Laundering Framework*, Law, Governance and Technology Series 76,
https://doi.org/10.1007/978-3-031-94698-1_1

the (debated) opinion that a public display of transactions in combination with redundant storage can replace the need to trust individual third-parties.[5]

Despite the deep fascination that they caused, these concepts and their applications quickly started generating significant legal challenges. While the non-centralised nature of (many of) these networks played a key role in supporting the socio-economic claims that accompanied their uptake, it easily defies the regulatory need to pinpoint accountable entities.[6] Although in practice the development of crypto-asset ecosystems does not always mirror the most common image of a DLT-based system, also in terms of ledger transparency, the supposed impossibility to reach (some of) them by regulatory and supervisory means stirs up considerable controversies.[7] Indeed, their perceived level of anonymity and ubiquity fuels strong fears of borderless illicit exploitation.[8] In particular, the debate on the legal consequences of anonymity in online communications intensified when the anonymous exchange of information started to have a financial content.[9] Meanwhile, scandals linking crypto-assets to darknet markets spurred the exploration of advanced forensic techniques to trace these funds.[10]

Nowadays, crypto-assets belong to an enigmatic set of ecosystems whose traits of anonymity and transparency range across a spectrum of combinations and degrees. Hence, pressing regulatory questions are generated by the twofold nature of crypto-asset transactions. These fears are related primarily to the regulatory framework to prevent the misuse of the financial system for purposes of money laundering and financing of terrorism and proliferation (AML/CFT). The final goal of these measures is to prevent criminals from enjoying the profit of illicit activities, thwarting their capacity to disguise the origin of funds, and from financing terrorist activities or the proliferation of weapons of mass destruction. The domain is overseen by the Financial Action Task Force (FATF), in its function of international standard setter. The FATF Recommendations have been transposed in the European Union through a process of harmonisation started in 1991 and climaxed with the 2021 proposal to establish a directly applicable single rulebook, finally adopted in 2024.[11]

The AML/CFT framework relies on a set of regulated entities to implement preventive measures and to monitor financial transactions to timely report suspicions of illicit activities to the authorities. Inherently, their oversight duties assume

---

[5] Casey et al. (2018). The concepts of IoM and ledger transparency are described in more detail in Chaps. 2 and 3, respectively.

[6] Finck (2019).

[7] Johnstone (2021); Massari and Catalini (2021).

[8] Financial Action Task Force (2021).

[9] A broad conceptualisation of the IoM was at the core of prior analysis conducted in Pocher (2023). It included cryptocurrency ecosystems, thus covering the part of the Internet of Value (IoV) that relates to payment-type crypto-assets. The present work focuses instead more broadly on crypto-asset ecosystems as a whole—i.e., not only those serving a payment purpose.

[10] Pocher et al. (2023a, 2023b).

[11] Financial Action Task Force (2012). Regulation (EU) 2024/1624.

a condition of financial transparency, where specific actors can access certain information to perform compliance and/or supervisory checks. The nature of this regime as intermediary-based seems inadequate to confront the crypto-asset space, where the recent events concerning the crypto-asset mixer Tornado Cash showcased some of the existing tension points.[12] To mitigate the current pitfalls in the AML/CFT approach to crypto-asset transactions, new methodological and compliance approaches are investigated. The most promising methods are grounded on a proactive use of technological solutions and on innovative interpretations of the interplay between regulation and technology.[13]

Meanwhile, the crypto-asset space has witnessed a consistent growth of industry-led stablecoin initiatives, where the price volatility of traditional cryptocurrencies is managed by tying the coin value to a reference asset.[14] Further, in recent years public and private stakeholders have been experimenting with the design of sovereign digital money, to be used for retail transactions or in wholesale scenarios between financial institutions. The various models of central bank digital currency (CBDC) spurred debates on their regulatory repercussions, chiefly in terms of user privacy, security and fight against illicit misuse. The global interest in these initiatives provides insights into the elements to be considered when addressing the relationship between regulation and the design of digital currency ecosystems.[15]

Against this multi-faceted backdrop, this research addresses the following research question: *In crypto-asset ecosystems, anonymity and transparency purportedly coexist in ever-evolving combinations and to varying degrees. How can the EU regulatory framework to prevent the misuse of the financial system for purposes of money laundering and terrorist and proliferation (AML/CFT) legitimately and effectively respond to the consequent twofold nature of crypto-assets?*

In its conclusions, this work provides EU-level regulatory recommendations to address the AML/CFT challenges posed by crypto-assets. The methodological foundation of the analysis pursues the mitigation of the risk of (regulatory) overfitting in a fast-changing environment, while acknowledging specificities in compliance with a key element of the AML/CFT regime, the risk-based approach (RBA), pivoting on tuning compliance measures to the principle of proportionality.

1.2 Research Objectives and Methods

The Law and Technology research domain encompasses the "variety of scholarly discourses concerning the intersections of law and technology, as to distinguish the object of analysis from specific laws and specific technologies themselves", thereby

---

[12] Nadler and Schär (2023).

[13] Schrepel (2021); Finck (2019).

[14] Bank for International Settlements (2019).

[15] Pocher and Veneris (2022a, 2022b).

including notions such as technology law, technology and law, legal tech, and techlaw.[16] While legal scholars typically situate their work in specific branches of the law that are each equipped with established and recognised methodologies, Law and Technology houses substantially divergent research communities and methods. In this regard, Kanevskaia and Pałka (2023) provide an overview of the angles from which legal questions can be asked with regard to technological advances—ranging from analysing the relationship between given technologies and the law and whether and how they should be regulated, to the automation of legal reasoning and the legitimacy challenges brought about when technology takes a regulatory role. Amidst this diversity, for a Law and Technology researcher "[t]he methods of research are often themselves an opportunity for experimentation".[17] Along these lines, this work often borrows notions and concepts from other disciplines to perform a holistic analysis of the research problem. The following remarks seek to clarify the ambiguities that may derive from the consequent complexities in terms of terminology and interdisciplinary research methods.

Kestemont (2018) clarifies that "the different types of research objectives that legal scholars can pursue in their research [are] descriptive, classifying, comparative, theory-building, explanatory, evaluative and recommendatory".[18] In the case of this work, the final objective is to put forward framework-level regulatory suggestions—that is, the final objective is recommendatory, i.e., one that "aims to formulate recommendations on how the law should be".[19] The intermediary steps feature methods that range from descriptive (i.e., where the goal is to "systematically analyze legal constructs in all their components in order to present them in an accurate, significant and orderly manner") and classifying (i.e., "to conceptualise or classify (legal) phenomena in the existing legal system") to evaluative (i.e., an objective "to evaluate/assess legal constructs in view of a norm").[20] The normative criteria are both internal—e.g., analysis of EU AML/CFT provisions in the context of the global financial system—and, as typical in interdisciplinary legal research, external—e.g., effectiveness vis-à-vis the evolving phenomenology of crypto-assets.

In this way, the work can accommodate the legal, technical and socio-economic aspects, which need to be scrutinised in a way that can reflect their specificity while safeguarding consistency in terms of structure. It follows that the deployed methodologies range from deductive (drawing deductive inferences from regulatory provisions and policy documents), to inductive (deriving general principles from the observation of phenomena), to abductive reasoning (inferring the most likely (i.e., probable) conclusion from observations). Abimbola (2002) offers an overview on the debated meaning of abduction and of how the claim to have the 'best'

[16] Kanevskaia and Pałka (2023), p. 1.

[17] Kanevskaia and Pałka (2023), p. 3.

[18] Kestemont (2018), p. 7.

[19] Kestemont (2018), p. 63.

[20] Kestemont (2018), pp. 19, 33, 60.

explanation is difficult to prove in real life for legal scholars—defining "abduction as inference to the best viable (actual) explanation".[21]

This publication remains primarily a legal work. Technical and socio-economic aspects are thus explored within the framework of a legally oriented reasoning, to the extent they can inform legal considerations from both a descriptive and normative standpoint. Notably, to determine whether the current regulatory approach is tailored to the specifics of the evolving phenomenology of crypto-assets, a domain inherently shaped by technology but whose development has a mutual relationship with socio-economic elements. Hence, this work does not deploy sociological, economic and financial methodologies, nor does it follow a criminological method when analysing phenomena of money laundering and terrorist financing.

When the term 'regulation' is used with no further specification, it refers in a comprehensive fashion to different legal sources—i.e., legislation, regulation, standards, soft law, self-regulatory initiatives, case law—and to their interplay. Evidently, this is a process of abstraction that must be performed carefully. To ease cross-disciplinary communication, when their qualification bears no relevance to the given argument, the term 'regulation' (e.g., not 'law and regulation') is used in an inclusive fashion. This choice does not dismiss the differences among legislative and regulatory methodologies, which are analysed in different parts of the book (e.g., Chaps. 5 and 7). Rather, it keeps the narrative anchored to the multi-layered compound of AML/CFT rules that exert effect on regulated entities—e.g., EU legislation, domestic legislation, soft law, EU standards, international standards.[22] Speaking of 'compliance with all relevant provisions' does not equate to an implicit claim that they have the same qualification, exert the same effects, are enforced in the same way and by the same actors.

Often, this research addresses a mutually reinforcing combination of terminological and conceptual conundrums. Namely, there are (a) terms strictly related to the investigated topics, that assume a particular connotation because of the context: e.g., crypto-asset ecosystems, non-centralisation, disintermediation; and (b) notions that do not exclusively pertain to this research area but must be contextualised to avoid ambiguities: e.g., anonymity, transparency. Because many crucial concepts are currently lacking universally agreed-upon definitions, it is not possible to delve into

---

[21] Abimbola (2002), p. 1689. The pragmatic standpoint of abductive reasoning is useful when tackling the complexities of the issues at hand. When abduction is deployed in this work, reference is to the legitimacy and effectiveness of EU regulatory actions as well as to pivotal principles in the research domain—e.g., RBA, avoidance of overfitting.

[22] In this sense, 'regulation' was broadly interpreted as "the process of writing the rules that apply to the regulated entities" (Auer, 2022, p. 2) and also as "intentional, organised attempts to manage or control risk or the behaviours of a different party through the exercise of authority, usually through the use of mechanisms of standard-setting, monitoring and information-gathering and behaviour modification to address a collective tension or problem" (Yeung & Ranchordás, 2024, p. 6), hence referring also to the resulting compound of rules applicable to AML/CFT regulated entities. For a deeper analysis of the controversial definition of what is 'regulation', the interested reader is referred to the valuable insights by Bennett and Raab (2020); Black (2002, 2012); Finck (2019); Hofmann et al. (2017); Pagallo et al. (2019), among others.

them without clarifying the terminology. For this reason, each chapter attempts the disambiguation of specific notions. Alternatively, the ultimate risk is to regulate 'by streetlight'—i.e., on the basis of what can be easily seen or (mis)understood—,[23] but also to incorporate common misconceptions into regulatory frameworks.

1.3 Methodological Building Blocks

The following six pillars underpin this research from a methodological perspective.

Socio-Technical Systems This work pivots on the interpretation of crypto-asset ecosystems as socio-technical systems (STSs)—thus, of the crypto-asset space as an ecosystem of interconnected socio-technical ecosystems. As such, they comprise interdependent human, social, organisational and technical components cooperating to achieve a task. The group of entities composing a crypto-asset system is called 'ecosystem' and these entities belong to one of four areas: (a) hardware (e.g., nodes), (b) business (e.g., developers, users, miners, investors), (c) software development (e.g., financial, semi-financial, non-financial), (d) protocol development (e.g., developers, academia). (ITU-T FG DLT, 2019, pp. 2–4).

While the literature applies the concept of STSs to domains close to crypto-assets and the AML/CFT regime (Chap. 2),[24] the notion was originally coined in the context of organisational studies and work/enterprise systems. The concept used in this work is drawn from the 'sociotechnical systems theory/approach', focusing on the holistic and interconnected mutual contributions of technology and the human systems that interact with it and vice versa.[25] In this sense, the complex network composed of blockchain nodes, crypto-asset users and miners, exchanges and tumblers/mixers was described as cooperating "within a complex system of social and informational relationships".[26]

Although there is no interdisciplinary consensus on what an STS is, the core revolves around the interdependency of humans, machines and context where they interact, and on the related possibility to make design choices. As pointed out in literature, the definition of the suitable level of abstraction when describing STSs is a primary challenge.[27] In information systems (IS) research, for example, the notions of *ecosystem* and of *socio-technical system* are conceptualised in a specific fashion. In particular, the socio-technical perspective has been referred to as the 'axis of cohesion' of the IS discipline (Sarker et al., 2019), and STS theory assumes that information systems consist of both a social and a technical part, nested in a

[23] Walch (2019), p. 25.

[24] Desmond et al. (2019); De Domenico and Baronchelli (2019); Poblet et al. (2020); Renwick and Gleasure (2020).

[25] Baxter and Sommerville (2010), p. 5.

[26] Desmond et al. (2019), p. 487.

[27] Baxter and Sommerville (2010), p. 8.

complex environment (Bostrom & Heinen, 1977a, 1977b). While this publication does not necessarily take an IS approach to crypto-asset ecosystems, it is partially inspired by these perspectives.

From a regulatory standpoint, the value of a 'system approach' lies in comprehensively embracing all the elements at play when devising a strategy to approach these ecosystems, thus avoiding reaching conclusions refuted by phenomenology. Hence, when tackling the design of an STS—e.g., of a crypto-asset ecosystem or of a CBDC model—, this book does it through a selective (i.e., teleologically-oriented, as defined below) analysis of the aspects that exert impacts on anonymity and on the privacy-transparency trade-off of the given ecosystem or proposed design. Notably, it leverages the STS concept to heed the different elements that influence the definitions of crypto-asset features, and exert consequences from a regulatory standpoint, chiefly in terms of AML/CFT rules and compliance strategies.

Teleologically-Oriented Methodology This work deploys a teleologically-oriented methodology when disambiguating the notions of anonymity and transparency in crypto-assets from an AML/CFT viewpoint. In other words, the analysis is informed by the specifics of the context, composed by crypto-asset ecosystems and the AML/CFT framework. The concept of 'teleological approach' draws from philosophy, ethics, and law. In broad terms, if an approach is teleological it means it involves "the explanation of phenomena in terms of the purpose they serve rather than of the cause by which they arise".[28] In scientific literature, an explanation can be described as teleological "when it resorts to notions such as ends, goals, purposes, or objectives",[29] and in ethics a teleological approach is results-oriented in defining ethical behaviour emphasising outcomes over process.[30] In the legal domain, teleological or purposive interpretation "interprets a legal provision in view of the legislator's original objective(s): protecting specific interests, obtaining a particular social or economic outcome, stimulating a specific type of behaviour, etc.".[31] The value of this approach emerges in EU law from the frequent deployment by the Court of Justice of the European Union (CJEU) to provide an explanation by reference to purposes or goals.[32] To the same end, the CJEU often applies 'teleological argumentation'.[33]

In a broader fashion, the teleological approach is deployed in two distinct but related legal and non-legal contexts: (a) when interpreting the features of crypto-

[28] Oxford Languages Dictionary (2024).

[29] González Galli and Meinardi (2011).

[30] The Arthur W. Page Center (2022).

[31] Kestemont (2018), p. 28.

[32] "A goal is an extralegal element such as needs, interests and values, which are also considered an object of teleological argumentation" (Kuch, 2022, p. 2).

[33] Because every legal provision has a goal, "among its possible meanings, the most significant one is why it has been adopted in the first place (its purpose)" (Kuch, 2022, pp. 3–4).

asset ecosystems having regard to the regulatory purpose for which they come into play in this research (i.e., AML/CFT regulation)—e.g., when interpreting the notion of crypto-asset anonymity having regard to the AML/CFT perspective when using this term; (b) when interpreting the details provided by the AML/CFT rules about the definitions of those concepts—e.g., taking into account the objective pursued by those norms while referring to anonymity and relevant risks.

Risk of Overfitting The structure and content of this work responds to the need to shape the regulatory approach to crypto-asset ecosystems. In other words, the need to strike a balance between a case-specific approach, to acknowledge the existing differences among crypto-asset ecosystems, and the risk of overfitting—i.e., the risk of rules becoming technologically outdated soon after their entry into force, or even beforehand. This risk manifests when rules are over-tailored to the state of evolution of the technology at the time of their conception, which generates a mismatch with later developments. Indeed, this is a recurring issue when regulating new technologies,[34] but it is more pressing in the case at hand: on the one hand the domain is ever-evolving in ways that disrupt both the domain to be regulated and the regulatory framework, and on the other hand the EU-level legislative process—although the same consideration could be raised at the domestic level—is bound to take a considerable amount of time from the start of the initiative to the entry into force of the rules. It is worth noting that regulatory overfitting does not overlap with the concept of overfitting that is commonly used in data science, statistics and mathematics.[35] Nonetheless, from an abstract perspective the two notions express similar considerations.

Risk-Based Approach The regulatory analysis and the framework recommendations are informed by the overarching role of the risk-based approach (RBA). This is a common concept in regulatory compliance, conducive to adopting implementation measures in a flexible way. This is especially true when the framework features a certain complexity and a disproportionate deployment of the same approach in all circumstances would overburden the stakeholders involved and originate inefficiency. In the AML/CFT sphere, both authorities and regulated entities can optimise the use of their resources if they adopt supervisory methods and preventive measures, respectively, in a way that is commensurate to the nature of the different risks. From a domestic perspective, when authorities identify higher risks, they must make sure they are adequately addressed with stricter rules within their jurisdiction, while in cases of lower risk simplified measures can be allowed. For regulated entities, internal controls and procedures, but also everyday activities, must mirror the preliminary risk assessment and the risks identified in the concrete compliance exercise in a proportionate manner—i.e., in brief, the identification of higher risks

[34] Hacker et al. (2019), p. 33.

[35] In mathematics and data science, an overfitting model fits too closely to a dataset (e.g., a machine learning model fits too closely to its training data) and is not reliable when applied to other contexts.

must originate enhanced controls and monitoring, up to the decision to discontinue (or not engage in) a given activity.[36] The matter is detailed in Chap. 5.

Regulation by Design This work is based on the possibility to conceive regulation 'by design' by focusing on the interplay of legal rules and technology, and to embed compliance measures into an application or tool. In recent years, these considerations gave rise to manifold methodological approaches, at times divergent. In brief, they are at the root of design-based regulatory and compliance techniques, which have been labelled as embedded regulation/compliance and regulation/compliance by/through design. These concepts and their variety, as well as the specific approach taken in this book based on a literature review, is outlined in Chap. 7. In broad terms, this method is conceived not in terms of leveraging the opportunities offered by technological design to replace regulatory provisions and their essence, but on the contrary as a specific techno-regulatory methodology to think about the mutual interaction between regulation and technology when drafting regulation whose compliance can be eased by design. Considering the outcomes of this research, these strategies may arguably aid an efficient deployment of the RBA and mitigate the risk of overfitting in the regulatory and phenomenological domains under consideration.

Taxonomies Finally, various parts of this work refer to the role of schemes known as 'taxonomies'—for instance, the conclusions advocate for the creation of a taxonomy instrument to assess the levels and types of anonymity risk posed by crypto-asset ecosystems. Indeed, complex fields often require the development of "classification schemes, or taxonomies, which provide ways to understand the similarities and differences among objects under study".[37] The notion of taxonomy is inherently cross-disciplinary, as it derives from biology studies and is largely used in social and management sciences, but also in law.[38] The method is widely adopted in neighbouring disciplines such as IS, where Nickerson et al. (2013) and Kundisch et al. (2022) devised and expanded, respectively, established methods for taxonomy development. While the core of a taxonomy lies in its classification endeavour to organise knowledge, the same was argued for typologies, ontologies, and frameworks,[39] and various disciplines confer varying importance to relevant distinctions, as well as abide by different rules for what concerns their development. In this work, taxonomies are seen as enablers of cross-disciplinary knowledge transfer and collaboration, but specific techno-legal rules for their development are left to future research.

---

[36] For an analysis of the concept of risk and its complex (and contested) role in regulation, the interested reader may refer to Black (2010) and Yeung and Ranchordás (2024), pp. 41–77.

[37] Nickerson et al. (2009), p. 1.

[38] For instance, see Mattei (1997), and UNCITRAL (2023).

[39] They are all "systems for grouping objects of interest in a domain based on common characteristics." (Nickerson et al., 2013, p. 3).

1.4 Structure of the Book

This work is divided into eight chapters. Besides offering an introduction to the crypto-asset space, the framework to prevent money laundering and the financing of terrorism and proliferation (AML/CFT) and other key components of this publication, Chap. 1 outlines the methodological foundations underpinning the analysis. It attempts contextualised clarifications regarding the approach chosen by the author to engage in interdisciplinary research from a techno-legal perspective. In doing so, this chapter seeks not only to guide the readers towards an understanding of specific elements of this work, but also to contribute to the methodological discussion ongoing in the Law and Technology research community.

Chapter 2 outlines the phenomenological foundations of crypto-asset ecosystems. Accordingly, it introduces their key traits by exploring their underlying combination of technologies and the role played by various stakeholders and architectures. It outlines the background against which crypto-asset-related concepts were devised, starting from P2P transfers and tokenisation, up to the advent of stablecoins and CBDCs. It defines crypto-asset ecosystems, highlighting the value of terminological disambiguation for what concerns crypto-assets and tokens. It explores the landscape of crypto-asset transfers by deploying a teleological and accountability-based approach. It underlines the nature of crypto-asset ecosystems as ecosystems of interconnected socio-technical ecosystems, and the need to focus not only on the interplay of their components but also on the developments in terms of non-centralisation and disintermediation. Finally, it outlines methodology benchmarks to address crypto-asset ecosystems from a regulatory perspective while heeding conceptual, ideological, and technical evolutions.

Against this backdrop, Chap. 3 presents the first part of the analysis of the concepts of anonymity and transparency in crypto-asset ecosystems. In doing so, it pursues the conceptual clarity on which to ground the following investigation and the final conclusions. It addresses the role of encryption and the multifold concepts of anonymity and transparency in crypto-assets and related transactions, while attempting disambiguation at the crossroads between different conceptual levels pertaining to the cyberspace, crypto-asset ecosystems, financial transactions. It explores the traits featured by anonymity and transparency within an AML/CFT context and provides an analysis of several features of crypto-asset anonymity. Meanwhile, it addresses the twofold notion of transparency, torn by the fact that the concept of transparency of the ledger and ledger operations is constitutively distant from the notion of financial transparency. Accordingly, it reframes the alleged paradox of public blockchains being both anonymous and transparent. Finally, it addresses enhanced disintermediation, showing the impact on accountability.

Chapter 4 provides the second part of the analysis of the concepts of anonymity and transparency, focusing on the socio-technical concepts of obfuscation and traceability. It heeds the impact of anonymity-enhancing strategies applied by different actors, and of transaction analytics tools. It shows how cryptocurrencies can be deployed in the laundering process in multiple ways, and how this hampers identification and categorisation of risks. Relatedly, it focuses on red flag indicators released by the FATF, phrased without a clear separation between the ways in which anonymity is enhanced. The chapter argues in favour of a teleologically oriented methodology when evaluating the meaning of features such as anonymity—i.e., it vouches for the consideration of the context, composed by crypto-asset ecosystems and the AML/CFT framework. Meanwhile, it suggests the identification of specific benchmarks to differentiate between the various degrees of anonymity without running into the risk of overfitting. It is in this context that the concept of accountability, ensured by the auditability of relevant transactions, emerges as pivotal.

Chapter 5 investigates the AML/CFT regulatory context and the evolution of the regime. It provides insights into the perceived risks related to crypto-assets and the (purported) anonymous character of the sphere. The chapter heeds the importance of the activity of the FATF as a sector-specific player within the dynamics of global financial regulation, and analyses its Recommendations as instruments of soft-law. Meanwhile, it outlines the main obligations, through the lens of their EU-level implementation, and underlines the importance of the RBA that underpins all duties imposed on regulated entities. Moreover, it analyses selected technical standardisation initiatives on cryptocurrencies, blockchain technologies or DLTs, underlining the interplay between technical and regulatory standards. It expands on the nature of the EU regulatory methodology in the AML/CFT field as minimum harmonisation, while addressing the more recent shift towards a single rulebook to overcome fragmentation. Starting from the relationship between EU law and international standards, this chapter addresses the new Anti-Money Laundering Authority (AMLA) and its task of drafting regulatory technical standards (RTSs). It displays the problematic application of the intermediary-based approach to the crypto-asset space, vis-à-vis the revolution brought about by decentralised finance (DeFi) platforms and decentralised exchanges (DEXes) also in terms of laundering trends. The matter is exemplified by the difficulty of ensuring compliance with the crypto travel rule.

Chapter 6 overviews sovereign digital currencies and a selection of debates on digital fiat money elicited in publications by leading institutions and private actors. CBDC explorations provide a revolutionary insight into cross-disciplinary efforts, while CBDC projects feature various approaches, designs and architectures. The chapter focuses on interoperability and standardisation, and on the impact of public-private interplays and cross-border models. It explores regulatory issues raised by CBDCs from an AML/CFT perspective and contextualises the debate within the broader cash-related anonymity problem and the establishment of relevant limits. It tackles privacy and data protection concerns and the competence for AML/CFT compliance in different public-private designs. It builds on the other chapters to introduce the existing trade-offs between anonymity and transparency in CBDCs, whose designs can embed various balances between confidentiality and auditability. It underlines the interplay between technology, regulation, and standardisation, to provide benchmarks for thinking about anonymity and transparency in CBDCs.

Chapter 7 explores key aspects of a possible novel methodology to be applied at the EU level in the AML/CFT sphere. Chiefly, it heeds the ever-evolving presence of manifold assets, technologies, innovative and traditional stakeholders in crypto-asset socio-technical ecosystems, the approaches put forward to regulate new technologies and their interplay with the AML/CFT regime. The analysis reviews the types of interplay DLT-based applications can have with regulatory frameworks, focusing on how proactive instances could replace reactive approaches. It overviews a set of methodological features of AML/CFT regulation, tailoring the analysis to anonymity-transparency trade-offs. It proposes the creation of a taxonomy instrument to evaluate the levels of anonymity risk posed by crypto-asset ecosystems and suggests the creation of a 'transposition model' of risk indicators to techno-regulatory standards. It investigates the shift from the criticised 'code is law' to a compound concept of 'regulation-enabled compliance through design' and advocates for the establishment of a multi-stakeholder co-regulatory model. It provides a case study of the proposed approach. Finally, it reviews methodological elements for the intervention of EU law in terms of legitimacy and effectiveness, overviewing its role in the design and implementation of the proposed methodology.

Finally, Chap. 8 mirrors the multi-layered approach of the previous sections and provides a combination of recommendatory elements as the final output of the work. The findings concern: (a) the anonymity-transparency trade-offs featured by crypto-asset socio-technical ecosystems, (b) the application of a holistic approach to draft a risk-based taxonomy, (c) the value of establishing an EU-level polycentric techno-regulatory standardisation model, methodologically grounded on (d) 'regulation-enabled compliance through design. In doing so, the chapter concludes this work by offering guidance for a possible methodology for an EU AML/CFT approach that accounts for the socio-technical interpretation of anonymity-transparency trade-offs present in crypto-asset ecosystems.

References

Abimbola, K. (2002). Abductive reasoning in law: Taxonomy and inference to the best explanation. In M. MacCrimmon & P. Tillers (Eds.), *The dynamics of judicial proof: Computation, logic, and common sense* (pp. 337–342). Physica-Verlag HD. https://doi.org/10.1007/978-3-7908-1792-8_17

Antonopoulos, A. M. (2016). *The Internet of money - Volume one*. Merkle Boom.

Antonopoulos, A. M. (2017a). *The Internet of money - Volume two*. Merkle Boom.

Antonopoulos, A. M. (2017b). *Mastering bitcoin* (2nd ed.). O'Reilly Media.

Auer, R. (2022). *Embedded supervision: How to build regulation into decentralised finance*. https://www.bis.org/publ/work811.pdf

Bank for International Settlements. (2019). *Investigating the impact of global stablecoins*. https://www.bis.org/cpmi/publ/d187.pdf

Baxter, G., & Sommerville, I. (2010). Socio-technical systems: From design methods to systems engineering. *Interacting with Computers*, *23*(1), 4–17. https://doi.org/10.1016/j.intcom.2010.07.003

Bennett, C. J., & Raab, C. D. (2020). Revisiting the governance of privacy: Contemporary policy instruments in global perspective. *Regulation and Governance, 14*(3), 447–464. https://doi.org/10.1111/rego.12222

Black, J. (2002). Critical reflections on regulation. *Australian Journal of Legal Philosophy, 27*, 1–46.

Black, J. (2010). The role of risk in regulatory processes. In R. Baldwin, M. Cave, & M. Lodge (Eds.), *The oxford handbook of regulation* (pp. 301–348). Oxford University Press. https://doi.org/10.1093/oxfordhb/9780199560219.003.0014

Black, J. (2012). Paradoxes and failures: 'new governance' techniques and the financial crisis. *Modern Law Review, 75*(6), 1037–1063. https://doi.org/10.1111/j.1468-2230.2012.00936.x

Bostrom, R. P., & Heinen, J. S. (1977a). MIS problems and failures: A socio-technical perspective. Part I: The causes. *MIS Quarterly, 1*, 17–32. https://doi.org/10.2307/248710

Bostrom, R. P., & Heinen, J. S. (1977b). MIS problems and failures: A socio-technical perspective. Part II: The application of socio-technical theory. *MIS Quarterly, 1*, 11–28. https://doi.org/10.2307/249019

Casey, M., Crane, J., Gensler, G., Johnson, S., & Narula, N. (2018). *The impact of blockchain technology on finance: A catalyst for change*. https://cepr.org/publications/books-and-reports/geneva-21-impact-blockchain-technology-finance-catalyst-change

De Domenico, M., & Baronchelli, A. (2019). The fragility of decentralised trustless socio-technical systems. *EPJ Data Science, 8*(1), 4–9. https://doi.org/10.1140/epjds/s13688-018-0180-6

Desmond, D. B., Lacey, D., & Salmon, P. (2019). Evaluating cryptocurrency laundering as a complex socio-technical system: A systematic literature review. *Journal of Money Laundering Control, 22*(3), 480–97. https://doi.org/10.1108/JMLC-10-2018-0063

Financial Action Task Force. (2012). *International standards on combating money laundering and the financing of terrorism & proliferation: The fatf recommendations*. Last updated: January 2025. https://www.fatf-gafi.org/publications/fatfrecommendations/documents/fatf-recommendations.html

Financial Action Task Force. (2021). *Virtual assets and virtual asset service providers - Updated guidance for a risk-based approach*. https://www.fatf-gafi.org/publications/fatfrecommendations/documents/guidance-rba-virtual-assets-2021.html

Finck, M. (2019). *Blockchain regulation and governance in Europe*. Cambridge University Press. https://doi.org/10.1017/9781108609708

González Galli, L. M., & Meinardi, E. N. (2011). The role of teleological thinking in learning the darwinian model of evolution. *Evolution: Education and Outreach, 4*, 145–152. https://doi.org/10.1007/s12052-010-0272-7

Hacker, P., Lianos, I., Dimitropoulos, G., & Eich, S. (2019). *Regulating blockchain: Techno-social and legal challenges*. Oxford University Press. https://doi.org/10.1093/oso/9780198842187.001.0001

Herian, R. (2019). *Regulating blockchain: Critical perspectives in law and technology*. Routledge. https://doi.org/10.4324/9780429489815

Hofmann, J., Katzenbach, C., & Gollatz, K. (2017). Between coordination and regulation: Finding the governance in internet governance. *New Media and Society, 19*(9), 1406–1423. https://doi.org/10.1177/1461444816639975

ITU-T FG DLT. (2019). *Technical report FG DLT D1.2 distributed ledger technology overview, concepts, ecosystem*. https://www.itu.int/en/ITU-T/focusgroups/dlt/Documents/FGDLT-D1.2.pdf

Johnstone, S. (2021). Regulatory building blocks and other concerns. In S. Johnstone (Ed.), *Rethinking the regulation of cryptoassets. Cryptographic consensus technology and the new prospect*. Edward Elgar. https://doi.org/10.4337/9781800886797.00015

Kanevskaia, O., & Pałka, P. (2023). Introduction to the research handbook on law and technology. In B. Brożek, O. Kanevskaia, & P. Pałka (Eds.), *Research handbook on law and technology*. Edward Elgar. https://doi.org/10.4337/9781803921327.00007

Kestemont, L. (2018). *Handbook on legal methodology. From objective to method*. Intersentia. https://lib.ugent.be/catalog/rug01:002488086

Kuch, P. (2022). Teleology - The missing piece to solving the GDPR puzzle. *Journal of Data Protection & Privacy*, *5*(1). https://doi.org/10.2139/ssrn.3675617

Kundisch, D., Muntermann, J., Oberländer, A. M., Rau, D., Röglinger, M., Schoormann, T., & Szopinski, D. (2022). An update for taxonomy designers. *Business and Information Systems Engineering*, *64*. https://doi.org/10.1007/s12599-021-00723-x

Massari, J., & Catalini, C. (2021). *DeFi, disintermediation, and the regulatory path ahead*. https://www.theregreview.org/2021/05/10/massari-catalini-defi-disintermediation-regulatory-path-ahead/

Mattei, U. (1997). Three patterns of law: Taxonomy and change in the world's legal systems. *The American Journal of Comparative Law*, *45*. https://repository.uclawsf.edu/faculty_scholarship/525/

Nadler, M., & Schär, F. (2023). Tornado cash and blockchain privacy: A primer for economists and policymakers. *Federal Reserve Bank of St. Louis Review*, 1–15. https://doi.org/10.20955/r.105.122-136

Nakamoto, S. (2008). *Bitcoin: A peer-to-peer electronic cash systems*. https://www.bitcoin.org

Nickerson, R., Muntermann, J., Varshney, U., & Isaac, H. (2009). Taxonomy development in information systems: Developing a taxonomy of mobile applications. In *HAL, Working Papers*. halshs-00375103

Nickerson, R., Varshney, U., & Muntermann, J. (2013). A method for taxonomy development and its application in information systems. *European Journal of Information Systems*, *22*. https://doi.org/10.1057/ejis.2012.26

Oxford Languages Dictionary. (2024). *Definition of "teleological"*. https://www.google.com/search?q=teleological

Pagallo, U., Casanovas, P., & Madelin, R. (2019). The middle-out approach: Assessing models of legal governance in data protection, artificial intelligence, and the web of data. *Theory and Practice of Legislation*, *7*(1), 1–25. https://doi.org/10.1080/20508840.2019.1664543

Poblet, M., Allen, D. W. E., Konashevych, O., Lane, A. M., & Diaz-Valdivia, C. A. (2020). From athens to the blockchain: Oracles for digital democracy. *Frontiers in Blockchain*. https://doi.org/10.3389/fbloc.2020.575662

Pocher, N. (2023). *Distributed ledger technologies between anonymity and transparency: AML/CFT regulation of cryptocurrency ecosystems in the EU*. PhD thesis, Alma Mater Studiorum Università di Bologna, KU Leuven, Universitat Autònoma de Barcelona. 10.48676/unibo/amsdottorato/10659.

Pocher, N., & Veneris, A. (2022a). Central bank digital currencies. In D. A. Tran, M. T. Thai, & B. Krishnamachari (Eds.), *Handbook on blockchain*. Springer. https://doi.org/10.1007/978-3-031-07535-3_15

Pocher, N., & Veneris, A. (2022b). Privacy and transparency in CBDCs: A regulation-by-design AML/CFT scheme. *IEEE Transactions on Network and Service Management*, *19*(2), 1776–1788. https://doi.org/10.1109/TNSM.2021.3136984

Pocher, N., Zichichi, M., & Ferretti, S. (2023a). The AML/CFT/CPF application of on-chain analytics and machine learning: Overview and open issues. In *Proceedings of Artificial Intelligence Governance Ethics and Law (AIGEL)*. https://ceur-ws.org/Vol-3531/SPaper_11.pdf

Pocher, N., Zichichi, M., Merizzi, F., Shafiq, M. Z., & Ferretti, S. (2023b). Detecting anomalous cryptocurrency transactions: An AML/CFT application of machine learning-based forensics. *Electronic Markets*, *33*(1). https://doi.org/10.1007/s12525-023-00654-3

Regulation (EU) 2024/1624. (2024). Regulation (EU) 2024/1624 of the European Parliament and of the Council of 31 May 2024 on the prevention of the use of the financial system for the purposes of money laundering or terrorist financing. http://data.europa.eu/eli/reg/2024/1624/oj

Renwick, R., & Gleasure, R. (2020). Those who control the code control the rules: How different perspectives of privacy are being written into the code of blockchain systems. *Journal of Information Technology*, *36*(1). https://doi.org/10.1177/0268396220944406

Sarker, S., Chatterjee, S., Xiao, X., & Elbanna, A. (2019). The sociotechnical axis of cohesion for the IS discipline: Its historical legacy and its continued relevance. *MIS Quarterly*, *43*, 695–719. https://doi.org/10.25300/MISQ/2019/13747

Schrepel, T. (2021). *Blockchain + sntitrust: The decentralisation formula*. Edward Elgar. https://doi.org/10.4337/9781800885530

Swan, M. (2015). *Blockchain: Blueprint for a new economy*. O'Reilly.

The Arthur W. Page Center. (2022). *Ethical orientations: Teleology*. https://www.pagecentertraining.psu.edu/public-relations-ethics/core-ethical-principles/lesson-1-title/ethical-orientations-teleology/

UNCITRAL. (2023). *Taxonomy of legal issues related to the digital economy*. https://uncitral.un.org/sites/uncitral.un.org/files/media-documents/uncitral/en/digitaleconomytaxonomy.pdf

Walch, A. (2019). *Regulating blockchain: Techno-social and legal challenges*. In *Code(Rs) we trust: Software developers as fiduciaries in public blockchains*. Oxford University Press. https://doi.org/10.1093/oso/9780198842187.003.0004

Werbach, K. (2019). *The blockchain and the new architecture of trust*. The MIT Press. https://doi.org/10.7551/mitpress/11449.001.0001

Yeung, K., & Ranchordás, S. (2024). *An introduction to law and regulation: Text and materials* (2nd ed.). Cambridge University Press. https://doi.org/10.1017/9781009379007

Chapter 2
Phenomenology of Crypto-Asset Ecosystems

2.1 Introduction

October 31, 2008, marks a milestone in the history of the Internet and of the global socio-economic development. The publication of the Bitcoin whitepaper by the mysterious figure(s) of Satoshi Nakamoto launched a revolutionary trend in P2P networks and distributed computing, with vast cross-industry repercussions.[1] The design of Bitcoin, and its open-source software Bitcoin Core, included the first blockchain database. Notably, a blockchain is a type of distributed ledger where data is recorded in a tamper-proof chain of blocks linked cryptographically.[2]

For the first time, distributed ledger technologies (DLTs) were leveraged to allow groups of network participants, known as 'nodes', to agree on actions and states with no need of a central trusted authority.[3] Following the first bitcoin trade two months after the whitepaper's release, a plethora of cryptocurrencies and crypto-assets followed. The amount estimated today includes between 10,000 and 20,000 cryptocurrencies.[4] Although blockchain-based solutions are now deployed in a vast range of industries, the fact that the seeds of this disruptive wave were first sown in the financial world bears relevance to this day. Indeed, even though the field is still largely based on traditional infrastructures, the so-called 'blockchain hype' introduced the idea of an alternative economy in which citizens

[1] Nakamoto (2008). The term "Bitcoin" refers to the protocol, the concept and the technology, whereas "bitcoin(s)" (with no capitalisation) labels the unit of currency.

[2] ITU-T FG DLT (2019a), pp. 1–4. A distributed ledger is "shared, replicated, and synchronised in a distributed and decentralised manner", with distributed control among the participants in the system operation.

[3] Antonopoulos (2016, 2017b). A P2P system is a "network of peers that directly share information and resources with each other without relying on a central entity" (ITU-T FG DLT, 2019a, p. 4).

[4] Statista (2024).

N. Pocher, *Crypto-Asset Ecosystems and the EU Anti-Money Laundering Framework*, Law, Governance and Technology Series 76,
https://doi.org/10.1007/978-3-031-94698-1_2

and businesses can participate directly on a collective basis. While the development of the FinTech sector unlocked innovative scenarios,[5] the tokenisation of assets has been implemented since 2017 with initial coin offering (ICOs) projects.[6]

The Bitcoin whitepaper is often perceived as embodying the socio-political and techno-economic values of the cyber- and cypher-punk movements, in terms of heralding anonymity and people's freedom from authorities and intermediaries. However, in contrast to the work of May (1988), which explicitly fosters the crypto-anarchist movement, there is not a broad agreement in the literature as to the economic orientation of Nakamoto's whitepaper. In particular, idioms linked to the economy are absent and the work appears scientific in addressing computer security issues.[7] Although the controversy is not inconsequential, it largely falls outside the scope of this work. Over the past decade, the evolution of P2P monetary interactions has amounted to much more (and much more complexity) than pursuing anarchist ideas. While there are anonymity-enhanced use cases such as Monero (Chap. 4), there are also initiatives on stablecoins and CBDCs.[8] Together with the role still played by various types of service providers, this shows how the idea of complete disintermediation must be adequately contextualised.

2.1.1 From Distributed Consensus to the Internet of Value

The creator(s) of Bitcoin did not put forward previously unknown concepts. The whitepaper refers to a collection of existing ideas and technologies, and it builds on years of research in both distributed systems and cryptography.[9] Its value lies in being the first application of a powerful combination: (i) a decentralised P2P protocol,[10] (ii) a public transaction ledger, an append-only and auditable log (i.e., the blockchain), (iii) consensus rules for validating transactions and issuing currency independently, and (iv) the proof-of-work (PoW) algorithm to reach decentralised consensus on the state of transactions. In particular, Nakamoto's combination solves two problems of distributed computing: (a) 'Byzantine Generals' (a computer system needs to cope with the failure of one or more of its components, which may send conflicting information across the network) and (b) 'double-spending'

---

[5] On the evolution of FinTech: Alt et al. (2024).

[6] Arner et al. (2019a), p. 262. Werbach (2020), p. 4. ICOs are online crowdfunding schemes that involve the issuance of digital tokens. The first step is the publication of a whitepaper with the fundamentals of the investment.

[7] Poblet et al. (2020), p. 2. Quiniou (2019), p. xii.

[8] CBDCs and stablecoins are addressed in Chap. 6. 'Privacy coins' are investigated in Chap. 4.

[9] Werbach (2019), p. 3.

[10] A protocol is a system of rules describing how a computer "can connect to, participate in, and transmit information over a system or network. These instructions define code syntax and semantics that the system expects. Protocols can involve hardware, software, and plain-language instructions" (Dannen, 2017, p. 3, referenced by Schrepel, 2021, p. 26).

(i.e., a participant manages to spend the same money multiple times. Bitcoin averts it by verifying the inputs of each added transaction).[11] Additionally, the ecosystem employs encryption in the issuance and in the validation phases, and consent is expressed by network participants through verifiable digital signatures.[12] For the purposes of this analysis, the understanding of crypto-asset ecosystems goes beyond DLTs. The reason is not only that not all relevant applications are based on this set of technologies, but also that architectural aspects are just one of the elements to consider. Yet, the historical role of distributed consensus mechanisms is crucial.

The Bitcoin blockchain is public and permissionless, as explained below. In principle, in this type of systems participants are "mutually distrusting users that may only know each other by their public addresses", where an address is used as an identifier to the entity/entities that are performing activities.[13] In the Bitcoin system, the PoW algorithm incentivises participants to make use of their own processing power to validate transactions through solving cryptographic puzzles, hence becoming so-called miners.[14] This is achieved by offering rewards to whoever solves the problem first, where the reward is the validation of a block of outstanding transactions—i.e., the respective transaction fees.[15] In this way, participants reach a consensus over the order of the events recorded in the ledger. Prohibitive computational and operational (e.g., energy-related) costs aim to deter single (groups of) miners to take over the network and subvert it by creating multiple versions of the ledger or tampering with it. The Bitcoin blockchain is watched over by full-nodes, and in this way reliance on third parties is replaced by a system of (cryptography-based) supposed 'trustless trust'.[16] Indeed, if one can legitimately identify the final goal of consensus algorithms in the decentralisation of the source of truth—i.e., it is no longer necessary to rely on central authorities to agree on a

[11] Antonopoulos (2017b), pp. 1–4. Casey et al. (2018), p. 2.

[12] Cryptography is a form of applied mathematics. Here the applied technique is public-key cryptography or asymmetric encryption, "in which a public key and a corresponding private key are used for encryption and decryption, where public key is disseminated, and private key is known only to the key owner" (ITU-T FG DLT, 2019a, p. 5). In this way, "users can digitally sign data with their private key, and the resulting signature can be verified by anyone using the corresponding public key", while a digital signature consists of "data appended to data units, or cryptographic changes made to data units, which allows the recipient of the data unit to con-firm the origin and integrity of the data and protect the data from being forged" (ITU-T FG DLT, 2019a, pp. 2–5). For an analysis of the role of encryption in blockchains: Schrepel (2021).

[13] ITU-T FG DLT (2019a), p. 1.

[14] PoW is not the only consensus algorithm in the world of blockchains. Among other reasons, the long-term sustainability and environmental impact of its energy-intensive design prompted the development of other consensus protocols, e.g., Proof-of-Stake (PoS), Proof-of-Activity, Proof-of-Burn. Casey et al. (2018), pp. 2–3. Schrepel (2021), p. 24.

[15] ITU-T FG DLT (2019a), p. 8.

[16] Schrepel (2021), pp. 18–19. The correctness of the 'trustless trust' terminology is contested—e.g., Walch (2019a), pp. 1–27. Arruñada (2018). Werbach (2020).

univocal truth by a unique source of authenticity—,[17] the value of oracles in the blockchain sphere testifies to its limits.[18]

This innovative way of devising interactions is grounded on an understanding of online social dimensions that gave birth to a next generation of Internet compared to the 'Internet of Information': an 'Internet of Value (IoV)'.[19] While the first one allows information to be shared by online means, the IoV leverages DLT-based solutions to foster the direct participation of every user in the global economy by embedding an economic layer into the web. In this respect, the concept of asset tokenisation emerges as one the most disruptive, as it depicts the process of issuing a token that digitally represents another (physical or non-physical) asset or right, to the end of storing it and exchanging it on the DLT. It is by leveraging tokenisation and P2P transfers that everyone can exchange value online directly, and blockchain technology creates the conditions for a 'regulated' IoV, permeated by public and democratic values.[20] In comparison with the level of intermediation featured by the traditional financial system, this setup shows a conceptual disruption. Despite their fascination, the concepts underlying the IoV need to be crafted carefully to reach a state of maturity, and cause bundles of problems that need to be addressed, especially in terms of legal and governance dynamics.[21]

2.1.2 What Is the Internet of Money?

To refer to the monetary disintermediation and the dynamics of direct participation introduced by Bitcoin, Antonopoulos (2016, 2017a, 2017b)—one of the first knowledge disseminators in the field—conceived the term 'Internet of Money (IoM)', and infused it with a libertarian ideological connotation. Indeed, Bitcoin and other cryptocurrencies—referred to as 'altcoins', i.e., 'alternative' to Bitcoin—are contextualised within a broader movement that is inherently influenced by the architecture of DLTs and their blockchain subset. This movement, in turn, holds a socio-economic promise of a technology-driven shift towards freedom and efficiency by removing control bottlenecks—i.e., intermediaries—through open and decentralised mechanisms.[22] This ecosystem is "as akin to the internet of money,

[17] Freni et al. (2020), p. 1.

[18] In the DLT domain, an 'oracle' is a third-party service or decentralised data feed acting like bridges and providing external and off-chain information to the blockchain (since the latter cannot autonomously access them).

[19] Casey et al. (2018), p. 7. Chen et al. (2019), p. 1. Tapscott and Euchner (2019). The Cryptocurrency Consultant (2019).

[20] Herian (2019), p. 81.

[21] Casey et al. (2018), p. 7. Werbach (2020), p. 3.

[22] Werbach (2020).

a network for propagating value and securing the ownership of digital assets via distributed computation".[23]

More than a decade later, the set of ecosystems and applications that populate the cryptocurrency domain go well beyond Bitcoin itself. Meanwhile, new initiatives such as stablecoins and CBDCs have started leveraging value tokenisation to uphold various types of digital currencies that to a certain extent differ, ideologically and/or architecturally, from the first cryptocurrency projects. On the contrary, they grow near to the IoV and are often mentioned jointly.[24] Two major reasons for the lack of cohesion between the elements of the IoM is that there is no universal definition of it, and that it is influenced by constant evolutions.

When exploring the interplay of crypto-asset ecosystems and AML/CFT rules, one realises the topic is positioned within the ever-evolving phenomenological landscape where crypto-asset transfers take place.[25] Given the dynamics of the AML/CFT framework, outlined in Chap. 5, and specific traits of crypto-asset ecosystems such as their anonymity and their transparency, the regulatory analysis must be grounded on concrete considerations concerning the actors, elements and entities that populate these ecosystems. Moreover, the lack of terminological clarity in this sphere suggests making a preliminary disambiguation effort to define conceptual yardsticks that can act as foundations for the subsequent reasoning.

Accordingly, this chapter lays out the phenomenological setting of the investigation. To do so, it overviews (i) the concepts of tokens and crypto-assets in terms of definitional impacts, (ii) the role of taxonomy initiatives to understand various types of crypto-assets, (iii) the phenomenology of crypto-asset ecosystems from a static (i.e., architectural) and dynamic (i.e., transactional) perspective, (iv) the socio-technical nature of this sphere, (v) the need to challenge the 'blockchain hype' and distinguish between theory and practice, to safeguard accountability, (vi) the ambiguities surrounding disintermediation, (vii) the evolution of stablecoins and CBDCs, to finally (viii) provide preliminary remarks on how to approach the interplay between crypto-asset ecosystems and the regulatory domain.

2.2 On a Hunt for Definitions Between Tokens and Crypto-Assets

In the field of crypto-assets, terminological consensus is far from being established. Not only does a large array of terms identify relevant applications, but their use varies across jurisdictions and research communities. Tokens, digital tokens,

[23] Antonopoulos (2017b).

[24] Klarin (2020).

[25] 'Phenomenology' refers to crypto-asset ecosystems from a concrete perspective, i.e., what can be experienced observing relevant applications, stakeholders, implementations, features. This terminology highlights possible contrasts between abstract principles believed to be broadly applicable (e.g., anonymity, decentralisation), and what can be observed.

digital currencies, virtual currencies, cryptocurrencies, digital assets, virtual assets, crypto-assets, digital coins, virtual coins, are often used indistinctly to refer to ecosystems, platforms, protocols, and assets. Because the use of each of these options brings with it specific consequences, their interchangeability hinders the creation of a harmonised groundwork on which to build regulatory initiatives, rules for interpretation and enforcement schemes.

In particular, the establishment of a worldwide approach has been hampered by the pursuit of two partly opposite goals: safeguarding consumers, investors and the economy at large from new risks, while reaping the benefits from these ubiquitous markets.[26] These two sentiments originated inconsistent and frequently imprecise methodologies: (i) a general acquiescence and a wait-and-see attitude, sponsoring a general abstention from invasive initiatives, and (ii) caution and fear in front of the (partially) unknown, which led to domain-specific definitions and terminological fragmentation. Almost fifteen years after the advent of Bitcoin and given the considerable developments of the sphere, however, a reactive approach is no longer justifiable. On the contrary, it is pivotal to employ a teleological and pragmatic reasoning anchored to the specific aim pursued when setting a definition. In this way, one can avoid over-simplifications but also steer clear of inconsequential arguments.

2.2.1 Terminological Notes from an EU and FATF Perspective

The financial domain harboured the first large-scale applications of DLTs. Thus, it offers the most comprehensive set of terminological insights in this regard. A vast number of studies showed multiple ways to approach these ecosystems from a regulatory standpoint, with institutions across the financial landscape providing a considerable, albeit divergent at times, set of definitions. They largely made use of the term crypto-assets, in line with the approach employed by standard-setting bodies. Because of the sense of urgency spurred by the fast development of these tools, however, most initiatives have been a reaction to fear of abuses rather than to a structured desire to achieve consistency and grasp connecting factors between the technical and the legal essence of these instruments. Therefore, regulatory and policy documents offer definitions whose degree of specificity differs substantially.

An example is featured by the 2018 FinTech Action plan, whereby the European Commission (EC) requested the European Banking Authority (EBA) and the European Securities and Markets Authority (ESMA) to provide an assessment of whether the EU framework was suitable for ICOs and crypto-assets.[27] On that occasion, the EC referred to 'market developments in crypto-assets', 'speculative investment in crypto-assets and ICO-tokens', while exchanges and service providers

[26] Athanassiou (2019).

[27] European Commission (2018).

"allow investors to purchase crypto-assets and tokens, hold them and trade them".[28] In their January 2019 reports, the EBA and the ESMA fell in line with this terminology.[29] The EBA report defined a crypto-asset as an asset that "(a) depends primarily on cryptography and DLT or similar technology as part of its perceived or inherent value; (b) is neither issued nor guaranteed by a central bank or public authority, and (c) can be used as a means of exchange and/or for investment purposes and/or to access a good or service".[30] ESMA, on its part, identified 'cryptocurrencies or virtual currencies' and 'digital tokens issued through ICOs' as two sub-groups. In May 2019, the European Central Bank (ECB) referred to crypto-assets as "a new type of asset recorded in digital form and enabled by the use of cryptography that is not and does not represent a financial claim on, or a liability of, any identifiable entity".[31] This definition was consistent with the EU concept of virtual currencies, albeit the latter is deemed to be broader.[32] Terminological malleability was confirmed by a December 2019 note of the International Monetary Fund (IMF), according to which "the term crypto asset denotes digital assets that use cryptography for security and are coins or tokens of distributed ledgers and/or blockchains, including asset-backed tokens", thus honouring the fact that "the definition of a crypto asset is far from globally uniform".[33] Moreover, although the terms were interchangeably employed in the document, a distinction between coins and tokens was acknowledged.[34]

The preference of EU institutions for the term crypto-assets was confirmed by the Digital Finance Package adopted in September 2020.[35] Among the actions encompassed by its timeline, the EC put forward two legislative proposals explicitly labelled to be 'on crypto-assets'—later adopted as Regulation on Markets in Crypto-Assets (MiCA) and Regulation on a Pilot Regime for Market Infrastructures Based on DLT.[36] While the first one states that a crypto-asset is "a digital representation of a value or of a right that is able to be transferred and stored electronically using distributed ledger technology or similar technology", the original text of its proposal used to specify that "any definition of crypto-assets should [...] correspond to the definition of virtual assets set out in the recommendations of the Financial

[28] European Commission (2018), p. 6.

[29] European Banking Authority (2019); European Securities and Markets Authority (2019).

[30] European Banking Authority (2019), pp. 10–11. The distinction sub (c) introduces the most widespread categorisation in the area.

[31] European Central Bank Crypto-Assets Task Force (2019), p. 3.

[32] European Central Bank Crypto-Assets Task Force (2019), p. 7.

[33] Cuervo et al. (2019).

[34] More specifically, "coins refer to bitcoin and altcoins, which were originally issued with a main purpose to serve as 'currency', that is, with money and payments-related functions. Tokens have more functions than coins, for example, permitting the coin holders to participate in the service provided or the returns offered by the token issuer" (Cuervo et al., 2019).

[35] European Commission (2020).

[36] Regulation (EU) 2023/1114 and Regulation (EU) 2022/858.

Action Task Force". This is worth noting because a partial discrepancy can be found between EU terminology and that of the FATF, the most important international authority in the AML/CFT domain.[37]

Indeed, the international standard-setter used first the term virtual currencies, and later introduced the notions of virtual assets (VAs) and virtual assets service provider (VASPs) in line with the evolution of the space. While in 2015 the FATF published a Guidance for a risk-based approach: virtual currencies, in 2019 the scope changed to Guidance for a risk-based approach for virtual assets and virtual asset service providers, and the following reports reiterated the choice.[38] According to the provided definition, a virtual asset is a "digital representation of value that can be digitally traded, or transferred, and can be used for payment or investment purposes. Virtual assets do not include digital representations of fiat currencies, securities and other financial assets that are already covered elsewhere in the FATF Recommendations".[39] This is the definition included in the Glossary from 2019 and referenced in October 2021 by the Updated guidance for a risk-based approach to virtual assets and virtual asset service providers.[40] The document testifies to the importance of monitoring the impacts of definitions, and one of its goals is the clarification of the definitions of VA and VASP to ensure they are "expansive and there should not be a case where a relevant financial asset is not covered by the FATF Standards (either as a VA or as another financial asset)".[41] The main question is related to the qualification of stablecoin arrangements, whose uncertain definition had been addressed by several institutions,[42] and in the EU MiCA Regulation.

The virtual choice can also be found in EU legislation. Directive (EU) 2015/849 (the so-called 4AMLD), as amended by Directive (EU) 2018/843 (the 5AMLD), does not mention crypto-assets, but defines virtual currencies as "a digital representation of value that is not issued or guaranteed by a central bank or a public authority, is not necessarily attached to a legally established currency and does not possess a legal status of currency or money, but is accepted by natural or legal persons as a means of exchange and which can be transferred, stored and traded electronically".[43] After the release of the AML Package addressed in Chap. 5, however, it can be argued the EU is converging towards the crypto option also in the AML field. Indeed, Article 2(7) of Regulation (EU) 2024/1624 on the prevention of the use of the financial system for the purposes of money laundering and terrorist financing refers to the definition of crypto-asset of the MiCA Regulation. Crypto-

[37] The Financial Action Task Force (FATF) is an intergovernmental organisation whose mandate focuses on setting standards to combat threats to the international financial system.

[38] Financial Action Task Force (2015, 2019, 2020a, 2020c).

[39] Financial Action Task Force (2019), p. 47.

[40] Financial Action Task Force (2021), p. 109.

[41] Financial Action Task Force (2021), p. 5.

[42] Financial Action Task Force (2020b); Financial Stability Board (2019); Bank for International Settlements (2019).

[43] Directive (EU) 2015/849 as amended by Directive (EU) 2018/843.

asset service providers (CASPs) are also at the core of the recast of Regulation (EU) 2015/847 to expand traceability requirements to crypto-assets, namely Regulation (EU) 2023/1113.

Against this backdrop, preliminary conclusions may be drawn. Provided the context is clearly outlined, the terms crypto-assets, digital assets and virtual assets may be used interchangeably. Ostensibly, however, the wording digital assets has a more generic nuance, and can cause confusion.[44] Other expressions such as cryptocurrencies or virtual currencies identify a subset of the assets. This is the way they are used in this work. Nevertheless, in early documents they were used to refer to the global set of crypto-assets. The term digital currencies is used in several cases, but lacks specificity when compared to virtual currencies or cryptocurrencies.

For the sake of structure and clarity, one may distinguish between two parts of these compound words: (a) crypto, virtual, digital, and (b) their possible objects—currencies, assets, tokens, and coins. The part sub (a) is often employed interchangeably, which leads to interpret crypto-assets, virtual assets and digital assets as synonyms. Literally, however, crypto is a subcategory of virtual, which is a subgroup of digital. Hence, cryptocurrencies are the subset of virtual currencies whose functioning relies on cryptography. Following this reasoning, digital assets is the most comprehensive expression, although the literature also defines crypto-assets as a neutral choice.[45] Undeniably, most of the retrievable definitions are sector-specific, and focus on financial regulation, crypto-assets market structure and relevant risks. This approach can cause discrepancies and may not relate to the architectural nature of these assets. In these cases, the use and usefulness of the definitions is limited to the specific framework, and they cannot be used as general benchmarks. As these inconsistencies hardly fit the legal need for certainty, in some jurisdictions (e.g., United States) the tendency is to ignore the formal qualification of a specific instrument when establishing applicable rules, and they rather refer to the concrete activity or transaction undertaken in each case.[46]

2.2.2 *Tokens: Bridging Techno-Legal Definitional Gaps*

Concurrently, the terms tokens or digital tokens are often used as a synonym of crypto-asset or, in conjoined expressions, to identify a subset of them—e.g., ICO-tokens or asset-backed tokens. This is not wholly incorrect, but a useful distinction can be made. Seemingly, these items are referred to as tokens when a technological approach is employed, or when there is an attempt to visualise these instruments

[44] Allen et al. (2020), p. 7, provided a narrower definition of crypto-assets as "digital tokens exclusively issued and transferred via open, permissionless DLT systems that play an indispensable role in the economic incentive design of the underlying shared ledger or application." They do not represent any external rights or things, and, consequently, do not constitute a financial asset.

[45] Brummer (2019), p. 1.

[46] For instance, the Howey Test deployed by the US Supreme Court to determine if a transaction qualifies as a security.

to describe them. Nonetheless, it was argued that "digital assets, sometimes called tokens, are poorly understood. That may be why they are used to describe a variety of things, some of which are contradictory", as well as "the different interpretations and uses of the word token are many, varied, and collectively confusing".[47]

The past years showcased how these terminological aspects are far from trivial. Indeed, the increasing variety of DLT-based assets is posing cross-disciplinary problems. Having no clear regulatory box in which to place an entity is not inconsequential, and technological development suffers from the causal link between the lack of (harmonised) definitions, lack of interdisciplinary dialogue, and lack of standardisation. In other words, the perception different communities have of new technologies is influenced by regulatory regimes. This public perception, in turn, is susceptible to shaping technological development.

If these uncertainties undermine cross-disciplinary cooperation in the field of crypto-assets, one can only imagine the extent to which the lack of a reference framework impairs public understanding.[48] The complexity of the DLT space, complemented by the impossibility of explaining the basics with a common language, can block communication with society. Under these circumstances, some perceived risks grow exponentially and are not caused as much by the features of crypto-assets as by widespread misconceptions. Since the average consumer is fascinated by this sphere, this calls for efforts by cross-disciplinary communities. In this respect, a valuable initiative finds tokens more suitable than other concepts to establish a common reference framework. While the expression tokenisation is gaining a foothold, in line with a shift from economics to tokenomics,[49] tokens were described as one of the building blocks of the blockchain world.[50] Above and beyond, "far from being just a means of payment, tokens are the critical data structure that could underpin every aspect of the future society".[51]

There is a general agreement that tokens are crypto-assets. Besides, tokens have been conceptualised as the 'legal wrap-up' of crypto-assets and depicted as crucial in the tokenised economy, while their legal validity might be ensured through smart contracts.[52] In a more descriptive way, tokens would be the way a legal right is embedded into a crypto-asset. The value of this idea lies in linking the two concepts of tokens and crypto-assets without forcing them into an unstable and undefined unicum. Crypto-assets can be digital or digitised assets, which means a token can represent a primary digital asset (the asset exists exclusively on the blockchain) or

[47] Tapscott (2020), pp. 3–5.

[48] Tapscott (2020), p. 5.

[49] Sandner (2020). Tokenisation: conversion of a physical or non-physical asset into a digital token on a blockchain. Token economics: a type of economy reflected by the design of an ecosystem in a blockchain environment.

[50] Athanassiou (2019).

[51] Skalex (2019). Arguably, tokens do not actually 'exist', either physically or in code. In fact, there is no code that specifically refers to a coin, a blockchain token is just a series of receipts.

[52] In the token economy, medium of exchanges feature embedded incentives and disincentives, while smart contracts and decentralised apps enable preprogrammed, (purportedly) trustless, interactions (Casey et al., 2018, p. 5).

be issued by tokenising existing assets (e.g., physical assets or rights).[53] Arguably, tokens represent architecturally what crypto-assets are, which explains a broader use of the latter in legal discourse. The tokenisation process consists of encapsulating "value in tradeable units of accounts".[54] Legal components embedded in a token define what kind of crypto-asset is originated, as the token can be seen as a digitised version of the underlying value.

Whether and how a token is also a coin from a strict definition perspective, however, is not straightforward. Yet, every digital coin is a crypto-asset and also a token, given that every digital coin technologically appears as a token. The matter rests on the meaning given to coin and token, which goes back to the definitory levels of assets and tokens. Clearly, these terms need clearer scopes of application, which explains the relevance of the taxonomy efforts described below. These initiatives single out types and uses of tokens, as well as their properties, from a legal and a technical standardisation perspective.

2.2.3 *Taxonomy Initiatives*

When trying to establish what crypto-assets are, focus has been mainly on identifying sub-groups.[55] A key angle from which to distinguish crypto-assets is their purpose, although over time this approach was complemented by others. From this so-called 'functional' perspective, three categories of underlying tokens were pinpointed:[56] (i) exchange tokens, also labelled as payment tokens or currency tokens, (ii) security or investment tokens, and (iii) utility tokens. Cryptocurrencies fall within the category sub (i) and can be defined as payment-type crypto-assets. Hence, as per the reasoning above, payment tokens are the architectural representation of what payment-type crypto-assets (i.e., cryptocurrencies) are. They are used as a means of payment or exchange for goods and services, where the latter are typically external to the DLT ecosystem on which the tokens are built. When a token is used to access goods and services, with these being internal to the DLT ecosystem they are built on, it belongs to the group sub (iii). In practice, utility tokens can also feature investment purposes; when they are legally defined as financial instruments, however, they are deemed security tokens.[57] When a token falls into more than one category, it is hybrid.

[53] Inozemtsev (2021).

[54] Freni et al. (2020), pp. 1–2.

[55] Examples of academic studies include Oliveira et al. (2018); Euler (2018).

[56] HM Treasury (2018); Euler (2018); Garrido (2023).

[57] In the United States, a security token is one that passes the 'Howey Test'; in this case, the mentioned transaction-oriented approach is employed, and the activity taking place is assessed. According to the 'Howey Test', the securities regime is applied in presence of all the following requirements: "an investment of money, [. . .] in a common enterprise, [. . .] in which the investor is led to expect profits, [. . .] derived from the entrepreneurial or managerial efforts of promoters or third parties" (Garrido 2023, referring to SEC v. W.J. Howey Co., 328 U.S. 293 (1946)).

In crypto-oriented publications, utility or security may refer to two extremes that are construed instrumentally and are complementary features of a collective whole. In this respect, the perception is that tokens should be touched by the law only if they are of the security type. On the contrary, if a token is of the utility kind, or presented as such, regulatory legitimacy would be lacking.[58] However, it is common for a crypto-asset to be hybrid, and ever-evolving features may be the basis of different interpretations. This may explain why terms like cryptocurrencies and digital coins are sometimes used with a broader scope, to include utility or security tokens.[59]

Further, a crypto-asset can be either native to its own blockchain, like Bitcoin or Ether, or non-native—i.e., built on top of another blockchain (e.g., a utility token built on Ethereum)—and acting as a proxy, representing assets that exist outside the given ledger.[60] Another label derives from Ethereum enabling projects and decentralised applications (dApps) to be developed through smart contracts deployed on its platform: application or platform token. When a token is created to be used on a dApp, its purpose depends on the application itself.[61] These tokens can be used as 'facilitators' for users external and unrelated to the operation of the network that has created them.

The idea of coins and tokens being antithetical concepts is seemingly simplistic. However, it leads to a better understanding of the different levels these remarks should be attached to. As the crypto-economy evolved, especially through Ethereum-based options, some uses of the term token started to part from cryptocurrencies. Tokens started to be used to represent both real world objects (e.g., land, artwork, vehicles) and rights (e.g., intellectual property), and tokenisation processes allowed decentralisation to be applied to value-based heterogeneous contexts beyond the monetary sphere.[62] Accordingly, tokens were phrased to be fungible or non-fungible. Whereas the first group refers to money-related fungibility (i.e., interchangeability or functional equivalence), the creation of unique crypto-items was enabled by the Ethereum ERC-721 standard.[63] While a popular traditional example is that of crypto-collectibles like CryptoKitties, Non-Fungible Tokens (NFTs) have more recently reached not only the headlines and an impressive share of worldwide interest, but also incredible evaluations.

In the words of the FATF, NFTs are "digital assets that are unique, rather than interchangeable, and that are in practice used as collectibles rather than as payment

[58] Tapscott (2020), p. 4.

[59] Tapscott (2020), p. 4. After the 2017 boom, certain Initial Coin Offerings were ruled as 'unlicensed sales of securities' by the US Securities and Exchange Commission (SEC); later, the term 'Security Token Offerings' (STOs) emerged.

[60] Athanassiou (2019), p. 3. In a slightly inconsistent way with the approach supported here, the words 'coins' and 'tokens' have been respectively linked to these two categories; only crypto-assets having their own platform can be 'coins', while 'token' identifies non-native assets.

[61] Distefano et al. (2020).

[62] Freni et al. (2020), p. 2.

[63] Ethereum request for comments (ERCs) are a set of technical standards used to create and manage tokens on the Ethereum blockchain.

or investment instruments".[64] In brief, while one bitcoin, or one ether, are equal, respectively, to another bitcoin or another ether, every CryptoKitty is one of a kind, and an NFT can represent anything in a unique form as an Ethereum-based asset. They represent ownership of unique items—e.g., they allow digital fine art to be sold to collectors, leveraging the capacity of NFTs to ensure proof-of-ownership.[65] NFTs themselves have been object of interdisciplinary and multi-layered taxonomy efforts.[66]

A typical criticism to functional classifications of tokens is that it often falls short in resolving key regulatory questions.[67] Yet, the concept of token has over time appeared not only familiar to technology-oriented domains, but also useful to connect legal arguments to it. The Token Taxonomy Initiative (TTI) by the Blockchain Research Institute addresses these issues. It pursues standardisation and meta-standardisation,[68] not only to suit socio-legal needs of oversight and accountability, but also for technical and interoperability reasons. To make sense of what a token is, the Token Taxonomy Framework (TTF) was launched in 2019. The idea was to create a composition scheme from the ground up, by making use of concepts and terms that can define and describe token projects in a modular, flexible and expandable template in a way that is both intuitive and technical.[69]

The TTF identified a set of token features: valuable (value can be determined), representative (of a claim to an asset, resource, right), digital (digitally stored), discrete (existence and number do not rely on observers), and authentic (authenticity can be verified). It also defined token types, behaviours and properties. Token types are its first foundation; beside fungible and non-fungible tokens, the idea of hybrid tokens is introduced when both fungible and non-fungible features are embodied (e.g., a reserved ticket). As to compositional elements, tokens can have different behaviors: rules for how they behave (e.g., singleton, indivisible vs. divisible); and properties/property sets: descriptive values they must have, but only have external meaning (e.g., a serial number).[70]

The fast-growing variety of tokens, however, does not only need classification templates; to increase security and avoid scams, they must be uniquely identified. The decentralised nature of the token-based economy makes it hard to distinguish between legitimate and fraudulent projects and to unambiguously refer to an

[64] Financial Action Task Force (2021), p. 24.

[65] Ethereum (2022).

[66] Hartwich et al. (2024).

[67] Garrido (2023), p. 23. After all, "[i]n the absence of legal rules, it is challenging to characterize the connection between tokens and rights" (Ibid., p. 30).

[68] Meta-standardisation refers to the characteristics of being chain-agnostic and technology-neutral (Tapscott, 2020, pp. 8–9).

[69] Tapscott (2020), p. 7. A specific syntax allows tokens to be defined by using a string of characters and a design tool eases the creation of puzzle-piece-looking tokens (Tapscott, 2020, p. 14).

[70] Tapscott (2020), pp. 10–12. Notably, the TTF outlined a set of behaviours that highlight features of a token behaving like money (Tapscott, 2020, pp. 12–13). More information is provided below.

item—e.g., in sale and purchase agreements. Arguably, "any service that neglects to maintain unique references is contributing to corrupt the entire subsequent ecosystem relying on its data", which prevents market maturation.[71] The International Token Standardisation Association (ITSA) tackled the issue and developed holistic market standards as unique identifiers. The scope included all DLT-based cryptographic tokens; the goals were identification, classification, and analysis.[72] Accordingly, the International Token Identification Number (ITIN) was created—for decentralised items identification is pivotal; their being software-defined and fork-susceptible demands to adequately locate their addresses across protocols.[73] The ITIN framework addressed the different levels of the token and asset definitions in an elaborate way. The term asset was used to identify the form of economic value represented by tokens.[74] In contrast to other identifiers, it did not assign a 'name' to an asset. The ITSA interface allowed reference to all information about the token and the transaction.

Taxonomy projects pursued by the BRI and ITSA show the concept of token is as crucial as multi-layered. Arguably, the token definition addresses two elements: their function and the essence of the asset they represent.[75] Hence, there are no inherent or self-standing definitions, and classification frameworks ought to focus on mapping value representations.[76]

2.2.4 *The Regulatory Role of Tokens*

Taxonomy initiatives show the importance of token definitions to convey a meaningful image of the crypto-asset space. If one considers that a token is the representation, from an architectural viewpoint, of what a crypto-asset is, their legal value is easier to grasp. Indeed, the creation and exchange processes, the rights they symbolise, the difference and/or similarity to traditional assets, are all

---

[71] Sandner (2020).

[72] ITSA (2022).

[73] The concept recalls Uniform Resource Locators (URLs) to locate web resources. ITINs build on the Uniform Token Locator standard, consisting of genesis hash, post-fork hash, recent hash, smart contract address, token sub-address. Most tokens are identifiable through post fork hashes and smart contract addresses; for NFTs sub-address can be used. Reliability and unambiguity are guaranteed by recent hashes. ITIN acts as a UTL shortener.

[74] ITSA represented the relationship between tokens and assets by using three layers: asset layer, protocol layer, token layer (token address, location and definition). The asset layer refers to the referenced asset, in terms of its economic value, e.g., for a share it would be dividend payments or voting rights, for physical assets their value.

[75] Freni et al. (2020), p. 2.

[76] The proposed approach is grounded on General Morphological Analysis and aims to map all dimensions of the problem (i.e., token identification and definition) and possible relationships to identify patterns (Freni et al., 2020, p. 3).

legally impactful topics. In broader terms, the perception of the role of tokens is increasing, and there is an emerging call to use them as regulatory benchmarks. Not many legal systems, however, explicitly follow this approach. It was argued that when the usefulness of tokens is not recognised, there is usually a lack of technical knowledge, and two consequences arise: an intensification of existing uncertainties and ambiguities and regulating intermediaries remains the only feasible methodology.[77] The last aspect is relevant to the AML/CFT domain, where current regulatory attempts are tainted by the insufficiency of applying 'active cooperation' strategies to new socio-legal ecosystems. Meanwhile, most tokens remain unregulated, as they do not meet the standards of a type of recognised asset.

In this respect, valuable insights can be drawn from a legislative initiative adopted in Liechtenstein in October 2019: the so-called Blockchain Act.[78] Its scope of application are Tokens and Trustworthy Technologies (TT), which are "technologies through which the integrity of Tokens, the clear assignment of Tokens to TT Identifiers and the disposal over Tokens is ensured".[79] A Token is defined as "a piece of information on a TT System which: (1) can represent claims or rights of memberships against a person, rights to property or other absolute or relative rights; and (2) is assigned to one or more TT Identifiers", i.e., public keys, enabling token assignment.[80] In brief, Liechtenstein did not regulate DLTs but focused on tokens, treated as 'containers of rights' and whose ownership/transfer is grounded on the interdependence between tokens and private keys. Meanwhile, the obligation of service providers to register depends on their functional relationship with tokens. Positive evaluations of the initiative consider that if it is through tokens that DLTs can unfold their potential and create new categories of assets and new ecosystems for their exchange, their regulation must be approached through the prism of tokens.[81] The EC's Digital Finance Package seemingly agrees, as it explicitly addresses tokenisation, and the MiCA Regulation largely refers to tokens—e.g., 'asset-referenced token', 'electronic money token', 'utility token'.[82]

2.2.5 *Cryptocurrencies and Qualification as Legal Tender*

Cryptocurrencies are payment tokens, also known as currency or exchange-type tokens. They are the prime implementation of blockchain technology and at the roots of its hype. A popular distinction is the one between convertible and non-convertible cryptocurrencies, which is based on the possibility to exchange them with fiat

[77] Athanassiou (2019), pp. 3–7.

[78] Token- und VT-Dienstleister-Gesetz (2019).

[79] Article 1(1)(a) of Token- und VT-Dienstleister-Gesetz (2019).

[80] Article 1(1)(c) and (d) of Token- und VT-Dienstleister-Gesetz (2019).

[81] Athanassiou (2019).

[82] Regulation (EU) 2023/1114.

currency or not.[83] The prevalence of convertibility over other categorisations mirrors a regulatory approach focused on the impact on the traditional financial system—i.e., on funds entering/leaving the crypto-asset space through an intermediary. Although the evolution of regulatory frameworks shows an increasing awareness of how the convertibility argument may be simplistic, the perception that non-convertibility per se entails dwarfed risks stems from the fact that there is no agreement on legally classifying cryptocurrencies as money. Indeed, as of today the only two jurisdictions that qualify Bitcoin—only Bitcoin, not any cryptocurrency—as legal tender are El Salvador, which did so with a controversial initiative known as Ley Bitcoin (or Bitcoin law),[84] and more recently the Central African Republic.[85]

As far as El Salvador is concerned, in September 2021 the country adopted "bitcoin as unrestricted legal tender with liberating power, unlimited in any transaction, and to any title that public or private natural or legal persons require carrying out" (Article 1), hence "all obligations in money expressed in USD, existing before the effective date of this, may be paid in bitcoin" (Article 13).[86] Accordingly, "tax contributions can be paid in bitcoin" (Article 4) and "exchanges in bitcoin will not be subject to capital gains tax, just like any legal tender" (Article 5). Although "every economic agent must accept bitcoin as payment when offered to him by whoever acquires a good or service" (Article 7), the Decree acknowledges the country's structural issues, and provides that "those who, by evident and notorious fact, do not have access to the technologies that allow them to carry out transactions in bitcoin are excluded from the obligation expressed in Art. 7 of this law. The state will promote the necessary training and mechanisms so that the population can access bitcoin transactions" (Article 12). Technical standards were later drawn up by the local central bank—e.g., wallets, educational measures.

The Central African Republic adopted Bitcoin as legal tender in April 2022. Controversies ensued, due to the dramatic socio-economic and geopolitical situation of the country, and its being a member of the Central African Monetary Union. Further, the country features comparatively low Internet access and digital literacy,[87] while Bitcoin's volatility discourages merchants from accepting bitcoins as a means of payment even if mandated by Article 10 of Law No. 22.004.[88]

These cases show how the legal qualification of cryptocurrencies is an issue inherently addressed at the (supra)national level, in line with elements of 'monetary law' and 'central bank law' explored in Chap. 6. This generates fragmentation that stems from different interpretations, while when supranational and international

[83] Fiat currency has no intrinsic value and is legal tender by means of a governmental act.

[84] Decreto N°57/2021. A comment was published by Gorjón (2021). An English translation of the Bitcoin Law can be found at Roy (2021).

[85] Kabré (2022). The qualification of Bitcoin as legal tender was introduced by Law No. 22.004.

[86] The US Dollar is the official currency of El Salvador.

[87] It was estimated 15% of the population has access to electricity and 10% to the Internet (Kabré, 2022).

[88] Kabré (2022) Law No. 22.004.

frameworks deal with exchange-type crypto-assets they tend to do so in silos, limiting their actions to the scope of their individual mandates. Generally, however, their goal is to prevent and mitigate risks and negative socio-legal impacts posed by these instruments. The preferred approach is not to state whether cryptocurrencies are legal tender, but to determine whether specific rules for monetary or financial transactions apply to them. This generates an intertwinement of fragmentations that adds to—and partially derives from—the difficulty in connecting the conceptual levels of being money from a legal perspective and a token from a technical standpoint. This is made even harder by the linguistic impact of token discourse originating from the Bitcoin world, which developed in opposition to traditional monetary systems. Above all, traditional legal concepts of money and currency do not relate to technology, as they are built on conventions.

Against this backdrop, a major problem posed by DLT-based implementations lies in asking the law to apply unconventional reasonings. In the tokenised economy, however, it makes sense to distinguish tokens that behave like money from tokens that do not. If one wants to use the concept of token as a legal benchmark and provide it with tailored rules, the role of technology is inevitably stronger than usual. After all, (a set of) blockchain-based solutions were described as replacing the traditional concept of trust with an innovative type of trust that is placed on technology itself, in the form of computer protocols.[89] From a pragmatic standpoint, the TTI maps features that a token must display to behave as money; as acknowledged, the list is a work in progress. Namely, such a token must: (a) have roles that are definable and assignable, and be (b) delegable (i.e., the owner can delegate certain behaviours), (c) transferable and (d) holdable (i.e., every token has an owner that can transfer it), (e) compliant with legal obligations (e.g., AML/CFT), (f) burnable, and (g) mintable.[90]

As far as payment tokens are concerned and depending on the source of their value, there is a difference between (i) intrinsic value tokens, and (ii) asset-backed or asset-referenced tokens. The first category derives its value from the activities (e.g., acquisition and use) undertaken by the users, while the value of the second group depends on the value of the mirrored assets, as in stablecoins. In this regard, the MiCA Regulation provides for a classification of crypto-assets that distinguishes between (1) utility tokens, which are "only intended to provide access to a good or a service supplied by (their) issuer";[91] (2) asset-referenced tokens, which aim "to maintain a stable value by referencing to any other value or right or a combination thereof, including one or more official currencies";[92] and (3) e-money tokens, which purport "to maintain a stable value by referencing to the value of one official currency".[93]

---

[89] Athanassiou (2019), p. 2.

[90] Tapscott (2020), pp. 12–13.

[91] Article 3(1)(9) of Regulation (EU) 2023/1114.

[92] Article 3(1) and (6) of Regulation (EU) 2023/1114.

[93] Article 3(1)(7) of Regulation (EU) 2023/1114.

2.3 The Accountability Conundrum: Architectures and Transactions

Antonopoulos (2016) coined the IoM label to discuss the innovative interplay between individual Internet users and disintermediated monetary transactions. His use of this expression features a strong ideologic characterisation, and in his speeches the disintermediation philosophy of the crypto-economy is an inspiration to change socio-economic dynamics, in line with the 'blockchain hype'.[94] Nonetheless, the concrete impact of crypto-assets on the general public has been as diverse as multifold. When new technologies meet established markets, they introduce both opportunities and risks. While some risks may be only perceived due to the fear of the unknown, others may exert concrete consequences. From a first perspective this work investigates dangers linked to the anonymity problem, tainting some crypto-asset ecosystems with risks of money laundering, fraud, tax evasion, and other forms of exploitation for illicit purposes. Secondly, this analysis weighs anonymity against the features of transparency that may inform DLTs architecturally.

This endeavour requires disambiguation of the features of these instruments, by first exploring their origin and various related understandings. When focusing on an architectural interpretation of cryptocurrencies that is mostly token-based, one may incur the risk of thinking they are deemed anonymous or transparent only because of how relevant tokens are construed. On the contrary, there are many aspects to be considered. The risks sketched above are not only inherent to tokens, but mostly relate to the structure of the systems that generate and exchange them, and to how governance is managed within them.[95] The main components that may influence such assessments are introduced below.

2.3.1 Crypto-Asset Ecosystems: Stakeholders and Socio-Technical Traits

Notwithstanding the role of architectural features in crypto-asset networks, important distinctions relate to the interplay of the actors involved in their lifecycle. A major example is that of the 'trustless' characterisation of these systems, where the general perception is of a thorough departure from trust among parties, leading to describe DLT-based implementations as inherently trustless—or at least substituting interpersonal trust with one in technology and algorithms. These arguments have been debated with reference to the roles concretely played by specific actors,[96] and legal literature has explored the impacts of participating stakeholders on accountability and liability within non-centralised and distributed networks.

[94] Hacker et al. (2019), pp. 3–12.

[95] Governance aspects are closely connected to the decentralisation debate (see below).

[96] Walch (2019a); Arruñada (2018); Werbach (2020).

Scholars refer to crypto-asset ecosystems, and to some related activities—e.g., cryptolaundering or platforms for digital democracy—, as socio-technical systems (STSs).[97] This expression compounds the interrelation between different levels of what the system is and does, as well as the way it interacts with other networks and/or external sources.[98] As the label suggests, they are complex systems that comprise elements belonging to the human, technological and technical sphere, organised to pursue a common goal (Chap. 1). To grasp their behaviours, one should not only examine separate components, but also their interactions—i.e., the overall system should be taken as unit of analysis.[99] Before delving into the interactions with external elements, this section outlines the basic stakeholders in a crypto-asset ecosystem.[100] These are: (a) users, (b) market participants, (c) nodes, (d) miners/forgers,[101] and (e) software developers. Their concrete roles are defined by the specific system, which means the extent of their power depends on structural and governance classifications. The role of these actors is key because regulatory efforts are constantly looking for targets to which their goals can be linked, especially when their traditional approach is based on intermediaries, such as in the AML/CFT sphere. In this respect, a substantial amount of literature provides analytical overviews of how their features may impact different DLT-based ecosystems, as well as of how technology itself prompts and encourages their participation and/or decisions, if any.

As an example, actors can be classified as per their relationship with the ecosystem, and were labelled as essential, native, or metamorphic. Essential stakeholders are necessary for the system to exist, but in principle do not exert control over the network. In permissionless systems this is usually the case for users, nodes, miners and developers. It was argued they cannot be held legally accountable because they may be unaware of their activity, which is constrained by code.[102] Consensus on this classification, however, has yet to be reached. Regarding miners and developers, well-known hard fork cases (e.g., Ethereum, Bitcoin) highlighted the power they may exert even within permissionless systems.[103] This circumstance is most likely

[97] Desmond et al. (2019), pp. 481–482. De Domenico and Baronchelli (2019), p. 1. Poblet et al. (2020), p. 3. Renwick and Gleasure (2020).

[98] Werbach (2019), pp. ix–x.

[99] Desmond et al. (2019), pp. 481–482.

[100] Capaccioli (2020). The blockchain-based subset is likely to influence the discussion more than others. The approach employed here is teleological, and concepts are mentioned when meaningful in terms of the accountability of those active in the ecosystems.

[101] In PoS, validators are known as forgers and ensure cooperation by putting holdings at stake.

[102] Capaccioli (2020), pp. 472–474. Arguably, the only approach is 'code as law' (see Chap. 7).

[103] A hard fork is a substantial change of the protocol of a blockchain network, whereby previously blocks and transactions are made invalid. It requires all validators to upgrade the software.

to occur when there is a participation of mining pools—i.e., groups of miners that join their computational power to increase the likelihood of mining a block.[104]

Indeed, native actors are not essential for the system to exist, but they originate within the cryptocurrency domain. Examples may refer to mining pools, a subset of entities that provide wallets and mixing services, consensus systems other than PoW. Finally, metamorphic actors are providers of services that can also be provided outside of the cryptocurrency sphere.[105]

2.3.2 *Multi-Layered Dynamics: Remarks on Access Control and Governance*

The actual operational weight exerted by the players active in DLT-based ecosystems is influenced by (i) the overall network and platform structure, and (ii) the link with external off-chain elements or other on-chain layers belonging to the same ecosystem. Hence, leading factors to consider pertain to (a) the off-chain or the on-chain world, and (b) the network or the application/protocol level. Significant misunderstandings stem from the phenomenological integration between these elements, which exerts a great impact on accountability. In this respect, a specification is needed. On the one hand, although DLT and blockchain are often used interchangeably, blockchain is a subset of DLTs and other types of distributed ledgers exist. This approach poses limitations and overlooks alternative structures, such as IOTA's directed acyclic graph (DAG), known as the Tangle.[106] Nonetheless, crypto-asset ecosystems are significantly based on blockchains.

On the other hand, in the dynamics of a blockchain ecosystem some distinctions impact regulatory methodologies and enforcement actions. A distributed ledger system can be public (i.e., "accessible to the public for use") or private (i.e., accessible "only to a limited group of DLT users", hence the label 'consortium blockchains' when multiple organisations are involved).[107] Meanwhile, it can be permissionless or permissioned; in the first case to maintain and operate a node it is not necessary to have permissions, which are required in a permissioned system.[108] A permissionless system such as the Bitcoin network is a decentralised ledger "open

[104] Since mining pools are usually managed by companies/individuals who relieve other participants from managing a full node, they are deemed native stakeholders. Walch (2019b), pp. 52–58. Walch (2019a), p. 5. Arruñada (2018), pp. 59–61.

[105] Capaccioli (2020), pp. 474–475. Arguably, their involvement with crypto-assets is just a diversification of their non-crypto activities. Hence, they can be addressed by traditional legal means.

[106] Saa et al. (2023).

[107] ITU-T Focus Group on Digital Currency (2019), p. 5.

[108] ITU-T Focus Group on Digital Currency (2019), p. 4. A permission refers to "intended allowable user actions (e.g., participate, read, write, execute)".

to anyone validating blocks, without needing permission from any authority", while in permissioned ones "users validating blocks shall be authorised".[109]

While these are conceptual distinctions grounded on architectural differences, the phenomenology of these ecosystems shows that even when self-organisation is pursued and control is supposed to be exerted by the algorithms, less visible and self-evident forces influence the management of these structures. Some of them depend on the relationship between the actors involved in the network and exerting impact on it. This group of entities is called an 'ecosystem'. As introduced in Chap. 1, these entities may be described as belonging to one among four areas: (a) hardware (e.g., nodes), (b) business (e.g., developers, users, miners, investors), (c) software development (e.g., financial, semi-financial, non-financial), and (d) protocol development (e.g., developers, academia).[110]

2.3.3 *Decentralisation and Non-Centralisation: A Matter of Degree*

The decentralised element of the crypto-asset sphere played a key role in supporting the socio-economic claims that accompanied its uptake, while it troubles regulatory frameworks that rely on accountability. However, the development of this space shows how these ecosystems are increasingly complex and do not always mirror the traditional image of a DLT-based monetary system—i.e., (the public understanding of) the Bitcoin network. Values and technologies, no matter how closely linked at initial stages, develop independently, especially when a plethora of actors pursue several goals by employing similar tools. It follows that crypto-asset discourse is affected by over-generalisations.

In this respect, decentralised is not always an accurate description of DLT-based STSs. While the underlying network is distributed and features a P2P architecture, with nodes communicating in a direct and equal way, a system is decentralised only when it is not controlled by a (single) central authority—i.e., no single user controls the data. In most legal fields, control can be exerted in different ways. In the DLT context, it can be measured using various criteria, and the quality of being (de)centralised is dynamic, multi-level and non-binary. Hence, the term non-centralised is more appropriate.[111] In this way, one can avert the risk of referring the concept to both the network itself and internal power dynamics (i.e., governance). Indeed, "blockchains are not by definition decentralised. Rather, they

[109] ITU-T Focus Group on Digital Currency (2019), p. 8. The topic is further explored in Chap. 3.

[110] ITU-T FG DLT (2019b), pp. 2–4. Mining pools are an example of a less-evident influential factor. Even in permissionless blockchains there is power recentralisation when individual actors are coordinated by a pool manager. This generates key governance consequences. As non-expert users seem to trust developers considerably, computer scientists and miners become partially trusted fiduciaries (Walch, 2019a, pp. 9–10. Szabo, 2017).

[111] Quiniou (2019), pp. 6–11. Schrepel (2021), pp. 24, 56. Allen et al. (2020), p. 16. Bodó and Giannopoulou (2019).

can be centralised at both the software and the hardware levels. First, one may have a blockchain that runs only on very few nodes, which can all be located in the same room. Second, even when DLT is highly decentralised at hardware level, it can still be centralised at the software governance level".[112]

A recent analysis conceptualised the degree of decentralisation of a given blockchain by identifying nine layers: (i) 'real space', (ii) cyberspace and the Internet, (iii) blockchain and ledger, (iv) blockchain infrastructure, (v) governance mechanism, (vi) applications, (vii) users, (viii) interaction/competition with other blockchain ecosystems, and (ix) interaction/competition with other technologies, services and applications. Hence, a blockchain ecosystem is a "set of levels".[113] With regard to governance, even in permissionless ledgers deemed fully decentralised (e.g., Bitcoin), an evaluation of decentralisation cannot disregard the possible presence of embedded governing structures, who ensure a degree of (re)centralisation. Furthermore, consortium systems (e.g., Corda, Hyperledger) are permissioned, but labelled as semi-decentralised, because centrally coordinated changes are allowed. Parallelly, centralised systems can be equipped with features that limit the overall decentralisation.[114]

Indeed, there is an interplay of different dimensions. Beyond the specificity of decentralisation analyses, failing to notice the complexity of the notion may generate an ambiguity that can be exploited to infer unaccountability from a perceived diffusion of power. This gives rise to the 'veil of decentralisation', mirroring the 'corporate veil' that severs rights/duties of a corporation from those of its shareholders.[115] In this respect, "the degree of centralisation reflects the accumulation of interacting decisions and tradeoffs at various layers", and "the fluctuating nature of a system's level of decentralisation is worth emphasising, as every passing second could bring massive changes to it. So many factors affect how decentralised a blockchain system is, so a change to any of those factors can shift the blockchain on the decentralisation spectrum".[116] Hence, the centralisation vs. decentralisation debate does not account for the structure of STSs, which are, ultimately, governed by human behaviour.[117]

The topic can be represented visually. A study addressed the evolution of cryptocurrency systems as 'interconnected systems of agents', quantitively measuring their centralisation.[118] The analysis focuses on the interactions of network entities

[112] Finck (2019).

[113] Schrepel (2021), pp. 59–62. The author defines decentralisation as "a dynamic and multi-level concept that measures the autonomy enjoyed by a given subject in determining its competence", where competence refers to "the ability to determine the spheres of action within which a given individual can decide" (Schrepel, 2021, p. 56).

[114] Casey et al. (2018), p. 6. Allen et al. (2020), pp. 18–21.

[115] Quiniou (2019), pp. 10–11, 28–29.

[116] Walch (2019b), p. 14.

[117] De Domenico and Baronchelli (2019), p. 1.

[118] Campajola et al. (2022), p. 1. The study investigates the networks Bitcoin, Ethereum, Bitcoin Cash, Litecoin, Dogecoin, Monacoin and Feathercoin.

through transactions, representing the nodes and using direct links to represent transaction flows. The work considered the effect exerted by (i) clustering;[119] (ii) degree distributions;[120] (iii) core-periphery structure;[121] (iv) mining concentration;[122] and (v) wealth inequality and spatial distribution.[123] It shows major cryptocurrencies are significantly centralised despite a supposed technological decentralisation and are transforming into something different from their original design. Indeed, the narrative of decentralised payment solutions, over which financial institutions exert no power in terms of money creation and distribution, is largely false: both miners and intermediaries exert considerable powers both from a technical and an economic perspective.[124] Likewise, an empirical analysis of the distribution of voting powers in non-custodial projects of Decentralised Finance (DeFi) suggested a significant degree of concentration.[125] Indeed, in this field centralisation tendencies were deemed inevitable due to structural elements (e.g., consensus mechanism) and governance needs.[126] The DeFi ecosystem is addressed in Chap. 4.

Given the difference between the ideological decentralisation and its actual implementations, legal experts ought to tread warily. Indeed, treating a system as thoroughly decentralised when it is not—i.e., when it houses significant control points—leads to incorrect statements concerning accountability.[127] On the contrary,

---

[119] Clustering is explored in Chap. 3 and shows the economic structure of these networks. Switching to an entity-based perspective shows a centralisation process, proven by a decrease in the average amount of addresses per entity, in conjunction with the use of cryptocurrencies as speculative assets and the advent of big intermediaries. Consistently, centralised platforms are increasingly used to enter the systems (Campajola et al., 2022, pp. 3, 7).

[120] A node's degree shows the number of counterparts and measures the importance of the entity within the given network. The distribution of degrees shows the way in which the network functions (Campajola et al., 2022, p. 3).

[121] The minority of nodes are highly interconnected, and the others are connected to the core and scarcely linked to peripheral nodes. This resembles "other trading networks from traditional economic and financial systems, and as time goes on the cores become increasingly smaller compared to the total size of the network" (Campajola et al., 2022, pp. 4, 8).

[122] Since the analysed networks are based on PoW, ledger's consistency needs mining power to be both distributed and decentralised, to avoid a "51% attack" where the majority adds false information to the ledger. The 'Nakamoto index' measures the distance from possible "51% attacks". Mining power is worryingly concentrated and there is stark wealth inequality, incompatible with the narrative of decentralised P2P systems (Campajola et al., 2022, pp. 5, 8).

[123] It concerns the distribution of tokens among entities, where wealth refers to the balance held by an address (or cluster). Most wealth is in the hands of relatively few entities, in the immediate vicinity of miners (Campajola et al., 2022, pp. 6–7).

[124] Campajola et al. (2022), pp. 7–8.

[125] Barbereau et al. (2023).

[126] Aramonte et al. (2021), p. 21. The authors argue that even in DeFi projects full decentralisation seems to be nothing but an illusion. This is because "platforms have groups of stakeholders that take and implement decisions, exercising managerial or ownership benefits" (Aramonte et al., 2021, p. 33). Meanwhile, "operating in a decentralised way is not incompatible with market power-creating reconcentration" (Zunzunegui, 2022, p. 10).

[127] Walch (2019b), p. 29. Walch (2019a), p. 3. Zetzsche et al. (2023), p. 16.

the term non-centralised allows for more room to consider that even if the network features no single central authority, some stakeholders may exert influence on the internal governance system—e.g., at times they may be in a privileged position to edit code as well. This means this set of actors ought to be considered as potential access points to extend regulatory reach over these ecosystems.[128] In this respect, applying a critical approach may mitigate a dangerous regulatory tendency identified in the area of new technologies. The complexity of these domains may lead to the temptation of regulating 'by streetlight'—i.e., making regulatory determinations limiting the scope to what can be easily seen or (mis)understood.[129] Arguably, the most dangerous risk is not that of building frameworks around more visible sides of the crypto-asset sphere, but that of incorporating common misconceptions that continue to persist in the public and academic discourse.

2.4 Theory and Practice at Ever-Changing Crossroads

The dynamic and multi-layered features of crypto-asset ecosystems hinder the attempts to conceptualise its defining traits. This worryingly leaves the crypto-asset space vulnerable to being (mis)defined in different ways by various internal and external actors, mainly depending on their underlying motive. Although a portion of this dilemma is arguably inherent to the composability of the set of technologies that compose crypto-asset ecosystems, it is paramount to limit the negative effects on the efforts to devise regulatory strategies that fit the target domain. From this viewpoint, the disintermediation element, originally crowning blockchain technologies and relevant value exchanges, exemplifies the value of scrutinising the adequacy of given regulatory frameworks against the actual characteristics of the sphere and its evolution.

2.4.1 Disintermediation Riddles

In light of the previous sections, it is crucial to test the narratives of decentralisation and disintermediation against the phenomenology of crypto-asset ecosystems. In other words, "separate fact from fiction".[130] This critical approach leads to challenge the description of all crypto-asset exchanges as disintermediated, as

[128] In this respect, "the view that nobody controls the network cannot be accepted, because each network is controlled by somebody: by a more or less wide group of community members, coordinated by software (code) and the developed rules of off-chain governance" (Karasek-Wojciechowicz, 2021, p. 6). Likewise, the abovementioned groups of actors that take and implement decisions in DeFi projects, together with their governance protocols, were described as natural entry points for policymakers (Aramonte et al., 2021, p. 33).

[129] Walch (2019a), p. 25.

[130] Finck (2019).

opposed to markets intermediated by financial institutions.[131] What makes this assessment more complex is that these features are not only influenced by matters that are internal to each platform. Indeed, a very important role is played by the ways in which different networks communicate—e.g., the ways in which they execute transactions, among themselves or with the traditional financial system—and the actors that enable this. Stakeholders such as crypto-asset exchanges or providers of wallet services are the most common way to interact with the crypto-asset space, where "most exchanges are centralised third parties that must be trusted with the custody of users' cryptocurrency balances".[132] These entities are acting as 'chokepoints' and '(re)centralisation points'.[133] Indeed, the history of the Internet itself can be conceptualised as "the history of the recentralisation of networks which were initially designed to be decentralised. DLTs are no exception to this rule".[134] Further, a substantial recentralisation can be witnessed at different layers—e.g., mining power, core code developers, major exchanges—, which generates "unexpected recentralisation of a technological infrastructure designed to be decentralised out of pure ideological reason".[135]

Concurrently, however, in the past years the advent of specific applications, products, and services—e.g., decentralised exchanges (DEXs), other types of DeFi projects, self-hosted wallets or atomic swaps (Chap. 3) can be seen as a transformation of the crypto-asset space towards true disintermediation. These events can be interpreted in two complementary ways: as a sign that there is room to challenge the actual disintermediation degree of previous more traditional (re)centralised crypto-asset dynamics, and that the world of crypto-assets is developing beyond gatekeepers bringing disintermediation to a new level. The importance of these considerations is overarching in terms of regulatory strategies, given that aspects such as AML/CFT are still gatekeeper-based and largely rely on the 'active cooperation' of a set of stakeholders (Chap. 5). Meanwhile, the feasibility of handling true disintermediation by regulatory means is highly debated. It may also be limited to outlawing certain activities or imposing regulatory burdens on stakeholders that may or may not have the capacity to exercise actual 'control' over the relevant networks. In this respect, the concept of embedded regulation, together with the corresponding value and challenges, is addressed in Chap. 7.

---

[131] New forms of intermediation emerged, also in an automated fashion (Quiniou, 2019, p. 18).

[132] Allen et al. (2020), p. 26.

[133] Their advent bridged the gap between cryptographic keys and human identities (Allen et al., 2020, p. 26).

[134] Bodó and Giannopoulou (2019), p. 4. See also Barbereau and Bodó (2023).

[135] Bodó and Giannopoulou (2019), p. 12.

2.4.2 *The (R)evolution of (Global) Stablecoins and Digital Fiat Money*

A major hindrance to the spread of cryptocurrencies lies in the high volatility of their value, which generates notable and unexpected fluctuations. Volatility prevents the 'first wave of crypto-assets' from efficiently serving the three traditional functions of money: store of value, means of payment, and unit of account. Over the years, this issue has been addressed through the creation of stabilisation mechanisms by backing the value of their coins with (an)other (less volatile) asset(s). The resulting instruments were labelled stablecoins.[136] They are a type of crypto-asset that aims "to maintain a stable value relative to a specified asset, or a pool or basket of assets".[137] Indeed, stablecoins are pegged to another asset, that can be: (a) another currency or set of currencies—in this case, they are known as tokenised funds (e.g., Tether); (b) securities and/or commodities—i.e., off-chain collateralised (e.g., gold); (c) other crypto-assets—i.e., on-chain collateralised; and (d) expectations users have of future value—i.e., algorithmic stablecoins.[138] The MiCA Regulation defines asset-referenced tokens as those aiming "to maintain a stable value by referencing to any other value or right or a combination thereof, including one or more official currencies",[139] and e-money tokens as those that purport "to maintain a stable value by referencing to the value of one official currency".[140]

As far as terminology is concerned, the FATF highlighted how stablecoins are not a clear legal and/or technical category. In practice, they can be 'retail or general purpose' or 'wholesale', depending on the target user(s); either anyone can access them, or only a selection of actors can.[141] From a legal perspective, each category of stablecoins can be classified according to whether it provides for decentralisation of responsibilities, and accountability of the issuer. In general, these instruments are "inherently at the edge of the decentralised crypto world in the sense that the price stabilisation aspect, whatever its form, usually requires some kind of trusted intermediation or other centralised infrastructure".[142] For tokenised funds (whose value is pegged to currency) and off-chain collateral (pegged to other off-chain assets) responsibilities are centralised, and the issuer can be held accountable. On the contrary, for algorithmic stablecoins, linked to on-chain assets, responsibilities are decentralised, and in principle no party can be held accountable. A hybrid situation relates to on-chain collateral, pegged to the mentioned expectations; there

[136] Bank for International Settlements (2019), pp. 1–3. Bullmann et al. (2019). Dabrowski and Janikowski (2018).

[137] Financial Action Task Force (2020b), p. 6. Financial Stability Board (2019), p. 4.

[138] Bullmann et al. (2019), pp. 1–3.

[139] Article 3(1)(6) of Regulation (EU) 2023/1114.

[140] Article 3(1)(7) of Regulation (EU) 2023/1114.

[141] Financial Action Task Force (2020b), p. 6. Bank for International Settlements (2019), pp. 1–2.

[142] Bank for International Settlements (2019), p. 24.

is no accountable issuer although responsibilities may not be decentralised. The more innovative potential is embodied by these instruments, the less it is possible to control the volatility risk—e.g., algorithmic stablecoins feature a high volatility risk.[143]

Stablecoins have not only attracted the attention of the public and regulators, but also spurred companies and organisations to explore the underlying concepts in order to create new regional and worldwide payment ecosystems. When stablecoins have this potential, they are addressed as global stablecoins. Their nature emerges from the wording of the MiCA Regulation, according to which "some asset-referenced tokens and e-money tokens should be considered significant when they meet, or are likely to meet, certain criteria, including a large customer base, a high market capitalisation, or a high number of transactions".[144] These arrangements are usually sponsored by the private sector—e.g., big technology, telecommunications or financial companies.[145] It is primarily the case of the Libra/Diem initiative, first announced by Facebook and the other 27 members of the Libra Association in June 2019. A second whitepaper followed in May 2020, but the project was abandoned in 2022. The initiative was perceived as a controversial monetary revolution from various technical, political and legal angles, further addressed in Chaps. 5 and 6.

The advent of global stablecoins showed how the crypto-asset sphere could potentially threaten financial stability due to the exploitation of network effects.[146] Hence, as per MiCA's text, when 'significant' asset-referenced or e-money tokens "could raise specific challenges in terms of financial stability, monetary policy transmission or monetary sovereignty should be subject to more stringent requirements than other asset-referenced tokens or e-money tokens".[147] Accordingly, when within a single currency area an asset-reference token becomes widely used as a means of exchange—i.e., number and value of transactions per day is higher than one million and EUR 200 million, respectively—its issuer should be required to reduce the activity level".[148] Global stablecoin adoption was also deemed to increase the risks of anonymity and money laundering and terrorist financing, but the intensity of these concerns depends on the design (e.g., (de)centralisation degrees of governance features), while a centralisation tendency is foreseeable.[149]

If the launch of Bitcoin marked the beginning of a new digital era, the Libra/Diem initiative revolutionised the ideological perception of the crypto-asset space. The clash between the disintermediated (in theory, at least) and decentralised (supposedly) ecosystems and the evolution of the domain reached a new level with the investigations into digital fiat money known as CBDCs (Chap. 6). Although one

[143] Bullmann et al. (2019), pp. 3–6, 9.

[144] Recital 59 of Regulation (EU) 2023/1114.

[145] Financial Action Task Force (2020b), p. 6.

[146] Bank for International Settlements (2019).

[147] Recital 59 of Regulation (EU) 2023/1114.

[148] Recital 61 of Regulation (EU) 2023/1114.

[149] Financial Action Task Force (2020b), pp. 11–14.

may argue they fall outside the crypto-asset sphere, the distinction is not clear-cut; seemingly, projects of cryptocurrencies, stablecoins and CBDCs are situated on a spectrum of ideological and architectural design choices.

2.5 Backing Phenomenology with Conceptual Frameworks

Against the backdrop of such complexity, it is crucial to devise an appropriate global methodology for analysis, assessment, research, regulation, and enforcement. From this perspective, it is not enough to acknowledge the aspects that influence a specific network with a cross-disciplinary approach, but there is a need to provide yardsticks that different stakeholders can use to ground analyses, application initiatives, and conclusions. The risk is otherwise that any finding could not be reutilised, as it would not be possible to reconstruct the underlying process and benchmarks taken as foundations of a specific suggestion. While this work aims to narrow the gap between legal and technological knowledge to pursue informed regulatory decisions, it seems unfeasible to ask all legal experts to develop a sound contextualised technical expertise. Moreover, crypto-assets are not only constantly evolving, but are also relevant to more and more legal domains, which makes it even more unrealistic to expect a sufficient evolution of all expertise domains involved.

Thus, flexible and sound theoretical frameworks can help understand the core elements of these worlds, in compliance with the scope of each action. This is in line with the goal of mitigating the risk that regulatory solutions, and underlying research findings, become technologically outdated soon after they are devised (or even before that): the 'risk of overfitting'.[150] In this respect, Chap. 7 explores the difference between rules-based and principles-based regulation, where principles-based rules were found to allow for flexibility and avoid never-ending regulatory vicious cycles.[151] Two conceptual benchmarks are introduced below.

2.5.1 Regulation and Crypto-Asset Ecosystems: Reaching Beyond the Complexity

The advent of crypto-assets marked a change in the way monetary transactions are envisioned. Distributed ledgers and blockchain introduced not only new mechanisms to handle major drawbacks of traditional means, but also seemingly safe alternatives to intermediation. The idea that computer systems, networks and algorithms can replace safeguards provided by trusted and regulated firms and professionals, however, is only a part of the picture. Indeed, the 'first wave of

[150] Hacker et al. (2019), p. 17.

[151] Black et al. (2007), p. 193.

cryptocurrencies' seems to have partially failed to deliver on what was promised, and their use has not met the expectations both quantitatively and qualitatively. Although a shift is to be detected in the perception of what monetary transactions should be, urging the setup of systems with less oversight, side effects have also arisen. Apparently, the price of disintermediation is higher than many people are willing to accept.

It was argued above that a major adoption challenge of cryptocurrencies is their unstable value. In this context, one can see clearly how technology and ideology can depart, and how similar implementations can address opposite needs. While it would not be possible to present the same argument for all technologies, in DLTs there is a remarkable fluidity in the way they can be shaped and tailored, and their properties exploited. As far as stablecoins and CBDCs are concerned, it is crucial to examine their interdisciplinary impacts, and the attention paid to them by institutions and entities piloting initiatives in this field. The AML/CFT domain represents a noteworthy benchmark, as many actors engaged in the implementation of these instruments are subject to compliance regimes, as addressed in Chap. 5. In some cases, the deployment of DLTs is just a diversification of traditional monetary activities. Even when this is not the case, consortia are often created with the participation of entities with financial expertise. This shows how regulatory frameworks can be shaped to suit the needs of traditional cryptocurrency instruments, albeit one should not overlook the fact that the 'second wave of cryptocurrencies' features striking differences when compared to the first one.

A partial exception is to be found in retail CBDCs (Chap. 6). Although central banks are evidently financial institutions, in some digital cash projects the possibility to engage in P2P transactions outlines the re-emergence of a new way for individuals to make use of monetary instruments. The following chapters focus on limitations and conceptual issues stemming from this approach, as did most pilot initiatives. Nonetheless, there is a tendency towards giving a greater share of freely disposable transaction power to the public. When it does not originate from institutions, it stems from technology itself, where certain digital skills are required to exploit it. From an AML/CFT perspective, it is necessary to evaluate regulatory impacts of phenomenological, ideological, and socio-technical distinctions featured by crypto-asset applications.

2.5.2 The Crypto-Asset Sphere as an Ecosystem of Socio-Technical (Eco)systems

The qualification of crypto-asset ecosystems as STSs was introduced above, and its elements were summarised by arguing that "the blockchain looks purely technical but, [. . .] like the Internet, it is sociotechnical in nature. Humans are essential to its performance: proof of work systems that support major platforms depend on miners, decisions about investing in blockchain hardware and software are made by humans, people are critical to blockchain operations in a variety of contractor and curator roles, and it is on the basis of human subjectivity that blockchains rise and fall".[152] Meanwhile, wallets linked to the network of nodes, users and miners, exchanges and mixers, were described to be all cooperating "within a complex system of social and informational relationships".[153]

Generally speaking, an STS is an articulated assemblage of technical and social elements in a given environment, interacting with one another in diverse ways and oriented towards a specific goal. Within an STS, various components are connected: actors, technology, structure, and tasks.[154] In a nutshell, multiple actors with different needs and backgrounds cooperate through an organisational structure to deploy a technology to perform specific tasks. Moreover, the level of abstraction at which an STS can be observed can vary. If—at a general level—cryptocurrency laundering and mobile banking can be viewed as STSs, the same is true for concrete technology implementations in specific socio-geographical and digital contexts.[155] Regardless of its conceptualisation, leveraging the STS notion is key from a methodological perspective. While technical and sociological perspectives view innovation from different angles, the key idea in socio-technical approaches is that "we should study the interactions between technological and social changes to enhance our understanding of innovation and that technology and social environment develop in a process of mutual shaping".[156]

The conceptualisation of crypto-asset systems as 'complex systems' is mirrored by considering them as ecosystems. Ostensibly "cryptolaundering occurs within a complex sociotechnical system. Such systems are defined as systems comprising human, techno-logical and technical elements working together to achieve a shared goal [. . .]. To understand the behaviour of complex sociotechnical systems, a so-called systems approach is required, which entails taking the overall system as the unit of analysis and examining the interactions between components (as opposed to only examining the components themselves). As such, a complex systems thinking perspective is required when attempting to understand and prevent cryptolaundering processes".[157] From an architectural standpoint, crypto-assets can be defined as ecosystems of interconnected STSs. The Ethereum platform itself was described as one element that belongs to an ecosystem of (interconnected) STSs.[158] In practice, from a technical standpoint the degree of their (direct) interconnection is strongly linked to the issue of blockchain interoperability (Chaps. 3 and 6).

---

[152] Werbach (2019), pp. ix–x.

[153] Desmond et al. (2019), pp. 481–482.

[154] Borrás and Edler (2020); Kopackova and Libalova (2017); Leavitt (1965); Bostrom and Heinen (1977a, 1977b).

[155] For instance, Desmond et al. (2019); Ambore et al. (2016); Gonsalves et al. (2012); De Domenico and Baronchelli (2019).

[156] Meijer and Thaens (2018), p. 366.

[157] Desmond et al. (2019), pp. 481–482.

[158] De Domenico and Baronchelli (2019).

The regulatory value of the socio-technical approach lies in embracing the elements at play when devising a strategy to approach these ecosystems. The concurrent presence of social and technical components in the qualification of a crypto-asset transaction as anonymous will be explored in Chaps. 3 and 4. Without this sensitivity, the risk is to reach conclusions refuted by phenomenology. Accordingly, a 'systems approach'—the consideration of the socio-technical components of crypto-asset ecosystems when evaluating their features—is used throughout this work, and explored in different directions.

2.6 Conclusions

This chapter outlined the foundations of the ecosystems that form the scope of this analysis. The traits of the crypto-asset sphere were introduced by exploring multi-layered aspects, ranging from the combination of technologies that led to the advent of Bitcoin, to the role played by various stakeholders and architectures. Accordingly, this chapter outlined the background against which the concepts of IoM and IoV were devised, leveraging P2P transfers and tokenisation, up to the advent of the 'second wave of cryptocurrencies' (i.e., stablecoins) and CBDCs. The importance of terminology and disambiguation efforts was highlighted, by leveraging definitional remarks on crypto-assets, tokens, and relevant taxonomies, as benchmarks for grounding cross-disciplinary remarks.

The architectural interpretation of crypto-asset ecosystems is mostly token-based, which may suggest they are (purportedly) anonymous or transparent only due to how tokens are construed. On the contrary, other aspects are to be considered, and actual risks mostly relate to the way the systems that generate and exchange them are construed and governed. Thus, the chapter explored the landscape in which crypto-assets are transferred by deploying a teleological and accountability-based approach. Moreover, it explored a set of elements portrayed by crypto-asset ecosystems to provide theoretical yardsticks for AML/CFT measures. Different levels of features were addressed, underlining the nature of the crypto-asset space as an ecosystem of interconnected socio-technical ecosystems, the need to focus on the interplay between the different dimensions, and paying special attention to the concept of non-centralisation. Parallelly, the notion of disintermediation went through a process of disambiguation, and new trends were outlined. Finally, methodology benchmarks were provided to address crypto-asset ecosystems from a regulatory perspective while heeding conceptual, ideological, and technical evolutions.

In summary, this chapter elaborated on several important threads: (i) the role of terminology in pursuing regulatory clarity, (ii) the development of taxonomies to enable interdisciplinary cooperation, (iii) the selection of yardsticks on which to ground legal reasonings, (iv) the disambiguation of crypto-asset-related misconceptions, and (v) the interplay of theoretical schemes and empirical phenomena. Its findings can be seen as the first steps towards avoiding the 'streetlight' effect when assessing regulatory solutions for crypto-assets in the AML/CFT domain.

References

Allen, J. G., Rauchs, M., Blandin, A., & Bear, K. (2020). *Legal and regulatory considerations for digital assets*. https://www.jbs.cam.ac.uk/faculty-research/centres/alternative-finance/publications/legal-and-regulatory-considerations-for-digital-assets/

Alt, R., Fridgen, G., & Chang, Y. (2024). The future of fintech – Towards ubiquitous financial services. *Electronic Markets*, *34*(1). https://doi.org/10.1007/s12525-023-00687-8

Ambore, S., Richardson, C., Dogan, H., Apeh, E., & Osselton, D. (2016). A "soft" approach to analysing mobile financial services socio-technical systems. In *Proceedings of the 30th International BCS Human-Computer Interaction Conference*. https://doi.org/10.14236/ewic/HCI2016.103

Antonopoulos, A. M. (2016). *The Internet of money - Volume one*. Merkle Boom.

Antonopoulos, A. M. (2017a). *The Internet of money - Volume two*. Merkle Boom.

Antonopoulos, A. M. (2017b). *Mastering bitcoin* (2nd ed.). O'Reilly Media.

Aramonte, S., Huang, W., & Schrimpf, A. (2021). Defi risks and the decentralisation illusion. *BIS Quarterly Review*. https://www.bis.org/publ/qtrpdf/r_qt2112b.pdf

Arner, D. W., Buckley, R. P., Didenko, A., Park, C.-Y., Pashoska, E., Zetzsche, D. A., & Zhao, B. (2019a). Policy and regulatory challenges of distributed ledger technology and digital assets in Asia. In C. Brummer (Ed.), *Cryptoassets: Legal, regulatory, and monetary perspectives*. Oxford University Press. https://doi.org/10.1093/oso/9780190077310.003.0011

Arruñada, B. (2018). Blockchain's struggle to deliver impersonal exchange. *Minnesota Journal Law Science & Technology*, *19*(1), 55–105. https://scholarship.law.umn.edu/mjlst/vol19/iss1/2

Athanassiou, P. (2019). Tokens and the regulation of distributed ledger technologies: Where Europe stood in the last quarter of 2018. *Journal of International Banking Law and Regulation*, *34*(3), 105–114.

Bank for International Settlements. (2019). *Investigating the impact of global stablecoins*. https://www.bis.org/cpmi/publ/d187.pdf

Bank of England HM Treasury, Financial Conduct Authority. (2018). *Cryptoassets task-force: Final report*. https://assets.publishing.service.gov.uk/government/uploads/system/uploads/attachment_data/file/752070/cryptoassets_taskforce_final_report_final_web.pdf

Barbereau, T., & Bodó, B. (2023). Beyond financial regulation of crypto-asset wallet software: In search of secondary liability. *Computer Law & Security Review*, *49*, 105829. https://doi.org/10.1016/j.clsr.2023.105829

Barbereau, T., Smethurst, R., Papageorgiou, O., Sedlmeir, J., & Fridgen, G. (2023). Decentralised finance's timocratic governance: The distribution and exercise of tokenised voting rights. *Technology in Society*, *73*, 102251. https://doi.org/10.1016/j.techsoc.2023.102251

Black, J., Hopper, M., & Band, C. (2007). Making a success of principles-based regulation. *Law and Financial Markets Review*, 191–206. https://doi.org/10.1080/17521440.2007.11427879

Bodó, B., & Giannopoulou, A. (2019). The logics of technology decentralisation: The case of distributed ledger technologies. In *Blockchain and Web 3.0: Social, economic, and technical challenges*. Routledge. https://doi.org/10.4324/9780429029530-8

Borrás, S., & Edler, J. (2020). The roles of the state in the governance of socio-technical systems' transformation. *Research Policy*, *49*(5), 103971. https://doi.org/10.1016/j.respol.2020.103971

Bostrom, R. P., & Heinen, J. S. (1977a). MIS problems and failures: A socio-technical perspective. Part I: The causes. *MIS Quarterly*, *1*, 17–32. https://doi.org/10.2307/248710

Bostrom, R. P., & Heinen, J. S. (1977b). MIS problems and failures: A socio-technical perspective. Part II: The application of socio-technical theory. *MIS Quarterly*, *1*, 11–28. https://doi.org/10.2307/249019

Brummer, C. (2019). Introduction. In *Cryptoassets: Legal, regulatory, and monetary perspectives*. Oxford University Press. https://doi.org/10.1093/oso/9780190077310.003.0001

Bullmann, D., Klemm, J., & Pinna, A. (2019). *In search for stability in crypto-assets: Are stablecoins the solution?* https://www.ecb.europa.eu/pub/pdf/scpops/ecb.op230~d57946be3b.en.pdf

Campajola, C., Cristodaro, R., De Collibus, F. M., Yan, T., Vallarano, N., & Tessone, C. J. (2022). *The evolution of centralisation on cryptocurrency platforms.* https://arxiv.org/abs/2206.05081

Capaccioli, S. (2020). Blockchain, bitcoin and stigmergy: An explanation and a new perspective for regulation. *BioLaw Journal, 2020*(2), 467–476. https://ssrn.com/abstract=3645044

Casey, M., Crane, J., Gensler, G., Johnson, S., & Narula, N. (2018). *The impact of blockchain technology on finance: A catalyst for change.* https://cepr.org/publications/books-and-reports/geneva-21-impact-blockchain-technology-finance-catalyst-change

Chen, W., Zheng, Z., Edith C.-H. Ngai, Zheng, P., & Zhou, Y. (2019). Exploiting blockchain data to detect smart Ponzi schemes on Ethereum. *IEEE Access, 7*(c), 37575–37586. https://doi.org/10.1109/ACCESS.2019.2905769

Cuervo, C., Morozova, A., & Sugimoto, N. (2019). *Regulation of crypto assets.* https://www.imf.org/en/Publications/fintech-notes/Issues/2020/01/09/Regulation-of-Crypto-Assets-48810

Dabrowski, M., & Janikowski, L. (2018). *Virtual currencies and central banks monetary policy: Challenges ahead.* https://www.europarl.europa.eu/cmsdata/149900/CASE_FINAL

Dannen, C. (2017). *Introducing Ethereum and solidity: Foundations of cryptocurrency and blockchain programming for beginners.* Apress. https://doi.org/10.1007/978-1-4842-2535-6

De Domenico, M., & Baronchelli, A. (2019). The fragility of decentralised trustless socio-technical systems. *EPJ Data Science, 8*(1), 4–9. https://doi.org/10.1140/epjds/s13688-018-0180-6

Decreto N°57/2021. (2021). *Decreto nº57, del 8 de junio del año 2021. ley bitcoin.* Available at: https://www.diariooficial.gob.sv/diarios/do-2021/06-junio/09-06-2021.pdf

Desmond, D. B., Lacey, D., & Salmon, P. (2019). Evaluating cryptocurrency laundering as a complex socio-technical system: A systematic literature review. *Journal of Money Laundering Control, 22*(3), 480–97. https://doi.org/10.1108/JMLC-10-2018-0063

Directive (EU) 2015/849. (2015). Directive (EU) 2015/849 of the European Parliament and of the Council on the prevention of the use of the financial system for the purposes of money laundering or terrorist financing, amending regulation (EU) no 648/2012 of the European Parliament and of the Council, and repealing Directive 2005/60/EC of the European Parliament and of the Council and Commission Directive 2006/70/EC. http://data.europa.eu/eli/dir/2015/849/oj

Directive (EU) 2018/843. (2018). Directive (EU) 2018/843 of the European Parliament and of the Council amending Directive (EU) 2015/849 on the prevention of the use of the financial system for the purposes of money laundering or terrorist financing, and amending Directives 2009/138/EC and 2013/36/EU. http://data.europa.eu/eli/dir/2018/843/oj

Distefano, B., Pocher, N., & Zichichi, M. (2020). Moatcoin: Exploring challenges and legal implications of smart contracts through a gamelike DApp experiment. In *Proceedings of the 3rd Workshop on Cryptocurrencies and Blockchains for Distributed Systems*, CryBlock '20, New York, NY, USA, 2020 (pp. 53–58). Association for Computing Machinery. https://doi.org/10.1145/3410699.3413798

Ethereum. (2022). *Non-fungible token (NFT).* https://ethereum.org/en/nft/

Euler, T. (2018). *The token classification framework: A multi-dimensional tool for understanding and classifying crypto tokens.* http://www.untitled-inc.com/the-token-classification-framework-a-multi-dimensional-tool-for-understanding-and-classifying-crypto-tokens/

European Banking Authority. (2019). *Report with advice for the European Commission on crypto-assets.* https://www.eba.europa.eu/sites/default/documents/files/documents/10180/2545547/67493daa-85a8-4429-aa91-e9a5ed880684/EBA%20Report%20on%20crypto%20assets.pdf

European Central Bank Crypto-Assets Task Force. (2019). *Crypto-assets: Implications for financial stability, monetary policy, and payments and market infrastructures.* https://www.ecb.europa.eu/pub/pdf/scpops/ecb.op223~3ce14e986c.en.pdf

European Commission. (2018). *Fintech action plan: For a more competitive and innovative European financial sector.* https://eur-lex.europa.eu/legal-content/EN/TXT/?uri=CELEX%3A52018DC0109

European Commission. (2020). *Digital finance package.* https://ec.europa.eu/info/publications/200924-digital-finance-proposals_en

European Securities and Markets Authority. (2019). *Advice - Initial coin offerings and crypto-assets*. https://www.esma.europa.eu/sites/default/files/library/esma50-157-1391_crypto_advice.pdf

Financial Action Task Force. (2015). *Guidance for a risk-based approach: Virtual currencies*. https://www.fatf-gafi.org/media/fatf/documents/reports/Guidance-RBA-Virtual-Currencies.pdf

Financial Action Task Force. (2019). *Guidance for a risk-based approach: Virtual assets and virtual asset service providers*. https://www.fatf-gafi.org/publications/fatfrecommendations/documents/guidance-rba-virtual-assets.html

Financial Action Task Force. (2020a). *12-month review of the revised FATF standards – virtual assets and virtual asset service providers*. http://www.fatf-gafi.org/media/fatf/documents/recommendations/12-Month-Review-Revised-FATF-Standards-Virtual-Assets-VASPS.pdf

Financial Action Task Force. (2020b). *FATF report to the g20 finance ministers and central banks governors on so-called stablecoins*. http://www.fatf-gafi.org/media/fatf/documents/recommendations/Virtual-Assets-FATF-Report-G20-So-Called-Stablecoins.pdf

Financial Action Task Force. (2020c). *Virtual assets red flag indicators of money laundering and terrorist financing*. https://www.fatf-gafi.org/media/fatf/documents/recommendations/Virtual-Assets-Red-Flag-Indicators.pdf

Financial Action Task Force. (2021). *Virtual assets and virtual asset service providers - Updated guidance for a risk-based approach*. https://www.fatf-gafi.org/publications/fatfrecommendations/documents/guidance-rba-virtual-assets-2021.html

Financial Stability Board. (2019). *Regulatory issues of stablecoins*. https://www.fsb.org/wp-content/uploads/P181019.pdf

Finck, M. (2019). *Blockchain regulation and Governance in Europe*. Cambridge University Press. https://doi.org/10.1017/9781108609708

Freni, P., Ferro, E., & Moncada, R. (2020). Tokenization and blockchain tokens classification: A morphological framework. In *Proceedings of the IEEE Symposium on Computers and Communications (ISCC)* (pp. 1–6). https://doi.org/10.1109/ISCC50000.2020.9219709

Garrido, J. M. (2023). Digital tokens: A legal perspective. In *International Monetary Fund Working Paper*. https://www.imf.org/en/Publications/WP/Issues/2023/07/28/Digital-Tokens-A-Legal-Perspective-537041

Gonsalves, T., Dittrich, Y., Vaidyanathan, L., & Jhunjhunwala, A. (2012). Prototyping socio-technical systems for banking services for rural India. In *Proceedings of the Conference: Learning from Marginalized Users: Reciprocity in HCI4D, Workshop at the Computer Supported Cooperative Work Conference 2012, Seattle Washington*.

Gorjón, S. (2021). *The role of cryptoassets as legal tender: The example of El Salvador*. https://www.bde.es/f/webbde/SES/Secciones/Publicaciones/InformesBoletinesRevistas/ArticulosAnaliticos/21/T4/Files/be2104-art35e.pdf

Hacker, P., Lianos, I., Dimitropoulos, G., & Eich, S. (2019). *Regulating blockchain: Techno-social and legal challenges*. Oxford University Press. https://doi.org/10.1093/oso/9780198842187.001.0001

Hartwich, E., Ollig, P., Fridgen, G., & Rieger, A. (2024). Probably something: A multi-layer taxonomy of non-fungible tokens. *Internet Research*, *34*(1). https://doi.org/10.1108/INTR-08-2022-0666

Herian, R. (2019). *Regulating blockchain: Critical perspectives in law and technology*. Routledge. https://doi.org/10.4324/9780429489815

Inozemtsev, M. (2021). Taxonomy and typology of crypto-assets: Approaches of international organisations. In *Engineering economics: Decisions and solutions from Eurasian perspective* (Vol. 139, pp. 122–33). https://doi.org/10.1007/978-3-030-53277-2_14

ITSA. (2022). *International Token Standardisation Association*. https://itsa.global

ITU-T FG DLT. (2019a). *Distributed ledger technology terms and definitions. FG DLT D1.1*. https://www.itu.int/en/ITU-T/focusgroups/dlt/Pages/terms-and-definitions.aspx

ITU-T FG DLT. (2019b). *Technical report FG DLT D1.2 distributed ledger technology overview, concepts, ecosystem*. https://www.itu.int/en/ITU-T/focusgroups/dlt/Documents/FGDLT-D1.2.pdf
ITU-T Focus Group on Digital Currency. (2019). *Taxonomy and definition of terms for digital fiat currency*. https://www.itu.int/en/ITU-T/focusgroups/dlt/Documents/FGDLT-D2.1.pdf
Kabré, R. J. (2022). Regulating cryptocurrencies in the Central African Republic: Has the cart been put before the horse? https://africlaw.com/2022/07/21/regulating-cryptocurrencies-in-the-central-african-republic-has-the-cart-been-put-before-the-horse/
Karasek-Wojciechowicz, I. (2021). Reconciliation of anti-money laundering instruments and European data protection requirements in permissionless blockchain spaces. *Journal of Cybersecurity*, 1–28. https://doi.org/10.1093/cybsec/tyab004
Klarin, A. (2020). The decade-long cryptocurrencies and the blockchain rollercoaster: Mapping the intellectual structure and charting future directions. *Research in International Business and Finance*, *51*. https://doi.org/10.1016/j.ribaf.2019.101067
Kopackova, H., & Libalova, P. (2017). Smart city concept as socio-technical system. In *Proceedings of the International Conference on Information and Digital Technologies* (pp. 198–205). https://doi.org/10.1109/DT.2017.8024297
Law No. 22.004. (2022). *Law no. 22.004 of 22 April 2022 governing cryptocurrency in the Central African Republic*. http://www.droit-afrique.com/uploads/RCA-Loi-2022-04-cryptomonnaie.pdf
Leavitt, H. J. (1965). Applied organisational change in industry: Structural, technological and humanistic approaches. In J. March (Ed.), *Handbook of organisations* (pp. 1144–1170). Routledge. https://doi.org/10.4324/9780203629130
May, T. C. (1988). *The crypto-anarchist manifesto*. https://nakamotoinstitute.org/authors/timothy-c-may/
Meijer, A., & Thaens, M. (2018). Urban technological innovation: Developing and testing a sociotechnical framework for studying smart city projects. *Urban Affairs Review*, *54*(2), 363–387 (2018)
Nakamoto, S. (2008). *Bitcoin: A peer-to-peer electronic cash systems*. https://www.bitcoin.org
Oliveira, L., Zavolokina, L., Bauer, I., & Schwabe, G. (2018). To token or not to token: Tools for understanding blockchain tokens. In *Proceedings of the International Conference on Information Systems*. https://aisel.aisnet.org/icis2018/crypto/Presentations/5
Poblet, M., Allen, D. W. E., Konashevych, O., Lane, A. M., & Diaz-Valdivia, C. A. (2020). From athens to the blockchain: Oracles for digital democracy. *Frontiers in Blockchain*. https://doi.org/10.3389/fbloc.2020.575662
Quiniou, M. (2019). *Blockchain: The advent of disintermediation*. Wiley-ISTE Ltd.
Regulation (EU) 2022/858. (2022). Regulation EU 2022/858 of the European Parliament and of the Council of 30 May 2022 on a pilot regime for market infrastructures based on distributed ledger technology, and amending Regulations EU No 600/2014 and EU No 909/2014 and Directive 2014/65/EU. http://data.europa.eu/eli/reg/2022/858/oj
Regulation (EU) 2023/1113. (2023). Regulation (EU) 2023/1113 of the European Parliament and of the Council of 31 May 2023 on information accompanying transfers of funds and certain crypto-assets and amending directive (EU) 2015/849 (recast). http://data.europa.eu/eli/reg/2023/1113/oj
Regulation (EU) 2023/1114. (2023). Regulation (EU) 2023/1114 of the European Parliament and of the Council of 31 May 2023 on markets in crypto-assets, and amending regulations (EU) no 1093/2010 and (EU) no 1095/2010 and directives 2013/36/EU and (EU) 2019/1937. http://data.europa.eu/eli/reg/2023/1114/oj
Regulation (EU) 2024/1624. (2024). Regulation (EU) 2024/1624 of the European Parliament and of the Council of 31 May 2024 on the prevention of the use of the financial system for the purposes of money laundering or terrorist financing. http://data.europa.eu/eli/reg/2024/1624/oj
Renwick, R., & Gleasure, R. (2020). Those who control the code control the rules: How different perspectives of privacy are being written into the code of blockchain systems. *Journal of Information Technology*, *36*(1). https://doi.org/10.1177/0268396220944406

Roy, A. (2021). *El Salvador's bitcoin law: Full English text.* https://freopp.org/el-salvadors-bitcoin-law-full-proposed-english-text-9a2153ad1d19

Saa, O., Cullen, A., & Vigneri, L. (2023). *IOTA 2.0 incentives and tokenomics whitepaper.* https://files.iota.org/papers/IOTA_2.0_Incentives_And_Tokenomics_Whitepaper.pdf

Sandner, P. (2020). *Unique referencing and identification in the token universe: Cross-chain, worldwide, and fork-resilient.* Medium. https://philippsandner.medium.com/unique-referencing-and-identification-in-the-token-universe-cross-chain-worldwide-and

Schrepel, T. (2021). *Blockchain + Antitrust: The decentralisation formula.* Edward Elgar. https://doi.org/10.4337/9781800885530

Skalex. (2019). *Making sense of crypto token types.* https://www.skalex.io/crypto-token-types/

Statista. (2024). *Number of cryptocurrencies worldwide from 2013 to June 2024.* https://www.statista.com/statistics/863917/number-crypto-coins-tokens/

Szabo, N. (2017). *Money, blockchains, and social scalability.* http://unenumerated.blogspot.com/2017/02/money-blockchains-and-social-scalability.html

Tapscott, D. (2020). *Token taxonomy: The need for open-source standards around digital assets.* https://www.blockchainresearchinstitute.org/wp-content/uploads/2020/02/Tapscott_Token-Economy_Blockchain-Research-Institute.pdf

Tapscott, D., & Euchner, J. (2019). Blockchain and the Internet of value: An interview with Don Tapscott. *Research Technology Management, 62*(1), 12–19. https://doi.org/10.1080/08956308.2019.1541711

The Cryptocurrency Consultant. (2019). *What is the internet of values?* Medium The Startup.

Token- und VT-Dienstleister-Gesetz. (2019). *Liechtenstein's gesetz über token und vt-dienstleister (2019) vom 3. oktober 2019 (token- und vt-dienstleister-gesetz; tvtg).* https://www.regierung.li/media/medienarchiv/950_6_08_01_2020.pdf?t=2

Walch, A. (2019a). Regulating blockchain: Techno-social and legal challenges. In *Code(Rs) we trust: Software developers as fiduciaries in public blockchains.* Oxford University Press. https://doi.org/10.1093/oso/9780198842187.003.0004.

Walch, A. (2019b). Deconstructing 'decentralisation'. In C. Brummer (Ed.), *Cryptoassets: Legal, regulatory, and monetary perspectives.* Oxford University Press.

Werbach, K. (2019). *The blockchain and the new architecture of trust.* The MIT Press. https://doi.org/10.7551/mitpress/11449.001.0001

Werbach, K. (2020). The siren song: Algorithmic governance by blockchain. In K. Werbach (Ed.), *After the digital tornado: Networks, algorithms, humanity.* Cambridge University Press. https://doi.org/10.1017/9781108610018

Zetzsche, D. A., Buckley, R. P., Arner, D. W., & van Ek, M. (2023). *Remaining regulatory challenges in digital finance and crypto-assets after MiCA.* Technical report, Committee on Economic and Monetary Affairs (ECON), Policy Department for Economic, Scientific and Quality of Life Policies, European Parliament. https://www.europarl.europa.eu/thinktank/en/document/IPOL_STU(2023)740083

Zunzunegui, F. (2022). How to regulate digital financial platforms: A research agenda. *Journal of International Banking Law and Regulation.* https://doi.org/10.2139/ssrn.4262693

Chapter 3
Disintermediation and Anonymity

3.1 Introduction

Chapter 2 introduced the principles underpinning crypto-asset ecosystems, showing how their qualification as the realm of disintermediation is not as clear-cut as frequently advertised. Indeed, assessing the disintermediation of crypto-asset ecosystems requires to account for the newest developments. On the one hand, most legal and socio-economic impacts exerted by blockchain technology lie in reducing the role of 'trusted' intermediaries—better, replacing 'inter-individual' trust with one that is 'systemic' and 'algorithmic'.[1] On the other hand, the role played by centralised exchanges (CEXes) and other service providers, and the development of stablecoin and CBDC projects, testify to the significance of intermediation in the crypto-asset space. They also showcase an increasing interplay between intermediated and disintermediated scenarios—e.g., between CEXes and DEXes, or service providers intermediating access to DEX platforms.

Indeed, the crypto-asset space is populated by a considerable number of intermediaries, consisting of both new types of entities—e.g., crypto-asset exchanges, brokerage platforms—, and traditional financial and payment institutions offering crypto-asset services. Most users still interact with crypto-assets through intermediaries, and not in a P2P fashion. Given this 'continuing mediation', disintermediation was described as a possible myth.[2] Nonetheless, not all entities operating as intermediaries in this sphere are within the scope and reach of regulation, and in principle these entities are not even needed to transact in crypto-assets. On the contrary, although AML/CFT regulatory guidelines and standardisation efforts have traditionally focused on the 'on- and off-ramps'—i.e., gateways between crypto

[1] Quiniou (2019), pp. xiv–xv.

[2] Herian (2019), p. 113.

N. Pocher, *Crypto-Asset Ecosystems and the EU Anti-Money Laundering Framework*, Law, Governance and Technology Series 76,
https://doi.org/10.1007/978-3-031-94698-1_3

activities and the traditional financial system—over time the domain has evolved significantly towards a variety of innovative products, services, business models, interactions, including virtual-to-virtual transactions.[3]

Although the opportunities offered by DLTs are plentiful, their advent has been channeled into a narrative of pervasive technological change and socio-economic repercussions.[4] The expression 'blockchain hype' has come to describe the enthusiasm towards the application to every aspect of life of a technology allegedly able to end dilemmas ranging from governmental corruption to financial exclusion.[5] The main disruption lies in enabling network's participants to agree upon and record information without the need to rely on a trusted central authority. The absence of a 'single point of truth' is counterbalanced using encryption and methods to add data to the ledger after the network has agreed on it—i.e., the consensus mechanisms.[6]

The level of disintermediation enabled by DLTs in sectors traditionally grounded on the regulatory and supervisory role of intermediaries challenges laws and regulations.[7] Meanwhile, the advent of Bitcoin showed how encryption also protects the identity of users and transactions.[8] Indeed, the idea of enabling anonymous and pseudonymous transactions seems inherent to the crypto-asset sphere as a realm of individual freedom, which generated tensions related to the application and enforcement of regulatory regimes against misuses of the financial system. Yet, the entangled relationship between anonymous exchange of information and the digital sphere had been debated well before blockchains, and the reason can be phrased simply: on the one hand anonymity is conducive to safeguarding the right to privacy, data protection and other civil liberties, while on the other hand lack of identification hampers investigation, enforcement and accountability, hence is a fertile ground for illegal behaviour.[9]

It is not straightforward to grasp the meaning of the terms used in the debate. Besides the frequent reference to privacy, there is often an equation between anonymity and lack of identification. But one may wonder: does transacting anonymously equate to transacting privately? Is a transaction private (only) when it is anonymous, and in turn is it anonymous (only) when there is no identification? From parallel perspectives, transparency is deemed one of the defining traits of blockchain technologies. Does this originate a paradox?

---

[3] Financial Action Task Force (2021), p. 7.

[4] Finck (2019b), p. 211.

[5] Walch (2017), p. 13.

[6] Schrepel (2021), pp. 18ff.

[7] Nonetheless, even if disintermediation equals to the (partial) elimination of intermediaries, it does not necessarily imply the absence of mediation, that can be automated. A key impact of Internet platforms was indeed the gradual replacement of physical intermediation with a digital one (Quiniou, 2019, p. 52).

[8] Schrepel (2021), p. 35.

[9] Nicoll et al. (2003), pp. 6–8.

3.1.1 *Encryption, Cyberspace Anonymity and Crypto-Assets*

The Bitcoin network was the first large-scale embryonic showcase of an economic system in which users could participate directly and anonymously, with no need of intermediaries and authorities. Although the extent to which Nakamoto's work embodied an ideologic and financial orientation is up for debate, the idea of exchanging value in an anonymous way was addressed throughout the whole history of telecommunication. The transmission of funds by electronic means, first by cable and later over the Internet, was introduced in the second part of the twentieth century, and cryptographic techniques and encryption—i.e., the application of cryptography for a message to be understood only by the intended readers—started to be implemented to safeguard its security.[10] Most importantly, after public-private key encryption was invented, in 1978 the RSA algorithm multiplied its applications and created digital signatures that were highly resistant to forgery.[11] It is the combination of public-private key cryptography and digital signatures that planted the theorical seed for "electronic cash, pseudonymous reputation, and content distribution systems, as well as new forms of digital contracts".[12] Hence, encryption, that can be applied to obtain anonymity, played a key role in the development of crypto-assets.

This line of cryptographic research partially overlaps with a broader cyber-libertarian movement that was underlining surveillance risks arising from the fast development of the Internet in sharing information, if left in the controlling hands of governmental powers.[13] There was a strong belief individuals' privacy rights were under existential threat by the hands of the excessive power exerted by governments and corporations.[14] Trying to find a privacy-preserving solution, in 1988 Timothy C. May, an electronic engineer, argued in his Crypto Anarchist Manifesto that computers could allow anonymous communication between individuals and groups.[15] Hence, people could "exchange messages, conduct business, and negotiate electronic contracts without ever knowing the True Name, or legal identity" of their counterparty. Similarly, he claimed these interactions could be untraceable.[16]

[10] Geva (2018), p. 24. In cryptography, the status in which only the intended reader can read and process stored or transmitted data is called 'secrecy'.

[11] De Filippi and Wright (2018), pp. 14–15. The Rivest–Shamir–Adleman (RSA) algorithm generates a mathematically linked set of public and private keys by multiplying two large prime numbers.

[12] De Filippi and Wright (2018), p. 16.

[13] Magnuson (2020), p. 17.

[14] Magnuson (2020), p. 34. Cyberpunks argued that "without proper checks and balances, the deployment of modern information technology would narrow the sphere of personal privacy, resulting in pervasive government and corporate surveillance" (De Filippi & Wright, 2018, p. 18).

[15] May (1988).

[16] May (1988).

Anonymous cash and untraceable payments fitted cyber-libertarian goals perfectly and seemed necessary to attain them.[17] Indeed, encryption does not suffice to save virtual interactions from the monitoring eye of the Government, due to the need to rely on a bank.[18] The work of David Chaum, founder of the International Association of Cryptologic Research, is a great example of early privacy-preserving discussions. In early 1980s, he proposed pseudonymous solutions to the pervasiveness of computerisation that was hampering individuals from controlling the use of the information about themselves.[19] In 1983, Chaum conceived the anonymous electronic money system known as Ecash, to be used for micropayments and based on RSA blind signatures, albeit still relying on a centralised operator.[20] Meanwhile, new models for exchanging information were emerging: one-way client-server models were joined by experiments with P2P networks, decentralised infrastructures composed of participants acting as both suppliers and consumers of informational resources.[21] The concept of resilient and decentralised P2P systems resonated well with cyberpunks, while the conjunction with encryption fostered freedom and liberty. Indeed, a decentralised currency seemed a perfect solution.[22] Nonetheless, as described in Chap. 2, the dream only became feasible with Bitcoin.

Anticipating risk assessments by international and (supra)national institutions, in his Manifesto May had foreseen the government was going to fight the spread of cryptographic solutions to protect national security—e.g., to avoid the use of these technologies by drug dealers and tax evaders. He acknowledged these concerns and even the possibility of aiding the establishment of an "anonymous computerised market" to deal in assassinations and extortions, apart from national secrets and illicit and stolen materials. He argued, however, this was not going to stop the movement.[23] The link between anonymity and illegal activities, which emerged from the early days of the cyberpunk movement, was deemed a minor side effect

[17] De Filippi and Wright (2018), p. 19.

[18] Magnuson (2020), p. 26.

[19] Chaum (1985), p. 1. Chaum (1981). Chaum (1983) argued that "the ultimate structure of the new electronic payments system may have a substantial impact on personal privacy as well as on the nature and extent of criminal use of payments. Ideally a new payments system should address both of these seemingly conflicting sets of concerns". The solution relied on an anonymous payments system that could safeguard privacy and mitigate theft risk (Magnuson, 2020, p. 28), by enabling transfer of e-cash without providing personal information (De Filippi & Wright, 2018, p. 19).

[20] ECash (1997). Chaum et al. (1990). Nicoll et al. (2003), pp. 34–42. De Filippi and Wright (2018), p. 20. Micro-payments involve very small sums, usually e-commerce transactions where the good/service is available online (e.g., applications, services, web-based contents).

[21] De Filippi and Wright (2018), pp. 16–18.

[22] Magnuson (2020), p. 34. De Filippi and Wright (2018), p. 18.

[23] May (1988).

in comparison to the benefits arising from safeguarding individual privacy against the government.[24]

Nonetheless, the application of advanced cryptography to payments and its impacts on illicit finance did not see the light with DLTs. The debate has a wider scope and the use of other technologies and of a wide variety of tools can be tailored to different goals. The issue of evaluating the impact of anonymous transactions on the financial system, and debates on whether and to what extent to allow them, did not originate from crypto-assets, nor is it inextricably linked to the Internet or digitisation per se. Hence, one may wonder why crypto-assets are permeated by concerns about their anonymity levels, to the extent that most regulatory activity in this field has targeted the prevention of misuses of the financial system.

3.1.2 Defining the Scope of the Conundrum

At the beginning of an investigation into the anonymity and transparency traits of crypto-asset ecosystems, one can notice the following elements:

- Anonymity and transparency are pivotal notions in the world of DLTs, and they are both considered inherent features of the crypto-asset world. Both encryption and ledger transparency have played a foundational role in the advent of Bitcoin and development of the crypto-asset space.
- Anonymity and transparency are key notions for AML/CFT as well, where anonymity generates considerable risks of financial systems being misused for illicit purposes. Meanwhile, transparency aids compliance, supervision, investigation, and enforcement.
- This twofold perspective is not new and does not relate to the crypto-asset sphere or AML/CFT exclusively. Anonymity and transparency have long been pivotal in the spheres of online communication and financial transactions, as testified by respective lines of literature.
- In the cyberspace, technology can be leveraged to undermine anonymity with analytics, but also to anonymise or pseudonymise activities,[25] which reduces users' accountability.
- Anonymity is double-edged: it can foster illegality, but the lack of it can violate human rights.[26] This prompted AML/CFT and privacy concerns, respectively. Cyber-libertarians testify to the tension between safeguarding individuals from surveillance and averting illicit deeds. Crypto-assets exemplify how these dimensions concretely play out.

---

[24] Magnuson (2020), p. 19. As explored below, anonymity and privacy are often placed on the same side of the debate, which requires a disambiguation effort.

[25] Nicoll et al. (2003), p. v. Article 19 (2015).

[26] Nicoll et al. (2003), pp. 6–8.

- crypto-asset ecosystems are not necessarily DLT-based, but the properties of DLTs substantially shaped the crypto-asset space. Many regulatory issues of crypto-asset ecosystems were linked to the properties of DLTs, a neutral tool susceptible to pursue good and illicit purposes.[27]

Against this backdrop, further analysis leads to observe the following:

- The crypto-asset discourse generally lacks terminological precision: different notions are (mis)used, within the DLT context and beyond it. The primary cause is the tendency of the 'blockchain hype' to generalise—e.g., insufficient distinction between anonymity and privacy.
- The AML/CFT framework makes use of the notions of anonymity and transparency in a way that relates to the mitigation of risks generated by financial transactions that fall outside traditional supervision and accountability mechanisms. This concept of anonymity, albeit crucial to the regulatory system, is not defined.
- Despite the belief that there are two distinct worlds—one of anonymity and irresponsibility, and one of transparency, identification, accountability—, the dichotomy between irresponsible anonymity and accountable identification was challenged.[28] Along a spectrum from complete anonymity to full transparency, at any given point they coexist in a balance.
- The socio-technical nature of crypto-asset ecosystems generates a granularisation of the concepts of anonymity and transparency. The features of crypto-assets are multi-layered, which spills into the dichotomy between anonymity and transparency—i.e., the traits of an ecosystem depend on technical and social elements,[29] as well as on their interaction.
- Crypto-asset ecosystems have levels of anonymity that vary significantly.[30] When measuring technical anonymity, various studies often anchor their assessments to the same metrics, but rely on different interpretations of the attributes, giving different meanings to the benchmarks.[31] Consequently, it appears that "there is no theoretical model up to now, which could model anonymity across different cryptocurrency schemes in a systematic way".[32] In this context, "modelling anonymity of cryptocurrencies involves a complex process of studying different notions of anonymity and their relationships and dependencies".[33]

[27] ITU-T FG DLT (2019), p. 26.

[28] Clarke (1999), de Koker (2015).

[29] Rogaway (2016). Sardá et al. (2019).

[30] Amarasinghe et al. (2019), p. 1.

[31] Amarasinghe et al. (2019), p. 3. Attribute describes "an essential, definitional property [of a person] that qualifies it as a member of a given set (or class) [of persons]" (Wang & De Filippi, 2020, p. 2). The same can be argued for crypto-asset ecosystems.

[32] Amarasinghe et al. (2019), p. 8.

[33] Amarasinghe et al. (2019), p. 9.

- Due to the complex interplay of the crypto-asset sphere and the AML/CFT dimensions, notions of anonymity and transparency commonly used in adjacent domains of legal research—e.g., privacy and data protection—are not useful and at times not applicable.
- A disambiguation effort is required when transposing AML/CFT concepts to the crypto-asset sphere. It is key to clarify which aspects of anonymity and transparency are important when fighting money laundering and terrorist financing performed within and/or through crypto-asset ecosystems.

Against this backdrop, after introducing the role of encryption in the crypto-asset space, this chapter (a) investigates the features of anonymity and transparency in crypto-asset transactions at the crossroads of the digital world, financial transactions, and AML/CFT, and (b) outlines the impact on accountability of enhanced disintermediation. In doing so, it lays the foundations to introduce a holistic perspective in Chap. 4, where the scope of the analysis encompasses socio-technical elements affecting anonymity and transparency levels of crypto-asset ecosystems.

3.2 Making Sense of Anonymity and Transparency: Two Sides of the Same (Crypto)Coin

The goals of this section are to disambiguate the notions of anonymity and transparency in the context of crypto-assets and in the AML/CFT domain. On the one hand, the relevant regulation does not define anonymity as such, but rather how to avert it.[34] On the other hand, the application of the term to crypto-asset ecosystems requires consideration of their features for any conceptualisation of anonymity to mirror their reality. Arguably, the use of a teleological approach, focused on the objective of the definitions, is useful to this end. One may wonder: why is it dangerous that a subject engages in anonymous transactions over the Internet? How are AML/CFT rules challenged by anonymity? In what ways does transparency mitigate those risks and what can be transparent in a crypto-asset transaction? What is the end-goal of prohibiting or restricting anonymous activities?

Well before the advent of crypto-assets, different conceptualisations had emerged in the realm of online anonymity. Ever since the issue spilled over to the financial domain and to the blockchain space, it has been increasingly complex for a definition to encompass all influential elements. Indeed, scholars adjusted the theory of anonymity in data communication—a topic that grounds diverse theoretical frameworks—to single out attributes to capture the different aspects of the concept of anonymity in the crypto-asset sphere.[35] In this respect, it is possible to identify

[34] de Koker (2015).

[35] Amarasinghe et al. (2019), p. 2.

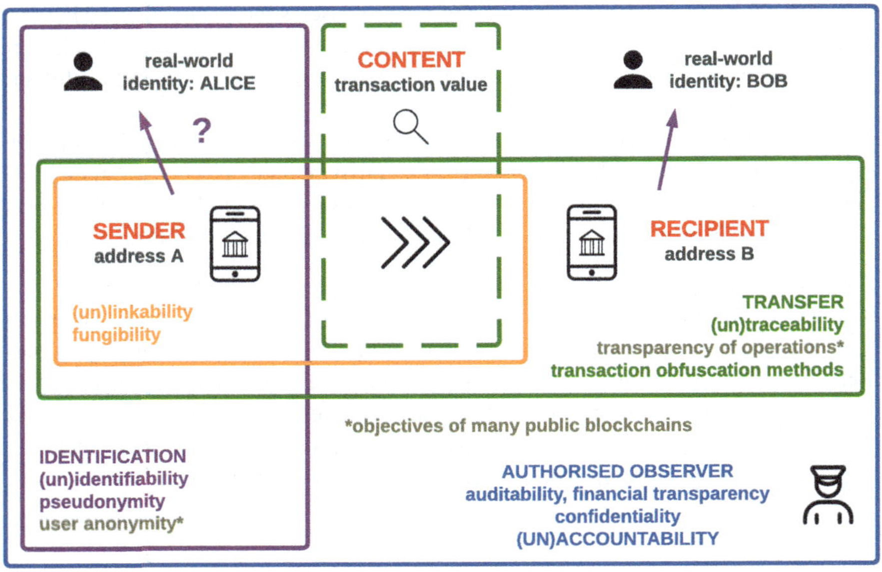

Fig. 3.1 A simplified depiction of the features related to anonymity and transparency relevant to a crypto-asset transaction. Based on Pocher (2023)

elements deemed as benchmarks to evaluate the anonymity construction of a crypto-asset scheme.[36]

This type of approach shows the granularity of anonymity, which emerges as composed of different features whose importance depends on the perspective of the analysis. This notion is often addressed in a 'static' way and evaluated using a series of metrics. While this approach is useful to ground any further analysis, a 'dynamic' methodology may prove more suitable to the AML/CFT context. This is chiefly because crypto-asset transactions are performed within (and across) socio-technical ecosystems populated by many stakeholders, services, and technical layers, where the concept of anonymity comes into play in different forms. While there are fewer perspectives on the notion of transparency, its analysis benefits from a 'dynamic' transaction-oriented approach as well. Indeed, the twofold nature of transparency outlined below arises from the application of DLTs to financial transactions.

Hence, the analysis begins from the perspective of a crypto-asset transaction. Figure 3.1 displays notions used in literature to describe anonymity and transparency, showing their different meanings and roles, as well as the layers and conceptual differences among them. The remainder of the section addresses the rectangles showed in the figure, highlighting traits within an AML/CFT context. According to this reconstruction, in the AML/CFT sphere anonymity emerges as (a) conceptually granular, (b) context-specific, (c) observer-dependent, and (d) a

[36] Amarasinghe et al. (2019), p. 3.

broader concept than the ones of other regulatory frameworks. Meanwhile, the notion of transparency appears twofold and split by the fact that, as explored below, the concept of transparency of the ledger and ledger operations appears distant from the constitutive elements of financial transparency.

3.2.1 *Conceptual Granularity of Anonymity*

This investigation focuses on the notions typically found in the literature, and at times used interchangeably with anonymity itself: (un)traceability, (un)linkability, (un)identifiability, identification (or lack thereof), pseudonymity, confidentiality, transparency, privacy. The goal is to outline their relationship with anonymity, as interpreted from the specific perspective of AML/CFT purposes. It was argued that "technical anonymity exists when individuals are untraceable: there is no link between their actions and a singular identifiable and accountable persona",[37] and that 'privacy coins' have "revealed that fungibility and anonymity are effectively synonymous".[38] In these statements, we see references to anonymity, untraceability, unlinkability, unidentifiability, unaccountability and fungibility. While the conveyed message is valuable from the perspective of their authors, it may be argued the mentioned concepts are not appropriately distinguished for (techno-)legal analysis.

As a preliminary note, the analysis of these properties assumes the transaction is detectable and observable—i.e., it is possible for the 'attacker/observer' (the subject trying to reach identification, as outlined below) to sufficiently distinguish the fact that it exists.[39] If not, the transaction is not relevant to this work and does not warrant further evaluation for its purposes.

A transaction such as the one in Fig. 3.1 is performed between a sender, with address A, and a recipient, with address B. As explored below, crypto-asset addresses act as pseudonyms for their users. In this context, there are three chief elements to consider: (a) the parties, (b) their addresses, and (c) the transfer, with its content. These aspects can be analysed separately to show how different features linked to anonymity are presented by literature.

When looking at the transfer of funds (green rectangle), the notion of traceability refers to the possibility to trace the transfer, where methods of obfuscation, addressed in Chap. 4, pursue the untraceability (or limited traceability) of fund flows—i.e., their obfuscation. Untraceability is defined as the impossibility to trace transactions back to their senders.[40] In the AML/CFT domain, the concept of anonymity is strongly related to that of opaqueness of financial flows, by influencing the possibility to retrieve information on the origin of funds, underlying reasons

---

[37] Bancroft (2020), p. 180.

[38] Berg (2019), p. 11.

[39] Torra (2017), p. 13.

[40] Amarasinghe et al. (2019), p. 3.

for business/financial operations and identity of beneficial owners. Meanwhile, the possibility to transact anonymously,[41] and in general the reduction of transparency of fund flows, facilitate collection and laundering of the proceeds of (cyber)crimes such as ransomware attacks, which are often in the headlines in recent years.

Considering the relationship between the transfers and the accounts that originated or received them (yellow rectangle), the notion of linkability describes the possibility to link two or more transfers to an address—i.e., given two or more transactions, it is possible to refer them to the same user. In this sense, literature equates anonymity with unlinkability, and accountability with maximum linkability.[42] In this context, the notion of recipient anonymity refers to the impossibility to link transactions to their recipients.[43] Another type of (un)linkability is used to define a property between transactions and other types of data, such as transaction metadata. For instance, metadata (un)linkability can refer to the (un)linkability of IP addresses to transactions and crypto addresses, which could single out geographical locations and uncover real-world identities. When looking at the content of the transaction (dotted green rectangle), specific techniques can hide transaction values. In this way, it is harder or impossible to link transactions to addresses through an analysis of transaction flow patterns.[44]

3.2.2 *Context-Specificity of Anonymity: Identifiability and Identification*

In the AML/CFT field there is a foundational concept that mirrors a necessary step to avoid anonymity: identification. Reaching identification, in turn, depends on the quality of identifiability—i.e., the possibility to link the address to a real-world identity. It is self-evident that the address acting as a pseudonym, in the absence of any connection to other data, is not enough to hold real-world users accountable. From an operational perspective, AML/CFT provisions regarding customer due diligence (CDD) and know your customer (KYC), analysed in Chap. 5, pivot on two concepts: (a) identification of a subject and (b) verification or authentication of a subject's identity. In this context, identification means establishing the real-world identity, while verification entails verifying the authenticity of said identity against previously pinpointed identifying information—i.e., an identifier or a set of identifiers.[45] In other words, verifying that the two details—i.e., the data provided

[41] This chapter and the following investigate the extent to which, and the conditions under which, a transaction can correctly be considered anonymous and the relationship with other notions.

[42] Torra (2017), p. 14.

[43] Amarasinghe et al. (2019), p. 3.

[44] Transaction analytics techniques are explored in Chap. 4.

[45] Other authors have described (biometric) identity-based systems starting with the concept of authentication, defined as a process that takes place after registration to a specific system, by which

and that used to verify it—relate to the same subject.[46] Indeed, the same existence of financial institutions was linked to identity-related regulatory requirements such as KYC in terms of 'identity cost economising'.[47]

As mentioned above, it is not like something is either identified or anonymous. Rather, these traits range on a spectrum. Nonetheless, frameworks such as AML/CFT provide criteria that impose a degree of identification conducive to the prevention (or risk mitigation) of illegal transactions or to ensure traceability. Hence, in this context one can argue a subject is identifiable for a specific purpose when the entity in charge of the identification process can access the information required by the framework. Thus, a subject is identifiable or non-identifiable only with reference to a specific actor. Since the concept of identifiability is the negation of anonymity, if a subject cannot identify another subject—or identify and verify the identity, if so required—, the latter is anonymous with regard to the first one.[48]

It follows that two seemingly opposite goals—(i) for a person to choose if/when to be identified, to safeguard fundamental rights,[49] and (ii) to ensure identifiability for the sake of accountability and enforcement—can be assessed only in light of the specific situation. For this reason, anonymity is arguably a context-specific notion. In other words, its definition varies depending on the (regulatory) context. In the case at hand, the applicable AML/CFT framework lays out the criteria against which it should be evaluated whether identification has been reached. In this respect, anonymity can be evaluated only with respect to specific requirements.

Taking a further step, one can notice that assessing compliance is not only a question of the regulated entity being able to identify and verify an identity—i.e., of the subject being identifiable. What is important is doing it—i.e., identification. Indeed, a regulated entity may simply not do it even when able to. This explains why in early AML/CFT initiatives 'anonymous funding' was defined as "cash funding or third-party funding through virtual exchangers that do not properly identify the funding source", and an 'anonymous transfer' is a situation where "sender

the system checks whether the individual has permission to access the service. In this scenario, there are two stages in authentication: identification and verification. While "verification is the process of verifying one's identity" (in the case at hand, by biometric means, a one-to-one matching process), "identification is the process of retrieving the identity of a particular individual, based on an identifier" (a one-to-many matching process) (Wang and De Filippi (2020), p. 8).

[46] Grijpink and Prins (2001), p. 381. The eIDAS framework—i.e., Regulation (EU) 910/2014 as amended by Regulation (EU) 2024/1183, colloquially known as eIDAS 2.0—provides valuable definitions: 'person identification data' is "a set of data that is issued in accordance with Union or national law and that enables the establishment of the identity of a natural or legal person, or of a natural person representing another natural person or a legal person" (Article 3(1)(3)) and 'authentication' is "an electronic process that enables the confirmation of the electronic identification of a natural or legal person or the confirmation of the origin and integrity of data in electronic form" (Article 3(1)(5)).

[47] Berg (2019), p. 2.

[48] Pfitzmann and Hansen (2010), p. 22.

[49] Lindsey (1999), p. 1.

and recipient are not adequately identified".[50] In these cases, anonymity may not originate from the entity being unable to perform the required identification and verification but stems from the entity neglecting its duty to perform one or more relevant activities.

When addressing anonymity and identifiability in the AML/CFT sphere, one cannot forget they are also at the core of data privacy and data protection law. In this case, the concept of anonymity is related to that of 'personal data', and the approach resembles the one described above with regard to the importance of identification and identifiability. The notion of anonymous information is not explicitly defined, but refers to the result of the conversion process of personal data to which data protection rules no longer apply—i.e., so-called 'anonymisation techniques' explored below.[51] In other words, "anonymous information is data which does not relate to an identified or identifiable individual (i.e., data that is not personal data)".[52] A similar reasoning, in conjunction with the arguments provided above, can be applied to an AML/CFT scenario—after all, a transaction is an exchange of information. Accordingly, an anonymous transaction is one that cannot be related, or in any case is not related—i.e., it does not relate—to an identified (hence, identifiable) individual.

3.2.3 *User Anonymity and Ledger Transparency*

When it comes to assessing ledger transparency, the distinction between private and public blockchains is most relevant. As introduced in Chap. 2, blockchains can be public or private, and permissioned or permissionless. The first concept concerns reading restrictions, while the latter pertains to writing permissions. In other words, a public blockchain is publicly readable, while a private blockchain can be read only by authorised actors; in a permissionless blockchain all the participants can add transactions to the ledger, while in a permissioned blockchain this is available only to authorised participants. It follows that private ledgers are usually permissioned—i.e., often, if there are reading restrictions there are also writing restrictions.[53] When the network can be freely accessed for reading and viewing purposes, it is public. If not, it is private. In this respect, the (un)restricted access is 'to' something, namely to a set of data. These distinctions come into play from two different, albeit related, perspectives.

[50] Financial Action Task Force (2014), p. 6.

[51] Information Commissioner's Office (2021).

[52] Information Commissioner's Office (2021).

[53] There are specific cases of private permissionless systems—e.g., Holochain, LTO Network—where generally anyone can become a node, but information is shared on private sidechains. Daniels (2018); LTO Network (2019).

On the one hand, different ledger types have been related to divergent approaches to identity and identification. In public permissionless blockchains with no intermediary or centralised authorities, such as Bitcoin and Ethereum, the nodes that maintain the network "operate without association to a particular given identity".[54] In this respect, public blockchains "are structurally designed as devices allowing anonymous transactions between peers. Blockchains are generally intended to provide users with evidence with no disclosure of knowledge".[55] Because in public ledgers all transaction data is publicly available, the anonymity of a public ledger could be defined as a situation in which "an outsider cannot link the transaction data to the participants involved in corresponding transactions".[56] Being a public ledger, we assume the outsider can see the transaction data, and anonymity is then referred to the possibility to connect this data to the parties involved. This is the feature of (un)linkability addressed in the previous section. By contrast, in permissioned blockchains, where there is a centralised entity or consortium that identifies the nodes, their key-pair is usually associated with a real-world identity. This enables policing and renders unnecessary some security measures employed in permissioned blockchains—e.g., consensus mechanisms such as PoW or PoS.[57]

On the other hand, allowing individuals to perform transactions directly and without being identified was one of the core elements pursued by the monetary application of DLTs. In this context, the goal of many public blockchains like Bitcoin is a combination between user anonymity—better, as outlined below, pseudonymity—with transparency of operations. In other words, the ledger is transparent, and the complete transaction history is available for everyone to read. Network participants, however, are not related to their real-world identities, but to addresses that act as pseudonyms.[58] The combination of user anonymity and transparency of operations may seem paradoxical. Indeed, part of the 'blockchain hype' is centred on the praise of these networks for the privacy they seem to offer, where privacy is intended as a product of the purported 'trustless trust' and lack of centralised control. By contrast, in principle data is published for all participants to see—i.e., the ledger is transparent.[59] While the two objectives may appear opposed at a first glance, they are in practice compatible.[60] The combination, pursued by public blockchains, between user anonymity and transparency of operations was further enhanced by AECs (see Chap. 4). In this context, key opportunities to combine these objectives are offered by zero-knowledge proofs (ZKPs).

[54] Wang and De Filippi (2020), p. 4.
[55] Quiniou (2019), p. 22.
[56] Amarasinghe et al. (2019), p. 2.
[57] Wang and De Filippi (2020), p. 4.
[58] Amarasinghe et al. (2019), p. 2.
[59] Marthews and Tucker (2019).
[60] Quiniou (2019), p. 18.

3.2.4 Transparency of Operations and Financial Transparency

Transparency of operations, however, is a type of transparency that does not ensure accountability, and starkly differs from financial transparency, grounded on the connection to real-world identities—i.e., it relies on identifiability. Indeed, transparency itself is a concept prone to embodying different understandings when related to accountability in information networks.[61] This distinction is important because the value of transparency is significant in the financial world as well. A long-lived debate has investigated the (in)compatibility of financial transparency with the concepts of financial privacy and banking secrecy, interpreted as the principle of confidentiality in financial transactions.[62] In this context, (financial) confidentiality also refers to the limited number of actors with access to financial information, as it is also in the context of AML/CFT-related data.[63] The digitisation of financial services generated new challenges in this regard, and a turning point was identified in 2008, when macroprudential concerns produced by the financial crisis urged regulators to balance core principles such as financial stability, consumer protection, inclusion, growth, and innovation.[64] A prior permissive approach to digitisation known as 'deregulation' was replaced by a more structured analysis, which was met by the FinTech revolution and its evolving risks.[65]

Against this backdrop, it is naïve to thrust on crypto-assets the burden of having first meddled with the relationship between transacting privately and being accountable for financial operations. Also in the financial services sector, a situation of 'full transparency' would cause significant turmoil, as on a fully transparent DLT platform "all information would be disclosed to the public such as the players involved, the pricing and the timing of the transactions along with other relevant information that would reveal much of the investment strategies of the institutions or people involved in the process. Such a level of disclosure would probably greatly affect the competitive advantage that some institutions have over their competitors".[66] The fact that the transparency of compliance regimes differs from the one praised in DLTs advocates for applying the teleological approach, focused on context and purpose of the definition of transparency.

As introduced above, a situation of transparency is often equated to one where there can be accountability. From this perspective, the quest for transparency to ensure accountability has long been a commonplace goal in information networks,

---

[61] Herian (2019), pp. 77–79.

[62] Lindsey (1999), pp. 171–172. ABA Bank Compliance (1999), pp. 147–158. Le Nguyen (2018), pp. 53–54.

[63] Fanti and Pocher (2022), p. 19.

[64] In financial regulation, the 'macroprudential/systemic' perspective focuses on the overall impact of inter-relationships between financial institutions, thus pinpointing those exerting influence from a systemic perspective.

[65] Zetzsche et al. (2017), pp. 6–8.

[66] ITU-T FG DLT (2019), p. 24.

frequently challenged by surveillance criticism. In this sense, the interplay between transparency and accountability does not only transcends the financial sphere—e.g., it also concerns the activity of public administrations—but is also complex.[67] The general understanding of transparency was linked to openness and visibility, as opposed to secrecy. This, however, proved insufficient in the normative dimension, where it was argued the concept of transparency can no longer be limited to revealing information, and should address issues of "usage, legitimacy, respect to privacy, accountability, as well as data integrity".[68] For this reason, a modern understanding of transparency is based on the presentation of information being "open, comprehensive, clear and understandable".[69] Hence, it is not enough to have access to information thanks to transparency requirements, it has to be presented in a way qualitatively conducive to establishing accountability.

In the AML/CFT sphere and related blockchain literature, one may find statements inspired by a teleological approach. Accordingly, the notion of transparency is the one that aims to fight money laundering and terrorist financing, and this understanding of transparency is focused on information on the origin of funds and on the identification of clients and intermediaries. Although the issue of transparency is key in blockchain protocols, the type of transparency offered by public blockchains is a type of transparency useful for user interaction, not for oversight bodies.[70] Indeed, non-centralised systems embody (and leverage) a concept of transparency radically opposed to the one useful for regulatory purposes, such as in the AML/CFT sphere. Hence, there would be a structural incompatibility between blockchain technologies and the rules on transparency set by regulators.[71] Indeed, "it is questionable whether this approach to user anonymity and transparency of operations adopted by public blockchains is compatible with regulations".[72] A clear example is that of the General Data Protection Regulation (GDPR), which pursues the "objective of conferring to the individual control of their own personal data, therefore not allowing it to be fully transparent and open to everyone".[73]

3.2.5 Pseudonymity and Monetary Fungibility

The accuracy of defining the Bitcoin system as anonymous was challenged extensively and there is widespread consensus that, despite its evolutions, it has yet

[67] Herian (2019), p. 77.

[68] ITU-T FG DLT (2019), p. 23.

[69] ITU-T FG DLT (2019). The definition is per ISO 16759:2013.

[70] Quiniou (2019), p. 20.

[71] Quiniou (2019), p. 20.

[72] Quiniou (2019), p. 18.

[73] ITU-T FG DLT (2019), p. 24. For an overview of related challenges and possible solutions in an organisational setting, please see, for instance, Rieger et al. (2019); Sedlmeir et al. (2022).

to provide an 'acceptable' degree of anonymity. This 'acceptability' in terms of cyber-libertarian ideals relates to monetary fungibility—i.e., the property of the units of a currency system that are all identical—according to its criteria of 'anti-individuation' and 'anti-reidentification'.[74] If it is possible to trace transactions back to senders/recipients and retrace the history of specific currency units, the currency scheme loses credibility and quality. This is because the history of a specific coin affects its nominal value and actual worth—i.e., it affects the fungibility of the units of currency.[75] If the history of currency units can be retraced, the outcome is similar to a banknote bearing on its surface dots representing the types of transactions it was involved in.

In this respect, the concept of 'identity of money' refers to the history of the exchanges: when a unit of currency has an identity, as a result of regulatory provisions and activities of authorities—e.g., a red dot is drawn on the banknote when it is used to perform an illicit payment—, monetary fungibility is threatened.[76] In this case, it is not true any longer that all banknotes are equal, as their identity is defined by the dots drawn over time, and a recipient may reject a specific banknote if a specific dot is present. Accordingly, the banknote loses connection with the nominal value, and the currency scheme loses credibility.

From the perspective of the possibility to link a given transfer—better, the specific coins involved—to a specific address and thus to the previous activities performed by that address and those coins, in Fig. 3.1 the quality of fungibility is placed in the yellow rectangle. Indeed, public distributed ledgers were proving tricky in maintaining user privacy, due to the possible exploitations of identifiers in terms of linkability and traceability. Accordingly, Bitcoin itself was found not to possess the properties of unlinkability and untraceability.[77] Hence, an analysis of the transactions could allow identity-related conclusions to be inferred: "if Account A sends a specific amount at a specific time to Account B it is sometimes possible to triangulate and determine the offline identities of the people associated with the transaction".[78]

The reasons for this depend on the way Bitcoin was designed, and in particular:

- Bitcoin transactions are based on two key concepts: inputs, the amounts spent on a transaction, 'spent state', and outputs, the amounts received, 'unspent state'. Hence, the balance of a wallet is equal to all the outputs not yet spent—i.e., 'unspent transaction outputs (UTXOs)'.[79] As depicted in Fig. 3.2, each transaction refers to one or many previous UTXOs with their own unique recipient addresses. Since these UTXOs become inputs for new transactions, to

[74] Berg (2019), p. 11.

[75] Berg (2019), p. 1.

[76] Berg (2019), p. 6.

[77] van Saberhagen (2013), cited by Amarasinghe et al. (2019), p. 3.

[78] Harvey and Branco-Illodo (2020), p. 109.

[79] Silva Ramalho and Igreja Matos (2021), p. 490. Furneaux (2018), p. 73.

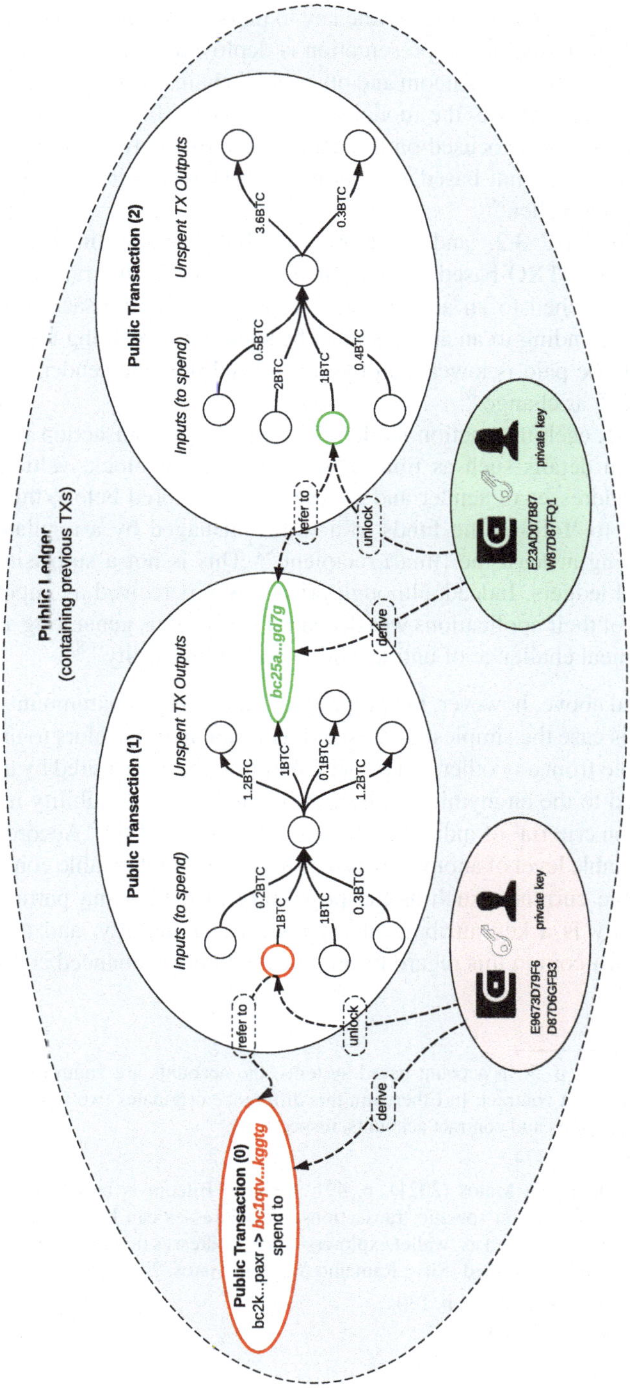

Fig. 3.2 Anatomy of a transaction in a UTXO-based system. Based on Pocher et al. (2023)

know the balance held by a specific user we can add up the UTXOs related to the addresses the person has the private key to unlock. When this type of UTXO-based or address-based data representation is deployed, there are no accounts at the protocol level. Besides Bitcoin and other blockchains such as Litecoin, Zcash, Dash, and Cardano, this is the model used by IOTA's Tangle. Other networks, especially blockchains focused on the deployment of smart contracts, primarily Ethereum, use an account-based accounting method, where coins are represented as a balance of a wallet.[80]

- As shown in Fig. 3.2, and contrary to what happens in account-based blockchains, in UTXO-based systems it is not possible to transfer only part of the coins attached to an address. Hence, in a UTXO transaction the entire amount corresponding to an address must be spent when making the transfer. If the amount to be paid is lower than the transferred one, the sender receives the remainder back as change.[81]
- In this context, each transaction is identified through a 'transaction ID (TXID)' equipped with details such as time of receipt, relevant block, values of input and output, addresses of sender and recipient. As explored below, this data can be leveraged to 'follow' the funds to a wallet managed by a regulated entity, thus identifying at least the (final) recipient.[82] This is not a surprising feature of distributed ledgers. Indeed, although privacy was perceived as important, the primary aim of their applications was decentralisation, thus generating a "double-headed technical challenge of untraceability and unlinkability".[83]

As mentioned above, however, the property of anonymity is paramount for a currency, and in this case the simplest understanding of anonymity refers to units being undistinguishable from any other.[84] The degree of fungibility featured by a currency is closely related to the anonymity it offers, while to satisfy fungibility it must fail the 'identification criteria' of individuation and re-identification.[85] Accordingly, the lack of an acceptable level of anonymity brings about the "undesirable consequences of a non-fungible currency, such as the possibility of ostracising participants".[86] Hence, fungibility is a key attribute of crypto-asset anonymity, and the claimed insufficiency of Bitcoin in this regard prompted anonymity-enhanced coins.

---

[80] Pocher et al. (2023), p. 3. In account-based systems, the accounts are controlled either by a private key or by a smart contract. In Ethereum, this difference originates two types of accounts: externally owned accounts and contract accounts, respectively.

[81] Furneaux (2018), pp. 73–74.

[82] Silva Ramalho and Igreja Matos (2021), p. 491. Because Bitcoin is based on transparency a significant amount of data on specific transactions and addresses can be obtained from open sources. In this respect, tools such as 'wallet explorers' allow addresses tied to gambling platforms, exchanges or mixers to be identified (Silva Ramalho & Igreja Matos, 2021, p. 493).

[83] Harvey and Branco-Illodo (2020), p. 130.

[84] Amarasinghe et al. (2019), p. 1.

[85] Berg (2019), pp. 1–3.

[86] Amarasinghe et al. (2019), p. 1.

Bitcoin is pseudonymous, and the same is true for other cryptocurrencies.[87] Pseudonymity is "the use of pseudonyms as identifiers", where a pseudonym is an "identifier of a subject other than the subject's real names".[88] A parallel was drawn between public and private keys and the idea of username and password,[89] where crypto addresses (public keys) act as usernames, a common example of pseudonyms. In a cryptocurrency transaction, the sender and/or recipient are pseudonymous, and not anonymous, when they are identified by their respective addresses. Indeed, the gap between cryptographic keys and human identities was one of the elements leading to the establishment of intermediaries in the crypto-asset sphere—e.g., centralised exchanges and related businesses.[90] The concept of pseudonymity primarily relates to the case in which it is possible to link public addresses (pseudonyms) to real-world identities. Hence, the purple rectangle in Fig. 3.1. Pseudonymity, however, can also be interpreted in a broader sense. Generally, a pseudonymous trait can be conceived even in those networks with no access requirements such as identification. This is because the linkage to a real-world identity can exploit data that is external to the ecosystem at hand.[91]

A blockchain system generally manages identifiers through pairs of public/private keys that identify the wallet holder uniquely.[92] In Bitcoin "the complete history of the transactions is transparent to the network participants, yet they are not related to specific identities, but addresses".[93] Bitcoin's pseudonymity means that even if identifiers "do not communicate any personal identifying information about the person, unless additional information is associated with them",[94] they can be used to connect transactions to their history. In other words, although Bitcoin seemed to fit cyberlibertarian goals of a monetary system supporting ideals of unaccountability, its actual anonymity level proved insufficient. In line with the socio-technical nature of the crypto-asset sphere, there are several elements to consider. A significant influence in the evolution of the anonymity levels was exerted by forensics. This is because the deployment of advanced investigative techniques, and certain transactions being trackable, generated significant distrust of the privacy degree of DLT ecosystems, while undermining fungibility.[95] Against

[87] Biryukov and Tikhomirov (2019); Li et al. (2019); Wachsman (2019).

[88] Pfitzmann and Hansen (2010), pp. 21–22. In a more ambiguous fashion, pseudonymity was equated with the use of a false name (Weber & Heinrich, 2012, p. 1), where 'false' assumes the chosen identifier is also a name.

[89] Sun and Zhang (2018).

[90] Allen et al. (2020), p. 26. Blockchain scholars explored identity using different methodologies. It was underlined how it is inherently 'digital', encompassing four elements: 'registration information', 'transactional identity', 'transaction history', and 'digital history' (Marthews & Tucker, 2019, p. 246). For AML/CFT purposes, it shall be a verifiable 'legal identity'.

[91] This can be done through blockchain forensic strategies (see Chap. 4).

[92] Wang and De Filippi (2020), p. 3.

[93] Amarasinghe et al. (2019), p. 2.

[94] Wang and De Filippi (2020), p. 3.

[95] Casey et al. (2018); Berg (2019).

this backdrop, other authors investigated parameters such as k-anonymity and taint resistance,[96] whose relevance emerged in the context of intelligence techniques addressed in Chap. 4.

3.2.6 *Observer-Dependency and Broadness of the Notion of Anonymity*

Because identifiers alone "do not communicate any personal identifying information about the person, unless additional information is associated with them",[97] the quality of being pseudonymous does not necessarily imply identifiability. A pseudonymous subject is identifiable only if from the point of view of the actor trying to identify the subject—e.g., providers of exchange or forensic services, law enforcement agencies (LEAs), authorities—, it is possible to discover its real-world identity. At this point, the literature accounts for the interplay between identifiability and traceability. In this sense, however, the meaning of traceability is referred to the identity of the parties, not to the transaction itself, as outlined above and displayed in the green rectangle of Fig. 3.1. Indeed, from this additional perspective the link been identifiability and traceability emerges from four 'forms of identification'—that could be better defined, perhaps, as degrees of identifiability—described by Froomkin (1995) with regard to email communication:

1. traceable anonymity: the originator sends no identity data, but this information can be retrieved by contacting the intermediary;
2. untraceable anonymity: the sender is unidentifiable;
3. traceable pseudonymity: the pseudonym can be traced back to the sender;
4. untraceable pseudonymity: the originator uses a false and untraceable identity.

These concepts explain why pseudonyms can be used to "cover the range between anonymity (no linkability) to accountability (maximum linkability)",[98] and to pursue anonymity.[99]

---

[96] K-anonymity was explained by stating that "in a system of k users, for any given user in the system, if the actions of any of the remaining k-1 users cannot be differentiated from said user, then that user is regarded as k-anonymous. K represents the size of the anonymity set and a larger k value corresponds to a higher level of anonymity" (Amarasinghe et al., 2019, p. 3). Taint resistance was defined as a "measure of the identifiability of the ownership of a Bitcoin by analysing its past transactions and hence is related to the properties of traceability and fungibility". In particular, the analysis is of the "relationships among Bitcoin addresses based on the transaction history corresponding to those addresses" (Meiklejohn & Orlandi, 2015, cited by Amarasinghe et al. (2019), p. 3).

[97] Wang and De Filippi (2020), p. 3.

[98] Torra (2017), p. 14.

[99] Pfitzmann and Hansen (2010), p. 22.

Against this backdrop, one can argue that the concept of anonymity is observer-dependent, insofar as it can be assessed only with respect to a specific actor trying to reach identification. Indeed, the anonymity of an entity was defined in the literature as the situation in which an outsider is unable to adequately identify it within a group of entities, where the latter is its 'anonymity set'. In the context of data privacy, the cybersecurity perspective is that of an 'attacker' engaged in a deanonymisation attack, where this is a negative concept—i.e., an attempt to compromise the integrity of a system to pursue illegal goals such as data protection violations. Nevertheless, the same techniques are deployed by LEAs to 'follow the money' and uncover illicit schemes (see Chap. 4). Evidently, when transferred amounts and other metadata are permanently and publicly stored on the ledger it is easier to gather information. Similarly, some networks leak information that can be used for de-anonymisation purposes.[100]

As suggested above, when speaking of anonymity in AML/CFT literature there is less terminological precision than in other fields such as data protection. It is also noticeable, however, that in the AML/CFT domain the meaning of the concept of anonymity is broader. Indeed, consistently with the purpose of the framework (i.e., teleological approach) AML/CFT provisions lean towards an understanding of anonymity that does not distinguish between anonymisation and strong pseudonymisation. Hence, in AML/CFT anonymity encompasses both "(i) the impossibility or near impossibility of linking data on a ledger with (an) identified person(s), and also (ii) a situation when such a linking is 'only' significantly hampered".[101] Thus, methodologically this work builds on a broad understanding of anonymous data and anonymisation technologies. Accordingly, it acknowledges that it is possible to qualify the same data as pseudonymous for what concerns the GDPR and as anonymous for AML/CFT purposes.[102]

The literature on crypto-asset anonymity does not usually enshrine an AML/CFT-oriented methodology, nor does it feature the perspective to strictly identify anonymity metrics relevant for AML/CFT compliance purposes. However, intelligence strategies and AECs show how the two perspectives may be closer than one would think. Hence, it can be argued that the increasing complexity of new applications, networks, or service providers, is making a broad technical understanding of their anonymity levels—and relevant metrics—more relevant also from an investigative and enforcement viewpoint. Indeed, there is an important connection between anonymity in crypto-assets and anonymisation techniques applied in data privacy. Their application to personal data happens in the context of frameworks such as the GDPR in the EU. When these techniques are applied to personal data, this is no longer considered personal, thus making the relevant regime not applicable. As per Recital 26 of the GDPR, the principles of data protection are not applicable to anonymous information, defined as information that is not related

[100] Airfoil (2019).

[101] Karasek-Wojciechowicz (2021), p. 3.

[102] Karasek-Wojciechowicz (2021), p. 3.

"to an identified or identifiable natural person", nor to personal data "rendered anonymous in such a manner that the data subject is not or no longer identifiable". Although anonymisation techniques have been supported for many years, their limitations have been recently underlined, such as that their effectiveness requires irreversibility.[103]

It goes beyond the scope of this work to dive into anonymisation techniques and their historical background. However, some have a strong connection to crypto-assets from an AML/CFT perspective, especially considering AECs. A special role is played by pseudonymisation, which is considered an anonymisation technique in data privacy, although its effectiveness is debated.[104] It is defined by Article 4(5) of the GDPR as "the processing of personal data in such a manner that the personal data can no longer be attributed to a specific data subject without the use of additional information, provided that such additional information is kept separately and is subject to technical and organisational measures to ensure that the personal data are not attributed to an identified or identifiable natural person".

Further, anonymisation techniques encompass concepts such as k-anonymity, l-diversity and t-closeness,[105] as well as approaches of data perturbation or noise addition such as differential privacy. Meanwhile, other methodologies employ synthetic/artificial datasets or apply homomorphic encryption, which allow encrypted data to be processed without decrypting it. Although these concepts prove useful to assess anonymity levels in crypto-asset ecosystems, in recent times these techniques were replaced by the application of distributed systems and blockchains. Indeed, centralised and trust-based systems are argued to be possibly insufficient to provide users with control over their personal data.[106] Albeit the compatibility of blockchain technology with data protection frameworks is debated,[107] its use to implement data protection systems is also investigated. To date, it has largely relied on ZKPs, as detailed in the following chapters.

3.2.7 Contextualisation: Privacy and Anonymity

Often, in crypto-asset discourse the terms anonymity and privacy are used in a way that may seem interchangeable. A typical example is to say that anonymity is dangerous but can safeguard individual privacy against governmental surveillance practices. This is not incorrect, but it is important to specify that in data privacy, anonymity—better, anonymisation—is only one of the available techniques to enhance privacy. In particular, anonymity requires the absence of identifiers. If there

103 Capraz and Ozsoy (2021), p. 110.

104 See, for instance, Article 29 Data Protection Working Party (2014).

105 L-diversity was described with reference to the idea of generating and using a diverse enough set of possible values to represent data. T-closeness uses distributed systems to parse and distribute sensitive data (Capraz and Ozsoy, 2021, p. 110).

106 Capraz and Ozsoy (2021), pp. 110–111.

107 Finck (2019b).

are identifiers, there is pseudonymity. Hence, both anonymity and pseudonymity relate to identity. By contrast, privacy is a much broader concept and can also be safeguarded in ways other than anonymity, and to different extents. Hence, the two terms, although possibly at the same side of the debate involving surveillance vs. privacy, are not synonyms. From this perspective, it was argued that a correct conceptualisation of anonymity does not define it as a subset of privacy, but as its perfect realisation or product.[108] To clarify, in the context of a transaction such as the one depicted in Fig. 3.1, from the perspective of data privacy the scope of the concept of anonymity only relates to the address—that acts as a pseudonym—and to the real-world identity—identifiability and identification.

The same interchangeable use of terms can be detected in privacy-enhancing techniques (PETs) and their implementation in AECs, also known as ‘privacy coins’. AECs and the application of PETs in the crypto-asset sphere are addressed in Chaps. 4 and 6, respectively. From the perspective that is relevant here, ‘privacy coin’ projects are focused on enhancing their privacy level, and they do so by enhancing (also) their anonymity level. Nonetheless, there is no single way to assess the privacy level of a given application, and three different aspects of privacy have been explored when looking at a blockchain architecture:

1. *privacy of identity or user-identity privacy*: it follows from what was argued before that this type of privacy relates to anonymity and pseudonymity. At times, this concept is labelled user anonymity. Indeed, user-identity privacy concerns the link between identity-related data stored on the blockchain, and a real-world identity. From this perspective, scholars explored the structural difference between anonymity and privacy in respect to identification, namelessness, and new technologies.[109] Relatedly, enhancing privacy does not necessarily impact on identification, as exemplified by the use of pseudonymity to protect privacy in the cyberspace long before the advent of Bitcoin;
2. *privacy of information* or, in the financial context, also privacy of transaction data: it refers to the green rectangle in Fig. 3.1. In this sense, privacy is a mutable concept, as data is represented differently in the different blockchain types, various elements may be public or private from different third-party observers (the observer-dependency argued above), and different types of information can be private to different extents;
3. *privacy of the total blockchain state*: this is a separate aspect that pertains to the total ledger state. In this context, specific attributes can be private to different extents.[110] Although more frequently mentioned use cases are blockchain-based, privacy assessments have been carried out for other distributed ledgers. In this respect, a notable example concerns IOTA’s DAG.[111]

[108] Helms (2001). The concept is most relevant to current debates on CBDC designs, explored in Chap. 6.

[109] Skopek (2015), pp. 717–723.

[110] Sun and Zhang (2018).

[111] Tennant (2017), pp. 14–15. Saa et al. (2023).

Against this backdrop, it can be argued that the concepts of anonymity and user privacy are overlapping, and most studies investigate "privacy and anonymity in conjunction and find an intrinsic relationship between the two terms".[112] Indeed, some of the metrics mentioned in this section in relation to anonymity have been leveraged to calculate the level of user privacy of different networks. For instance, the level of user privacy offered by Bitcoin was assessed through the metrics of unlinkability of activities and indistinguishability of user profiles.[113]

3.2.8 Anonymity and Transparency: A Paradox or a Combination?

Public blockchains tend to enshrine an alleged 'paradox' in which "while the information on the ledger is transparent for everyone to see or read, it is also private, thus ensuring the anonymity of the players involved. The balance between transparency and privacy is paramount for DLTs to comply with norms and regulations".[114] In a distributed and non-centralised environment, transparency is used to generate or bypass 'trust', avoiding the need of a trusted third party. To some extent, transparency enables the kind of privacy that follows the absence of a central authority. Nonetheless, transparency has a twofold impact, since it fosters accountability and allows surveillance and traceability. This is not a surprising feature of distributed ledgers: although privacy was politically important, the primary aim of their applications was decentralisation, which generated a "double-headed technical challenge of untraceability and unlinkability".[115] Hence, reaching higher levels of anonymity required specific techniques known as PETs, addressed in Chaps. 4 and 6. While PETs can be used to 'design' privacy, their application to DLTs generates regulatory problems: while in intermediated systems there is a gateway that "has no technical restraints in providing access to the information and in deciding when to delete it", the use of PETs may produce considerable challenges when there is a change in compliance rules, or the requirements entail "a differentiation of disclosure of the information".[116] PETs display different features, and are often implemented in a joint fashion to mitigate their respective shortcomings.

Against this backdrop, crypto-asset networks offering architectural transparency and (some) transactions being anonymous does not seem paradoxical, but a combination of multi-faceted elements. The combination does not exclusively concern crypto-assets, as these concepts have long coexisted in the areas of online

[112] De Haro-Olmo et al. (2020), p. 11.

[113] Androulaki et al. (2013).

[114] ITU-T FG DLT (2019), p. 24.

[115] Harvey and Branco-Illodo (2020), p. 130.

[116] ITU-T FG DLT (2019), p. 24.

communication and financial transactions. Still, one shall not forget two aspects. On the one hand, the impact exerted on DLT-based monetary ecosystems by techno-libertarian views is debated; the topic should neither be ignored nor overestimated. On the other hand, the crypto-asset sphere has long overcome Bitcoin, and the possible contrast between ideology and architecture is not mirrored in the same way by the variety of current use cases, with more than 10,000 cryptocurrencies deployed to date.[117]

Indeed, today one may distinguish between two types of crypto-asset ecosystems:

1. The ones actively rejecting any intervention of the law and authorities, and only regulating themselves (if so) through code, a topic addressed in Chap. 7.
2. The ones yielding to accountability needs, mainly to interact with the traditional financial system. In this context, research is investigating whether it is feasible for crypto-assets and CBDCs to comply with both privacy and accountability requirements.[118]

3.3 The Uptake of Enhanced Disintermediation, Atomicity and Impacts on Accountability

Many new intermediaries are involved in crypto-asset transactions, while enticing business prospects prompt also traditional financial intermediaries to offer related services. From a regulatory perspective, both categories of players can be reached by compliance measures. As suggested in Chap. 2, however, the crypto-asset space is witnessing new trends in non-centralisation and disintermediation, which can be described as cases of enhanced disintermediation as opposed to the more traditional disintermediation cherished by the 'blockchain hype'. These innovations are generating anonymity concerns and show how the fluid nature of the crypto-asset sphere alters the landscape in terms of (un)accountability and transaction opaqueness. In this respect, since 2019 the FATF has been voicing a downward trend.[119] In particular, these solutions are challenging identifiability, linkability, and traceability as depicted above in Fig. 3.1. While Chap. 4 addresses reduced transparency and increased obfuscation of crypto-asset flows, this section focuses on key developments in techniques and tools of enhanced disintermediation. In doing so, it attempts a typology of these trends, by identifying four major breakthroughs fostering a new era for crypto-asset transfers: (1) atomic cross-chain swaps; (2)

---

[117] Statista (2024).

[118] Goodell and Aste (2019); European Central Bank and Bank of Japan (2020); European Central Bank (2019); Berberich and Steiner (2016); Finck (2019a); Karasek-Wojciechowicz (2021).

[119] Financial Action Task Force (2019, 2020a, 2020b, 2020c).

multi-layered applications; (3) unhosted or self-hosted wallets; and (4) decentralised exchanges (DEXes).[120]

These developments have a profound impact on the anonymity level of crypto-asset ecosystems and leverage technologies that must be analysed in terms of their concrete implementations. From a basic perspective, the degree of actual disintermediation depends on the technical capacity to support interoperability between different blockchains and DLTs. Indeed, (intra-blockchain) interoperability is needed to allow the transfer of the increasing number of assets, platforms, and projects from an ecosystem to another.[121] As an example, trading bitcoins with ether without relying on conversion services offered by a third party—e.g., a centralised cryptocurrency exchange (CEX). While providers of crypto-asset portfolios can manage ledgers compatible with multiple systems, intra-blockchain interoperability still poses technical issues.[122] Notwithstanding multi-blockchain compatibility schemes, the result is still not the same as direct, disintermediated, and non-centralised exchanges. The four mentioned breakthroughs aim to change this paradigm and raise regulatory concerns.

3.3.1 Atomic Cross-Chain Swaps and Multi-Layered Protocols

Atomic swaps are key to true disintermediation, as they feature a smart contract technology that enables P2P cryptocurrency exchanges without third-party intervention. In particular, the notion of atomic cross-chain swap or on-chain atomic swap defines the case in which the protocol is embedded in a distributed ledger. In this case, the mechanism works as a "distributed coordination task where multiple parties exchange assets across multiple blockchains, for example, trading bitcoin for ether".[123] The model consists of a directed graph, where vertexes and arcs represent parties and proposed asset transfers, respectively.[124] Transactions are instant, and are either both finalised or cancelled. Indeed, the atomicity of a series of database operations refers to their indivisibility and irreducibility, and their sequence is called

[120] The order of these instances of enhanced disintermediation mirrors the one used in this section and serves a narrative purpose only. Nonetheless, atomic cross-chain swaps play a key role in obtaining disintermediation.

[121] Interoperability can be described as the feature of a system able "to provide services to and accept services from other systems and to use the services so exchanged to enable them to operate efficiently together" (ISO/IEC 30182:2017, cited by Zeuch et al. (2019), p. 155).

[122] Quiniou (2019), pp. 62–64. While intra-blockchain interoperability defines the "overall capacity of blockchains to exchange information with other blockchains", interoperability refers more broadly to the "capability of blockchains to exchange information with other systems, outside of blockchains" (Tasca & Tessone, 2018, p. 21).

[123] Herlihy (2018), p. 245.

[124] Herlihy (2018), p. 247.

a distributed atomic transaction.[125] Evidently, the lack of third-party intervention implies lack of monitoring.

The disruptive idea underlying atomic swaps is that they provide a way to engage in these transactions even if there is no trust among participants. The protocol guarantees not only that all swaps shall take place, but also that for it to happen they must all conform to the system—if not, no transfer occurs. This means no participant can end up in advantageous circumstances by breaking the rules, and everyone is incentivised to adhere to the protocol.[126] This explains another definition of an atomic swap protocol as a "trust-free Byzantine-hardened form of distributed commitment".[127] Clearly, there is an important distinction between transacting crypto-assets through centralised platforms—i.e., 'gatekeepers' addressed by regulation—and the situation in which users can do so while remaining in control of their crypto-assets.[128] Hence, P2P trading causes a remarkable operational and architectural shift.

Atomic swaps are useful to grasp the relationship between multi-layered protocols and enhanced disintermediation. Indeed, besides (i) on-chain atomic swaps—e.g., the 2017 on-chain swap between Dacred and Litecoin—the crypto-asset space houses atomic swaps that take place (ii) off-chain, and (iii) on the second layer of a blockchain.[129] This last category enables exchanges between selected currencies that take place on a secondary layer of nodes,[130] and suggests there is communication between different layers. Indeed, decentralisation can be enhanced by adding new 'layers' of application protocols and often "interdependent forces shape the degree of centralisation in often more than one layers of DLTs".[131] Common examples are known as layer-2 solutions, such as the Lightning Network, used for the first off-chain atomic swap between Bitcoin and Litecoin.[132] As already argued, decentralisation is not a siloed trait and impacts on other features of a crypto-asset ecosystem such as anonymity. Hence, anonymity is influenced by the presence of a multi-layered structure. While a network architecture can comprise multiple

---

[125] Herlihy (2018), p. 246.

[126] The goal is achieved through hash timelocked contracts, which are deployed by the transacting parties and take temporary control over the assets until the finalisation of the transaction is triggered by the contract receiving matching secrets. If not, a refund takes place (Herlihy, 2018, p. 249; Satoshi, 2019.). With atomic swaps the crypto-asset exchange "will initially be locked and can only be retrieved by the relevant counterparty using a cryptographic hash function. Thereby, a time-lock function ensures the refund of the two crypto-assets to the original counterparty in the case that one of the counterparties did not retrieve the crypto-asset within a predefined time period" (European Securities and Markets Authority, 2019, p. 15).

[127] Herlihy (2018), p. 246.

[128] European Securities and Markets Authority (2019), p. 15.

[129] Choo (2019).

[130] European Securities and Markets Authority (2019); Choo (2019).

[131] Bodó and Giannopoulou (2019), p. 5.

[132] Choo (2019).

on-chain and off-chain layers for diverse reasons, this mechanism can be exploited to add one or more anonymity-enhancing layer(s) on top of an existing network.

3.3.2 Peer-to-Peer Transactions and the FATF

Atomic cross-chain swaps enable P2P transfers across different blockchains or DLT networks without the intervention of a central entity. As mentioned in Chap. 2, P2P systems are networks of peers sharing information with each other directly and without relying on a third-party service.[133] Although the 'blockchain hype' pivots around disintermediation, the crypto-asset sphere turns out to be more centralised and intermediated than expected, at least until enhanced disintermediation started to arise. In a truly disintermediated transaction, no monitoring activity can take place, nor it is possible to regulate an intermediary. Depending on the circumstances it may not even be feasible to know the transfers are taking place, let alone to identify senders, recipients, amounts, or to trace them. Although the "visibility of P2P transactions on public ledgers might support financial analysis and law enforcement investigations, especially when combined with other information sources", these techniques can be hampered by anonymity-enhancing technologies.[134]

From an AML/CFT perspective, the FATF defines P2P crypto-asset transactions as transfers performed without the involvement of a regulated entity.[135] When users perform this type of transfers, they do not rely on the services of third parties. As outlined in Chap. 5, current AML/CFT frameworks are intermediary-based and P2P transactions fall outside their scope. Nonetheless, the FATF stressed the risk they can be used to bypass controls, as P2P transfers can be both used for legitimate activities and exploited for criminal purposes, which is even more worrisome given the rapid evolution of the sector.[136]

Data provided by analytics companies on P2P transfers is significant, but there is no consensus on the size of the sector. The difficulty in obtaining precise data mirrors "the challenges and limitations inherent in this kind of research with blockchain analytics, in terms of coverage, timeliness, accuracy and reliability, even if P2P transactions are recorded on public ledgers".[137] If it were to become

[133] ITU-T FG DLT (2019), p. 4.

[134] Financial Action Task Force (2021), p. 18.

[135] "VA transfers conducted without the use or involvement of a VASP or other obliged entity" (Financial Action Task Force, 2021, p. 18).

[136] The FATF urges jurisdictions and service providers to single out those P2P transfers that pose higher and lower risk, and to understand the different risk profiles, where "relevant factors that could, depending on the design of the VA, potentially impact the extent to which users engage in P2P transactions include the VA's accessibility and protocols that control the VA's privacy, transparency, security and associated transaction fees" (Financial Action Task Force, 2021, p. 18).

[137] Financial Action Task Force (2021), p. 18.

mainstream for a significant portion of crypto-asset activity to take place P2P, the effectiveness of AML/CFT measures would be challenged radically.

3.3.3 *Self-hosted Wallets and Decentralised Custody*

Despite enhanced disintermediation, to this day the crypto-asset world remains more intermediated and centralised than the hype would suggest. In this respect, although a blockchain system is decentralised when the history of transactions is recorded and maintained immutably by a distributed network of nodes, the "decentralised nature of a blockchain network does not, however, apply to the custody and secure storage of the keys that control the individual wallets on that network".[138] Indeed, most users hold their coins in so-called custodial wallets, also known as hosted wallets. The value of crypto-assets never leaves the network, and they are stored in wallets that resemble more keychains than traditional wallets. It is well-known there are different types of crypto wallets, whose function is to help manage addresses and private keys.[139] The choice among the different options depends on individual preferences and expertise. A user accesses and spends the coins associated with a given address through the corresponding private key, as outlined in Chap. 2. Because private keys act as an authentication code that grants access to funds, the different options come with strings attached in terms of privacy and security.[140]

From a first perspective, wallets are 'hardware' when they consist of devices like USB pen drives (e.g., Ledger Nano, Trezor), or 'software'. In turn, 'software' wallets can be 'desktop', 'mobile' or 'web' wallets.[141] 'Desktop' and 'mobile' wallets are applications installed on a computer (e.g., Bitcoin Core, Electrum) or on a smartphone (e.g., Mycelium, Coinomi), respectively. They do not involve the services of an intermediary, and the software is executed only on the device. On the contrary, 'web' wallets are accessed through Internet browsers or apps, and can be either 'hosted' (e.g., Coinbase) or 'non-hosted' (e.g., MetaMask). This means the wallet can be 'custodial', where a third party offers storage services and has custody of users' private keys, or 'non-custodial', when users retain custody of their private keys. Given the differences among 'software' wallets, the fact that users interact with their wallet through an app does not mean the wallet is 'hosted'—i.e., that a third-party entity is storing their private keys. Lastly, wallets can be classified as 'hot', when they are connected to the Internet, or 'cold', when private keys are stored offline.[142] The decision to make use of a 'hot' or 'cold' wallet is significant in terms

138 Wang and De Filippi (2020), p. 6.

139 Whitehouse-Levine and Kelleher (2020), p. 5.

140 Pocher (2021).

141 Another subcategory of 'software' wallets is that of "paper" wallets, although this type is argued to be obsolete. It consists of a printed QR code or a hand-written piece of paper.

142 Smith (2024).

of privacy and security, as 'cold' solutions are not constantly exposed to the dangers stemming from connectivity to the Internet (e.g., cyberattacks, thefts).

Hence, custodial wallets are not the only available means to store and use crypto funds. On the contrary, a type of P2P transaction that is currently worrying AML/CFT regulators and enforcement agencies relates to "VA transfers between two unhosted wallets whose users are acting on their own behalf".[143] These wallets are known as self-hosted or unhosted or private and are non-custodial, which means users are the sole holders of their private keys and have full control of their funds. In this way they can perform P2P transactions, which achieves the disintermediation goal. To explain the importance of users retaining full custody it was argued that "from a purely technical perspective (notwithstanding legal and contractual obligations), ownership of assets on the blockchain is equated with control of the assets, which is managed through the private keys associated with a wallet that contains the assets". It follows that when exchanges control the private keys associated with the wallets of their customers, they also control their funds, given that "custody of these keys ultimately implies full control of the funds stored in that account".[144] From an AML/CFT perspective, in P2P transactions there is clearly no third party to hold accountable for monitoring, as no regulated intermediary is involved. Evidently, the traditional intermediary-based 'active cooperation' approach, outlined in Chap. 4, ends up empty-handed, which leaves a gap where illicit activities could potentially thrive.

These considerations prompted the FATF, the EU, and other authorities such as FinCEN to take a stand against such instruments, especially because of possible combinations with obfuscation methods (see Chap. 4)—e.g., 'privacy coins' and advanced services that reduce transaction transparency.[145] The topic of self-hosted wallets from a compliance perspective will be addressed in Chap. 5, also with reference to the impacts on the 'crypto travel rule' debate.[146] What is worth anticipating here is that the regulatory issue is twofold. On the one hand, self-hosted wallets ordinarily interact with regulated providers of crypto-related services.

[143] Financial Action Task Force (2021), p. 18.

[144] Wang and De Filippi (2020), pp. 6–7. The impact is not limited to the financial sphere. It more generally relates to individuals exerting control on their digital IDs, which is pivotal in the 'self-sovereign identity' debate. While the topic falls outside the scope of this work, digital ID systems are strongly linked to AML/CFT—e.g., from the KYC perspective. The related 'principle of control' is that per which "individuals must control their identities, they should always be able to refer to it, update it, or even hide it—even if others can make claims about these identities" (Wang & De Filippi, 2020, p. 10). The private law impacts of different types of wallets on ownership and custody, and considerations on the legal treatments of these instruments, are not addressed in this work. An overview of the importance of self-storage and self-custody is provided by Barresi and Zatti (2020). Key issues related to the ownership of DLT-based crypto-assets are addressed by Siena (2022).

[145] The Financial Crimes Enforcement Network (FinCEN) belongs to the US Department of the Treasury and is responsible for collecting and analysing information about financial transactions to combat money laundering, terrorism financing and other types of financial crimes.

[146] Pocher (2025).

Indeed, funds can originate from a self-hosted wallet and be sent to a hosted wallet, or vice versa. In these cases, regulated entities are required to comply with specific AML/CFT rules (see Chap. 5). On the other hand, true P2P transactions, taking place between two self-hosted wallets, are equally possible and largely fall outside regulatory mechanisms.

Against this backdrop, regulators are considering restrictions on the use of non-custodial wallets, in the form of bans or threshold limits. These initiatives are starkly criticised by some crypto communities and by defenders of anti-surveillance. In their view, a restrictive attitude would be detrimental to values such as individual freedom, privacy, autonomy, and financial inclusion, as well as it would hamper the use of self-hosted wallets as non-monetary value holders and the use of cryptocurrencies as true digital cash.[147]

3.3.4 Decentralised Exchanges and Decentralised Finance

The most common ways to buy and exchange crypto-assets still relies on centralised trading venues, known as CEXes. The use of this type of intermediary services is at odds with the description of the crypto-asset space as an ecosystem for people to dispose of their own money without intermediaries.[148] Thus, it does not come as a surprise that the field has witnessed the emergence of a new type of trading venues with no central authority, free from regulatory constraints—known as decentralised exchanges (DEXes)—and of so-called decentralised protocols. These projects fall within the domain of DeFi applications, which include stablecoin projects (e.g., DAI), lending platforms (e.g., Aave, Compound), crypto-asset DEXes (e.g., Bancor, Kyber, Uniswap, Sushiswap, Pancakeswap), derivative services/DEXes (e.g., Synthetix, dYdx).[149] More recently, the space witnessed the emergence of other DeFi business models such as yield farming (e.g., Yearn Finance, Alpaca Finance) and prediction markets (e.g., Polymarket, Aduro).[150]

The DeFi space has largely developed on the Ethereum blockchain, although specific projects were implemented on networks such as EOS, TRON, Cosmos and Curve.[151] DeFi represents "a whole ecosystem of financial services realised through smart contracts deployed on public distributed ledgers",[152] where "the role

[147] Pocher (2021); Whitehouse-Levine and Kelleher (2020).

[148] Choo (2019).

[149] Amler et al. (2021), p. 182. Aramonte et al. (2021), p. 23. Beinke et al. (2024).

[150] Beinke et al. (2024); Xu and Feng (2023); Wang (2023).

[151] Katona (2021); Nassr et al. (2024).

[152] Amler et al. (2021), p. 181. Despite the growing importance of the sphere, there is no widespread agreement on a common understanding of DeFi (Gramlich et al., 2023, p. 2). However, in broad terms, DeFi is "an ecosystem of decentralised applications which is built on top of permissionless smart contract platforms to mimic and extend traditional financial services" (Eikmanns et al., 2023, p. 1).

of the financial intermediary is taken over by the self-executing computer code".[153] Along similar lines, it was defined as "a decentralised financial system that enables financial services and instruments to be offered and used without the need for intermediaries as the system is based on public blockchains and smart contracts".[154]

The composability of the DeFi space warranted the label 'financial Lego' or 'money Lego'—i.e., protocols and applications can interact with each other and be combined to reach the optimal transaction experience for the users.[155] The total value of DeFi projects reportedly amounted to USD 1 billion in January 2020, USD 27 billion in January 2021, USD 60 billion in April 2021, almost USD 180 billion USD in November 2021. It then plummeted to USD 50 billion in the first half of 2023, in the aftermath of the so-called 'crypto winter'.[156] During the first half of 2024, the total value locked in DeFi projects has steadily increased again up to over USD 100 billion.[157] DEXes, among the primary DeFi applications, are governed by online communities of anonymous stakeholders,[158] and offer marketplaces of crypto-assets and/or other tokens built directly on DLT networks. The opposite happens with CEXes, which are centrally operated by (for-profit) entities—e.g., Coinbase, Binance, Kucoin, FTX, CEX.io, OKEx, Kraken.[159]

The basic concept in DEXes is that trading on them only requires a self-hosted wallet.[160] The Ethereum-based DEX landscape is significantly concentrated, and Uniswap dominates the market share of volume with more than 80% of total market activity.[161] The service is non-custodial and transactions are not intermediated in any way, but rather governed by smart contracts,[162] which serve the purpose of depositing the assets users want to exchange.[163] While they present a series of advantages, their use undoubtedly requires specific skills.[164]

---

[153] Katona (2021), p. 78.

[154] Gramlich et al. (2023), p. 8.

[155] Amler et al. (2021), p. 181. Katona (2021), p. 81.

[156] Zetzsche et al. (2023).

[157] Chainalysis (2022, 2024).

[158] Barbereau et al. (2023).

[159] A CEX operates like any other exchange. There is a matchmaking algorithm that regulate supply and demand, and an order book that stores the users' orders. Wiesflecker (2021).

[160] Yazdanparast (2021); Choo (2019); Wiesflecker (2021).

[161] This is not unexpected, as trading activity tends to gravitate towards markets with higher liquidity (Nassr et al., 2024, p. 12).

[162] European Securities and Markets Authority (2019), p. 44. Indeed, DEXes offer the key functions of CEXes, including "order books (or Automated Market Maker (AMM)), a trading venue, a matching system, and security functions. The difference to centralised exchanges is that all these functions are decentralised. To this end, a DEX is not based on internal servers and its own IT infrastructure but acts as a decentralised application (dApp) on a blockchain" (Wiesflecker, 2021).

[163] Wiesflecker (2021).

[164] Choo (2019). DEXes make use of atomic swaps. Real-time on-chain trading is currently hampered by transactions being processed by miners.

The world of DEXes is populated by different species of platforms. From a first perspective, the specific setup of a DEX impacts the type of crypto-assets it can offer. In this respect, they can be currency-centric or currency-neutral. To date, they can offer only crypto-to-crypto exchanges, and most of them trade only Ethereum-based tokens. In the early stages, DEXes did not support cross-chain transfers,[165] and still cannot access the market of fiat money. The development of cross-chain bridges,[166] however, started to offer new opportunities. In particular, cross-chain bridge protocols received almost 750 million USD (in crypto) from illicit addresses in 2023, up from around 310 million USD in 2022.[167] Meanwhile, users can usually trade a wider variety of assets on a DEX than on a CEX, as in DEXes there is typically no preliminary verification of the safety of listed assets.[168]

Secondly, while some projects pursue the creation of platforms for a decentralised token exchange—e.g., Uniswap, Airswap—, others pursue the combination of multiple models of DEX swaps—e.g., MetaMask.[169] Parallelly, DEXes such as Bancor and Kyber are 'simplified', while other projects are not. More specifically, the architecture of DEXes can feature either (i) an off-chain order book and order matching with on-chain settlement—by smart contracts or by relayers/miners—, such as IDEX and EtherDelta, or (ii) an on-chain order book, order matching, and settlement by miners, such as OasisDEX. This means DEXes can vary substantially in their decentralisation levels. When the order book is held off-chain, in the architecture of a DEX there is a centralisation point. In these cases, they might be within regulatory reach.[170] In this respect, it was noted how often DEXes "don't collect KYC information on their users and have no way of freezing funds like a centralised exchange; sometimes, this power lies with the individual DeFi projects themselves".[171] DEXes, however, developed beyond the use of order books, in favour of 'liquidity pools'—in brief, "smart contracts that hold balances of two unique tokens and enforce rules around depositing and withdrawing them".[172]

In light of their activities, DEXes would in theory fall within the FATF's and the EU understanding of providers of crypto-asset services. Because they are not single entities, however, it is challenging to impose compliance on them. That is, at least, through traditional gatekeeper-based models and despite the considerations regarding their actual degree of centralisation and power re-concentration put forward in

---

[165] Choo (2019); Lin (2019).

[166] Cross-chain bridges are a type of decentralised application that allows the transfer of crypto-assets from one blockchain to another.

[167] Chainalysis (2024), p. 32.

[168] Yazdanparast (2021).

[169] World Economic Forum (2020), pp. 18, 28.

[170] EtherDelta was charged by the US SEC for exchanging unregistered securities. Choo (2019).

[171] CipherTrace (2021), pp. 11–12.

[172] On liquidity pools and role of liquidity providers: Dex & Cex (2021); Beinke et al. (2024). Liquidity providers lock crypto-assets in the pools in exchange for fees, paid by traders that make use of the pools' liquidity (Nassr et al., 2024, p. 6).

Chap. 2. In this respect, notwithstanding the value of embedded regulation explored in Chap. 7, in the context of DeFi communities and stakeholders its implementation could indeed prove difficult.[173] Additionally, to use the services offered by a DEX there is no need to undergo a registration procedure, the possession of a self-hosted wallet is enough. It is for this reason they are usually described as anonymous,[174] and indeed anonymity in the form of absence of authentication and KYC is described as one of the core reasons to trade on a DEX, together with a claimed higher security when compared to CEXes.[175]

3.4 Conclusions

Leveraging the overview of the socio-technical nature, foundations and development of crypto-asset ecosystems, this chapter presented a first part of considerations on the concepts of anonymity and transparency in the crypto-asset space. In Chap. 4, the analysis will focus on obfuscation and traceability. In particular, this chapter addressed the role of encryption in the early stages of crypto-assets against the backdrop of the cyber-libertarian movement and introduced the relation between anonymity and the impacts of allowing transactions that cannot be monitored. After singling out the scope of this analysis, it explored the multifold concepts of anonymity and transparency in the crypto-asset space and related transactions, attempting disambiguation efforts at the crossroads between different conceptual levels pertaining to the cyberspace, crypto-asset ecosystems, financial transactions. This chapter focused primarily on achieving a higher level of conceptual clarity about constitutive elements of the domain, on which to ground the following investigation and the final conclusions. In doing so, the analysis pivoted around the notion of accountability and on how it is affected by enhanced disintermediation.

Through an exploration of the characteristics featured by crypto-related anonymity and transparency within an AML/CFT context, the analysis differentiated anonymity from privacy, and defined crypto-asset anonymity as: (a) 'conceptually granular', compounding the technical metrics of traceability, linkability, identifiability, identification, pseudonymity, confidentiality, privacy, (b) 'context-specific', on the grounds of the role played by identifiability in AML/ CFT frameworks, (c) 'observer-dependent', as it can be assessed only with respect to a specific actor trying to reach identification, as well as (d) presenting a broader meaning than the understandings of anonymity featured by other regulatory frameworks (e.g., data protection), since it does not distinguish between anonymisation and strong pseudonymisation. Meanwhile, the notion of transparency relevant to crypto-asset ecosystems emerged as twofold and torn by

[173] Barbereau et al. (2023); Zetzsche et al. (2023).

[174] Choo (2019).

[175] Wiesflecker (2021).

the fact that the concept of transparency of the ledger and ledger operations is constitutively distant from the notion of financial transparency. Thus, the alleged paradox of blockchains featuring anonymity and transparency traits was reframed into a combination of features whose interplay can be explored and measured by using a teleological methodology. Finally, the part of the crypto-asset world that pursues enhanced disintermediation was addressed, in terms of P2P transfers, major techniques such as atomic cross-chain swaps and multi-layered protocols (e.g., layer 2 solutions), self-hosted wallets and DEXs, showing the impact on accountability from an AML/CFT standpoint.

Some threads can be identified in this chapter: (i) crypto-asset anonymity is situated at the crossroads of online anonymity and financial confidentiality, (ii) the issue of anonymous exchange of information precedes the 'blockchain hype'; (iii) crypto-assets are not the first instance of tension between private transactions and accountability; (iv) the quest for transparency to ensure accountability is common in information networks; (v) the transparency of compliance regimes differs from the one of public blockchains; (vi) the issue of cyberspace and crypto-asset anonymity is of socio-technical nature; (vii) AML/CFT provisions pivot around the concepts of identification and verification of an identity; (viii) a subject or an item is not identified or anonymous: these traits range on a spectrum; (ix) anonymity is a concept dependent on the observer; (x) a subject is identifiable if the entity in charge of identification can access the information required by the applicable framework; (xi) anonymity and transparency can be reconciled by using benchmarked trade-offs and a teleological methodology; (xii) in AML/CFT, an anonymous transaction is one that cannot be related to an identified or identifiable individual; (xiii) AML/CFT and data protection embody different understandings of anonymity; and (xiv) the crypto-asset sphere is more intermediated than expected, but disruptive new trends of enhanced disintermediation pose substantial anonymity risks.

References

ABA Bank Compliance. (1999). Privacy crossfire: Money laundering hearings refocus privacy debate. *ABA Bank Compliance, 20*(10), 1–2.

Airfoil. (2019). *De-anonymising anonymous crypto services*. Medium DDI. https://medium.datadriveninvestor.com/de-anonymizing-anonymous-crypto-services-a80258132e5b

Allen, S., Capkun, S., Eyal, I., Fanti, G., Ford, B., Grimmelmann, J., Juels, A., Kostiainen, K., Meiklejohn, S., Miller, A., Prasad, E., Wuest, K., & Zhang, F. (2020). *Design choices for central bank digital currency: Policy and technical considerations*. https://ftp.iza.org/dp13535.pdf

Amarasinghe, N., Boyen, X., & McKague, M. (2019). A survey of anonymity of cryptocurrencies. In *Proceedings of the Australasian Computer Science Week Multiconference*. https://doi.org/10.1145/3290688.3290693

Amler, H., Eckey, L., Faust, S., Kaiser, M., Sandner, P., & Schlosser, B. (2021). DeFi-ning DeFi: Challenges & pathway. In *IEEE 3rd Conference on Blockchain Research & Applications for Innovative Networks and Services (BRAINS)*. https://doi.org/10.1109/BRAINS52497.2021.9569795

Androulaki, E., Ghassan O. Karame, Roeschlin, M., Scherer, T., & Capkun, S. (2013). Evaluating user privacy in bitcoin. In A.-R. Sadeghi (Ed.), *Proceedings of the International Conference on Financial Cryptography and Data Security*, Berlin, Heidelberg (pp. 34–51). Springer Berlin Heidelberg. https://doi.org/10.1007/978-3-642-39884-1_4

Aramonte, S., Huang, W., & Schrimpf, A. (2021). Defi risks and the decentralisation illusion. *BIS Quarterly Review*. https://www.bis.org/publ/qtrpdf/r_qt2112b.pdf

Article 19. (2015). *Right to online anonymity - Policy brief.* https://www.article19.org/data/files/medialibrary/38006/Anonymity_and_encryption_report_A5_final-web.pdf

Article 29 Data Protection Working Party. (2014). *Opinion 05/2014 on anonymisation techniques*. Available at: https://ec.europa.eu/justice/article-29/documentation/opinion-recommendation/files/2014/wp216_en.pdf

Bancroft, A. (2020). *The darknet and smarter crime: Methods for investigating criminal entrepreneurs and the illicit drug economy*. Palgrave Macmillan. https://doi.org/10.1007/978-3-030-26512-0

Barbereau, T., Smethurst, R., Papageorgiou, O., Sedlmeir, J., & Fridgen, G. (2023). Decentralised finance's timocratic governance: The distribution and exercise of tokenised voting rights. *Technology in Society*, *73*, 102251. https://doi.org/10.1016/j.techsoc.2023.102251

Barresi, R. G., & Zatti, F. (2020). The importance of where central bank digital currencies are custodied: Exploring the need of a universal access device. https://doi.org/10.2139/ssrn.3691263

Beinke, M., Beinke, J. H., Anton, E., & Teuteberg, F. (2024). Breaking the chains of traditional finance: A taxonomy of decentralized finance business models. *Electronic Markets*, *34*(1), 29. https://doi.org/10.1007/s12525-024-00704-4

Berberich, M., & Steiner, M. (2016). Blockchain technology and the GDPR - How to reconcile privacy and distributed ledgers? Technical core features and use cases of the blockchain technology. *European Data Protection Law Review*, *2*(3), 422–426. https://doi.org/10.21552/EDPL/2016/3/21.

Berg, A. (2019). The identity, fungibility, and anonymity of money. *Economic Papers*, 1–16. https://doi.org/10.2139/ssrn.3211011

Biryukov, A., & Tikhomirov, S. (2019). Deanonymisation and linkability of cryptocurrency transactions based on network analysis. In *Proceedings of the 4th IEEE European Symposium on Security and Privacy*, 172–184. https://doi.org/10.1109/EuroSP.2019.00022

Bodó, B., & Giannopoulou, A. (2019). The logics of technology decentralisation: The case of distributed ledger technologies. In *Blockchain and web 3.0: Social, economic, and technical challenges*. Routledge. https://doi.org/10.4324/9780429029530-8

Capraz, S., & Ozsoy, A. (2021). Personal data protection in blockchain with zero-knowledge proof. In S. Patnaik, T.-S. Wang, T. Shen, & S. Kumar Panigrahi (Eds.), *Blockchain technology and innovations in business processes, smart innovation, systems and technologies* (Vol. 219). Springer Nature. https://doi.org/10.1007/978-981-33-6470-7_7

Casey, M., Crane, J., Gensler, G., Johnson, S., & Narula, N. (2018). *The impact of blockchain technology on finance: A catalyst for change*. https://cepr.org/publications/books-and-reports/geneva-21-impact-blockchain-technology-finance-catalyst-change

Chainalysis. (2022). *The 2022 crypto crime report. original data and research into cryptocurrency-based crime*. https://go.chainalysis.com/2022-Crypto-Crime-Report.html

Chainalysis. (2024). *The 2024 crypto crime report. the latest trends in ransomware, scams, hacking, and more*. https://go.chainalysis.com/crypto-crime-2024.html

Chaum, D. (1981). Untraceable electronic mail, return addresses, and digital pseudonyms. *Communication of the ACM*, *24*(2), 1981. https://doi.org/10.1145/358549.358563

Chaum, D. (1983). *Blind signatures for untraceable payments*. http://www.hit.bme.hu/~buttyan/courses/BMEVIHIM219/2009/Chaum.BlindSigForPayment.1982.PDF

Chaum, D. (1985). Security without identification: Transaction systems to make big brother obsolete. *Communications of the ACM*, *28*(10), 1985. https://www.cs.ru.nl/~jhh/pub/secsem/chaum1985bigbrother.pdf

Chaum, D., Fiat, A., & Naor, M. (1990). *Untraceable electronic cash*. https://chaum.com/wp-content/uploads/2021/12/Untraceable_Electronic_Cash.pdf

Choo, H. (2019). *Blockchain application: Dex (decentralized exchange)*. https://syssec.kaist.ac.kr/~yongdaek/courses/ee817/Presentation/DEX_final.pdf

CipherTrace. (2021). *Cryptocurrency crime and anti-money laundering report*. https://ciphertrace.com/wp-content/uploads/2021/05/CipherTrace-Cryptocurrency-Crime-and-Anti-Money-Laundering-Report-May-2021-051221b.pdf

Clarke, R. (1999). Identified, anonymous and pseudonymous transactions: The spectrum of choice. In *Proceedings of the User Identification & Privacy Protection Conference*. https://www.rogerclarke.com/DV/UIPP99.html

Daniels, A. (2018). *The rise of private permissionless blockchains – part 1*. https://medium.com/ltonetwork/the-rise-of-private-permissionless-blockchains-part-1-4c39bea2e2be

De Filippi, P., & Wright, A. (2018). *Blockchain and the law: The rule of code*. Harvard University Press. https://doi.org/10.2307/j.ctv2867sp

De Haro-Olmo, F. J., Varela-Vaca, Á. J., & Álvarez Bermejo, J. A. (2020). Blockchain from the perspective of privacy and anonymisation: A systematic literature review. *MDPI Sensors*, *20*, 7171. https://doi.org/10.3390/s20247171

de Koker, L. (2015). Anonymous clients, identified clients and the shades in between – perspectives on the FATF AML/CFT standards and mobile banking. 10.2139/ssrn.2634305

Dex & Cex. (2021). *Dex & cex*. https://ghoststaking.com/dex-cex/

ECash. (1997). *Introduction to ecash*. https://web.archive.org/web/19971009044558/http://digicash.com/publish/ecash_intro/ecash_intro.html

Eikmanns, B. C., Mehrwald, P., Sandner, P. G., & Welpe, I. M. (2023). Decentralised finance platform ecosystems: Conceptualisation and outlook. *Technology Analysis and Strategic Management*, 1–13. https://doi.org/10.1080/09537325.2022.2163886

European Central Bank. (2019). *Exploring anonymity in central bank digital currencies*. https://www.ecb.europa.eu/paym/intro/publications/pdf/ecb.mipinfocus191217.en.pdf

European Central Bank and Bank of Japan. (2020). *Balancing confidentiality and auditability in a distributed ledger environment*. https://www.ecb.europa.eu/paym/intro/publications/pdf/ecb.miptopical200212.en.pdf

European Securities and Markets Authority. (2019). *Advice - Initial coin offerings and crypto-assets*. https://www.esma.europa.eu/sites/default/files/library/esma50-157-1391_crypto_advice.pdf

Fanti, G., & Focher, N. (2022). *Privacy in cross-border digital currency: A transatlantic perspective*. https://www.atlanticcouncil.org/in-depth-research-reports/issue-brief/privacy-in-cross-border-digital-currency-a-transatlantic-approach/

Financial Action Task Force. (2014). *Virtual currencies – key definitions and potential AML/CFT risks*. https://www.fatf-gafi.org/media/fatf/documents/reports/Virtual-currency-key-definitions-and-potential-aml-cft-risks.pdf

Financial Action Task Force. (2019). *Guidance for a risk-based approach: Virtual assets and virtual asset service providers*. https://www.fatf-gafi.org/publications/fatfrecommendations/documents/guidance-rba-virtual-assets.html

Financial Action Task Force. (2020a). *12-month review of the revised FATF standards – virtual assets and virtual asset service providers*. http://www.fatf-gafi.org/media/fatf/documents/recommendations/12-Month-Review-Revised-FATF-Standards-Virtual-Assets-VASPS.pdf

Financial Action Task Force. (2020b). *FATF report to the G20 finance ministers and central banks governors on so-called stablecoins*. http://www.fatf-gafi.org/media/fatf/documents/recommendations/Virtual-Assets-FATF-Report-G20-So-Called-Stablecoins.pdf

Financial Action Task Force. (2020c). *Virtual assets red flag indicators of money laundering and terrorist financing*. https://www.fatf-gafi.org/media/fatf/documents/recommendations/Virtual-Assets-Red-Flag-Indicators.pdf

Financial Action Task Force. (2021). *Virtual assets and virtual asset service providers - Updated guidance for a risk-based approach*. https://www.fatf-gafi.org/publications/fatfrecommendations/documents/guidance-rba-virtual-assets-2021.html

Finck, M. (2019a). *Blockchain and the GDPR: Can distributed ledgers be squared with European data protection law?* European Parliamentary Research Service. https://www.europarl.europa.eu/RegData/etudes/STUD/2019/634445/EPRS_STU(2019)634445_EN.pdf

Finck, M. (2019b). *Blockchain regulation and governance in Europe*. Cambridge University Press. https://doi.org/10.1017/9781108609708

Froomkin, A. M. (1995). Anonymity and its enmities. *Journal of Online Law*. https://ssrn.com/abstract=2715621

Furneaux, N. (2018). *Investigating cryptocurrencies: Understanding, extracting, and analyzing blockchain evidence*. Wiley. https://ieeexplore.ieee.org/servlet/opac?bknumber=9820817

Geva, B. (2018). Banking in the digital age – who is afraid of payment disintermediation? In *European Banking Institute Working Paper Series*. https://digitalcommons.osgoode.yorku.ca/cgi/viewcontent.cgi?article=1329&context=all_papers

Goodell, G., & Aste, T. (2019). Can cryptocurrencies preserve privacy and comply with regulations? *Frontiers in Blockchain*, *2*(4). https://doi.org/10.3389/fbloc.2019.00004

Gramlich, V., Guggenberger, T., Principato, M., Schellinger, B., & Urbach, N. (2023). A multivocal literature review of decentralized finance: Current knowledge and future research avenues. *Electronic Markets*, *33*(1), 11. https://doi.org/10.1007/s12525-023-00637-4

Grijpink, J., & Prins, C. (2001). Digital anonymity on the Internet: New rules for anonymous electronic transactions? An exploration of private law implications of digital anonymity. *Computer Law and Security Review*, *17*(6), 379–389. https://doi.org/10.1016/S0267-3649(01)01105-0

Harvey, J., & Branco-Illodo, I. (2020). Why cryptocurrencies want privacy: A review of political motivations and branding expressed in "privacy coin" whitepapers. *Journal of Political Marketing*, *19*(1–2), 107–136. https://doi.org/10.1080/15377857.2019.1652223

Helms, S. C. (2001). Translating privacy values with technology. *Boston University Journal of Science and Technology Law*, *7*. https://www.bu.edu/law/journals-archive/scitech/volume72/helms.pdf

Herian, R. (2019). *Regulating blockchain: Critical perspectives in law and technology*. Routledge. https://doi.org/10.4324/9780429489815

Herlihy, M. (2018). Atomic cross-chain swaps. In *Proceedings of the ACM Symposium on Principles of Distributed Computing* (pp. 245–54). https://doi.org/10.1145/3212734.3212736

Information Commissioner's Office. (2021). *Introduction to anonymisation*. https://ico.org.uk/media/about-the-ico/consultations/2619862/anonymisation-intro-and-first-chapter.pdf

ISO 16759:2013. (2013). *16759:2013, concerning graphic technology – quantification and communication for calculating the carbon footprint of print media products*. https://www.iso.org/standard/50344.html

ISO/IEC 30182:2017. (2017). *ISO/IEC 30182:2017, smart city concept model, guidance for establishing a model for data interoperability*. https://www.iso.org/standard/64656.html

ITU-T FG DLT. (2019). *Distributed ledger technology regulatory framework*. Technical report FG DLT D4.1. https://www.itu.int/en/ITU-T/focusgroups/dlt/Documents/FGDLT-D4.1.pdf

Karasek-Wojciechowicz, I. (2021). Reconciliation of anti-money laundering instruments and European data protection requirements in permissionless blockchain spaces. *Journal of Cybersecurity*, 1–28. https://doi.org/10.1093/cybsec/tyab004

Katona, T. (2021). Decentralized finance: The possibilities of a blockchain 'money lego' system. *Financial and Economic Review*, *20*(1). https://doi.org/10.33893/FER.20.1.74102

Le Nguyen, C. (2018). Preventing the use of financial institutions for money laundering and the implications for financial privacy. *Journal of Money Laundering Control*, *21*(1), 47–58. https://doi.org/10.1108/JMLC-01-2017-0004

Li, Y., Susilo, W., Yang, G., Yu, Y., Du, X., Liu, D., & Guizani, N. (2019). Toward privacy and regulation in blockchain-based cryptocurrencies. *IEEE Network*, *33*(5), 111–17. https://doi.org/10.1109/MNET.2019.1800271

Lin, L. X. (2019). Deconstructing decentralized exchanges. *Stanford Journal of Blockchain Law and Policy*, *2*(1), 58–77. https://stanford-jblp.pubpub.org/pub/deconstructing-dex/release/1

Lindsey, L. B. (1999, Nov). *The money-laundering conundrum: Mugging privacy in the assault on crime? The future of financial privacy*. https://www.cei.org/wp-content/uploads/2000/01/2372.pdf
LTO Network. (2019). *Permissionless private blockchain*. https://blog.ltonetwork.com/permissionless-private-blockchains-lto-network/
Magnuson, W. (2020). *Blockchain democracy: Technology, law and the rule of the crowd*. Cambridge University Press. https://doi.org/10.1017/9781108687294
Marthews, A., & Tucker, C. (2019). Blockchain and identity persistence. In C. Brummer (Ed.), *Cryptoassets: Legal, regulatory, and monetary perspectives*. Oxford University Press.
May, T. C. (1988). *The crypto-anarchist manifesto*. https://nakamotoinstitute.org/authors/timothy-c-may/
Meiklejohn, S., & Orlandi, C. (2015). Privacy-enhancing overlays in bitcoin. In M. Brenner, N. Christin, B. Johnson, & K. Rohloff (Eds.), *Proceedings of the International Conference on Financial Cryptography and Data Security* (pp. 127–141). Springer. https://doi.org/10.1007/978-3-662-48051-9_10
Nassr, I. K., Kostika, E., & Melachrinos, A. (2024). Concentration of DeFi's liquidity. In *OECD Working Papers on Finance, Insurance and Private Pensions* (Vol. 49). https://doi.org/10.1787/4ed08440-en
Nicoll, C., Prins, J. E. J., & van Dellen, M. J. M. (2003). *Digital anonymity and the law: Tensions and dimensions*. T.M.C. Asser Press.
Pfitzmann, A., & Hansen, M. (2010). *A terminology for talking about privacy by data minimisation: Anonymity, unlinkability, undetectability, unobservability, pseudonymity, and identity management*. https://dud.inf.tu-dresden.de/literatur/Anon_Terminology_v0.28.pdf
Pocher, N. (2021). *Self-hosted wallets: The elephant in the crypto room?* https://www.law.kuleuven.be/citip/blog/self-hosted-wallets/
Pocher, N. (2023). *Distributed ledger technologies between anonymity and transparency: AML/CFT regulation of cryptocurrency ecosystems in the EU*. PhD thesis, Alma Mater Studiorum Università di Bologna, KU Leuven, Universitat Autònoma de Barcelona. 10.48676/unibo/amsdottorato/10659
Pocher, N. (2025). Traceability of crypto-asset transfers under the new EU AML/CFT regime: The crypto travel rule between challenges and open issues. In J. Lee & A. Darbellay (Eds.), *A research agenda for financial law and regulation* (pp. 197–220). Edward Elgar. https://doi.org/10.4337/9781803929996.00017
Pocher, N., Zichichi, M., & Ferretti, S. (2023). The AML/CFT/CPF application of on-chain analytics and machine learning: Overview and open issues. In *Proceedings of Artificial Intelligence Governance Ethics and Law (AIGEL)*. https://ceur-ws.org/Vol-3531/SPaper_11.pdf
Quiniou, M. (2019). *Blockchain: The advent of disintermediation*. Wiley-ISTE Ltd.
Regulation (EU) 2024/1183. (2024). Regulation (EU) 2024/1183 of the European Parliament and of the Council of 11 April 2024 amending Regulation (EU) no 910/2014 as regards establishing the European digital identity framework. http://data.europa.eu/eli/reg/2024/1183/oj
Regulation (EU) 910/2014. (2014). Regulation (EU) 910/2014 of the European Parliament and of the Council of 23 July 2014 on electronic identification and trust services for electronic transactions in the internal market and repealing directive 1999/93/EC. http://data.europa.eu/eli/reg/2014/910/oj
Rieger, A., Guggenmos, F., Lockl, J., Fridgen, G., & Urbach, N. (2019). Building a blockchain application that complies with the EU general data protection regulation. *MIS Quarterly Executive*, *18*(4), 263–279. https://doi.org/10.17705/2msqe.00020
Rogaway, P. (2016). *The moral character of cryptographic work*. https://web.cs.ucdavis.edu/~rogaway/papers/moral-fn.pdf
Saa, O., Cullen, A., & Vigneri, L. (2023). *IOTA 2.0 incentives and tokenomics whitepaper*. https://files.iota.org/papers/IOTA_2.0_Incentives_And_Tokenomics_Whitepaper.pdf

Sardá, T., Natale, S., Sotirakopoulos, N., & Monaghan, M. (2019). Understanding online anonymity. *Media, Culture and Society, 41*(4), 557–64. https://doi.org/10.1177/0163443719842074

Satoshi. (2019). *Hash time locked contracts (HTLCs) explained.* Medium Liquality. https://medium.com/liquality/hash-time-locked-contracts-htlcs-explained

Schrepel, T. (2021). *Blockchain + Antitrust: The decentralisation formula.* Edward Elgar. https://doi.org/10.4337/9781800885530

Sedlmeir, J., Lautenschlager, J., Fridgen, G., & Urbach, N. (2022). The transparency challenge of blockchain in organizations. *Electronic Markets, 32*(3), 1779–1794 (2022). https://doi.org/10.1007/s12525-022-00536-0

Siena, J. (2022). Distributed ledger technology: Cutting through the paradox. *Journal of Securities Operations & Custody, 15*(1), 28–44. https://doi.org/10.69554/JCGG5975

Silva Ramalho, D., & Igreja Matos, N. (2021). What we do in the (digital) shadows: Anti-money laundering regulation and a bitcoin-mixing criminal problem. *ERA Forum, 22*, 487–506. https://doi.org/10.1007/s12027-021-00676-4

Skopek, J. M. (2015). Reasonable expectations of anonymity. *Virginia Law Review, 101*, 691–762. https://virginialawreview.org/wp-content/uploads/2020/12/Skopek_Book.pdf

Smith, A. (2024). *Types of crypto wallets explained.* https://www.blockchain-council.org/blockchain/types-of-crypto-wallets-explained/

Statista. (2024). *Number of cryptocurrencies worldwide from 2013 to June 2024.* https://www.statista.com/statistics/863917/number-crypto-coins-tokens/

Sun, Y., & Zhang, Y. (2018). *Privacy in cryptocurrencies: An overview.* Medium. https://medium.com/@yi.sun/privacy-in-cryptocurrencies-d4b268157f6c

Tasca, P., & Tessone, C. J. (2018). Taxonomy of blockchain technologies. principles of identification and classification. *Ledger, 4.* https://doi.org/10.5195/ledger.2019.140

Tennant, L. (2017). *Improving the anonymity of the IOTA cryptocurrency.* https://laurencetennant.com/papers/anonymity-iota.pdf

Torra, V. (2017). *Data privacy: Foundations, new developments and the big data challenge.* Springer. https://doi.org/10.1007/978-3-319-57358-8

van Saberhagen, N. (2013). *Cryptonote v 2.0.* https://bytecoin.org/old/whitepaper.pdf

Wachsman. (2019). *Answering one of blockchain's biggest questions: Anonymity or pseudonymity?* Medium.

Walch, A. (2017). Blockchain's treacherous vocabulary: One more challenge for regulators. *Journal of Internet Law, 21*(2). https://ssrn.com/abstract=3019328

Wang, F., & De Filippi, P. (2020). Self-sovereign identity in a globalized world: Credentials-based identity systems as a driver for economic inclusion. *Frontiers in Blockchain.* https://doi.org/10.3389/fbloc.2019.00028

Wang, Y. (2023). Prediction markets, automated market makers, and decentralized finance (DeFi). In P. Pardalos, I. Kotsireas, Y. Guo, & W. Knottenbelt (Eds.), *Mathematical research for blockchain economy* (pp. 213–231). Springer International Publishing. https://doi.org/10.1007/978-3-031-18679-0_12

Weber, R. H., & Heinrich, U. I. (2012). *Anonymisation.* SpringerBriefs in cybersecurity. Springer London. https://doi.org/10.1007/978-1-4471-4066-5

Whitehouse-Levine, M., & Kelleher, L. (2020). *Self-hosted wallets and the future of free societies.* Blockchain Association. https://theblockchainassociation.org/wp-content/uploads/2020/11/Self-Hosted-Wallets-and-the-Future-of-Free-Societies.pdf

Wiesflecker, L. (2021). *Cex vs. dex – here are the differences.* Medium. https://medium.com/coinmonks/cex-vs-dex-here-are-the-differences-143fae4c33d4

World Economic Forum. (2020). *Crypto, what is it good for? An overview of cryptocurrency use cases.* https://www3.weforum.org/docs/WEF_Cryptocurrency_Uses_Cases_2020.pdf

Xu, J., & Feng, Y. (2023). Reap the harvest on blockchain: A survey of yield farming protocols. *IEEE Transactions on Network and Service Management, 20*(1), 1–1. https://doi.org/10.1109/TNSM.2022.3222815

Yazdanparast, E. (2021). *Cex vs dex: A comprehensive comparison of features*. Medium. https://medium.com/coinmonks/cex-vs-dex-a-comprehensive-comparison-of-features-bb398d416d4f

Zetzsche, D. A., Buckley, R. P., Arner, D. W., & Barberis, J. N. (2017). *Regulating a revolution: From regulatory sandboxes to smart regulation*. https://ir.lawnet.fordham.edu/jcfl/vol23/iss1/2/

Zetzsche, D. A., Buckley, R. P., Arner, D. W., & van Ek, M. (2023). *Remaining regulatory challenges in digital finance and crypto-assets after MiCA*. Technical report, Committee on Economic and Monetary Affairs (ECON), Policy Department for Economic, Scientific and Quality of Life Policies, European Parliament. https://www.europarl.europa.eu/thinktank/en/document/IPOL_STU(2023)740083

Zeuch, K., Wöhnert, K. H., & Skwarek, V. (2019). Derivation of categories for interoperability of blockchain and distributed ledger systems. *Informatik*. https://doi.org/10.18420/inf2019_20

Chapter 4
Obfuscation and Traceability

4.1 Introduction

The unsatisfactory level of Bitcoin's anonymity prompted the implementation of new techniques both within the same network and to design other ecosystems. In this way, developer communities pursued fungibility and user unaccountability for cyberspace transactions, bypassing regulatory constraints and governmental surveillance. The advent of complex and anonymity-oriented models was accompanied by an increasing interest of institutional and corporate stakeholders in the crypto-asset space, which transformed into the emergence of stablecoins and CBDC projects (Chap. 6). In this context, the array of privacy concerns grew wider and generated new sensitivities to the possible exploitation of financial data by a vast range of actors—e.g., if transactions are not performed anonymously, "a malicious merchant may sell customers' transaction information to third parties for financial benefit".[1]

The onset of anonymity-enhanced trends is also linked to the intelligence techniques applied to the blockchain space. As Bitcoin transactions became popular and AECs were developed, experts and law enforcement professionals devised specific investigative strategies to trace these transfers through blockchain forensics. Later, these analytics solutions were requested by newly regulated entities—e.g., exchanges and custodian wallet providers. As it often happens with innovation, new opportunities gave rise to a race where "in response to a new technological shift, criminals and consumers alike are increasingly finding new ways to evolve".[2]

This evolution of the crypto-asset space caused an overall enhancement of the obfuscation level of crypto-asset transactions, which challenges the AML/CFT framework. The FATF frequently reported this, noting how the crypto-asset sphere

[1] Li et al. (2021), p. 679.

[2] Reynolds and Irwin (2017), p. 1.

N. Pocher, *Crypto-Asset Ecosystems and the EU Anti-Money Laundering Framework*, Law, Governance and Technology Series 76,
https://doi.org/10.1007/978-3-031-94698-1_4

is increasingly populated by AECs, "mixers and tumblers, decentralised platforms and exchanges, privacy wallets, and other types of products and services that enable or allow for reduced transparency and increased obfuscation of financial flows", as well as innovative "business models or activities such as initial coin offerings (ICOs) that present ML/TF, fraud and market manipulation risks". In this context, there is a worrying rise of new typologies of illicit financing such as "virtual-to-virtual layering schemes that attempt to further obfuscate transactions in a comparatively easy, cheap, and secure manner".[3]

The laundering process provides benchmarks to understand the debate on the degree of obfuscation and traceability of crypto-asset transfers. Hence, the following sections will provide an overview that contextualises the regulatory analysis of Chap. 5. Indeed, the link between obfuscation, traceability and money laundering is clearly showcased by the literature and legal initiatives. This is not surprising, since crypto-asset anonymity has been mostly addressed in terms of possible misuses of the financial system. Meanwhile, forensic activities are a major source of insights into crypto-asset anonymity from a socio-technical perspective.

4.1.1 Transaction Obfuscation and the Money Laundering Process

From an objective-oriented standpoint, the goal of AML/CFT measures is to prevent criminals from enjoying and profiting from ill-gotten proceeds, hindering their capacity to benefit from the revenues of illicit activities, thereby also reducing the incentive to engage in them. The strategy is to thwart the capacity to 'wash' these proceeds, thus making it difficult to provide them with a legitimate appearance. This explains why the first prevention and repression measures originated from enforcement operations against crimes that produce substantial returns—e.g., organised crime, trafficking in drugs and firearms, corruption.[4] In the 1970s and 1980s, U.S. investigators started considering 'follow the money' techniques as a key part of their effort to unravel criminal organisations.

In crypto-asset ecosystems, the relationship between money laundering, obfuscation and anonymity pivots on two aspects: (i) money laundering is a 'process', and (ii) the regulatory response consists of two complementary approaches. From the first perspective, money laundering does not consist of a single act, but of a process usually described as composed of three phases depicting the steps illicit profits go through to be 'laundered' and come out 'clean': placement, layering and integration. Briefly put, in the (i) placement phase ill-gotten proceeds are introduced into the financial system, if needed (i.e., if not already there); in the (ii) layering stage their origin is concealed through as many complex transactions as possible; and finally

[3] Financial Action Task Force (2021b), p. 7.

[4] de Koker and Goldbarsht (2024), pp. 2–5. Gelemerova (2009), pp. 34–36.

(iii) integration sees cleansed funds being (re)integrated into the system.[5] Evidently, this threefold layout is a simplification, and in real-life scenarios these stages are not siloed.[6] Laundering methods are often complex—e.g., they may involve the use of different corporate vehicles and be performed at a global scale. Because it is difficult to find a clear separation between these phases, and the actions pursuing the three different goals tend to overlap, nowadays they are not considered a comprehensive representation of laundering dynamics. Nonetheless, they can play a benchmarking role when analysing the risks tainting the crypto-asset space.

The added value of using crypto-assets reportedly stems from three elements that enable the exploitation of blind corners of the prevention system and allow these funds to covertly go through the laundering stages.[7] They are: (a) decentralisation, in terms of operating (partially, at least) outside the regulated financial system; (b) pseudonymity, that provides opportunities to conceal real-world identities; and (c) instant conclusion of transactions and speed of payment, that challenge the effectiveness of due diligence checks.[8] Chapters 2 and 3 outlined the differences between crypto-asset ecosystems and the actors involved, focusing on enhanced disintermediation, cross-blockchain exchanges and DeFi. Hence, the elements sub (a), (b) and (c) should be interpreted flexibly; the same arguments do not apply in the same way to all crypto-asset transactions. Different ecosystems feature various levels of vulnerabilities to illegal exploitation. On top of this, significant concerns affect areas currently unregulated and/or where effective compliance, implementation and/or enforcement are harder to attain—e.g., DEXes, self-hosted wallets, the 'crypto-travel rule'.

Crypto-assets seem to be most useful in the layering phase, where their use is more frequent. Layering is a key component in all studies on their criminal use and is facilitated by the cross-border nature of their ecosystems and the growing variety of options in terms of service providers.[9] In this respect, in schemes of virtual-to-virtual layering illicit actors engage in multiple exchanges from/to different crypto-assets to conceal the origin and transaction history of their funds, making

[5] Ecorys and Centre for European Policy Studies (2017), p. 57.

[6] Matanky-Becker (2024).

[7] Silva Ramalho and Igreja Matos (2021), p. 501.

[8] Silva Ramalho and Igreja Matos (2021), p. 501. The recast of the Fund Transfers Regulation reads as follows. Recital 30: "Compared to transfers of funds, transfers of crypto-assets can be carried out across multiple jurisdictions at a larger scale and higher speed due to their global reach and technological characteristics. In addition to the pseudo-anonymity of crypto-assets, those features of transfers of crypto-assets offer criminals the opportunity to carry out at high speed large illicit transfers while circumventing traceability obligations and avoiding detection, by means of structuring a large transaction into smaller amounts, using multiple seemingly unrelated DLT addresses, including one-time use DLT addresses, and using automated processes.".

[9] In trade-based laundering, the complexity of international trade and the interconnection of supply chains are exploited to transfer value—e.g., false invoices (e.g., over-/under-invoicing) or representations of goods (e.g., over-/under-shipment or false descriptions)—and violate customs and tax regulations (i.e., smuggling and fraud).

use of manifold service providers. Nonetheless, crypto-assets can be used effectively throughout the whole laundering cycle.[10] Indeed, also for placement and integration launderers can leverage the almost instantaneous and cross-border nature of these transfers to avert the time-consuming and regulated traditional financial paths. From a placement perspective, they may exploit the low-risk opportunity to swiftly open and access crypto-asset accounts, which allows them to convert and consolidate their profits easily and (pseudo)anonymously. Indeed, pseudonymity allows flagged or blacklisted actors—i.e., people or entities that cannot enjoy the services of regulated entities because of previous flagging or blacklisting (e.g., sanctioned entities or individuals)—to bypass restrictions posed by authorities to their operations.[11] Finally, in the integration phase they can be used to buy an increasing variety of goods and/or services, options bound to increase in the future. Reportedly, 'privacy coins' are increasingly adopted in darknet markets and by ransomware actors, while for settlement bitcoins or fiat currencies are usually chosen.[12]

From a second point of view, the regulatory response to the money laundering risk encompasses two complementary approaches. On the one hand, criminal sanctions are imposed on launderers—i.e., money laundering is a crime in most jurisdictions.[13] In this respect, an important evolution affected predicate offences—i.e., crimes that generate the proceeds whose 'washing' is deemed by law as money laundering.[14] By expanding the list of predicate offences, regulators widen the scope of application of the AML/CFT framework itself. On the other hand, a set of AML/CFT provisions are included in civil/administrative regulatory frameworks, depending on the legal system.[15] These norms thrust compliance duties on specific entities, thus partially decentralising oversight—i.e., regulated entities cooperate

[10] Irwin and Dawson (2019); Fanusie (2020); Mabunda (2018); CipherTrace (2021); Desmond et al. (2019).

[11] Silva Ramalho and Igreja Matos (2021), p. 501.

[12] Financial Action Task Force (2021a), p. 23. Reportedly, while cybercriminals usually want to be paid in bitcoin, at times ransomware operators offer discounts to victims willing to pay in 'privacy coins' to reduce transparency.

[13] The issue concerning the definition of 'money laundering' and the role of international and EU initiatives in respect to criminal law efforts—with specific reference to Directive (EU) 2018/1673—is addressed in Chap. 5.

[14] 'Predicate offences' are components of a larger crime—e.g., money laundering or terrorist financing. While initially focused on drugs-related offences, the scope was later expanded to a plethora of serious crimes. Today, as per Directive (EU) 2018/1673, "any kind of criminal involvement in the commission of any offence punishable, in accordance with national law, by deprivation of liberty or a detention order for a maximum of more than one year or, as regards Member States that have a minimum threshold for offences in their legal systems, any offence punishable by deprivation of liberty or a detention order for a minimum of more than six months" can be a predicate offence for money laundering. A list of crimes is included per se (Article 2(1)(1)).

[15] Boundaries between civil, administrative and criminal frameworks may not be as explicit. Frequently, the same piece of legislation provides for different kinds of sanctions for violations of different norms.

with authorities by monitoring financial activities. What these entities have in common is a substantial involvement in financial and business operations, in various ways and to different extents, and their 'active cooperation' is deemed conducive to alerting authorities if suspicions arise. Hence, businesses such as banks, law firms, notaries or casinos are tasked to follow the measures such as KYC and CDD (Chap. 5). The publications released by the FATF and supervisory organisations often address these entities to help them fulfil their role. Moreover, these 'active cooperators' and law enforcement bodies are the actors that benefit the most from improvements in the services of analytics companies. This has contributed to the development of new strategies and technologies, striving to make it easier for regulated stakeholders to comply with the ever-expanding AML/CFT regime.

Besides considering crypto-assets as one of the possible means to launder funds—i.e., focusing on their use within this process—it is also possible to look at how they can be laundered themselves. This means considering cases in which criminals are not (only) trying to cleanse fiat money by means of crypto-assets, but (also) want to conceal the illegal origin of their crypto funds—i.e., crypto-asssets themselves are proceeds of the predicate offence. This dynamic is called 'cryptocurrency laundering' or 'crypto-cleansing', and originated from the uptake of 'mixing/tumbling' techniques, initially labelled 'Bitcoin mixing'. More recently, the phenomenon has spread to other major networks such as Ethereum. Specifically, Ethereum-based mixers recently gained regulatory and supervisory attention.[16]

Instances of crypto laundering can take place within a process initiated with fiat proceeds, for instance in the layering phase, or independently. Laundering 'of' and 'through' crypto-assets often happen in a conjoined fashion—e.g., proceeds originally in fiat money can be converted into crypto-assets that are later 'crypto-cleansed' in the layering phase. This testifies to the intricate interlinks between the three stages. It is in this context the FATF highlighted the risks posed by virtual-to-virtual operations performed by/through unregulated providers.[17] Nonetheless, both in laundering 'through' and 'of' crypto-assets the goal is to obfuscate the chain of transactions and hinder investigations and enforcement.

4.1.2 Anonymity as a Red Flag Indicator

Chapter 2 introduced the socio-technical nature of crypto-asset anonymity and transparency, and the value of applying a teleological approach to their definition. As noted there, the AML/CFT framework does not provide a definition of anonymity, but insights can be drawn from the understanding of anonymity that emerges from the FATF's 'red flag indicators'. In this context, the organisation outlines benchmarks to signal regulated entities and authorities to proceed with care in

[16] Barbereau et al. (2023).

[17] Fruth (2018).

certain situations. These 'red flag indicators' are typical of frameworks grounded on the RBA. At the national level, self-regulating authorities issue indicators for their supervisees. The goal is to help identify risky and suspicious operations and/or customers based on a list of circumstances. Accordingly, regulated entities are required to apply enhanced CDD, submit an STR or even refuse to perform an operation (Chap. 5).

The FATF published a comprehensive list of indicators related to activities in virtual assets in 2020, with a subsection on anonymity, and complementary risk factors in 2021.[18] These risks are vulnerabilities inherent to the technology or generated by the dynamics of the ecosystem. However, the FATF does not consider anonymity alone as an automatic suggestion that a transaction is illicit. Indeed, legitimate reasons can drive behaviours that are indicated as suspicious by the risk factors—e.g., hardware wallets are also means of protection against thefts—, but in these cases further scrutiny is required. Hence, in compliance with the RBA, the risk must be assessed considering the specific customer and business relationship (Chap. 5).

Figure 4.1 lists FATF's risk factors, with a summary of the suspicious elements and the type of anonymity that comes into play—e.g., what is the aspect that grounds FATF's risk evaluation. In particular, this includes an assessment whether each case of anonymity is linked to the type of crypto-asset (e.g., privacy coins, coins linked to fraud), service (e.g., DEXes, mixing services, crypto ATMs),[19] communication (e.g., VPNs, proxies), wallet (e.g., self-hosted), and/or wallet use (e.g., shell wallets). In turn, an evaluation is provided of whether the case of anonymity is an example of obfuscation (grey shading), enhanced disintermediation (green shading), or is of another specific kind. These categories can be tied to untraceability and/or unidentifiability and/or unlinkability. While a single risk indicator can include at the same time more anonymity types, for each risk indicator it is possible to identify one that comes across as more evident as the targeted one.

Based on these benchmarks provided in 2020, the "market for anonymity-enhancing tools and methods is in rapid flux" and poses considerable concerns.[20] In 2021, the FATF referred to other obfuscation techniques such as the use of chain-hopping and dusting (i.e., transfer of small amounts of crypto-assets to random

[18] Financial Action Task Force (2020), pp. 9–10. Financial Action Task Force (2021b).

[19] The risk of crypto ATMs emerges in the recast of the Fund Transfers Regulation (see Chap. 5): Crypto-ATMs "can enable users to perform transfers of crypto-assets to a crypto-asset address by depositing cash, often without any form of customer identification and verification. Crypto-ATMs are particularly exposed to money laundering risks because the anonymity they provide and the possibility of operating with cash of unknown origin make them an ideal vehicle for illicit activities" (Recital 25 of Regulation (EU) 2023/1113). Meanwhile, Ponzi schemes, prohibited in many countries, are a "fraudulent investment operation where the operator generates return for older investors through revenue paid by new investors, rather than from legitimate business activities or profits of financial trading. In a Ponzi scheme, many participants, especially those posteriors, are doomed to lose most of their invested money". The blockchain-based form exploits the lack of specific knowledge of users and investors (Chen et al., 2019).

[20] Financial Action Task Force (2021a), p. 23.

	Text of the Risk Indicators:	It is suspicious when:	Anonymity is tied to:
1	"Transactions by a customer involving more than one type of VA, despite additional transaction fees, and especially those VAs that provide higher anonymity, such as anonymity-enhanced cryptocurrency (AEC) or privacy coins"	a customer transacts in more than one type of cryptoasset and AECs, even if doing so requires the payment of additional transaction fees	Type of Cryptocurrency (obfuscation): Privacy Coins
2	"Moving a VA that operates on a public, transparent blockchain, such as Bitcoin, to a centralised exchange and then immediately trading it for an AEC or privacy coin"	a customer moves assets from a public and transparent blockchain to a CEX and then exchanges it with AECs	Type of Cryptocurrency (obfuscation): Privacy Coins
3	"Customers that operate as an unregistered/ unlicensed VASP on peer-to-peer (P2P) exchange websites, particularly when there are concerns that the customers handle huge amount of VA transfers on its customer's behalf and charge higher fees to its customer than transmission services offered by other exchanges. Use of bank accounts to facilitate these P2P transactions"	a customer operates on P2P platforms as an unregistered service provider, especially when there are concerns the customer handles a significant number of transfers and charges high fees	Type of Service (disintermediation): P2P exchanges / DEXes
4	"Abnormal transactional activity (level and volume) of VAs cashed out at exchanges from P2P platform-associated wallets with no logical business explanation"	there is abnormal activity in terms of level and volume of transactions, cashed out from wallets tied to P2P platforms	Type of Service (disintermediation): P2P exchanges / DEXes
5	"VAs transferred to or from wallets that show previous patterns of activity associated with the use of VASPs that operate mixing or tumbling services or P2P platforms"	cryptoassets are transferred to/from wallets tied to mixing services or P2P platforms	Type of Service (disintermediation): P2P exchanges/DEXes (obfuscation): Mixing services
6	"Transactions making use of mixing and tumbling services, suggesting an intent to obscure the flow of illicit funds between known wallet addresses and darknet marketplaces"	mixing services are used, suggesting the goal of obfuscating the flow between wallet addresses and darknet markets	Type of Service (obfuscation): Mixing services
7	"Funds deposited or withdrawn from a VA address or wallet with direct and indirect exposure links to known suspicious sources, including darknet market-places, mixing/tumbling services, questionable gambling sites, illegal activities (e.g. ransomware) and/or theft reports"	funds are deposited or withdrawn to/from an address/wallet directly or indirectly exposed to sources known as suspicious, e.g., darknet marketplaces, mixing services	Type of Service (obfuscation): Mixing services
8	"The use of decentralised/unhosted, hardware or paper wallets to transport VAs across borders"	funds are moved across borders through decentralised/unhosted, hardware/paper wallets	Type of Wallet (disintermediation): Self-hosted wallets
9	"Users entering the VASP platform having registered their Internet domain names through proxies or using domain name registrars (DNS) that suppress or redact the owners of the domain names"	users use proxies or DNS suppressing/redacting their owners	Type of Communication (obfuscation): Anonymisers / proxies
10	"Users entering the VASP platform using an IP address associated with a darknet or other similar software that allows anonymous communication, including encrypted emails and VPNs. Transactions between partners using various anonymous encrypted communication means (e.g. forums, chats, mobile applications, online games, etc.) instead of a VASP"	users use an IP address associated with a darknet or a software enabling anonymous communication or transactions take place between users communicating through encrypted methods instead of regulated providers	Type of Communication (obfuscation): Anonymizers / proxies
11	"A large number of seemingly unrelated VA wallets controlled from the same IP-address (or MAC-address), which may involve the use of shell wallets registered to different users to conceal their relation to each other"	there are many wallets, seemingly unrelated, controlled from the same IP or MAC address	Type of wallet use (obfuscation): Shell wallets
12	"Use of VAs whose design is not adequately documented, or that are linked to possible fraud or other tools aimed at implementing fraudulent schemes, such as Ponzi schemes"	schemes whose design is not properly documented or is linked to fraudulent mechanisms such as Ponzi schemes	Type of Cryptocurrency (specific): New Asset / Ties to fraud
13	"Receiving funds from or sending funds to VASPs whose CDD or know-your-customer (KYC) processes are demonstrably weak or non-existent"	transfers from/to providers whose CDD/KYC is weak or non-existent	Type of Service (specific): Non-compliant providers
14	"Using VA ATMs/kiosks despite the higher transaction fees and including those commonly used by mules or scam victims; or in high-risk locations where increased criminal activities occur. A single use of an ATM/kiosk is not enough in and of itself to constitute a red flag, but would if it was coupled with the machine being in a high-risk area, or was used for repeated small transactions (or other additional factors)"	repeated use of cryptocurrency ATMs/kiosks for small transactions, even if fees are high and they are used by mules or scam victims, or in locations at high-risk for criminal activities	Type of Service (obfuscation): ATMs / kiosks

Fig. 4.1 Classification of FATF's VA Red Flag Indicators related to anonymity. Based on Pocher (2023). The text of the indicators is from: Financial Action Task Force (2020), pp. 9–10

wallets), cases of enhanced disintermediation linked to decentralised applications, atomic swapping exchanges, and reported an increase in 'privacy wallets' transfers that combine into a single transaction those of multiple people—e.g., CoinJoin. In this context, the FATF identified two sets of actions to mitigate enhanced anonymity: (i) enforcement initiatives to close mixing platforms for operating as unregistered providers, and (ii) registered providers delisting products such as AECs.[21]

Against this backdrop, to avoid or mitigate the risk of overfitting, this work heeds the socio-technical and ever-evolving nature of the traits of anonymity and transparency of crypto-asset ecosystems. To structure the analysis accordingly, the concepts of obfuscation and traceability are at the core of the analysis. These notions are the key to explore:

- the interaction and possible combinations between the types of anonymity risks and the difference between laundering 'of' and 'through' crypto-assets;
- the 'social' elements contributing to the anonymity and transparency level of a crypto-asset ecosystem, with reference to the impacts exerted by (i) techniques pursuing the obfuscation of crypto-asset flows, and (ii) intelligence strategies such as blockchain analysis;
- their repercussions of the specific methods deployed sub (i) and (ii) on the accountability level of the actors involved in crypto-asset transactions.

Hence, the remainder of this chapter (a) addresses the multi-layered nature of obfuscation techniques in their relationship with money laundering, where a key role is played by AECs, PETs and mixing, (b) contextualises their action vis-à-vis intelligence strategies, as well as (c) provides a socio-technical framework to define an AML/CFT-specific concept of crypto-asset anonymity.

4.2 Methods to Obfuscate Financial Flows and the Role of Traceability

When it comes to the ways in which obfuscation and traceability come into play in the crypto-asset space from an AML/CFT perspective, it is important to consider the phenomenological interaction between the types of anonymity risks emerging from FATF's guidelines, and the difference between laundering 'of' and 'through' crypto-assets. Methods to obfuscate the flow can be combined in many ways, and it is useful to visualise a process composed of different stages, each of them corresponding to the activities performed by a launderer.

[21] Financial Action Task Force (2021a), p. 23.

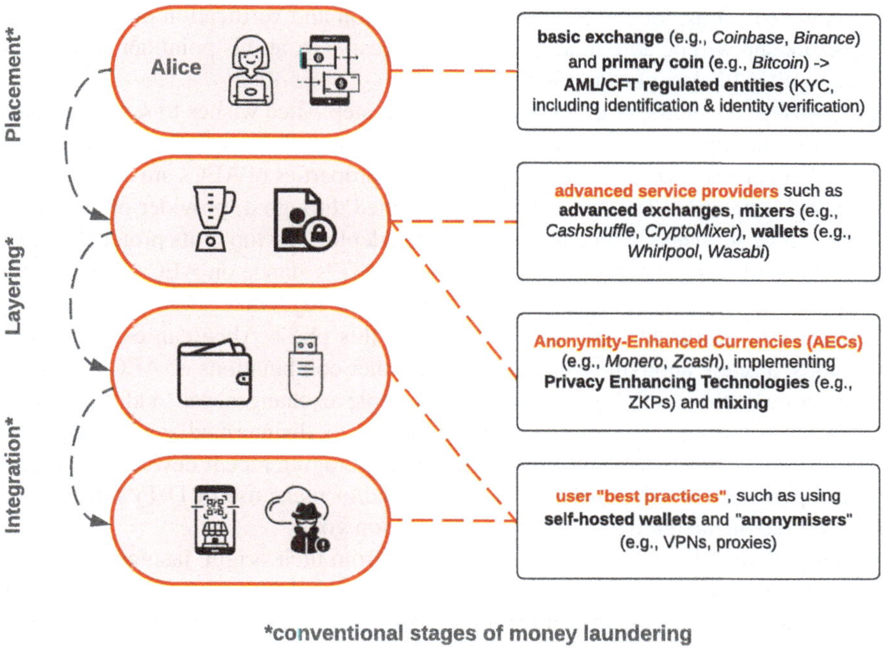

Fig. 4.2 Simplified example of obfuscation of crypto-asset flows. Based on Pocher (2023)

The laundering process could involve the steps taken by Alice in Fig. 4.2, where the proceeds are originally in fiat money.[22] As mentioned above, a key step is layering. In particular:

1. *Placement/Layering*. Alice exchanges ill-gotten funds from fiat currency to a 'primary' type of cryptocurrency through a provider of basic exchange services. A 'primary coin' is a coin that is not anonymity-enhanced (i.e., as opposed to AECs), and a 'provider of basic exchange services' is a regulated provider that does not make use of anonymity-enhancing tools. In principle, in this example the first step consists either of a placement activity, if funds are not already in the financial system—in this case, they could be converted into a 'primary coin' from a cash-based crypto-ATM (hence the evaluation of crypto-ATMs as suspicious)—or already of a layering activity, with the fiat money to convert originating from bank accounts or accounts held at non-bank payment service providers (PSPs). If we assume Alice is a money launderer, the issue with this first stage is that the entities that perform fiat-to-crypto exchanges are usually

[22] This is not always the case. When crypto-asset funds are stolen from a DeFi project or a crypto exchange, the proceeds of the crime are already in the form of crypto-asset. Later the hackers engage in laundering activities to prevent LEAs and intelligence companies from tracing the stolen coins back to the hack.

regulated. Thus, they will perform identification and verification of her identity before she will be able to access their services—i.e., at this point her real-world identity is likely linked to the funds.

2. *Layering*. Given the circumstances, as a next step Alice wishes to sever her real-world identity from her funds.To this end, the 'primary coins' can be mixed and exchanged for AECs. As explored below, the properties of AECs are conducive to Alice's objective. The conversion is performed through a 'provider of advanced exchange services', which is a provider that deploys on top of its protocol and/or embeds obfuscation techniques. Given the FATF's stance on AECs and the link to mixing techniques, these providers may not be regulated.
3. *Layering*. To further obfuscate the trail, in this phase Alice can exchange her funds, already anonymity-enhanced, with other combinations of AECs, through layering techniques that can rely on multiple exchanges and addresses (i.e., virtual-to-virtual layering). She can also try to disintermediate the trail, by making use of DEXes and P2P platforms. Leveraging recent developments, she can perform cross-blockchain exchanges, and/or make use of DeFi solutions to combine the disintermediation and obfuscation goal.
4. *Integration*. Alice's funds are now cleansed from their origin, insofar as she can trust the chain of obfuscated transactions not to unveil their history.[23] As a further step, they may be withdrawn from the crypto-asset space (but compliant crypto-to-fiat exchanges will ask information on the funds' origin) or spent directly to buy goods and services from sellers that accept cryptocurrencies. Meanwhile, the funds may be held on self-hosted wallets.

This process is far from rigid. Besides the overlapping of the different phases, the monetary flow may also proceed in the opposite way, starting with Alice holding crypto funds on a self-hosted wallet, passing through various anonymity-enhancements, and finally being converted into 'primary coins' and fiat currency through 'basic exchanges'. This is, however, hampered by the duties of regulated entities. Nevertheless, the goal of this section is to show how the different phases of the process can be interlinked in manifold ways. The interplay is a clear emblem of the threats posed by intricate layering schemes.

By retracing the phases of this illicit journey, certain steps appear crucial not only in disintermediating, but also in obfuscating, the trail, in terms of reducing traceability and accountability. These loopholes can be specific assets such as AECs, or service providers such as 'advanced exchanges' or 'mixers'. In early regulatory initiatives, the compound of these instruments was addressed as anonymisers, broadly described as "tools and services, such as darknets and mixers, designed to obscure the source of a Bitcoin transaction and facilitate anonymity".[24] They emerged in the analysis of the FATF's 'red flag indicators', but over time experts taxonomised the main methods to obfuscate crypto-asset flows: (1) mixing; (2) zero-

[23] Fruth (2018).

[24] Financial Action Task Force (2014), p. 6.

knowledge proofs (ZKPs) and other privacy-enhancing cryptographic techniques; (3) user best practices.[25] This work adds remarks on (4) network-level anonymity-enhancements.

4.2.1 Anonymity Enhanced Currencies

Bitcoin paved the way for an array of cryptocurrencies labelled 'altcoins', short form for 'alternative coins' in respect to Bitcoin.[26] The main driver of a subset of these systems—known as AECs or 'privacy coins'—was the desire to safeguard privacy. As reported in a comprehensive review of their whitepapers, many AECs share the ambition to be used as general-purpose money, although the political positions and justifications underlying the initiatives vary significantly.[27] Their privacy motive pivots around the concept of fungibility. Because money can be (mis)used for criminal purposes, throughout its history of transfers its owners' actions can taint it. This concerns both transactions that involve drugs, weapons, or laundering, but also those associated to activities in breach of rules posed by dictatorial regimes. From this perspective, obfuscating the transaction history aims at true fungibility, where "all coins are equally valued regardless of their historical trajectories and associated owners", a quality of physical coins and banknotes.[28]

Nonetheless, currency fungibility was not the only AEC driver. Privacy has also been pursued for personal security, consumer protection, safe acquisition/transaction, and compliance. Bitcoin's pseudonymity is equal to the publication of account numbers or credit card statements while keeping originators and beneficiaries' names hidden, and anonymity-enhancements are tasked to mitigate the relevant dangers.[29] While in AEC projects privacy is generally seen as 'as end in itself' and there is no consensus on its specifics, promoters agree on one aspect: the pursuit of anonymity. Reportedly, "the state of privacy which privacy coins aim to protect ... is, almost always, anonymity", and most whitepapers explicitly refer to it explicitly.[30] The link between privacy and anonymity is clear in the literature (Chap. 3).

Against this backdrop, AEC-related risks challenge the AML/CFT framework considerably, and in 2021 the FATF specified they fall within the scope of the regu-

[25] Sun and Zhang (2018a, 2018b); Zhang and Sun (2019).

[26] The first 'altcoin', Namecoin, was released in 2011 (Orr & Lancaster, 2018, p. 422).

[27] The motives behind 'privacy coin' projects have never ceased to develop. Arguably, they moved past anti-governmental and anti-establishment goals. Successful cryptocurrencies, in terms of the value creation, are now "explicitly branded and positioned to aid hegemonic political interests" (Harvey & Branco-Illodo, 2020, p. 108).

[28] Harvey and Branco-Illodo (2020), p. 122.

[29] Silva Ramalho and Igreja Matos (2021), p. 503.

[30] Harvey and Branco-Illodo (2020), p. 121.

latory regime. The major obfuscation concern lies in the evolution of the underlying technologies, which hampers effective monitoring on the types of transfers they enable. Despite extensive research on the anonymity of crypto-assets, a standardised mean to assess its levels has yet to be achieved (Chap. 3). By contrast, the efforts to identify anonymity in a unified manner across different implementations suggest "claims for anonymity cannot be made lightly in the presence of such granularity".[31] While the most basic type of privacy-enhancement is the use of a new address for every transaction—i.e., stealth addresses—, most AECs implement a combination of PETs, whose role is significant in terms of both safeguarding privacy and fostering anonymity-oriented set-ups.[32] Indeed, anonymity is one of the methods to pursue privacy. Accordingly, on the one hand PETs can be implemented to safeguard privacy against intrusions and for the sake of data protection (e.g., as per the GDPR), and on the other hand they can be exploited to cripple the traceability of funds.[33]

ZKPs, among the most complex and used PETs, are a perfect example of this twofold nature. User privacy is preserved by enabling a party to prove the possession of certain data without the need to disclose it, thanks to a cryptographic technique that allows a transaction to be validated while masking the content, preventing users not participating in it from accessing its original content.[34] The value of ZKPs lies in bridging the two objectives of public blockchains: user anonymity and transaction transparency.[35] Accordingly, research is exploring how to use ZKPs to reach a desirable level of user privacy, in the form of confidentiality, without thwarting accountability, measured in terms of auditability.[36]

The application of ZKPs entails data obfuscation—i.e., to mask/hide data. According to their specifics, and on the grounds of the effects on data confidentiality and auditability, PETs were classified as segregating, hiding, or unlinking.[37] Accordingly, their effects were ranked from effective auditability to weak auditability, showing how some techniques may safeguard privacy but still enable oversight, while others do not leave room for effective auditing. In this respect, the level of auditability can be construed as the result of the degrees of: (a) accessibility to necessary information; (b) reliability of information; and (c) efficiency of the process.[38]

---

[31] Amarasinghe et al. (2021), pp. 206, 219.

[32] Torra (2017).

[33] Pocher and Veneris (2022), p. 7.

[34] De Haro-Olmo et al. (2020), p. 14.

[35] Quiniou (2019).

[36] European Central Bank and Bank of Japan (2020); Yuen (2020); Dashkevich et al. (2020); Puzis et al. (2019); Tian et al. (2020); Barbereau et al. (2022); Gross et al. (2021).

[37] European Central Bank and Bank of Japan (2020). Pocher and Veneris (2022), p. 8. Stealth addresses, one-time address and ring signatures based on homomorphic encryption are unlinking PETs. Homomorphic encryption is used in e-voting, "where each vote cast must not be related to the identity of its issuer, who must be anonymous. This is achieved by using ring signatures" (De Haro-Olmo et al., 2020, p. 15).

[38] European Central Bank and Bank of Japan (2020), p. 15.

To imagine an extreme scenario, if a specific technique leads to some data not being stored on the ledger in any form, this cannot be retrieved later. In particular, it was argued 'segregating PETs', 'Quorum's private transaction', 'Pedersen commitment' and 'centralised mixing' may allow for effective auditability, which means they can be applied to reach a suitable balance between privacy and transparency for AML/CFT. On the contrary, 'ZKP', 'one-time address' and 'multi/ring-signatures' make transaction information thoroughly inaccessible.[39] Chapter 6 addresses this distinction and the AML/CFT impacts within a more comprehensive analysis of trade-offs in PETs. By contrast, the following subsection takes a broader approach in heeding the elements at play when pinpointing anonymity benchmarks in 'privacy coins' that embed different techniques. To do so, it outlines four use cases of AECs—Zcash, Monero, Dash, Mimblewimble—, and their cryptographic mechanisms. Although these use cases are blockchain-based, privacy has been enhanced in non-blockchain scenarios as well.[40]

4.2.2 *Four AEC Use Cases*

Zcash was created drawing from two previous systems: Zerocoin and ZeroCash. On the one hand, Zerocoin relied on 'one-way accumulators' for value storage and on ZKPs for spending coins while breaking ties between transactions. On the other hand, ZeroCash introduced a type of ZKP known as zero-knowledge succinct non-interactive argument of knowledge (zk-SNARKs) for transaction verification, and schemes of 'decentralised anonymous payment' to pay directly and privately (i.e., concealing senders, recipients and amounts). Both systems presented serious drawbacks: they were not compatible with the Bitcoin network, their functioning relied on heavy cryptographic computation, they did not hide the IP addresses of their users.[41]

Zcash was developed on top of the ZeroCash model, to improve its level of confidentiality and the size of its anonymity set, while also using Bitcoin's transaction type.[42] The main anonymity feature of Zcash is the 'shielded pool', and also in this case the goal of the underlying ZKP protocol is to hide transaction data while allowing its verification. However, in Zcash privacy is enhanced selectively, which enables to preserve confidentiality of a subset of data. When coins are placed into the 'pool', senders are revealed but recipients are hidden by using 'z-addresses' to identify them. By contrast, when coins are withdrawn from the "pool", senders are hidden, and recipients are revealed. Hence, complete privacy can only be provided when transactions take place within the "shielded pool". In

[39] European Central Bank and Bank of Japan (2020), pp. 18–22.

[40] Tennant (2017), pp. 6–8. Ince et al. (2018), pp. 32–45.

[41] Amarasinghe et al. (2019), pp. 5–6.

[42] Amarasinghe et al. (2019), p. 6.

this case, senders, recipients and transferred value are all hidden.[43] Because zk-SNARKs are computationally expensive, only a minority of Zcash's addresses is shielded. The other ones are transparent (i.e., not anonymity-enhanced). The use of transparent addresses has the same outcome of Bitcoin transactions, described in terms of "t-addresses". Hence, the Zcash model is not "private-by-default",[44] and the unlinkability of its transactions is not complete due to the concurrent presence of transparent and shielded transactions, which means the system vulnerable to de-anonymisation.[45]

Monero, on its part, was initially deploying the CryptoNote protocol to achieve untraceability and unlinkability counterbalancing blockchain's transparency. The goal was pursued using 'one-time ring signatures' with non-interactive ZKPs, similar to 'non-interactive mixing'.[46] The expression 'ring signatures' refers to the presence of a 'ring of users', within which a user signs a message on behalf of the whole group without revealing the individual identity—i.e., the signature is verified using all the public keys of the group. This technique is considered less performant than zk-SNARKs, but was tested more intensely.[47] Nonetheless, it was vulnerable to de-anonymisation: some features made transactions partially linkable, values were not hidden, and cryptographic keys increased transaction size.[48]

Indeed, the anonymity of Monero has evolved over time, and the cryptocurrency is claimed to be one of the most anonymous given the deployed combination of PETs. Currently, it uses 'ring signatures' to hide senders' details and allows coins to be 'mixed' with so-called 'mixins'. Transaction values are hidden through 'ring confidential transactions', that allow verification through value commitments, to improve CryptoNote. Meanwhile, 'one-time addresses' or 'stealth addresses' are deployed to hide recipients, and 'linkable ring signatures' attain senders' privacy and avoid double spending.[49] In principle, transactions can still be de-anonymised because the 'mixing' sampling strategy allows linkability, and untraceability can be

[43] Yousaf et al. (2019), p. 13. In 'shielded' transactions, each address is equipped with a private spending key that enables the owner to spend the coins (notes) sent to that address. For each note, a unique nullifier is created using the spending key and a note commitment, made public upon creation of the note. The private key allows the note commitment to be linked to its nullifier. Hence, a Zcash unspent note is a note whose commitment is revealed and whose nullifier is hidden. The creation of a 'shielded' transaction entails the disclosure of (i) nullifiers of input notes and (ii) commitments of output notes. Values are also hidden, as they are revealed through value commitments related to inputs and out-put notes, whose balancing is performed as homomorphic operations. Zk-SNARKS primitives are deployed to prove the notes' ownership and to verify and validate transactions (Amarasinghe et al., 2021, p. 214).

[44] Biryukov and Tikhomirov (2019), pp. 1–2. Yousaf et al. (2019), p. 13.

[45] Amarasinghe et al. (2019), p. 6. Amarasinghe et al. (2021), p. 208.

[46] Altcoins such as ByteCoin and Aeon deploy CryptoNote (Amarasinghe et al., 2019, p. 6).

[47] Maupin (2017), p. 7.

[48] Amarasinghe et al. (2019), p. 6.

[49] Yuen (2019), pp. 225–227. Each Monero user has two pairs of private/public keys acting as spend/view keys. For each output, senders create a 'one-time public key/stealth address' using the recipients' public key. To generate the inputs' ring signature the input is mixed with random public

breached.[50] However, Monero deploys Dandelion++ to obscure the IP address of the device broadcasting the transaction. This protocol makes use of 'randomised routing algorithms' and 'graph topologies', and consists of a broadcast propagation method where new transactions pass through a Monero node, and later a probabilistic method decides whether the transaction is sent to one node or broadcasted to many.[51] Further, the ongoing project Kovri aims to further increase anonymity by encrypting the traffic and routing it through nodes of the Invisible Internet Project (I2P), whose nodes transfer messages without having visibility over them.

Thirdly, Dash embeds as its main anonymity feature a type of CoinJoin known as 'PrivateSend transactions'. It allows multiple users to make more transfers through a single transaction, in line with the 'mixing' concept outlined below. When a group of senders sends the same number of coins to the respective recipients, it becomes difficult to link input addresses to the corresponding outputs, which severs the link between individual senders and recipients. If CoinJoin methods usually require users to find each other, Dash finds users automatically and chains multiple mixers together. The actual level of anonymity depends on the number of transactions mixed in any given case,[52] and to hamper users from sending identifiable values the system restricts 'PrivateSend transactions' to specific denominations.[53] As in Zcash, the privacy of senders and recipients is achieved in the same way.[54] Dash deploys a secondary network of full nodes (i.e., Dash Masternode Network) on top of the Bitcoin network, therefore its privacy level is influenced by the presence of both regular nodes and 'masternodes'.[55]

Finally, Mimblewimble is a protocol that deploys a system of 'confidential transactions' and 'transaction aggregation'.[56] Its cryptographic method, named 'elliptic curve cryptography' is based on logarithms and allows the verification of transactions' amounts and involved parties without revealing any information. On top of this, other cryptographic protocols are deployed, such as the mentioned CTs and CoinJoin—to conceal transaction values and make transactions untraceable,

---

keys (i.e., mixins). Outsiders can only see the ring's public keys, each of them having the same probability of being the input (Amarasinghe et al., 2021, p. 216).

[50] Amarasinghe et al. (2019), p. 7. Amarasinghe et al. (2021), p. 208. Du et al. (2024).

[51] Amarasinghe et al. (2019), p. 7. Fanti et al. (2018), pp. 1–35.

[52] Yuen (2019), p. 225.

[53] Yousaf et al. (2019), p. 14. PrivateSend is an extension of the CoinJoin protocol and improves decentralisation and denominations. Remaining limitations are the need of at least three participants and the centralisation caused by the Masternode network (Amarasinghe et al., 2019, p. 5).

[54] Yuen (2019), p. 227.

[55] Biryukov and Tikhomirov (2019), p. 2. Amarasinghe et al. (2019), p. 5.

[56] Senders send input coins to recipients through an authenticated channel that adds commitments to output coins that include individual private keys, and a partial transaction's signature generated using a random nonce. This is sent back to the sender, who validates the signature, adds his/her portion of it, and broadcasts the transaction to the network. The transaction is verified and minted by the nodes, and the transaction graph is hidden through 'transaction aggregation' (Amarasinghe et al., 2021, p. 217).

respectively—, but also Dandelion and Cut-Through, where the first one hides the identity of senders and users and the second one improves 'scalability'.[57] Mimblewimble's features make it highly fungible when compared to other cryptocurrency schemes. Nonetheless, proposed corrections to enhance security turned out to lower fungibility insofar as the amount of preserved data increases.[58]

4.2.3 *Crypto-Mixing: The First Type of Crypto-Cleansing*

Since mixing was the first attempt to solve Bitcoin's lack of fungibility, in the early stages of crypto-assets 'crypto-laundering' and 'Bitcoin mixing' were considered synonyms. The mixing process consists of combining inputs and outputs of different transactions into a larger one, to sever the links between the addresses of senders and recipients.[59] Transactions are made unlinkable by shuffling them, which means the level of confidentiality depends on the amount of mixed data (the 'anonymity set') and the similarity of transfers' values.[60] From a related perspective, due to the fact that transaction amounts are usually stored in the clear on the blockchain mixing methods are often combined with hiding techniques.

The resulting degree of confidentiality is also influenced by whether the model is custodial—i.e., the mixing service is operated by a centralised provider—or not. Indeed, if the service is offered by a centralised provider, users must entrust it with their original information. In other words, the level of confidentiality depends on the way in which the provider disposes of the identifying data after the mixing operation.[61] New P2P schemes of non-custodial crypto-asset mixers allow the centralisation point to be removed, but in non-centralised and non-custodial scenarios users need to timely find others willing to mix their data.[62] An example of mixing method that does not rely on a third party is the CoinJoin protocol implemented by Dash, while significant turmoil was generated by Tornado Cash, which in the past was the most used non-custodial mixer on Ethereum.[63] It consists of a set of smart contracts and was proposed as a zkSNARK-based ERC-20 solution

[57] Shilina (2021).

[58] Amarasinghe et al. (2021), p. 208.

[59] Sun and Zhang (2018a). Chapter 6 will heed the classification of 'mixing' as an 'unlinking' PET (European Central Bank and Bank of Japan, 2020; Pocher & Veneris, 2022, p. 8).

[60] Pocher and Veneris (2022), p. 8. Amarasinghe et al. (2019), p. 4.

[61] Nadler and Schär (2023), p. 3.

[62] Pocher and Veneris (2022), p. 8.

[63] Wu et al. (2022), p. 2. Nadler and Schär (2023). The U.S. OFAC sanctioned Tornado Cash in 2022 for money laundering in connection with the Lazarus Group, a North Korea state-sponsored hacking group (U.S. Department of the Treasury, 2022). The developers/co-founders of Tornado Cash were charged in the U.S. for what concerns Roman Storm and Roman Semenov (Federal Bureau of Investigation, 2023) and convicted in the Netherlands for what concerns Alexey Pertsev (de Rechtspraak, 2024).

to the user privacy challenges in account-based blockchains.[64] Similarly, a method that provides trustless unlinkability deploys "ring signatures with elliptic curve digital signature algorithm" and can be integrated into Bitcoin to generate and verify signatures. However, if mixing operations are constructed by a server, the overall decentralisation level decreases.[65] Although mixing is neutral in principle, there is a negative aura surrounding these services, as they strongly inhibit detection of criminal revenues. Nonetheless, it was argued that even if they are usually used to dilute and disguise criminal proceeds, they can also serve legitimate purposes of self-protection.[66]

From an operational perspective, mixing can take various forms, and can be automatic or voluntary. Indeed, it can be offered as a service by centralised entities—i.e., as an external service, by providers such as the early BitLaundry and MixCoin, or Cashshuffle, Blender and CryptoMixer—, or it can be embedded into: (i) the currency design, implemented on top of the original protocol—e.g., layer-2 solutions; (ii) a wallet—e.g., Whirlpool, Wasabi; or (iii) an exchange platform. Overall, mixing services are often linked to the activities of custodian wallet providers.[67] Crypto-wallets with embedded mixing are dubbed privacy wallets or mixing-enabled wallets and perform transfers where multiple transactions are combined into a single transfer.[68] The FATF considers all these possible mixing strategies as tools that increase anonymity in the crypto-asset space.[69] Indeed, while these methods belong to different categories of anonymity-enhancements, the intermediary-based AML/CFT framework applies to regulated entities regardless of the specific embedded obfuscation techniques.[70]

---

[64] Béres et al. (2021), pp. 72, 76. Wu et al. (2022), pp. 2–3. Users make deposits of equal amounts (of Ether and a few Ethereum-based tokens) to a Tornado Cash smart contract, and later they withdraw the funds to a 'fresh' account by proving with a ZKP they were among the depositors. The new account is unlinkable to any unique depositor, albeit the level of confidentiality varies according to the size of the 'anonymity set', as outlined above.

[65] Amarasinghe et al. (2019), pp. 4–7.

[66] Silva Ramalho and Igreja Matos (2021), pp. 497, 503.

[67] Silva Ramalho and Igreja Matos (2021), pp. 497, 503.

[68] Financial Action Task Force (2021b), p. 7.

[69] Financial Action Task Force (2021a), p. 23.

[70] The framework applies to "covered VA activities and VASPs, regardless of the type of VA involved in the financial activity (e.g., a VASP that uses or offers AECs to another person for various financial transactions), the underlying technology (e.g., whether it uses the mainnet or the use of embedded layering or other scaling solutions), or the additional services that the platform potentially incorporates (such as a mixer or tumbler or other potential features for obfuscation)" (Financial Action Task Force, 2021a, p. 23). Chapter 5 addresses the concepts of 'covered VA activity' and the definition of VASP.

4.2.4 Users and a Diversified Bundle of 'Best' Practices

'Red flag indicators' do not only refer to the use of crypto-assets or services embedding or employing anonymity-enhancing methods or increasing disintermediation. While mixing and PETs are applied at a protocol level, a set of anonymity enhancements originate from user behaviour. In 2021 the FATF underlined the risk posed by "exposure to Internet Protocol (IP) anonymiser such as The Onion Router (TOR), the Invisible Internet Project (I2P) and other anonymising software or anonymity enhancements".[71] Indeed, users can deploy obfuscation strategies defined as 'best practices'—e.g., making use of anonymisers such as Virtual Private Networks (VPNs), and other strategies such as using new addresses for every payment.[72]

To conceal their IP address, users may access the Internet through a VPN, which generates an encrypted tunnel between the user and a remote server before accessing the Internet.[73] TOR, on its part, is the most popular anonymous communication network and it enables server-side anonymity through hidden 'onion services'. In this way, "a hidden service client and operator establish a communication tunnel, known as a circuit, between each other over multiple intermediate routers. Anonymity is maintained as long as the intermediate routers at the two ends of the tunnel are not controlled by an adversary who can use time or traffic analysis to link the source to the destination".[74] On top of more common solutions, such as VPNs but also TOR, other sophisticated methods can be deployed by skilled users active on darknet markets to avert any investigative and enforcement intervention.[75] The reason to deploy these strategies has emerged above: even if AEC schemes have reached 'acceptable' anonymity levels in terms of unlinkability and untraceability, complete unlinkability has yet to be attained with regard to IP addresses.[76]

4.2.5 Network-Level Anonymity-Enhancements: On-Chain and Off-Chain Layers

The decentralisation level of a DLT application can be affected by the addition of one or more on-chain or off-chain 'layers' to the protocol—e.g., the Lightning Network in Bitcoin (Chap. 3). Accordingly, the properties of privacy and anonymity can be altered by the specifics of a multi-layered structure—i.e., by the design of the network. In particular, one or more layers can be added to an existing network,

[71] Financial Action Task Force (2021b), p. 20.

[72] Furneaux (2018); Sun and Zhang (2018a).

[73] Furneaux (2018), pp. 229–230.

[74] Al Jawaheri et al. (2019), p. 3.

[75] Maupin (2017), p. 5.

[76] Amarasinghe et al. (2019), p. 7.

or introduced in the design of a new project, to the end of enhancing its privacy and/or its anonymity. The Dash Masternode Network, mentioned above, consists of a secondary network of full nodes deployed on top of the Bitcoin network that influences the overall privacy level of Dash transactions.[77]

As argued for 'best practices', the need to develop additional methodologies is linked to other techniques not having achieved full unlinkability of IP addresses—i.e., lack of metadata unlinkability. In this context, the creation of overlaying anonymous 'payment channels' was suggested to guarantee transaction anonymity by storing some transaction data off-chain, leveraging smart contracts. 'Payment channel networks (PCNs)' are also known as 'second layer' or 'layer 2' solutions, where 'layer-1' is the primary blockchain architecture (the 'mainnet' or 'root blockchain'). 'Second layer' solutions can consist of 'sidechains', 'state channels', or 'off-chain transaction networks', allowing instant off-chain transactions with minimal fees, which enhances efficiency and scalability. For this reason, they are used to experiment with (automatic) micro-payments,[78] for which traditional consensus mechanisms are unsuitable due to their comparatively high execution costs. The 'layer 2' can deploy specific anonymity enhancements, such as a mixing mechanism. From this perspective, the anonymity and transparency of the resulting network may be altered by the specifics of the tools deployed on overlaying networks or off-chain services.

Whenever a pair of users wishes to transact through a PCN, they can perform a funding transaction that locks funds on-chain, that are then to be used in the specific PCN opened between them. After this, PCN transactions do not involve (i.e., they are not recorded on) the blockchain, and consists only of exchanging a signed message containing the balance between the users. In addition, two users that do not have an open direct PCN can still transact with each other if a path of payment channels connects them—e.g., if Alice has a channel open with Bob, and Bob has a channel open with Charlie, Alice and Charlie can transact with each other through this path. This typically requires the payment of a fee (in this case, to Bob) for having the transaction forwarded, anticipating both the transaction amount and all the required fees for routing the payment. Atomicity is used as a guarantee: either all users along the path update their balances, or none of the balances is updated.[79] An example of the basics of the PCN technique can be found in Blind Off-chain Lightweight Transactions (BOLT). Besides the Lightning Network in Bitcoin, examples of 'second layer solutions' can be found in Ethereum's Raiden for intra-chain operations, and InterLedger or Atomic CrossChain for inter-blockchain transactions.[80] Another network-level solution is the one implemented by Dandelion ++, described above, using randomised routing algorithms and graph topologies.[81]

---

[77] Biryukov and Tikhomirov (2019), p. 2. Amarasinghe et al. (2019), p. 5.

[78] Pocher and Zichichi (2022) focus on micro-payments in device-to-device transactions.

[79] Avarikioti et al. (2021), pp. 1, 3.

[80] Amarasinghe et al. (2019), p. 7. Pocher and Zichichi (2022), p. 5.

[81] Fanti et al. (2018). pp. 1–35. Amarasinghe et al. (2019), p. 7.

4.3 Intelligence Strategies: Following Funds Across the Ecosystems

Chapter 2 introduced crypto-asset ecosystems as socio-technical, which affects the evaluation of their anonymity and transparency. Accordingly, among influential elements one should not only consider the technical ones—e.g., PETs, governance, architecture—, but also the social factors. As underlined when exploring fungibility, from a social perspective the essence of crypto-asset anonymity comprises the impacts exerted by investigative activities. In this context, forensic techniques are to be weighed against users' skills to limit traceability. The overall transparent nature of (public) blockchains makes them vulnerable to insufficient data privacy, de-anonymisation attacks and possible application of surveillance techniques. However, while deanonymisation is a concept that is often perceived negatively, it is the same mechanism that can be applied to 'follow the money' and comply with rules that aim to mitigate specific risks. In this respect, the combination of data that is accessible due to the nature of (certain types of) blockchain and the extracts of a given crypto wallet offers great material for investigative purposes—e.g., Bitcoin transactions generally associate more input addresses to an output address, and an analysis of these links provides useful insights in terms of tracking.[82]

Although in a public blockchain it is not difficult to retrieve information such as TXIDs, with details attached (e.g., time of receipt, input/output values, sender/recipient addresses), specific operative knowledge is needed to interpret it. Indeed, some traits of Bitcoin's inputs and outputs (e.g., transaction fees, transfers between addresses belonging to the same wallet) may be misleading.[83] Further, the trustworthiness of the retrieved data for what concerns the association between addresses and real-world identities should always be double-checked. In this sense, the private sector has been crucial in providing the technology to gather intelligence.[84]

This offer of 'visibility' into the crypto-asset space is the business of companies such as CipherTrace, Chainalysis, Elliptic, but also Coin Metrics, Elementus, ScoreChain, Blockseer, Neutrino, Crystal Blockchain, Blockchain Intel, TRM Labs. In broad terms, their activities consist of developing strategies of 'blockchain analytics', to be sold as a service to governments, supervisory authorities, LEAs, and entities regulated under compliance regimes. Because they analyse the different ecosystems and their relationships, these companies can provide insights to "bridge the gaps between regulation and the world of cryptocurrencies and blockchain".[85]

---

[82] Wu et al. (2020), p. 1231. Pocher et al. (2023a, 2023b).

[83] Silva Ramalho and Igreja Matos (2021), p. 491.

[84] Pocher et al. (2023a, 2023b).

[85] CipherTrace (2021), pp. 2, 6.

Further, they can help supervisory authorities identify unlicensed entities operating as service providers,[86] or regulated entities in assessing exposure to specific risks.[87]

4.3.1 *Blockchain Forensics: The Unfolding of Different Techniques*

As they benchmark the level of traceability, forensic techniques can be addressed as the trait d'union between pseudonymity and accountability. Their role lies in defining the possibility and/or likelihood to link a real-world identity to a specific (set of) crypto-asset transaction(s). This, in turn, depends on the efficacy of the given techniques vis-à-vis privacy-enhancing methods. At the same time, the efficacy of 'follow the money' strategies influence the evolution of anonymity enhancements, because they prompt the development of new means of obfuscation.

Forensic techniques started to be deployed in the crypto-asset space as 'blockchain analysis', informed by the specificities of blockchain technology. Accordingly, 'blockchain forensics' was defined as a "use of science and technology to investigate and establish facts in criminal or civil courts of law" that "deals primarily with the recovery and analysis of latent evidence left on the blockchain digital ledger as the results of transaction activities on a blockchain".[88] Although an analysis of crypto-asset transactions mainly focuses on blockchain data, and techniques were mostly tested on the Bitcoin network, data-exploitation strategies were deployed on Ethereum as well,[89] and debates are ongoing for non-blockchain-based DLTs.[90]

In addition, crypto-asset transactional data is usually analysed through a combination of on-chain and off-chain techniques—i.e., targeting also information that is not recorded on blockchains. In other words, although data generated by on-chain activity, related to the transactions cleared and settled on a blockchain layer, is a primary source of insights, it is necessary to turn to off-chain data to gather data on transactions performed outside the blockchain layer—e.g., transactions between two traders on an exchange's order-book, trading volumes or market data of exchanges, volumes of P2P platforms.[91] Off-chain information may also consist of data that is

---

[86] Financial Action Task Force (2021b), p. 45.

[87] Financial Action Task Force (2021b), p. 71. Enhanced CDD and risk assessment procedures are addressed in Chap. 5.

[88] Phan (2021). The criminal and/or procedural aspects of crypto-assets analytics fall outside the scope of this work. The analysis is limited to traceability and socio-technical impact on anonymity, privacy, and transparency.

[89] Chen et al. (2019), p. 1. Bartoletti et al. (2020). Li et al. (2021). Moreno-Sanchez et al. (2016), pp. 436–453. Ferretti and D'Angelo (2019). Wu et al. (2022).

[90] Tennant (2017), pp. 6, 7. Ince et al. (2018), pp. 32–45.

[91] Blandin et al. (2020), p. 36.

linked to on-chain activity but is not stored on-chain and is retrieved elsewhere—i.e., everywhere but on the given blockchain (hence, also on another blockchain).

The analysis of transactions is the main method to trace transfers in the crypto-assets sphere.[92] Before delving into existing approaches, a disclaimer is needed. In the overview provided below, the use of crypto-assets is an assumption, but in real-world investigations this may not be clear from the start. Hence, preliminary strategies encompass acquisition or extraction of private keys, public addresses and crypto-wallets files pertaining to a given subject, analysis of recovered addresses and wallets, to gather data on which to build 'follow the money' operations.[93]

In this context, the final goal of intelligence methods is to match users to transactions performed by 'cryptocurrency IDs'—in other words to connect users' pseudonyms (i.e., addresses) to real-world identities—, leveraging the presence of unique identifiers to specific individuals.[94] The structure of the crypto-asset world allows many sources of information to be exploited to this end—e.g., data extracted from a transaction can be leveraged to retrieve the transaction history of an address. Different techniques have been refined over time, according to the parallel development of anonymity enhancements, and methods based on Artificial Intelligence (AI) and machine learning, addressed below, are now broadly deployed.[95]

4.3.2 Analysis of the Transaction Network and the Role of Clustering

A considerable portion of forensic techniques deploy statistical approaches to collection and transaction analysis. Notably, they focus on the re-use of the same account for multiple transactions, or the co-use of more accounts for a single transaction, as well as their topologies, are elements that can be leveraged to match accounts to the same user.[96] Among these methods, several strategies try to link (pools of) addresses and transactions to specific users. They deploy techniques of 'address clustering' to cluster addresses owned by the same user,[97] and visualisation analytics such as 'transaction graphs'.[98] Some of these methods aim to identify

[92] Other methods rely on a 'central party' or on 'cryptographic tools', generally embedding certain features into an AEC to ensure its traceability by design (Li et al., 2021, pp. 680–681).

[93] Furneaux (2018), pp. 119–145, 147–173, 175–197.

[94] Airfoil (2019); The Cryptocurrency Consultant (2019). Paesano (2019), pp. 2–8. Pocher et al. (2023a, 2023b).

[95] Yin et al. (2019), pp. 37–73. Serena et al. (2022); Pocher et al. (2023b).

[96] Li et al. (2021), p. 680.

[97] Neudecker and Hartenstein (2017), pp. 1–12. Ince et al. (2018), p. 37. Wu et al. (2020), p. 1231.

[98] Fleder et al. (2015), pp. 1–7. Ober et al. (2013), pp. 237–249. Weber et al. (2019).

'idioms of use' in the network that can erode user anonymity.[99] In principle, these techniques do not (try to) de-anonymise an address or transaction (i.e., to link a given address or transaction to a real-world identity), but in case one of them is de-anonymised (in other ways) they allow the whole cluster to be de-anonymised. Likewise, the function of these strategies is not to identify and analyse transaction patterns, but to allow that "once an address is suspected in a cluster, other addresses are also suspected because they are very likely to belong to the same user or group".[100] However, 'transaction flow analysis' can be implemented to define patterns based on transaction features, to pinpoint suspected addresses.[101]

Clustering methodologies are grounded on heuristic models.[102] The concept behind 'clustering heuristics' is that users may be associated with addresses through two heuristic models: (1) "if two (or more) addresses are used as inputs to the same transaction, then they are controlled by the same user".[103] Indeed, one can assume that if a user owns the private keys to sign the transaction—i.e., all the private keys matching the public keys of the different inputs—then the same user owns all the addresses; (2) a "one-time change address—if one exists (a 'change address' is created for the sender to receive the excess from the input address)—is controlled by the same user as the input addresses".[104] As outlined above, in a transaction a 'change address' is created to receive the remaining funds unless the user owns the exact amount in one UTXO. Hence, at least one of a transaction's outputs is the 'change address'. Since a related 'idiom of use' is that the 'change address' is created internally and never re-used, if a transaction has a single output, this address usually has the same owner as the input address.[105] This approach is named 'wallet-closure analysis' and aims to establish a "unique many-one mapping between addresses and an identity".[106]

Another technique is known as 'behaviour-based clustering'.[107] 'Behaviour-based clustering' is defined as the "grouping of Bitcoin addresses with similar behavior patterns based on characteristics such as transaction values". Other clustering methods are 'co-spend clustering', when more addresses contribute inputs to

---

[99] Meiklejohn et al. (2016), p. 87.

[100] Wu et al. (2020), p. 1231.

[101] Wu et al. (2020), pp. 1231–1232.

[102] Lischke and Fabian (2016), p. 4. Androulaki et al. (2013), pp. 8–10. Reid and Harrigan (2011), pp. 8–11. A 'heuristic method' is a problem-solving approach deployed when an 'exhaustive search' methodology proves impractical. It is based on intuition, reasoning, problem context and past experiences. Although 'heuristics' pursues solutions not guaranteed to be optimal, they provide sufficient accuracy for the immediate goal.

[103] Meiklejohn et al. (2016), p. 89

[104] Meiklejohn et al. (2016), p. 90

[105] Meiklejohn et al. (2016), p. 90. Borreguero Beltrán (2019), p. 29.

[106] Al Jawaheri et al. (2019), p. 5.

[107] Amarasinghe et al. (2019), p. 3.

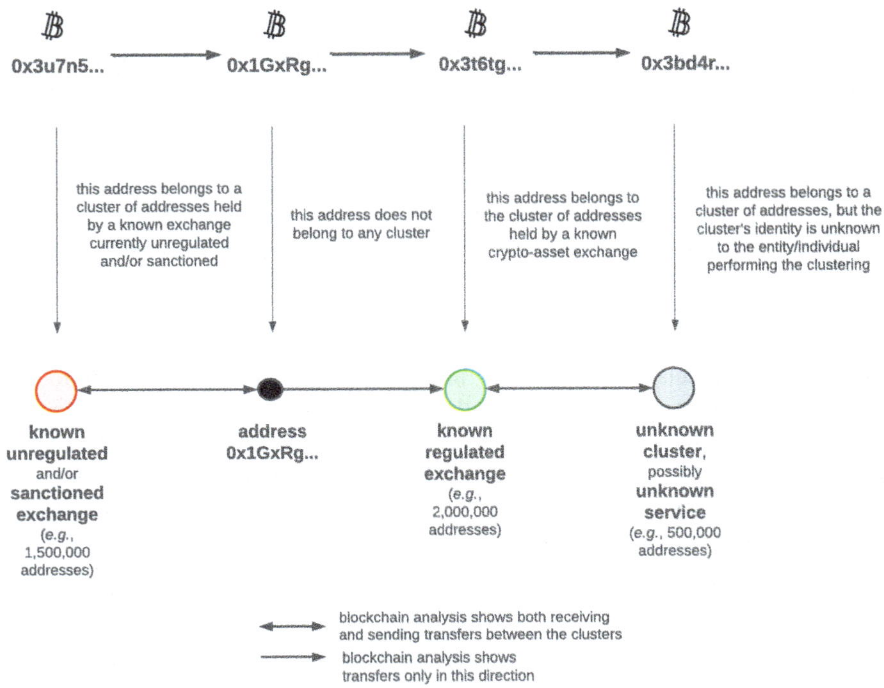

Fig. 4.3 An example of clustering in blockchain analytics. Based on Pocher et al. (2023a)

a single transaction, or 'intelligence-based clustering' when information is gathered from sources external to the transaction history, as outlined below.[108]

One of the practical examples of the value of clustering is displayed in Fig. 4.3 above. Given a series of cryptocurrency (in this case, bitcoin) transactions between four addresses, through the deployment of clustering algorithms—that are often proprietary and owned by the analytic companies offering RegTech applications—each of the addresses is pinpointed as either (i) belonging to a specific identified cluster (e.g., a service provider such as an exchange), (ii) belonging to a (yet) unidentified cluster (e.g., a possible service provider given the amount of addresses and relevant transactions), or as (iii) not belonging to any cluster (at least as far as the specific clustering algorithm is concerned). These findings allow the fund flow between the identified entities/clusters to be visualised, thus unveiling (a part of) the transaction history. Since forensic companies perform this process on as many cryptocurrency transactions as possible, the overall outcome shows the degree of receiving/sending relationships between the clusters. Although the example focuses on bitcoin transactions, the same approach is deployed on other blockchains and cross-chain (i.e., across different blockchains).

[108] Yin et al. (2019), pp. 37–73.

On the application level, other analytic methods exploit the information that leaks when it is possible to establish a correlation between transactions and the users' public profiles on social networks. Indeed, users do not only often post their crypto addresses (e.g., to receive donations, offer services) on social media, but also personal information related to their online identities (e.g., contact information, age, gender, location).[109] In this respect, there are methods of 'transaction fingerprinting' pegged on 'publicly available information',[110] or on 'off-network information',[111] and techniques involving web-scraping and OSINT tools.[112] Parallelly, a more proactive approach is 'illicit transactions mapping and prediction'.[113]

In light of the obfuscating role of mixing techniques, another forensic method analyses mixing services.[114] As introduced above, a 'coin-mixer' obfuscates funds by sending them to other addresses and shuffling them with those of other users. Clearly, users of mixing services are harder to trace if the number of inputs and outputs involved in a given process is larger.[115] Although intermediated third-party mixing services still tend to act as centralisation points also for traceability purposes, other disintermediated methods pursue a similar shuffling goal through more sophisticated approaches—e.g., the P2P mixing protocol CoinJoin. Against the backdrop of the enhanced disintermediation evolution (Chap. 3), an important role is played by the performance of disintermediated transactions between crypto-assets on different blockchains, and hence also by the related platforms. In this context, a new subset of blockchain analytics research efforts targets the analysis of cross-currency transactions and their traceability through exchanges such as ShapeShift.[116]

4.3.3 *Machine Learning-Based Approaches to Anomaly Detection*

Nowadays, tools of blockchain forensics are ordinarily deployed as part of RegTech solutions that support regulated entities in their compliance activities by providing alerts when unusual patterns are identified—e.g., when a transaction meets predefined standards of suspicion. In this context, 'anomaly detection' consists of processing data to detect patterns that suggest a change in system operations, thus

---

[109] Yin et al. (2019), pp. 1, 5.

[110] Fleder et al. (2015), p. 2.

[111] Lischke and Fabian (2016), p. 4. Reid and Harrigan (2011), pp. 15–17.

[112] Airfoil (2019); The Cryptocurrency Consultant (2019); Paesano (2019).

[113] The Cryptocurrency Consultant (2019); Weber et al. (2019); Koshy et al. (2014).

[114] Wu et al. (2020).

[115] Borreguero Beltrán (2019), p. 30.

[116] Al Jawaheri et al. (2019), p. 6.

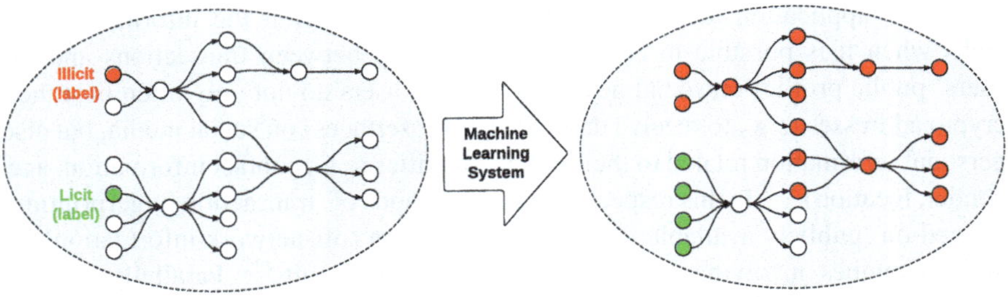

Fig. 4.4 Example of the application of supervised learning for transaction classification. Based on Pocher et al. (2023a)

pinpointing events that are significantly different from the dataset.[117] The important interplay between anomaly detection solutions and the red flag indicators mentioned above will be introduced in Chap. 5 and explored more extensively in Chap. 7. In this section, the goal is to complement the overview of crypto-asset-related analytic approaches by accounting for strategies based on AI and machine learning.

AI-based solutions are increasingly deployed in transaction analytics, and a line of research specifically focuses on machine learning-based forensics.[118] In machine learning, a key distinction is between unsupervised and supervised methods.[119] Unsupervised techniques are usually deployed when there is a lack of real-world labelled (i.e., tagged, annotated) datasets,[120] but the latter arguably guarantee better results when it comes to prediction—e.g., transaction classification. In the AML/CFT domain, there is an overall shortage of large-scale annotated blockchain transaction datasets, due to both the scale of the relevant phenomena but also to the timing of relevant investigations.[121] Hence, the role of analytic companies has emerged as crucial in labelling crypto-asset transaction data.

For instance, providers of RegTech services can annotate a transaction dataset tagging different transactions as licit or illicit based on previous investigations,

[117] Kamišalić et al. (2021).

[118] Machine learning is a part of AI "that exploits data and algorithms to imitate human learning processes, with gradual accuracy improvements [...] in the most diverse contexts, it provides tools that can learn and improve automatically leveraging the vast amount of data available in our age" (Pocher et al., 2023b; Kamišalić et al., 2021). These algorithms show promising results when applied in AML/CFT RegTech solutions, especially in terms of mitigating the shortcomings of rule-based systems, increasing detection rates and limiting false positives.

[119] In the first case, the learning model pursues the discovery of data and patterns previously undetected. In the second case, algorithms are trained using labelled datasets, which means the initial training data must be tagged and annotated by experts (Pocher et al., 2023a).

[120] To address lack of data, various strategies were proposed—e.g., fully synthetic data or simulating unusual accounts within a real-world dataset (Eddin et al., 2021.). Meanwhile, the shortage of real-life datasets led to the deployment of methods of unsupervised and active learning (Lorenz et al., 2021).

[121] Lorenz et al. (2021).

public information (e.g., scandals, scams) or their own proprietary data and methods—e.g., clustering algorithms. The resulting set of labelled transactions can be used to train machine learning algorithms to identify other transactions as licit or illicit—i.e., to perform transaction classification where the model provides a prediction output starting from an annotated dataset (Fig. 4.4). Indeed recent tools deploy supervised machine learning to detect anomalies based on rules of association to pinpoint suspicions. Since in AML/CFT-oriented applications the label of a transaction usually indicates whether it was identified as illicit,[122] a primary challenge is to identify proper classification criteria—e.g., defining how to reach the conclusion that if a transaction is illicit its neighbour transactions also are. Examples of supervised techniques are Decision Trees, Random Forests, Boosting Algorithms, Logistic Regression, Support Vector Classification, k-Nearest Neighbours.[123]

Since every crypto-asset transfer inherently involves a relationship between entities that can be represented using a graph structure, 'transaction graph analysis' emerged as key in blockchain forensics and focused on leveraging the structure of these graphs to identify illicit transactions.[124] Meanwhile, the broader field of machine learning has been experimenting with real-world structured datasets that take the form of graphs or networks—e.g., social networks and knowledge graphs.[125] Hence, some solutions focused on the possibility to create multiple graph types from blockchain data. A set of approaches are based on a variant of neural networks that operates directly on graphs—i.e., graph neural networks.[126] Convolutional neural networks, for instance, extract statistical patterns from large-scale and high-dimensional datasets and can be generalised to graphs.[127] In particular, graph convolutional networks (GCN) aim to learn a function of features on a dataset structured as a graph, and graph attention networks (GAT) can give different importance to each node's edge.[128]

In this context, a supervised learning approach was deployed on the Bitcoin blockchain to predict the type of entities yet not identified.[129] Relatedly, studies

---

[122] Yin et al. (2019); Lorenz et al. (2021).

[123] For an overview of the techniques: Pocher et al. (2023b), pp. 12–13.

[124] Because blockchain transactions are linked by nature, it is possible to create "a graph of transactions that can be of help in the classification process. Given a transaction t, it is possible to collect all the connected transactions and recursively search for other ones up to a certain depth level. Given such a connected graph centred at t, an inspection of the neighbouring transactions and their classified value can aid the classification of t. Each node of the graph (transaction) thus has a set of neighbours that will influence its classification" (Pocher et al., 2023b, p. 15). See also Serena et al. (2022).

[125] Pocher et al. (2023a), p. 10.

[126] You et al. (2020); Kipf and Welling (2016); Marasi and Ferretti (2024).

[127] Defferrard et al. (2016); Kipf and Welling (2016).

[128] Marasi and Ferretti (2024); Pocher et al. (2023b).

[129] Yin et al. (2019). The analytic company Chainalysis provided the dataset and had previously clustered, identified, and categorized a considerable number of addresses manually or through clustering techniques. The authors concluded it is possible to predict if a cluster belongs to predefined categories—e.g., exchange, gambling, mining pool, mixing, ransomware, scam.

benchmarked GCN against various supervised methods,[130] and leveraged random walks on a cryptocurrency graph to characterise distances to previous suspicious activity.[131] Parallelly, a set of works focused on graph-based scores of suspicion based on a detection system leveraging business knowledge on financial flows, without the use of any learning algorithm.[132] Against this backdrop, Pocher et al. (2023b) aim to improve the performance of classifier methods through a combination of machine learning and transaction graph analysis. Notably, this was pursued through the deployment of a GAT-based scheme for transaction classification and an innovative GCN implementation.[133] Relatedly, Marasi and Ferretti (2024) compare various graph neural networks classification methods.

4.4 An Accountability-Based Approach to a Socio-Technical Conundrum

Cyber-libertarians want a cyberspace free from regulatory constraints, where everyone operates anonymously, and nobody is held accountable for their actions (Chap. 3). Although the idea of transposing the anonymity of cash to the online world was appealing, they were not able to create a currency system that could underpin a cashless society, chiefly because Bitcoin's pseudonymity houses "an inherent tension between the two extremes of anonymity and accountability".[134] In all means of payment—more generally, in all means of information exchange—there is a trade-off between privacy (of which anonymity is one aspect) and transparency. Likewise, anonymity and transparency do not only ordinarily coexist, but also embody internal ambivalences. Transparency can bypass trust, but also aid de-anonymisation, and fosters both accountability and surveillance.[135]

Even before Bitcoin, new technologies allowed to pursue monitoring and anonymisation at the same time. Technology can be used to reach opposing goals, and this chapter displays how innovative techniques can generate new pathways to both accountability (e.g., forensics) and unaccountability (e.g., anonymity-enhancing methods). The evolution of the crypto-asset sphere helps single out the trade-offs featured by the Internet and develop an analytical framework to assess them.[136] Not all crypto-asset ecosystems within the anonymity-oriented subset

[130] Weber et al. (2019); Eddin et al. (2021).

[131] Oliveira et al. (2021). In mathematics and computer science, a 'random walk' is a frequently deployed "random process which describes a path including a succession of random steps in the mathematical space" (Xia et al., 2020, p. 95).

[132] Li et al. (2022); Sun et al. (2021).

[133] Pocher et al. (2023b), pp. 20–23.

[134] Yin et al. (2019), p. 64.

[135] Herian (2019).

[136] Magnuson (2020), p. 19.

are equally anonymous. However, it is possible to assess the impact of a given implemented technology on the risk of anonymity and the degree of accountability (or lack thereof). Relatedly, the technological solution underlying an application can embed a specific balance, which in turn is influenced also by aspects related to the ecosystem itself and stakeholder dynamics.

In this respect, the levels of anonymity and transparency are influenced by: (i) the technical side—i.e., privacy tools such as PETs, governance (e.g., centralised vs. decentralised systems), broader architecture of the system (e.g., relationship with other on/off-chain layers); and (ii) the social side—i.e., forensic techniques against the backdrop of users' skills to hinder their efficacy. It is difficult to apply such a detailed and layered account of anonymity and transparency to devise a compliance or regulatory approach. For this reason, it is useful to apply a teleological approach, referring to AML/CFT goals and to its benchmarks when evaluating different systems. After all, in AML/CFT the functional approach plays an important role in accommodating technological advances.[137]

4.4.1 Obfuscation Red Flags and Crypto-Asset Forensics

From a phenomenological perspective, transaction obfuscation depends on the interplay between (i) the combination between laundering 'through' or 'of' crypto-assets, and (ii) forensic techniques. The two types of crypto(-enabled) laundering pursue a similar end-goal: to obfuscate the flow and confuse the traceability chain. In this way, criminals strive to thwart investigative efforts and elude enforcement. Laundering 'through' crypto-assets often encompasses multiple layers of 'crypto-cleansing' because the transition from fiat money to crypto-assets alone does not ensure anonymity in terms of lack of identifiability and traceability, and further steps are necessary to reach obfuscation. To clarify this argument, reference can be made to the example of the illicit journey of the funds laundered by Alice (Fig. 4.2). Indeed, in that circumstance the following may have happened:

1. Assuming the proceeds of crime were originally in fiat money, Alice may have bought her bitcoins (a 'primary' cryptocurrency, that is not anonymity-enhanced, and thus does not feature unlinkability and untraceability) with her credit card or via a wire transfer on a 'basic exchange platform', such as Coinbase. At this point, the regulated entity acquired information on her identity, verified it, and possibly inquired about the origin of her funds.
2. Later she could have exchanged Bitcoins for Monero through an 'advanced/high risk exchange service', such as CryptMixer, that embeds a mixing service. The transaction that moves Bitcoins to the other exchange or to a self-hosted wallet (to then convert it, if the 'basic exchange platform' does not exchange to AECs

[137] Financial Action Task Force (2021b), p. 22.

or Monero specifically), performed from a Coinbase account to CryptMixer, is traced and evaluated by the regulated entity.
3. Most likely, now Alice was holding her Monero on a self-hosted wallet or at an entity offering services of cryptocurrency custody implementing anonymity-enhanced wallets such as Wasabi. Then she could have exchanged her Monero for combinations of Zcash and Dash, by making use of other 'advanced exchanges' and by creating multiple/stealth addresses. She could have also focused on DeFi products and/or made use of DEXes. The operations performed at this point increase the obfuscation of Alice's transaction trail substantially, to avert techniques such as graph analysis and be outside the monitoring eye of regulated entities or LEAs that implement RegTech tools implementing these solutions.
4. Finally, she could have used her funds, stored in a self-hosted wallet, to buy goods and services online. In this respect, Alice could have either made her online purchases on legitimate websites, if retailers accept cryptocurrencies or buy both legal and illegal goods and services on darknet marketplaces. In the latter case, possible purchases include drugs, weapons, human organs, counterfeited currency, cybercrime-as-a-service.
5. Along this journey, she could have likely deployed the array of mechanisms addressed as 'best practices', such as the basic measure to connect to the Internet through a VPN.

The steps taken by Alice aim to sever the links between her transactions and any association to her. She wants neither to be identified as the person making the transfers, nor for her transactions to be linked to one another. Further, her goal is that none of the activities can be traced back to her computer or to off-network information that may be available and possibly linked to her. To sum up, her actions strive to elude forensic methodologies of data-exploitation devised to de-anonymise crypto-asset transactions. Notably, these strategies are among the ones listed within FATF's anonymity-related 'red flag indicators' outlined above,[138] which testifies to how Alice is trying to heighten the degree of anonymity of her operations, in the form of both obfuscation and enhanced disintermediation. Indeed, Alice:

1. transacts in multiple crypto-assets, especially in AECs,
2. changes bitcoins through a centralised exchange and then into AECs,
3. makes use of mixing services,
4. keeps her funds on a self-hosted wallet,
5. deploys anonymous encrypted communication methods (i.e., a VPN service),
6. interacts with questionable service providers—e.g., 'high risk exchanges',
7. transacts on/through DEXes,
8. operates on DeFi platforms and/or buys DeFi products.

Alice's actions show how the teleological approach to the meaning of anonymity (and transparency)—i.e., one that focuses on the purpose, context and end-goal

[138] Financial Action Task Force (2020).

of a concept when defining it—may prove useful when it comes to identifying those elements that are more conducive to illicit activities. To this end, a primary reference can be made to FATF's 'risk indicators' themselves. Given the dangers posed by anonymity-enhanced applications, countries—through their regulatory and supervisory activities—must ensure regulated entities are able to manage and mitigate the risks arising from performing "activities that involve the use of anonymity-enhancing technologies or mechanisms, including but not limited to AECs, mixers, tumblers, privacy wallets and other technologies that obfuscate the identity of the sender, recipient, holder, or beneficial owner".[139] Alternatively, should they not be found able to manage and mitigate (or should they not be able to give sufficient assurances that they are indeed able to manage and mitigate) the risks that arise from performing or being exposed to these anonymity-enhanced activities, these providers should not be permitted to engage in them.[140]

While the crypto-asset sphere challenges existing measures to mitigate and/or prevent the risk of abuse for illicit purposes, techniques of forensic investigation engage in a race to disrupt dangerous dynamics. Because these opponents do not seem to be bound to outrun one another once and for all, any regulatory instrument needs to be constantly updated. Thus, they need to be conceived and drafted in a way that allows it. As the FATF suggests, money laundering is not a victimless crime, and the possibility to cleanse great amount of funds and/or to gather finances through anonymous and untraceable solutions poses a great threat to the international community and financial system. This is not to say cryptocurrencies ought to be collectively marked as shady or illegal. On the contrary, most stakeholders and ecosystems are less anonymous and more traceable than what could be expected. However, while lawmakers and LEAs deploy their forces to include these transactions in the scope of AML/CFT compliance, the online world reaches new heights of unaccountability. While it could be argued that anonymity-enhanced tools are not easy to use by individuals lacking specific expertise, the history of the Internet shows how the evolution of new solutions has over time the potential to provide a great variety of users with opportunities originally in the exclusive hands of experts.

4.4.2 The Multi-Layered Nature of Accountability in the Crypto-Asset Sphere

As outlined so far, in the crypto-asset space the techno-legal trade-off between complete anonymity and full transparency is socio-technical in nature. Thus, the evaluation of these traits may be challenging from an operational perspective. For instance, although the crypto-asset world may seem impenetrable because of

[139] Financial Action Task Force (2021b), p. 55.

[140] Financial Action Task Force (2021b), p. 55.

darknet operations, a given crypto-asset and its network should not be confused with what users or developers do on top of or in parallel to increase the anonymity level of a transaction. Physical cash is always anonymous, not only when used in the black market or hidden in a briefcase. Bitcoin is pseudonymous even if it is used in the dark web, and even if the degree of anonymity may be altered socially, through users' actions to hinder traceability vis-à-vis forensics.

Indeed, in any given use case that presents features of anonymity (or transparency) the trait can be referred to different aspects, such as the payment instrument, some specific elements of it, and/or the whole system. The features could then be influenced by the application of obfuscation techniques, hindering traceability and linkability, or by tools of enhanced disintermediation that deceive traditional intermediary-based regimes. Moreover, the anonymous trait may stem from embedded technologies (within layer 1), from processes that are implemented on top of it (as a layer 2 or as a component of layer 2) and/or from additional behaviours (e.g., user best practices). Accordingly, when evaluating crypto-asset ecosystems or specific transactions, it is possible to assess their levels of anonymity and transparency from different perspectives. For instance, one can focus on the concept of online exchange of information, and/or on their position within the financial services domain and/or on the specific implemented technologies such as DLTs and/or the given governance aspects displayed by a specific use case. Features such as anonymity, transparency and privacy present diversified meanings and degrees in the crypto-assets sphere, and they can pertain to conceptual, ideological, or structural levels of reasoning.

The interplay between the ambivalent principles informing online communication and the financial domain, coupled with the non-binary nature of traits such as anonymity and transparency, testify to the need to set appropriate balances policy-wise. Crypto-assets do not make any difference: the only way to overcome a tension between the traits of anonymity and transparency is to agree on a desirable trade-off. When setting or evaluating these trade-offs, there are elements that resemble issues arising in general from innovative products and services, and other aspects more closely linked to DLTs and crypto-asset specifics, such as cryptography. From this perspective, anonymity and transparency are coexistent values that shaped the crypto-asset sphere. DLTs, when applied in certain ways, exacerbate such traits.

DLTs retain ambivalent features, depending on the perspective. They have been analysed and implemented as solutions to reach seemingly conflicting goals, attempting to leverage their multifold properties to different ends. In addition, the debate between financial privacy and transparency shows how financial confidentiality was discussed before digital technologies. DLTs heightened an existing complexity more linked to the need to reach suitable trade-offs between opposing interests than to the technology. Hence, the regulatory urgency to agree on acceptable balances between non-binary states such as anonymity and transparency does not originate from DLTs. The latter, however, provide insights on the dynamics informing these values—i.e., the crypto-asset space shows how these technologies can unlock opportunities for both lawlessness and accountability—and ways to combine them.

In this context, accountability emerges as the conceptual trait d'union between the different developments. Both obfuscation and disintermediation generate a situation where users are not accountable for their transactions. Likewise, the socio-technical perspective accounts for players and techniques that pursue to increase or decrease accountability for crypto-asset transactions. Indeed, some actors are trying to (provide ways to) avoid regulatory constraints, and some others are trying to re-establish it, engaging in a race that is not likely to end soon. On the ground of the socio-technical nature of crypto-asset ecosystems, the activities performed by this plethora of actors influence the overall character of the domain. Hence, the added challenge brought by crypto-assets when addressing trade-offs between privacy and transparency is not their presence, but rather the composition of their socio-technical elements.

4.5 Conclusions

After the deep dive of Chap. 3 into the notions of anonymity and transparency in the crypto-asset space from an AML/CFT standpoint, this chapter addressed the impact of (a) available methods to obfuscate crypto-asset transactions and, by contrast, (b) forensic techniques deployed to trace these fund flows. To do so, the analysis started from how the unsatisfactory level of anonymity of the Bitcoin network fostered the evolution of (i) anonymity-enhancing strategies applied by different actors at various levels (e.g., application, network), and (ii) methods of transaction analytics to 'follow the money' across the crypto-asset sphere for investigation and compliance. Most of these elements consist of activities performed by stakeholders of crypto-asset ecosystems. Hence, they affect anonymity-transparency trade-offs of relevant crypto-asset socio-technical ecosystems from a 'social' standpoint.

This chapter furthered the application of the teleological approach when evaluating the meaning of features such as anonymity and transparency in the domain at hand. Accordingly, various types of anonymity enhancements were outlined with respect to the traditional phases of the laundering process. This highlighted not only the growing relevance of virtual-to-virtual layering schemes, but also the difference between laundering 'of' and 'through' crypto-assets. Relatedly, it outlined the understanding of anonymity that emerges from the risk indicators published by the FATF. Since various aspects are reported without a clear classification of the ways in which anonymity can be enhanced, it addressed the relevant risk factors individually and performed an assessment of whether their anonymous character pertains to obfuscation (e.g., AECs, mixing, PETs), enhanced disintermediation (e.g., DEXes, DeFi), or is related to other specific circumstances.

Moreover, this chapter argued that in different scenarios the anonymous trait may stem from embedded technologies, processes that are implemented on top of it and/or also additional behaviours (e.g., user best practices). Parallelly, it provided an overview of the main deployed forensic approaches, from the chief standpoint of the techniques of transaction network analysis, which usually leverage graph visualisation tools, underlining the role of clustering. Further, recent applications of AI for anomaly detection were introduced, outlining the value of the combination between machine learning-based approaches and graph analysis.

This investigation displays how anonymity enhancements and forensic techniques are engaging in a never-ending race. It follows that any regulatory instrument needs either to be constantly updated or conceived in a way that grants the flexibility to adapt to continuous technological advances. In this respect, specific benchmarks can be identified to differentiate between the various degrees of anonymity enshrined by crypto-asset ecosystems without running into the risk of overfitting. It is in this context that the concept of accountability, ensured by the auditability of relevant transactions, emerges as pivotal. Indeed, both obfuscation and disintermediation generate a situation where users are not accountable for their activity (in this case, for their transactions). Likewise, the socio-technical perspective accounts for players and techniques that pursue to increase or decrease accountability for crypto-asset activities.

In this scenario, the feature of auditability assumes that access to a given type of information is allowed in certain circumstances, by specific actors and for a specific purpose, in a way that does not breach confidentiality. Indeed, confidentiality and auditability, in the same way as anonymity/privacy and transparency, are not a zero-sum game, but generate different trade-offs that can be balanced depending on the intended objective. To this end, crypto-asset schemes and transactions can be assessed in term of their privacy-transparency and confidentiality-auditability trade-offs by referring to specific benchmarks such as the implementation of certain PETs. Chapter 6 elaborates on how these yardsticks can play out in the evaluation of CBDC use cases, and on what type of classifications can be built on top of it.

References

Airfoil. (2019). *De-anonymising anonymous crypto services*. Medium DDI. https://medium.datadriveninvestor.com/de-anonymizing-anonymous-crypto-services-a80258132e5b

Al Jawaheri, H., Al Sabah, M., Boshmaf, Y., & Erbad, A. (2019). Deanonymising Tor hidden service users through bitcoin transactions analysis. *Computers & Security, 89*. https://doi.org/10.1016/j.cose.2019.10168

Amarasinghe, N., Boyen, X., & McKague, M. (2019). A survey of anonymity of cryptocurrencies. In *Proceedings of the Australasian Computer Science Week Multiconference*. https://doi.org/10.1145/3290688.3290693

Amarasinghe, N., Boyen, X., & McKague, M. (2021). The complex shape of anonymity in cryptocurrencies: Case studies from a systematic approach. In N. Borisov & C. Diaz (Eds.), *Proceedings of the International Conference on Financial Cryptography and Data Security*, volume 12674 of LNCS. Springer. https://doi.org/10.1007/978-3-662-64322-8_10

Androulaki, E., Karame, G. O., Roeschlin, M., Scherer, T., & Capkun, S. (2013). Evaluating user privacy in bitcoin. In A.-R. Sadeghi (Ed.), *Proceedings of the International Conference on Financial Cryptography and Data Security*, Berlin, Heidelberg (pp. 34–51). Springer Berlin Heidelberg. https://doi.org/10.1007/978-3-642-39884-1_4

Avarikioti, Z., Pietrzak, K., Salem, I., Schmid, S., Samarth Tiwari, & Yeo, M. (2021). *Hide & seek: Privacy-preserving rebalancing on payment channel networks*. Cryptology ePrint Archive, Paper 2021/1401. Available at: https://eprint.iacr.org/2021/1401

Barbereau, T., Ermolaev, E., Brennecke, M., Hartwich, E., & Sedlmeir, J. (2023). Beyond a fistful of tumblers: Toward a taxonomy of Ethereum-based mixers. In *Proceedings of the 44th International Conference on Information Systems (ICIS)*. https://aisel.aisnet.org/icis2023/cyber_security/cyber_security/13

Barbereau, T., Sedlmeir, J., Smethurst, R., Fridgen, G., & Rieger, A. (2022). Tokenization and regulatory compliance for art and collectibles markets: From regulators' demands for transparency to investors' demands for privacy. In M. C. Lacity & H. Treiblmaier (Eds.), *Blockchains and the token economy*. Springer. https://doi.org/10.1007/978-3-030-95108-5_8

Bartoletti, M., Carta, S., Cimoli, T., & Saia, R. (2020). Dissecting Ponzi schemes on Ethereum: Identification, analysis, and impact. *Future Generation Computer Systems*, *102*, 259–277. https://doi.org/10.1016/j.future.2019.08.014.

Béres, F., Seres, I. A., Benczúr, A. A., & Quintyne-Collins, M. (2021). Blockchain is watching you: Profiling and deanonymising Ethereum users. In *Proceedings of the 3rd IEEE International Conference on Decentralized Applications and Infrastructures (DAPPS)*. https://doi.org/10.1109/DAPPS52256.2021.00013

Biryukov, A., & Tikhomirov, S. (2019). Deanonymisation and linkability of cryptocurrency transactions based on network analysis. In *Proceedings of the 4th IEEE European Symposium on Security and Privacy* (pp. 172–184). https://doi.org/10.1109/EuroSP.2019.00022

Blandin, A., Pieters, G., Wu, Y., Eisermann, T., Dek, A., Sean Taylor, & Njoki, D. (2020). *3rd global cryptoasset benchmarking study*. https://www.jbs.cam.ac.uk/wp-content/uploads/2021/01/2021-ccaf-3rd-global-cryptoasset-benchmarking-study.pdf

Borreguero Beltrán, Á. (2019). *A forensics approach to blockchain*. Master's thesis, Universitat Politècnica de Catalunya. http://hdl.handle.net/2117/168894. Master Thesis in Telecommunications Engineering

Chen, W., Zheng, Z., Ngai, E. C.-H., Zheng, P., & Zhou, Y. (2019). Exploiting blockchain data to detect smart Ponzi schemes on Ethereum. *IEEE Access*, *7*(c), 37575–86. https://doi.org/10.1109/ACCESS.2019.2905769

CipherTrace. (2021). *Cryptocurrency crime and anti-money laundering report*. https://ciphertrace.com/wp-content/uploads/2021/05/CipherTrace-Cryptocurrency-Crime-and-Anti-Money-Laundering-Report-May-2021-051221b.pdf

Dashkevich, N., Counsell, S., & Destefanis, G. (2020). Blockchain applications for central banks: A systematic mapping study. *IEEE Access*, *8*, 139918–139952. https://doi.org/10.1109/ACCESS.2020.3012295

De Haro-Olmo, F. J., Varela-Vaca, Á. J., & Álvarez Bermejo, J. A. (2020). Blockchain from the perspective of privacy and anonymisation: A systematic literature review. *MDPI Sensors*, *20*, 7171. https://doi.org/10.3390/s20247171

de Koker, L., & Goldbarsht, D. (2024). Towards a global approach to combating financial crime. In D. Goldbarsht & L. de Koker (Eds.), *Financial crime, law and governance: Navigating challenges in different contexts*, volume 116 of *Ius Gentium: Comparative perspectives on law and justice series*. Springer. https://doi.org/10.1007/978-3-031-59547-9_1

de Rechtspraak. (2024). *Developer of tornado cash gets jail sentence for laundering billions of dollars in cryptocurrency*. https://www.rechtspraak.nl/Organisatie-en-contact/Organisatie/Rechtbanken/Rechtbank-Oost-Brabant/Nieuws/Paginas/Developer-of-Tornado-Cash-gets-jail-sentence-for-laundering-billions-of-dollars-in-cryptocurrency.aspx

Defferrard, M., Bresson, X., & Vandergheynst, P. (2016). Convolutional neural networks on graphs with fast localized spectral filtering. In *Proceedings of 30th Conference on Neural Information Processing Systems*. https://doi.org/10.48550/arXiv.1606.09375

Desmond, D. B., Lacey, D., & Salmon, P. (2019). Evaluating cryptocurrency laundering as a complex socio-technical system: A systematic literature review. *Journal of Money Laundering Control*, *22*(3), 480–97. https://doi.org/10.1108/JMLC-10-2018-0063

Directive (EU) 2018/1673. (2018). Directive (EU) 2018/1673 of the European Parliament and the Council on combating money laundering by criminal law. http://data.europa.eu/eli/dir/2018/1673/oj

Du, H., Che, Z., Shen, M., Zhu, L., & Hu, J. (2024). Breaking the anonymity of Ethereum mixing services using graph feature learning. *IEEE Transactions on Information Forensics and Security*, *19*, 616–631. https://doi.org/10.1109/TIFS.2023.3326984

Ecorys and Centre for European Policy Studies. (2017). *Study on an eu initiative for a restriction on payments in cash*. https://ec.europa.eu/info/sites/default/files/economy-finance/final_report_study_on_an_eu_initative_ecorys_180206.pdf

Eddin, A. N., Bono, J., Aparício, D., Polido, D., Ascensão, J. T., Bizarro, P., & Ribeiro, P. (2021). *Anti-money laundering alert optimisation using machine learning with graphs*. https://arxiv.org/abs/2112.07508

European Central Bank and Bank of Japan. (2020). *Balancing confidentiality and auditability in a distributed ledger environment*. https://www.ecb.europa.eu/paym/intro/publications/pdf/ecb.miptopical200212.en.pdf

Fanti, G., Venkatakrishnan, S. B., Bakshi, S., Denby, B., Bhargava, S., Miller, A., & Viswanath, P. (2018). Dandelion++: Lightweight cryptocurrency networking with formal anonymity guarantees. In *Proceedings of the ACM on Measurement and Analysis of Computing Systems* (Vol. 2, No. 2, pp. 1–35). https://doi.org/10.1145/3224424

Fanusie, Y. J. (2020). Central bank digital currencies: The threat from money launderers and how to stop them. In *The Digital Social Contract: A Lawfare Paper Series* (pp. 1–23). https://www.lawfaremedia.org/article/central-bank-digital-currencies-threat-money-launderers-and-how-stop-them

Federal Bureau of Investigation. (2023). *Tornado cash co-founders accused of helping cyber-criminals launder stolen crypto*. https://www.fbi.gov/news/stories/tornado-cash-co-founders-accused-of-helping-cybercriminals-launder-stolen-crypto

Ferretti, S., & D'Angelo, G. (2019). On the Ethereum blockchain structure: A complex networks theory perspective. *Concurrency and Computation*, *32*(12). https://doi.org/10.1002/cpe.5493

Financial Action Task Force. (2014). *Virtual currencies – key definitions and potential AML/CFT risks*. https://www.fatf-gafi.org/media/fatf/documents/reports/Virtual-currency-key-definitions-and-potential-aml-cft-risks.pdf

Financial Action Task Force. (2020). *Virtual assets red flag indicators of money laundering and terrorist financing*. https://www.fatf-gafi.org/media/fatf/documents/recommendations/Virtual-Assets-Red-Flag-Indicators.pdf

Financial Action Task Force. (2021a). *Second 12-month review of the revised FATF standards on virtual assets and virtual asset service providers*. https://www.fatf-gafi.org/media/fatf/documents/recommendations/Second-12-Month-Review-Revised-FATF-Standards-Virtual-Assets-VASPS.pdf

Financial Action Task Force. (2021b). *Virtual assets and virtual asset service providers - Updated guidance for a risk-based approach*. https://www.fatf-gafi.org/publications/fatfrecommendations/documents/guidance-rba-virtual-assets-2021.html

Fleder, M., Kester, M. S., & Pillai, S. (2015). *Bitcoin transaction graph analysis*. https://arxiv.org/abs/1502.01657

Fruth, J. (2018). *Crypto-cleansing: Strategies fight digital money laundering and sanctions evasion*. https://www.reuters.com/article/bc-finreg-aml-cryptocurrency-idUSKCN1FX29I

Furneaux, N. (2018). *Investigating cryptocurrencies: Understanding, extracting, and analyzing blockchain evidence*. Wiley. https://ieeexplore.ieee.org/servlet/opac?bknumber=9820817

Gelemerova, L. (2009). On the frontline against money-laundering: The regulatory minefield. *Crime, Law and Social Change*, *52*(1), 33–55. https://doi.org/10.1007/s10611-008-9175-8

Gross, J., Sedlmeir, J., Babel, M., Bechtel, A., & Schellinger, B. (2021). Designing a central bank digital currency with support for cash-like privacy. *SSRN Electronic Journal*. https://doi.org/10.2139/ssrn.3891121

Harvey, J., & Branco-Illodo, I. (2020). Why cryptocurrencies want privacy: A review of political motivations and branding expressed in "privacy coin" whitepapers. *Journal of Political Marketing, 19*(1–2), 107–136. https://doi.org/10.1080/15377857.2019.1652223

Herian, R. (2019). *Regulating blockchain: Critical perspectives in law and technology*. Routledge. https://doi.org/10.4324/9780429489815

Ince, P., Liu, J. K., & Zhang, P. (2018). Adding confidential transactions to cryptocurrency IOTA with bulletproofs. In *Proceedings of the International Conference on Network and System Security* (pp. 32–45). https://doi.org/10.1007/978-3-030-02744-5_3

Irwin, A. S. M., & Dawson, C. (2019). Following the cyber money trail: Global challenges when investigating ransomware attacks and how regulation can help. *Journal of Money Laundering Control, 22*(1), 110–131. https://doi.org/10.1108/JMLC-08-2017-0041

Kamišalić, A., Kramberger, R., & Fister Jr., I. (2021). Synergy of blockchain technology and data mining techniques for anomaly detection. *Applied Sciences, 11*(17). https://doi.org/10.3390/app11177987

Kipf, T. N., & Welling, M. (2016). Semi-supervised classification with graph convolutional networks. In *Proceedings of the International Conference on Learning Representations*. https://arxiv.org/abs/1609.02907

Koshy, P., Koshy, D., & McDaniel, P. (2014). An analysis of anonymity in bitcoin using p2p network traffic. In *Proceedings of the International Conference on Financial Cryptography and Data Security* (Vol. 8437, pp. 469–85). https://doi.org/10.1007/978-3-662-45472-5_30

Li, Y., Yang, G., Susilo, W., Yu, Y., Ho Au, M., & Liu, D. (2021). Traceable monero: Anonymous cryptocurrency with enhanced accountability. *IEEE Transactions on Dependable and Secure Computing, 18*(2), 679–691. https://doi.org/10.1109/TDSC.2019.2910058

Li, Z., Xiang, Z., Gong, W., & Wang, H. (2022). Unified model for collective and point anomaly detection using stacked temporal convolution networks. *Applied Intelligence, 52*(3), 3118–3131. https://doi.org/10.1007/s10489-021-02559-0

Lischke, M., & Fabian, B. (2016). Analyzing the bitcoin network: The first four years. *Future Internet, 8*(1). https://doi.org/10.3390/fi8010007

Lorenz, J., Silva, M. I., Aparício, D., Ascensão, J. T., & Bizarro, P. (2021). Machine learning methods to detect money laundering in the bitcoin blockchain in the presence of label scarcity. In *Proceedings of the First ACM International Conference on AI in Finance*. https://doi.org/10.1145/3383455.3422549

Mabunda, S. (2018). Cryptocurrency: The new face of cyber money laundering. In *Proceedings of the International Conference on Advances in Big Data, Computing and Data Communication Systems* (pp. 1–6). https://doi.org/10.1109/ICABCD.2018.8465467

Magnuson, W. (2020). *Blockchain democracy: Technology, law and the rule of the crowd*. Cambridge University Press. https://doi.org/10.1017/9781108687294

Marasi, S., & Ferretti, S. (2024). Anti-money laundering in cryptocurrencies through graph neural networks: A comparative study. In *Proceedings of the IEEE Consumer Communications & Networking Conference (CCNC)* (pp. 272–277). https://doi.org/10.1109/CCNC51664.2024.10454631

Matanky-Becker, R. (2024). High-end and cash-based money laundering: Defining and disaggregating complex phenomena. *European Journal on Criminal Policy and Research*. https://doi.org/10.1007/s10610-024-09579-9

Maupin, J. (2017). Mapping the global legal landscape of blockchain technologies. In *CIGI Papers*. https://www.cigionline.org/sites/default/files/documents/Paper

Meiklejohn, S., Pomarole, M., Jordan, G., Levchenko, K., McCoy, D., Voelker, G. M., & Savage, S. (2016). A fistful of bitcoins: Characterizing payments among men with no names. *Communications of the ACM, 59*(4), 86–93. https://doi.org/10.1145/2896384

Moreno-Sanchez, P., Zafar, M. B., & Kate, A. (2016). Listening to whispers of ripple: Linking wallets and deanonymising transactions in the ripple network. In *Proceedings on Privacy Enhancing Technologies Symposium* (Vol. 4). https://doi.org/10.1515/popets-2016-0049

Nadler, M., & Schär, F. (2023). Tornado cash and blockchain privacy: A primer for economists and policymakers. *Federal Reserve Bank of St. Louis Review*, 1–15. https://doi.org/10.20955/r.105.122-136

Neudecker, T., & Hartenstein, H. (2017). Could network information facilitate address clustering in bitcoin? In *Proceedings of the International Conference on Financial Cryptography and Data Security* (pp. 155–169). https://doi.org/10.1007/978-3-319-70278-0_9

Ober, M., Katzenbeisser, S., & Hamacher, K. (2013). Structure and anonymity of the bitcoin transaction graph. *Future Internet*, *5*(2). https://doi.org/10.3390/fi5020237

Oliveira, C., Torres, J., Silva, M. I., Aparício, D., Ascensão, J. T., & Bizarro, P. (2021). *Guiltywalker: Distance to illicit nodes in the bitcoin network*. https://arxiv.org/abs/2102.05373

Orr, D. A., & Lancaster, D. M. (2018). Cryptocurrency and the blockchain: A discussion of forensic needs. *International Journal of Cyber-Security and Digital Forensics*, *7*(4), 420–435. https://api.semanticscholar.org/CorpusID:199006517

Paesano, F. (2019). *Regulating cryptocurrencies: Challenges & considerations*. https://baselgovernance.org/publications/working-paper-28-regulating-cryptocurrencies-challenges-and-considerations

Phan, T. (2021). *Exploring blockchain forensics*. https://www.isaca.org/resources/news-and-trends/isaca-now-blog/2021/exploring-blockchain-forensics

Pocher, N. (2023). *Distributed ledger technologies between anonymity and transparency: AML/CFT regulation of cryptocurrency ecosystems in the EU*. PhD thesis, Alma Mater Studiorum Università di Bologna, KU Leuven, Universitat Autònoma de Barcelona. 10.48676/unibo/amsdottorato/10659

Pocher, N., & Veneris, A. (2022). Privacy and transparency in CBDCs: A regulation-by-design AML/CFT scheme. *IEEE Transactions on Network and Service Management*, *19*(2), 1776–1788. https://doi.org/10.1109/TNSM.2021.3136984

Pocher, N., & Zichichi, M. Towards CBDC-based machine-to-machine payments in consumer IoT. In *Proceedings of the 37th ACM/SIGAPP Symposium on Applied Computing*. https://doi.org/10.1145/3477314.3507078

Pocher, N., Zichichi, M., & Ferretti, S. (2023a). The AML/CFT/CPF application of on-chain analytics and machine learning: Overview and open issues. In *Proceedings of Artificial Intelligence Governance Ethics and Law (AIGEL)*. https://ceur-ws.org/Vol-3531/SPaper_11.pdf

Pocher, N., Zichichi, M., Merizzi, F., Shafiq, M. Z., & Ferretti, S. (2023b). Detecting anomalous cryptocurrency transactions: An AML/CFT application of machine learning-based forensics. *Electronic Markets*, *33*(1). https://doi.org/10.1007/s12525-023-00654-3

Puzis, R., Barshap, G., Zilberman, P., & Leiba, O. (2019). Controllable privacy preserving blockchain: Fiatchain: Distributed privacy preserving cryptocurrency with law enforcement capabilities. In *Proceedings of the Cyber Security Cryptography and Machine Learning – 3rd International Symposium (CSCML)* (Vol. 11527). Springer. https://doi.org/10.1007/978-3-030-20951-3_16

Quiniou, M. (2019). *Blockchain: The advent of disintermediation*. Wiley-ISTE Ltd.

Regulation (EU) 2023/1113. (2023). Regulation (EU) 2023/1113 of the European Parliament and of the Council of 31 May 2023 on information accompanying transfers of funds and certain crypto-assets and amending directive (EU) 2015/849 (recast). http://data.europa.eu/eli/reg/2023/1113/oj

Reid, F., & Harrigan, M. (2011). An analysis of anonymity in the bitcoin system. In *Proceedings of the IEEE Third International Conference on Privacy, Security, Risk and Trust and 2011 IEEE Third International Conference on Social Computing* (pp. 1318–1326). https://doi.org/10.1109/PASSAT/SocialCom.2011.79

Reynolds, P., & Irwin, A. S. M. (2017). Tracking digital footprint: Anonymity within the bitcoin system. *Journal of Money Laundering Control*, *20*(2), 172–89. https://doi.org/10.1108/JMLC-07-2016-0027

Serena, L., Ferretti, S., & D'Angelo, G. (2022). Cryptocurrencies activity as a complex network: Analysis of transaction graphs. *Peer-to-Peer Networking and Applications, 15*, 839–853. https://doi.org/10.1007/s12083-021-01220-4

Shilina, S. (2021). *What is mimblewimble, and how does it work?* https://cointelegraph.com/news/what-is-mimblewimble-and-how-does-it-work

Silva Ramalho, D., & Igreja Matos, N. (2021). What we do in the (digital) shadows: Anti-money laundering regulation and a bitcoin-mixing criminal problem. *ERA Forum, 22*, 487–506. https://doi.org/10.1007/s12027-021-00676-4

Sun, X., Zhang, J., Zhao, Q., Liu, S., Chen, J., Zhuang, R., Shen, H., & Cheng, X. (2021). Cubeflow: Money laundering detection with coupled tensors. In *Proceedings of Pacific-Asia Conference on Knowledge Discovery and Data Mining*. https://api.semanticscholar.org/CorpusID:232320361

Sun, Y., & Zhang, Y. (2018a). *Privacy in cryptocurrencies: An overview*. Medium. https://medium.com/@yi.sun/privacy-in-cryptocurrencies-d4b268157f6c

Sun, Y., & Zhang, Y. (2018b). *Privacy in cryptocurrencies: Mixing-based approaches*. Medium. https://medium.com/@yi.sun/privacy-in-cryptocurrencies-mixing-based-approaches-ce08d0040c88.

Tennant, L. (2017). *Improving the anonymity of the IOTA cryptocurrency*. https://laurencetennant.com/papers/anonymity-iota.pdf

The Cryptocurrency Consultant. (2019). *Crypto forensics: How the blockchain convicts criminals*. Medium The Startup.

Tian, H., Luo, P., & Su, Y. (2020). A group signature based digital currency system. In Z. Zheng, H.-N. Dai, M. Tang, & X. Chen (Eds.), *Proceedings of the International Conference on Blockchain and Trustworthy Systems* (pp. 3–14). Springer Singapore.

Torra, V. (2017). *Data privacy: Foundations, new developments and the big data challenge*. Springer Cham. https://doi.org/10.1007/978-3-319-57358-8

U.S. Department of the Treasury. (2022). *Press release. U.S. treasury sanctions notorious virtual currency mixer tornado cash*. https://home.treasury.gov/news/press-releases/jy0916

Weber, M., Domeniconi, G., Chen, J., Weidele, D. K. I., Bellei, C., Robinson, T., & Leiserson, C. E. (2019). Anti-money laundering in bitcoin: Experimenting with graph convolutional networks for financial forensics. In *Proceedings of the Conference on Knowledge Discovery and Data Mining, Workshop on Anomaly Detection in Finance*. ACM. https://arxiv.org/abs/1908.02591

Wu, M., McTighe, W., Wang, K., Seres, I. A., Bax, N., Puebla, M., Mendez, M., Carrone, F., De Mattey, T., Demaestri, H. O., Nicolini, M., & Fontana, P. (2022). *Tutela: An open-source tool for assessing user-privacy on Ethereum and tornado cash*. https://arxiv.org/pdf/2201.06811.pdf

Wu, Y., Tao, F., Liu, L., Gu, J., Panneerselvam, J., Zhu, R., & Shahzad, M. N. (2020). A bitcoin transaction network analytic method for future blockchain forensic investigation. *IEEE Transactions on Network Science and Engineering, 8*(2). https://doi.org/10.1109/TNSE.2020.2970113

Xia, F., Liu, J., Nie, H., Fu, Y., Wan, L., & Kong, X. (2020). Random walks: A review of algorithms and applications. *IEEE Transactions on Emerging Topics in Computational Intelligence, 4*(2), 95–107. https://doi.org/10.1109/TETCI.2019.2952908

Yin, H. H. S., Langenheldt, K., Harlev, M., Mukkamala, R. R., & Vatrapu, R. (2019). Regulating cryptocurrencies: A supervised machine learning approach to de-anonymising the bitcoin blockchain. *Journal of Management Information Systems, 36*(1). https://doi.org/10.1080/07421222.2018.1550550

You, J., Ying, Z., & Leskovec, J. (2020). Design space for graph neural networks. In *Proceedings of the 34th Conference on Neural Information Processing Systems*. https://proceedings.neurips.cc/paper_files/paper/2020/file/c5c3d4fe6b2cc463c7d7ecba17cc9de7-Paper.pdf

Yousaf, H., Kappos, G., & Meiklejohn, S. (2019). Tracing transactions across cryptocurrency ledgers. In *Proceedings of the 28th USENIX Security Symposium*. https://www.usenix.org/system/files/sec19-yousaf_0.pdf

Yuen, T. H. (2019). Pachain: Private, authenticated and auditable consortium blockchain. In *Proceedings of the International Conference on Cryptology and Network Security* (pp. 214–234). Springer. https://doi.org/10.1007/978-3-030-31578-8_12

Yuen, T. H. (2020). Pachain: Private, authenticated & auditable consortium blockchain and its implementation. *Future Generation Computer Systems, 112*. https://doi.org/10.1016/j.future.2020.05.011

Zhang, Y., & Sun, Y. (2019). Privacy in cryptocurrencies: Zero-knowledge and zk-SNARKs (1/2). Medium. https://medium.com/@krzhang/privacy-in-cryptocurrencies-zero-knowledge-and-zk-snarks-1-2

Chapter 5
AML/CFT and Crypto-Assets: EU Law and Global Standards

5.1 Introduction

Some concepts underlying the AML/CFT regime were mentioned in the previous chapters, as they depict the fil rouge between the different parts of the analysis. Although this regulatory domain may be perceived as a single entity with clear goals and predefined objectives, however, despite international efforts it would be a mistake to think only one AML/CFT framework exists today. Indeed, jurisdictions hold discretionary powers in setting their own rules, and the motives of different regimes generate political debates and, at times, even heated controversies.

The measures to prevent and repress the misuse of the financial system for illegal purposes comprise two different angles: (i) criminal sanctions applied to those performing illegal deeds, generally on an individual basis and in some jurisdictions also at an entity-level;[1] and (ii) rules placing a set of compliance and 'active cooperation' duties on regulated entities, qualified in various ways depending on the legal system—e.g., civil, administrative.[2] The latter category of provisions is the main target of this work, but the two sets of norms share core goals and a certain share of definitions. Regulatory guidelines are given at the international level from

[1] Schemes of liability of legal persons are demanded by Articles 7 and 8 of Directive (EU) 2018/1673 (e.g., 'corporate liability for criminal offences'). Examples of frameworks of liability of legal entities are the Italian responsabilità amministrativa degli enti (derivante da reato) as per the Italian Legislative Decree 231/2001, as amended, and the Spanish responsabilidad penal de las personas jurídicas as per Article 31bis of the Spanish Criminal Code. Article 31bis was introduced by Organic Law 5/2010 and amended by Organic Law 1/2015.

[2] The boundaries between civil, administrative, and criminal frameworks may not be clearly delineated in all legal systems. Usually, there is a special substantial and procedural regime. Frequently, different sanctions (whose qualification depends on the severity of the deed) target violations of various norms, and different norms target different actors—e.g., individuals, corporate entities, intermediaries.

N. Pocher, *Crypto-Asset Ecosystems and the EU Anti-Money Laundering Framework*, Law, Governance and Technology Series 76,
https://doi.org/10.1007/978-3-031-94698-1_5

both perspectives, albeit with different degrees of bindingness depending on the instrument.

Both regulatory responses bear upon sensitive areas that are intertwined with the given socio-economic context—e.g., organised crime-related factors, tax crimes such as tax evasion, and fiscal policies. It follows that they tend to be in a political limelight and exposed to territorial-based fragmentation. Nonetheless, international efforts have been made towards cooperation and harmonisation. Criminal law features sovereignty concerns and is traditionally of national competence, which makes approximation of laws more complex. Illustratively, in the process of EU integration its harmonisation has been subject to specific conditions.

This chapter brings together different elements to provide the foundations for the arguments of Chap. 6 and the techno-regulatory analysis of Chap. 7. AML/CFT provisions are at the heart of it, together with their relationship with the crypto-asset space. The investigation is also based on the findings of the previous chapters: (i) the AML/CFT regime established at the EU level must be analysed considering its position within a regulatory system chaired by the global standardisation activity of the FATF, and (ii) the socio-technical and multi-layered nature of the anonymity trait of crypto-asset ecosystems must be taken into account when addressing the topic from a regulatory viewpoint. These considerations depict a hybrid nature of this chapter: it addresses on the one hand EU legislation and standardisation, and on the other hand technical and regulatory standardisation.

Accordingly, the chapter covers the following topics: (a) the core aspects of AML/CFT provisions affecting crypto-asset ecosystems and stakeholders; (b) the diachronic link between AML/CFT and the perception of crypto-asset anonymity; (c) the landscape of global financial regulation, where both FATF's and EU measures are positioned; (d) the presence of siloed technical and regulatory standardisation; (e) FATF's approach to the extension of its guidance to crypto-assets; (f) the main AML/CFT duties and the extent to which the framework suits crypto-assets; (g) the EU AML Package and the creation of a EU-wide Authority, its techno-regulatory role, and the crypto travel rule; and finally (h) how the challenge of attribution mirrors the problem of anonymity and unaccountability outlined in the previous chapters.

5.1.1 Ratio and Evolution of AML/CFT Regimes

The ultimate goal of AML/CFT measures is to prevent criminals from enjoying the economic profit of illicit activities, thwarting their capacity to disguise the origin of funds and provide them with a legitimate appearance. For this reason, when the framework was established in the 1970s and 1980s the focus was on proceeds of organised criminal activities with substantial returns—e.g., trafficking in drugs and illegal firearms and corruption.[3] The crimes that generate proceeds

---

[3] de Koker and Goldbarsht (2024b).

whose laundering is considered by law as money laundering are dubbed 'predicate offences'. Indeed, money laundering is a subsequent offence, or delictum subsequens, to a main offence, dubbed predicate offence or delictum principale. The FATF's Glossary defines 'proceeds' as "any property derived from or obtained, directly or indirectly, through the commission of an offence".[4] As explored below, predicate offences have gone through an important evolution.

Another key evolution in the criminal treatment of money laundering relates to the qualification of 'self-laundering'—i.e., the same person perpetrates both the predicate offence and the laundering. Traditionally, the latter was absorbed in the primary offence, as the secondary conduct is performed in relation to the first one. Later, at the international and EU levels the criminalisation of self-laundering emerged as advisable. The notions of predicate offences and self-laundering are not only useful in a criminal law context. The definition of what qualifies as money laundering is a prerequisite to apply AML/CFT measures; it qualifies the illicit nature of the proceeds themselves, which depends on how predicate offences are construed. Hence, attempts were made to establish a global minimum standard. Several treaties of the United Nations (UN) and the Council of Europe play a key role in this.[5]

According to the FATF, the international AML/CFT standard-setter, money laundering should be criminalised based on the Vienna and Palermo Conventions, terrorist financing as per the Terrorist Financing Convention, and financial sanctions should be implemented as per UN Security Council resolutions on the prevention and suppression of terrorism and terrorist financing, and the prevention, suppression and disruption of proliferations of weapons of mass destruction and its financing.[6] Likewise, money laundering must be interpreted to encompass "all serious offences, with a view to including the widest range of predicate offences".[7]

Well before the advent of the 'blockchain hype' and the popularisation of crypto-assets, the deployment of 'follow the money' techniques had emerged as a pivotal tool to investigate the activities of criminal groups and constrain their business. The subtraction of economic resources to criminals mostly consists of preventing them from disguising the nature of their income and re-investing clean

[4] Financial Action Task Force (2012).

[5] Vienna Convention Against Illicit Traffic in Narcotic Drugs and Psychotropic Substances (UN General Assembly, 1988), Convention for Suppression of Financing of Terrorism (UN General Assembly, 1999), Palermo Convention against Transnational Organised Crime and Protocols against human trafficking, migrants' smuggling, illicit manufacturing and trafficking in firearms (UN General Assembly, 2000a,b,c, 2001), Mérida Convention against Corruption (UN General Assembly, 2003), Strasbourg Convention on Laundering, Search, Seizure and Confiscation of the Proceeds from Crime (Council of Europe, 1990), Warsaw Convention (Council of Europe, 2005).

[6] FATF Recommendations 3, 5, 6 and 7. Financial Action Task Force (2012).

[7] FATF Recommendation 3. Financial Action Task Force (2012). Furthermore, not only the financing of criminal acts should be criminalised, but also that of terrorist organisations and individuals regardless of existing terrorist acts (FATF Recommendation 5). 'Proliferation financing risk' is strictly related to the "potential breach, non-implementation or evasion of the targeted financial sanctions obligations" (Interpretative Note to FATF Recommendation 1, Paragraph 3).

money in fruitful ways. In this regard, Chap. 4 addressed the laundering 'process', underlining its conceptual value. From this perspective, one may focus on the 'conducts/behaviours' that compliance frameworks aim to avoid.

The notion of money laundering comprises the efforts to hide the illegal origin of funds and those to channel into criminal activities funds earned in a lawful way.[8] Also by means of reference to Article 3(1–5) of Directive (EU) 2018/1673, Article 2(1) of Regulation (EU) 2024/1624 (the AML Regulation) defines as money laundering the following intentional conducts:[9]

(a) "the conversion or transfer of property, knowing that such property is derived from criminal activity, for the purpose of concealing or disguising the illicit origin of the property or of assisting any person who is involved in the commission of such an activity to evade the legal consequences of that person's action";
(b) "the concealment or disguise of the true nature, source, location, disposition, movement, rights with respect to, or ownership of, property, knowing that such property is derived from criminal activity";
(c) "the acquisition, possession or use of property, knowing at the time of receipt, that such property was derived from criminal activity";
(d) "aiding and abetting, inciting and attempting to commit that conduct, whether the activities which generated the property to be laundered were carried out on the territory of a Member State or on that of a third country".

As provided for by Article 1(3) of the 5AMLD,[10] Article 3(1)(5) of Directive (EU) 2018/1673 included self-laundering.[11] By means of reference to Article 11 of Directive (EU) 2017/541, Article 2(1)(2) of Regulation (EU) 2024/1624 defines terrorist financing as the intentional provision or collection of "funds, by any means, directly or indirectly, with the intention that they be used, or in the knowledge that they are to be used, in full or in part, to commit, or to contribute to the commission of, any of the offences referred to in Articles 3 to 10 of Directive (EU) 2017/541".

5.1.2 *What About Crypto-Assets? The Dark Web and the Silk Road*

The previous chapters already depicted how the crypto-asset sphere has been perceived as increasingly risky. This spurred regulatory initiatives targeting the

---

[8] Goforth (2021), p. 9.

[9] Article 2(5) provides that "knowledge, intent or purpose required as an element of that conduct may be inferred from objective factual circumstances".

[10] With the wording 5AMLD this work refers to the last consolidated version of Directive (EU) 2015/849 as amended by Directive (EU) 2018/843 and by Directive (EU) 2019/2177 (most recent changes were introduced by Regulation (EU) 2023/1113 and Directive (EU) 2024/1640, addressed below). The original text of Directive (EU) 2015/849 is the 4th AML Directive (4AMLD), while Directive (EU) 2018/843 is dubbed 5th AML Directive (5AMLD).

[11] The topic was addressed by the European Court of Justice (2001).

application of DLTs to the financial sector. Among the risk elements, this work focuses on those related to the alleged anonymity of these ecosystems. This is a key perspective in terms of regulatory drivers in the crypto-asset space, as the first concerns about the misuse of crypto-assets originated when their (purported) anonymity was leveraged to perform illicit transactions. A set of investigations made the headlines, prompting public fear towards these instruments. Because, especially in the early stages, their essence and ongoing evolution was remarkably difficult to convey to a non-expert audience, this overall mistrust was hard to mitigate.

On top of this, the (purported) anonymity of crypto-assets was mostly exploited on the 'dark web', unfamiliar to most people. Its understanding is grounded on the difference between the 'Internet' and the 'world wide web', often used as synonyms. While the Internet is a huge network of networks, the web is built on top of it as a model to access and share information. The web's content can be 'structured' or 'unstructured' and there are three 'layers of accessibility'. On the one hand, the 'visible/clear/surface web' is readily available to the public, accessible by regular browsers and searchable by main search engines. It makes up for about 4% of the web. On the other hand, there is the 'deep web'—roughly 96% of the web but growing exponentially—whose content is not indexed. Its content includes medical and financial records, social media files, other data that needs to be kept private and secure.[12] Within the 'deep web', the 'dark web' cannot be measured, because its content is intentionally hidden.[13] Special browsers are needed to access it: tools such as I2P, Freenet and TOR, transmitting data through multiple layers of encryption.[14] The anonymity of the dark web makes it perfect for activities people do not dare to perform on the visible web.[15]

These 'darknets' can be used for legitimate purposes—e.g., to avoid identity theft or censorship—, and software such as TOR and I2P was not developed to enable illegal activities. Nonetheless, its features of anonymity make it vulnerable to being exploited to trade illegal services or products, spread extremist ideas and/or share illegal content,[16] as well as orchestrating or contributing to terrorism financing.[17] Hence, the dark web has been increasingly at the heart of investigations, either proactively (i.e., LEAs looking for information and attempt indexing) or reactively (i.e., to gather information on a suspect, engaging in activities of de-anonymisation

---

[12] Kavallieros et al. (2021a), pp. 4–6.

[13] Goldbarsht (2024), p. 172

[14] TOR's technology was developed in the 1990s by US intelligence. In 2016, TOR had approximately 2.5 million daily users. The layers' number depends on the users acting as 'nodes' at a given time. The objective is to safeguard user anonymity and avert traffic analysis that could reveal messages' origin, destination and/or content. The decentralised and P2P I2P overlay network was created in 2003 and offers anonymity through garlic routing, a variant of onion routing. Freenet is arguably the third largest darknet user-wise (Kavallieros et al., 2021a, pp. 10, 14–15, 16–17).

[15] Many 'dark web' websites aim to be accessible only to people that already know of their existence (Kavallieros et al., 2021a, p. 6).

[16] Kavallieros et al. (2021a), pp. 7–8.

[17] Goldbarsht (2024); Burgess et al. (2024).

of dark web traces).[18] In this context, a significant win relates to the first 'scandal' related to the criminal use of crypto-assets: the Silk Road case.

The Silk Road was a 'darknet market' defined as an underground 'Amazon for drugs', operated as a TOR hidden service.[19] In facilitating the exchange of illicit products and services, darknet markets leverage Bitcoin's (perceived) anonymity to avoid regulatory oversight and law enforcement. Arguably, many people first heard of Bitcoin in relation to the Silk Road case, which explains how it came to be perceived as inextricably tied to criminal activities, if not a vehicle for them.[20] The Silk Road was founded in February 2011 and shut down in October 2013 after the arrest of its operators. In November 2013 the Silk Road 2.0 was launched, and one year later it was shut down by the FBI and Europol.[21] Other marketplaces such as Agora and Evolution thrived in the aftermath but were later closed voluntarily and with an exit scam, respectively. Meanwhile, AlphaBay became the most active darknet market, and Nucleus and Abraxas were successful but ended in exit scams in 2016 and 2015.[22] While Silk Road 3.0 emerged as a scam and was taken down in 2017 by its admins, Silk Road 3.1 was launched.[23]

5.1.3 The Rise and Fall of Darknet Markets and the Present Day

The 'dark web' appeared as a safe place for cybercriminals to trade illegal goods and services—e.g., also in terms of 'cybercrime-as-a-service', drugs, stolen information, corporate data theft, credit card fraud, child abuse material, human organs, weapons, malware, and advanced hacking. share information and criminal 'best practices', with payments in cryptocurrencies. Darknet marketplaces offer a platform to both monetise and fund cybercriminal activities (e.g., ransomware).[24] Hence, they were found to increasingly target victims with monetisation potential, as well as sensitive and valuable data. When criminals have access to sensitive data, they extort the

[18] Kavallieros et al. (2021a), pp. 20–22.

[19] Dark web/darknet/dark markets are terms that were introduced to refer to the online illicit marketplaces operating in the dark web environment (Kermitsis et al., 2021, p. 85).

[20] Goforth (2021), pp. 8–9. Adler (2018).

[21] 'Operation Onymous' arguably exploited both users' mistakes and TOR's technical limitations and security issues (Kavallieros et al., 2021a, pp. 22–23).

[22] Tsuchiya and Hiramoto (2021a), p. 2.

[23] Kermitsis et al. (2021), pp. 101–102.

[24] 'Malware' is any malicious software that intentionally harms a computer system, network or service. It includes viruses, ransomware, spyware. A 'ransomware' attack consists of locking users' files or encrypting their system until users pay a ransom to receive the decryption key. It can be downloaded unwittingly from a compromised website or delivered in a phishing email. The most famous ransomware attack is WannaCry in May 2017, affecting more than 300,000 computers in 150 countries (Irwin and Dawson, 2019, pp. 111–112).

victims threatening to disclose it publicly.[25] While a wide range of new technologies aid darknet operations, cryptocurrencies play a key role by facilitating payments, and the major players are Bitcoin and Monero.[26] The adoption of Monero is reportedly increasing, with 67% of darknet markets supporting it in 2021 as opposed to 45% in 2020, and some supporting it exclusively (e.g., Archetyp). Nonetheless, Bitcoin still leads the way, supported by 93% of darknet markets. Overall, the trend is worrying: although the number of markets has decreased, in 2021 their revenue set a record of a total worth of USD 2.1 billion.[27]

After the 2013 shutdown of the Silk Road, various darknet markets have been launched and other scandals impacted on the public perception of crypto-assets.[28] A few examples are useful to contextualise the remainder of this chapter's analysis. On the one hand, there were 'exit scams': once the owners and/or admins of a marketplace had gathered a significant amount of funds the site became unreachable and outgoing transfers were blocked (e.g., Nucleus Market, Sheep Marketplace, TheRealDeal, Abraxas).[29] On the other hand, some markets were taken down. This is the case of AlphaBay and Hansa Market, shut down in July 2017 by a joint operation of the FBI, the US Drug Enforcement Agency and the Dutch National Police, supported by Europol.[30] Parallelly, the 2014 scandal of the (alleged) hack of the Tokyo-based Mt Gox exchange led to the loss of around USD 473 million.[31] Similar events affected Bitfinex in 2015/2016, Coincheck in 2018, and Bitgrail in 2018, and the four hackings combined involved losses for more than USD 1.2 billion.[32] As outlined in Chap. 4, however, the abilities of LEAs are constantly evolving. In 2021, the FBI shut down the REvil ransomware strain and OFAC sanctioned two Russia-based service providers involved in laundering activities, Suex and Chatex.[33]

Against this backdrop, the FATF classified the most common instances of criminal crypto-asset misuse in three groups: (i) illicit trafficking in controlled substances,

---

[25] Kavallieros et al. (2021b), pp. 35–36.

[26] Kermitsis et al. (2021), p. 86.

[27] Chainalysis (2022), pp. 100, 109. More recently, Chainalysis (2024), pp. 57–68 elaborates on the role of Monero in the field of child sexual abuse material.

[28] Tsuchiya and Hiramoto (2021a), p. 1.

[29] 'Multisig' or 'Trusted Markets' (e.g., Wall Street Market) make the process safer via multi-signature (more than one key is needed to release payments). The Wall Street Market is also an 'Invite/Referral Market': users need an invite code or a referral link. In 2021 many closures were planned, perhaps to avoid investigation, but users could withdraw funds in advance. Kermitsis et al. (2021), pp. 87–89. Tsuchiya and Hiramoto (2021a), p. 2. Chainalysis (2022), p. 101.

[30] In the aftermath of this 'Operation Bayonet', vendors' active on AlphaBay and Hansa migrated to Dream Market. Kermitsis et al. (2021), pp. 112–113. Tsuchiya and Hiramoto (2021a), p. 3. Jardine (2021), pp. 992–994.

[31] Johnstone (2021e), p. 58.

[32] Johnstone (2021d), p. 121.

[33] Chainalysis (2022), p. 4. The Office of Foreign Assets Control (OFAC) is the agency of the US Department of the Treasury in charge of administering and enforcing economic and trade sanctions.

to perform sales or layering; (ii) frauds, scams, ransomware attacks, extortion; and (iii) use by professionals launderers to transfer, collect and/or layer proceeds.[34] More recently, the case of Tornado Cash displayed the full extent of crypto-asset misuse enabled by mixers (Chap. 4). In August 2022, it was blacklisted by OFAC due to the accusation of laundering more than USD 7 billion, including USD 455 million arguably stolen by a hacking group tied to the North Korean government.[35] The accuse was facilitation of illicit crypto-asset activity by sanctioned persons, such as receipt of ransomware payments and state-sponsored crypto-asset theft. The designation was controversial because sanctions were imposed for the first time on a decentralised protocol (i.e., a set of smart contracts on Ethereum). The goal of the sanctions is to prohibit any interaction with the application—i.e., regulated entities must monitor, investigate, prevent and/or report any direct or indirect exposure to it. In addition, the developers/co-founders of Tornado Cash were charged in the U.S. (Roman Storm and Roman Semenov),[36] and convicted in the Netherlands (Alexey Pertsev).[37] The use of crypto-assets to fund terrorist activities through donations and the organisation of crowdfunding via the dark web has also emerged significantly.[38]

At the beginning of 2022, crypto-asset addresses identified as illicit held a value of at least USD 10 billion.[39] In most cases, these wallets are associated with theft, darknet markets and scams. Crypto-related laundering appears heavily concentrated; most outgoing value from illicit addresses is sent to few services, some seemingly purpose-built. Given the amounts sent from illicit to hosted addresses, it was argued USD 8.6 billion (in cryptocurrency) was laundered in 2021. This concentration also means that, in principle, LEAs can hamper crypto crime significantly by disrupting these services. In 2022, the total cryptocurrency value received by illicit addresses was estimated at almost USD 40 billion (corresponding to 0.42 of the total on-chain transaction volume). In 2023, at USD 24 billion (the 0.34% of the total on-chain transaction volume), in line with the aftermath of the 'crypto winter'.[40] In 2023, sanctioned entities and jurisdictions accounted for almost USD 15 billion worth of transaction volume—i.e., around 60% of the illicit transaction volume for the same year.[41] Meanwhile, in 2023 ransomware payments surpassed USD 1 billion,[42] and in terms of money laundering illicit addresses sent more than USD 20 billion worth to services, which is a significant decrease from more than USD 30 billion worth

[34] Financial Action Task Force (2021b), p. 12.

[35] Marquardt et al. (2022); U.S.Department of the Treasury (2022).

[36] Federal Bureau of Investigation (2023).

[37] de Rechtspraak (2024).

[38] Goldbarsht (2024), pp. 174–181. Burgess et al. (2024), p. 205.

[39] A large portion does not originate from the criminal activity, but from the asset's value increase (Chainalysis, 2022, p. 8).

[40] Chainalysis (2024), pp. 3–6.

[41] Chainalysis (2024), pp. 8–9.

[42] Chainalysis (2024), p. 12.

in 2022. In particular, there was a huge increase in the volume of funds sent to blockchain bridges from addresses associated with stolen funds.[43]

5.1.4 Multi-Layered Efforts and Global Financial Standards

At the international level, AML/CFT efforts are coordinated by the FATF, a standard-setting organisation established in 1989. The scope of its activities is broad, as they consist not only of policy making, issuing guidance to governments, authorities, regulated entities, the public at large, but also include monitoring the relevant implementation and enforcement. Although FATF's Recommendations are instruments of soft law,[44] and as such not directly binding on individuals and organisations, participating jurisdictions committed to transposing them into national law.[45] In this regard, the FATF cooperates with FATF-Style Regional Bodies and observer organisations such as the IMF, the World Bank and the UN.[46]

This chapter addresses AML/CFT regulation starting from international standardisation efforts. In this context, both the regulatory scope and the methodology are close to the larger domain of financial regulation.[47] While a comprehensive analysis of the broad area of financial regulation falls outside the scope of this research, overlooking the role of soft law and global financial standardisation would insufficiently account for the role of the FATF and the impact of other institutions' regulatory and policy activities on the crypto-asset space. Indeed, regulatory actions targeting crypto-assets and their stakeholders, as well as their underpinning methodologies, were not created from scratch, but relied on established mechanisms of coordination.

International financial regulation consists of a compound of rules, standards, and best practices. Typically, its various ramifications (e.g., banking, securities, insurance) share as focal points the reduction of the information asymmetries and the systemic risk generated by financial institutions. However, there is a tendency to focus on the national implementations of the different sectors, each equipped with its areas of emphasis and objectives.[48] While standard-setting procedures run the risk of being neglected, starting from the late 1980s financial integration and increasing cross-border capital flows urged regulatory cooperation to protect

[43] Chainalysis (2024), pp. 23–25.

[44] The role of 'soft law' and 'standardisation' is explored below and in Chap. 7.

[45] Karasek-Wojciechowicz (2021), p. 2.

[46] Financial Action Task Force (2012), p. 8.

[47] For an in-depth critical analysis: Brummer (2015c), pp. 1–22. Indeed, "irrespective of the correctness of positioning cryptoassets in the arena of financial regulation, the fact is that the financial use of cryptoassets has been expanding rapidly" (Johnstone, 2021c, p. 157). For a broader context, please see Barbereau et al. (2024).

[48] Brummer (2015c), pp. 3–4, 7–10.

financial market stability and consumers.[49] In other words, the need to prevent market participants from escaping national supervision required the setting of prudential guidelines through international forums that could suit the evolving nature of capital markets.[50]

Nonetheless, while most areas of international economic law, such as tax and trade law, are construed on legally binding treaties, international financial regulation consists of global rules adopted as informal and non-binding agreements, either by regulatory agencies or by institutions with undefined legal status.[51] In this respect, soft law was defined as a compendium of "instruments or agreements that are not directly enforceable like treaties, but that nevertheless create powerful expectations",[52] and its role as regulatory mechanism is increasingly key.[53] In this sense, the global regulation of finance features a low degree of institutionalisation and widely relies on voluntary compliance.[54] However, the coerciveness of regulatory instruments is more a matter of enforcement than obligation. If compliance can be enforced, standards and best practices can be interpreted from a functional viewpoint as part of international law, even if not formally recognised as such.[55]

The architecture of relevant organisations provides valuable insights.[56] On the global financial market arena, the main institutions to create regulatory policies are the G-20, the Financial Stability Board (FSB), the International Organisation of Securities Commissions (IOSCO) and the Basel Committee on Banking Supervision (BCBS).[57] From a systematic viewpoint, different types of entities are involved in financial regulation: they (i) set the core agenda for the international regulatory system (e.g., G-20, FSB);[58] (ii) focus on standard-setting, issuing prescriptive guidance usually on specific sectors or issue areas (e.g., FATF), and/or (iii) monitor

---

[49] Brummer (2015c), pp. 10, 17. Kerwer (2005), pp. 613–614.

[50] Brummer (2015a), p. 62.

[51] Brummer (2015b), p. 3.

[52] Merchant and Allenby (2017), p. 108. In the area of international business governance, soft law was referred to as 'civil regulation', defined as "codes, regulations, and standards that are not enforced by the state and that address the social and environment impacts of global firms and markets" (Vogel, 2008, pp. 262–264).

[53] Casanovas et al. (2022), p. 78.

[54] Newman and Bach (2014), p. 432.

[55] Brummer (2015b), p. 5.

[56] While these entities enshrine models of P2P technocratic cooperation, they are institutional players belonging to a hierarchical system of influence and power, with sophisticated internal designs (Brummer, 2015a, p. 63).

[57] The BCBS, the oldest standard-setter, was created in the 1970s to address risks arising from changes in banking. The public perception of the role of these organisations has risen since the 2008 financial crisis and after the consequent review processes (Brummer, 2015c, p. viii, 1).

[58] The G-20 and the FSB are the primary setters of the financial regulatory agenda. Since G-20's role was revived as a response to the 2008 financial crisis, it has been the most visible political forum for economic coordination. The FSB operates as its technocratic extension, with a focus on macroprudential regulation (Brummer, 2015a, pp. 71–75).

the system and check compliance (e.g., World Bank, IMF). This is an integrated system where "broad-based and more-political institutions set agendas and assess gaps, whereas more-technocratic sectoral and specialist standard setters promulgate best practices and, in some instances, granularised rule".[59]

The 'agenda setters' sub (i) are not involved in the daily process of standard-setting. The definition of standards to be adopted or implemented at a national level is a task of less political bodies that are inherently 'sectoral'—i.e., their mandate focuses on specific financial sectors.[60] In this respect, the BCBS is tasked with overseeing banks and other financial institutions. The best-known activities of the BCBC relate to the 1988 rules on capital adequacy ('Basel I'), their refinement in 2004 ('Basel II'), and recent efforts for a 'Basel III'.[61] Other bodies have limited mandates, such as the International Accounting Standards Board (IASB) and the Committee on Payments and Markets Infrastructure (CPMI).[62] Meanwhile, the Bank for International Settlements (BIS), in its regulatory capacity, supports the other institutions by conducting economic, monetary, financial and legal research.[63]

5.2 International Standards and the Financial Action Task Force

The mandate of the FATF is to define standards and promote effective implementation of regulatory and operational measures to fight money laundering, terrorist financing and related threats to the international financial system.[64] The FATF Standards, known as Recommendations, relate to criminal justice, law enforcement,

[59] These bodies feature diverging governance, but highly developed institutional structures, with rules on membership, decisions, processes (Brummer, 2015a, pp. 18, 69–70, 115–116).

[60] Brummer (2015a), pp. 76–77.

[61] Basel I was adopted by all members and almost 100 non-members. It required banks to maintain 8% of their capital in risk-weighted assets. Basel II aimed to give the largest banks discretion regarding internal risk ratings. Basel III establishes a regime of capital requirements to identify financial institutions whose importance is systemic and determines practices of bank compensation and corporate governance with effects on financial stability. The BCBS is the primary standard-setter in the banking domain, IOSCO for securities, and the International Association of Insurance Supervisors (IAIS) for insurance (Brummer, 2015a, pp. 79–81).

[62] The IASB pursues the development of global accounting standards for investors, creditors, and regulatory authorities. The CPMI was created in 1990 to provide oversight and guidance on clearing and settlement—i.e., technologies, procedures, rules for fund transfers among participating entities (Brummer, 2015a, pp. 82–83, 86).

[63] Brummer (2015a), p. 93.

[64] The FATF has 39 Members: 37 members and 2 regional organisations (EC, Gulf Cooperation Council). It includes Associate Members (e.g., Council of Europe's Moneyval, the Asia/Pacific Group on ML) and Observers (e.g., Indonesia and bodies such as BCBS, Egmont Group, ECB, OECD, UN, IOSCO, IMF, World Bank, Europol, Interpol). The OECD cooperates closely and sanctions non-compliant institutions (Brummer, 2015a, pp. 88–90).

the financial system, its regulation, and international cooperation. They consist of a set of measures to be implemented by participating jurisdictions through individual regulatory and operational initiatives, and they are issued after consultation procedures.[65] Meanwhile, the FATF works with other international players to identify national vulnerabilities. Worldwide AML/CFT frameworks largely take after the FATF Standards, which include their Interpretative Notes and the definitions of the FATF's Glossary.[66] In terms of implementation, Member Jurisdictions are not expected to take identical measures on the grounds of their different legal, administrative, and operational frameworks, and diverse financial systems. Hence, the Recommendations are classified as 'global standards'.

The FATF Recommendations are under constant revision and were most recently amended in November 2023.[67] Due to the specificity of its monitoring and enforcement, the Recommendations are regarded as one of the most successful examples of international standards. The scope of the regime was first broadened in 1996 (so-called '40 Recommendations'). In October 2001, efforts to combat the financing of terrorism (CFT) were included, thus creating the Eight (later Nine) Special Recommendations—i.e., standards and common approaches for the detection, prevention, and suppression of the TF and terrorist acts—and establishing the current version of the framework, dubbed 'FATF 40+9 Recommendations'. Starting from 2008, the fight against the financing of proliferation of weapons of mass destruction (WMD) has been included by adopting a Recommendation to ensure effective implementation of targeted financial sanctions imposed by the UN Security Council.[68]

The contents of the Recommendations can be classified into six categories: (i) risk identification, development of policies and domestic coordination; (ii) pursuit of money laundering and terrorist financing; (iii) application of preventive measures for the financial domain and other designated sectors; (iv) establishment of powers and responsibilities for investigative, enforcement and supervisory authorities; (v) enhancement of transparency and availability of beneficial ownership information of legal persons/arrangements; and (vi) facilitation of international cooperation.[69]

The FATF Standards rely on participating countries having authorities and supervisors in place to regulate, monitor, supervise, and in some cases handle the licensing of, 'regulated entities' in different sectors.[70] Supervisors are expected to have the powers to impose sanctions (disciplinary and financial) and to with-

---

[65] Financial Action Task Force (2012), p. 7. Goforth (2021), p. 10. Brummer (2015a), pp. 88–90.

[66] Financial Action Task Force (2012), pp. 7–8.

[67] Financial Action Task Force (2012). The original Recommendations date back to the 1990s and focused on drug-related laundering, in the wake of the 1988 US efforts for a BCBS's Statement of Principles on Money Laundering and the Vienna Convention. While the frequent revision of principles is common for standard-setters, FATF also introduced a specific method to guide the application of the Recommendations—i.e., Interpretative Notes (Brummer, 2015a, pp. 88–89).

[68] Financial Action Task Force (2012), pp. 7–8. Brummer (2015a), pp. 88–89.

[69] Financial Action Task Force (2012), p. 7.

[70] Recommendation 26. Financial Action Task Force (2012).

draw, restrict or suspend the license, if applicable.[71] At the receiving end of the cooperation obligations imposed on regulated entities there are national Financial Intelligence Units (FIUs).[72] An FIU receives, assesses, and shares financial information (e.g., STRs/SARs, other data relevant for analysis and/or dissemination) with other national authorities or other FIUs.[73] As the FATF monitors implementation of its principles through a system of mutual evaluations, there is a list of codes and criteria to identify non-compliant jurisdictions, as well as a schedule of countermeasures.[74] In this context, the influence of FATF's guidance on national policies is complemented by the 'blacklist' of non-compliant nations,[75] according to which regulated entities have to perform enhanced CDD when dealing with individuals or entities of countries of 'higher-risk'.[76]

5.2.1 The FATF and Virtual Assets: Definitions and Timeline

Over the years, the focus of the FATF adjusted to the developments of the financial domain and the ways to transmit value over the Internet. It started to address crypto-asset risks in June 2014, issuing a document with background notions on 'virtual currencies (VCs)'.[77] A year later, the first guidance to the application of the RBA, defined below, to the crypto-asset sphere was released.[78] These documents were limited in two ways: (i) they addressed the subset of VAs labelled as VCs, and (ii) exclusively focused on the "on and off ramps" to the traditional (regulated) financial system. In other words, on the points of intersection between the latter and activities in VCs (e.g., VC-exchanges). Later, the FATF became increasingly aware of the

[71] Recommendation 27. Financial Action Task Force (2012). For DNFBPs, it can be a Self-Regulatory Body (Recommendation 28).

[72] Recommendation 29. Financial Action Task Force (2012). In the EU, FIU establishment and operations is governed by Chapter III of Directive Directive (EU) 2024/1640.

[73] The FATF establishes a framework of 'mutual legal assistance' (Recommendation 37), while in 1995 the Council of Europe established the Egmont Group to aid information exchange.

[74] Brummer (2015a), pp. 88–89.

[75] Goforth (2021), p. 10.

[76] Recommendation 19. Financial Action Task Force (2012). Jurisdictions with 'weak' AML/CFT measures are identified by two lists routinely updated: High-Risk Jurisdictions subject to a Call for Action, and Jurisdictions under Increased Monitoring. The first document is the so-called 'blacklist' (Financial Action Task Force, 2024b) and comprises countries with serious strategic deficiencies; currently, the Democratic People's Republic of Korea, Iran and Myanmar. The second one is the 'grey list' (Financial Action Task Force, 2024c) and includes countries taking committed steps to resolve their deficiencies—i.e., at the time of writing, Bulgaria, Burkina Faso, Cameroon, Croatia, Democratic Republic of the Congo, Haiti, Kenya, Mali, Monaco, Mozambique, Namibia, Nigeria, Philippines, Senegal, South Africa, South Sudan, Syria, Tanzania, Venezuela, Vietnam, Yemen.

[77] Financial Action Task Force (2014).

[78] Financial Action Task Force (2015).

evolution of crypto-assets towards "new products and services, business models, and activities and interactions, including virtual-to-virtual asset transactions".[79]

In October 2018, the FATF clarified the application of the Standards to 'financial activities involving VAs', to urge the implementation of the measures on crypto-asset-related service providers. The amended Recommendation 15 included 'virtual asset service providers (VASPs)' into the standards' scope, also in terms of licensing, monitoring and supervision systems. The development of new products and services, and the introduction of different types of providers, led the FATF to provide clearer definitions of VAs and VASPs and to specify the Standards apply "to both virtual-to-virtual and virtual-to-fiat transactions and interactions involving VAs".[80]

The most recent FATF's definition of a VA is "a digital representation of value that can be digitally traded, or transferred, and can be used for payment or investment purposes", excluding "digital representation of fiat currencies, securities and other financial assets that are already covered elsewhere in the FATF Recommendations".[81] The most recent definition of VASPs comprises natural or legal persons, otherwise not covered by the Recommendations, that as a business conduct—for or on behalf of another natural or legal person—one or more activities operations among: exchange between (i) VAs and fiat currencies or (ii) one or more VAs; (iii) transfer of VAs from one address or account to another; (iv) safekeeping and/or administration of VAs or instruments enabling control over VAs; (v) participation in and provision of financial services related to an offer and/or sale of a VA.[82]

In June 2019, the FATF adopted the Interpretative Note to Recommendation 15, to clarify the application of the RBA to VA activities and VASPs, supervision and monitoring mechanisms, licensing, preventive measures such as CDD, record-keeping, reporting, sanctions, enforcement, international cooperation. Relatedly, it issued the first comprehensive Guidance to apply its principles to VAs and VASPs, to aid national regulatory and supervisory responses, and to help the private sector understand the obligations.[83] This Guidance was revised in October 2021 after a public consultation. The update focused on (i) clarification and expansion of definitions; (ii) application of the Standards to stablecoins and conditions for the qualification of related entities as VASPs; (iii) risks posed by P2P transactions and countermeasures; (iv) VASP licensing/registration; (v) 'travel rule' implementation for the public and private sector; and (vi) information sharing and co-operation

[79] Financial Action Task Force (2021b).

[80] Financial Action Task Force (2021b). Goforth (2021), p. 10.

[81] Financial Action Task Force (2021b), p. 109. Financial Action Task Force (2012).

[82] Financial Action Task Force (2021b), p. 109.

[83] Financial Action Task Force (2019, 2012). Goforth (2021), p. 11. Financial Action Task Force (2021b), pp. 4, 8.

among VASP supervisors.[84] In July 2024, the FATF released its fifth Targeted Update on Implementation of the FATF Standards on VAs and VASPs.[85]

Meanwhile, in 2020 ransomware attacks had brought crypto-asset risks into the spotlight again.[86] The FATF noted how while some jurisdictions had implemented VAs-VASPs AML/CFT frameworks, in some cases these are not effective vis-à-vis the cross-jurisdictional development of crypto-assets, their growing adoption and functionalities. The ransomware-related use of VA emerged as a critical issue, especially when considering the growth of ransomware attacks on a global level.[87] Accordingly, in September 2020 the FATF published the Virtual Assets Red Flag Indicators of Money Laundering and Terrorist Financing, with a section on the concept(s) of anonymity.[88] Finally, a set of other documents bear influence on the FATF's regime for VAs and VASPs.[89]

5.2.2 *The Risk-Based Approach and Crypto Regulated Entities: The FATF and the EU*

The gist of AML/CFT measures tends towards global coherence in the form of compliance with the FATF Standards. The end-goal of their compliance efforts is to timely draw the attention of competent authorities in case suspicions of illicit activities arise—more specifically, suspicions of 'money laundering', 'terrorist financing', and 'proliferation financing', as defined above. To this end, the regimes established in different jurisdictions rely on a set of 'regulated entities', also labelled 'obliged entities', required to provide 'active cooperation' to the authorities, chiefly in terms of monitoring financial transactions and value exchanges. The number and type of regulated entities has increased over time. Their selection is grounded on

[84] Financial Action Task Force (2021b), pp. 5–6.

[85] Financial Action Task Force (2024a).

[86] It is estimated that in 2020 illicit actors received almost USD 700 million in crypto-assets as parts of ransomware attacks (Chainalysis, 2022).

[87] Financial Action Task Force (2021b), p. 10.

[88] Financial Action Task Force (2020d).

[89] In March 2020, the Guidance on Digital ID was released to help identification in digital contexts (Financial Action Task Force, 2020c). In June 2020, the 12-Month Review of the Revised FATF Standards on VAs and VASPs identified areas in need of further guidance, while the Report to the G20 on so-called Stablecoins outlined issues in applying the standards to stablecoins (Financial Action Task Force, 2020a,b). In March 2021, a Guidance on Risk-Based Supervision also targeted VASP supervision, and in June 2021 the Second 12-Month Review of the Revised FATF Standards on VAs and VASPs identified implementation loopholes (Financial Action Task Force, 2021c,a). A revision of the Recommendations took place in June 2021, where an amendment to the Interpretative Note to Recommendation 15 clarified the applicability of the requirements concerning proliferation financing (Financial Action Task Force, 2012). Another revision took place in November 2023.

the kind of involvement they have in financial transactions, thus on their (purported) oversight capacity in their daily activities.[90] Although the range of regulated entities goes beyond the financial sector, the latter has a one-of-a-kind relationship with the compliance regime. As addressed in the previous chapters, the tension between financial transparency and confidentiality precedes crypto-assets. Indeed, FATF Recommendation 9 opens its part on 'preventive measures' specifying that the presence of financial secrecy laws should not inhibit the implementation of the regime.[91]

The primary principle that sits at the core of all obligations and procedures comprised by the framework is the risk-based approach (RBA). While this work addresses duties imposed on 'regulated entities', international and supranational frameworks also thrust on their members and supervisory authorities a set of RBA-related obligations—e.g., in the EU risk assessments are to be issued EU-wide (by the EC), nation-wide and for specific sectors (by competent authorities). Accordingly, regulated entities are required to undertake preliminary assessments to be able to tune their compliance measures to the principle of proportionality—i.e., stricter if risk factors are higher and vice versa.[92] To do so, they must consider risk factors identified by the FATF, such as the 'red flag indicators', but also by the EU AMLD, national regulation, sector-specific and supervisory authorities. Consistently, they must set up internal policies, procedures, and controls.[93]

The RBA informs compliance in manifold ways. Besides obligations outlined below, the AML Regulation outlines the impact on internal structures and operations. The underlying reason is that "[i]t is important that AML/CFT requirements apply in a proportionate manner and that the imposition of any requirement is proportionate to the role that obliged entities are able to play in the prevention of money laundering and terrorist financing".[94] Pursuant to Article 10(1), the entity must perform a 'business-wide risk assessment' which means taking "appropriate measures, proportionate to the nature of their business, including its risks and complexity, and their size, to identify and assess the risks of money laundering and terrorist financing to which they are exposed, as well as the risks of non-

---

[90] The actual degree of oversight capacity of the different types of 'reporting entities' is subject to heated debates. Various stakeholders do not always agree on the extent of daily monitoring burdens thrust on these entities.

[91] Recommendation 9. Financial Action Task Force (2012).

[92] de Koker and Goldbarsht (2024a), pp. 247–248.

[93] They may encompass organising training activities, audits, appointing a compliance officer, etc. The content of the RBA is outlined in FATF Recommendation 1 also in relation to Member Jurisdictions, that should identify, assess, and understand the money laundering and terrorist financing risks they face, and adopt appropriate measures to mitigate them. Hence, countries can adopt a flexible set of measures, deploy their resources effectively and apply preventive measures commensurately (Financial Action Task Force, 2012, pp. 8, 10). It was noted how the FATF only provides a general description of risk as a function of threat, vulnerability and consequence (de Koker and Goldbarsht, 2024a, p. 248).

[94] Regulation (EU) 2024/1624. Recital 28.

implementation and evasion of targeted financial sanctions". This includes the indicative list of risk variables set out in Annex I (i.e., customer, product, service or transaction, delivery channel, life and other investment-related insurance) and the non-exhaustive list of lower and higher risk factors laid out in Annex II and III, as well as EU and national-level risk assessments, sector-specific risk assessments, risk-related data provided by key stakeholders (e.g., FATF, EC, AMLA, competent authorities) and information on the customer base.[95] These risk assessments must be documented, updated, and made available to authorities and self-regulatory bodies.[96]

As per Article 9(1), entities must have (proportionate) internal policies, controls and procedures in place to ensure compliance with Regulation (EU) 2024/1624, Regulation (EU) 2023/1113 and any supervisory act. As examples of RBA at national-level, pursuant to Articles 4, 5 and 6 of Regulation (EU) 2024/1624, Member States may decide to exempt a series of legal and natural persons (certain providers of gambling services, certain professional football clubs and certain financial services, respectively) from the requirements of the AML Regulation, provided a series of criteria are met—e.g., when financial activities are provided "on an occasional or very limited basis where there is little risk of money laundering or terrorist financing".[97]

According to FATF's terminology, regulated entities encompass financial institutions and designated non-financial businesses and professions (DNFBPs).[98] As per Interpretative Note to Recommendation 15 on 'new technologies', countries should apply the Standards to VAs and VASPs and carry out risk-based assessments. Further, VASPs should be licensed or registered, adequately regulated, supervised, or monitored; they should not be supervised by a self-regulatory body, but by an authority that should conduct risk-based supervision and monitoring. Within the EU framework, the array of regulated entities are defined by Article 3(1) of the AML Regulation—e.g., credit and financial institutions, professionals (e.g., auditors, lawyers, accountants, notaries), casinos, and art galleries. As per Article 2(1)(6)(i) of the AML Regulation, CASPs are included in the category of financial institutions. As per Article 2(1)(9) of the AML Regulation, they are defined in Article 3(1)(15) of the MiCA Regulation (Chap. 2). Previously, Article 2(1)(g) and (h) of the AMLD, added by the 5AMLD, included "providers engaged in exchange services between virtual currencies and fiat currencies" (i.e., fiat-to-crypto exchanges) and 'custodian wallet providers', respectively.

A comparison can be made with the US, where at the federal level FinCEN is the authority fighting the illicit use of the financial system. FinCEN first

---

[95] Article 10(1)(a-f). of Regulation (EU) 2024/1624.

[96] Individual documentation may be deemed unnecessary if the sector's risks are clear (Article 10(3) of Regulation (EU) 2024/1624).

[97] Article 6(1) of Regulation (EU) 2024/1624.

[98] DNFBPs comprise (insofar as they engage in specified activities) casinos, real estate agents, dealers in precious metals/stones, lawyers, notaries, accountants, trusts, and company service providers (Recommendation 22).

regulated cryptocurrency transactions in 2013, issuing a guidance on how to apply its rules to "persons administering, exchanging or using virtual currencies".[99] It targeted all stakeholders involved in the use, distribution, exchange, acceptance or transmission of VCs for another person, to clarify they can be regarded as 'Money Services Business (MSBs)'.[100] In particular, "any person engaged in the business of accepting and transmitting value, whether physical or digital, that substitutes for currency (including convertible virtual currency, whether virtual-to-virtual, virtual-to-fiat, or virtual-to-other value) from one person to another person or location by any means" is regulated.[101] MSBs are required to register and follow AML/CFT rules as provided for by the 'Currency and Foreign Transactions Reporting Act of 1970', as amended: the US Bank Secrecy Act (BSA).[102] The BSA is codified in 31 US Code §§5311 et seq. and lays out rules in line with the 'active cooperation' enshrined by FATF Standards. In 2019, FinCEN issued guidance on the application of its Regulations to 'Certain Business Models Involving Convertible Virtual Currencies'.[103] Other requirements are set at the state level—e.g., 'BitLicense', introduced in August 2015 by the New York Department of Financial Services.[104]

In June 2024, FinCEN issued a Notice of Proposed Rulemaking to strengthen the risk-based AML/CFT regulatory and supervisory regime by amending the BSA and notably the AML Act enacted in 2021. In particular, the proposed rule would require financial institutions "to establish, implement, and maintain effective, risk-based, and reasonably designed AML/CFT programs with certain minimum components, including a mandatory risk assessment process".[105]

5.2.3 *An Extensive Array of Obligations: The FATF and the EU*

The structure of the FATF Recommendations provides an overview of the foundational elements of AML/CFT obligations, while EU implementation offers

---

[99] Department of the Treasury FinCEN (2013).

[100] 31 CFR §1010.100(ff). Goforth (2021), p. 10.

[101] The obligations are equally thrust on "domestic and foreign-located money transmitters, even if the foreign-located entity does not have a physical presence in the United States and regardless of where it is incorporated or headquartered, as long as it does business in whole or substantial part in the United States" (Financial Action Task Force, 2021b, p. 98).

[102] Goforth (2021), pp. 9–10. Several acts, including the USA PATRIOT Act, amended the BSA.

[103] Department of the Treasury FinCEN (2019).

[104] Irwin and Dawson (2019), p. 116.

[105] Financial Crimes Enforcement Network (2024). In July 2024, FinCEN issued an Interagency Statement on the Issuance of the AML/CFT Program Notices of Proposed Rulemaking together with the Board of Governors of the Federal Reserve System, the Federal Deposit Insurance Corporation, the National Credit Union Administration, and the Office of the Comptroller of the Currency (Financial Crimes Enforcement Network et al., 2024).

insights into their interplay. The section of FATF Recommendations on 'preventive measures' outlines a primary set of obligations relating to CDD and record-keeping, as well as specific measures for certain customers or activities.[106] As per Recommendation 10, CDD must be carried out for new and existing (a) business relationships, and (b) under certain conditions such as a transfer above EUR/USD 15,000, for occasional transactions. In the EU, Article 2(1)(19) of the AML Regulation defines a 'business relationship' as "a business, professional or commercial relationship connected with the professional activities of an obliged entity, which is set up between an obliged entity and a customer, including in the absence of a written contract and which is expected to have, at the time when the contact is established, or which subsequently acquires, an element of repetition or duration".

Chapter III of the AML Regulation lays out CDD duties as outlined by FATF. As per Article 19(1–9), CDD is to be performed for an occasional transaction of "a value of at least EUR 10 000, or the equivalent in national currency, whether that transaction is carried out in a single operation or through linked transactions, or a lower value" when determined by the AMLA's RTSs (see below). It must also be performed in other cases, such as "when there is a suspicion of money laundering or terrorist financing, regardless of any derogation, exemption or threshold" or when there are doubts about either the veracity/adequacy of the customer identification or as to whether the person is the customer or is authorised to act on behalf of the customer.[107] As per Article 19(2), CDD must be performed for transfer of funds as per Regulation (EU) 2023/1113, addressed below, exceeding EUR 1000, while Article 19(3) lays out specific rules for CASPs.[108] This aligns with FATF's Interpretative Note to Recommendation 15, according to which the threshold above which VASPs must conduct CDD for occasional transactions is EUR/USD 1000.[109]

CDD measures comprise identification and verification of the identities of customers and beneficial owners.[110] In other words, CDD obligations include KYC

[106] E.g., Politically Exposed Persons (PEPs), correspondent banking, Money or Value Transfer Services (MVTS). As per FATF's Glossary, PEPs are individuals who are/have been entrusted with prominent public functions domestically or by a foreign country—e.g., "heads of state or of government, senior politicians, senior government, judicial or military officials, senior executives of state-owned corporations, important political party officials". MVTS are "financial services that involve the acceptance of cash, cheques, other monetary instruments or other stores of value and the payment of a corresponding sum in cash or other form to a beneficiary by means of a communication, message, transfer, or through a clearing network [. . .]".

[107] Article 19(1–9) of Regulation (EU) 2024/1624.

[108] Regulation (EU) 2024/1624.

[109] Pocher (2025).

[110] The concept of beneficial owner is crucial. As per FATF Glossary, it is "the natural person(s) who ultimately owns or controls a customer and/or the natural person on whose behalf a transaction is being conducted. It also includes those persons who exercise ultimate effective control over a legal person or arrangement". As per Interpretative Note to Recommendation 10, the beneficial owner of a legal person is the natural person(s) who ultimately have a controlling ownership interest in the legal person, depending on the ownership's structure—e.g., it can be based on a threshold,

but also see beneficial owners as primary targets. As per Article 23 of the AML Regulation, identity verification "shall take place before the establishment of a business relationship or the carrying out of an occasional transaction".[111] CDD must be applied to new and existing customers, on a risk-sensitive basis, at appropriate times, and in specific circumstances. CDD includes assessing purpose and intended nature of the business relationship or occasional transactions,[112] verifying if customer and beneficial owners are subject to targeted financial sanctions,[113] and ongoing monitoring (e.g., transaction scrutiny) to ensure the operations remain consistent with the collected information and resulting risk profile.[114]

As mentioned above, CDD compliance must be performed on a risk-sensitive basis—e.g., higher risks call for enhanced measures and low-risk situations may allow a simplified regime. Accordingly, Article 33 of the AML Regulation provides rules for simplified due diligence, while Articles 34–46 provide a series of enhanced due diligence measures to be detailed at Member State level, to be read in conjunction with the risk variables and factors laid out in the Annexes. Article 40, in particular, focuses on mitigating the risk arising for CASPs when transacting with self-hosted addresses, which align with the provisions of Regulation (EU) 2023/1113. Because the RBA applies also to identification and identity verification, "non-face-to-face business relationship or transactions" may constitute a risk factor, unless they rely on reliable and independent digital ID systems.[115]

Regulated entities, without displacing their responsibility, may rely on identification and verification performed by regulated third parties.[116] The AML Regulation lays out necessary requirements in Articles 48–50. As per Article 48(1), "[t]he ultimate responsibility for meeting the customer due diligence requirements shall remain with the obliged entity which relies on another obliged entity".

---

such as any person that owns more than 25%. If the ownership criterium is not conclusive, the beneficial owner is the natural person(s) that exercise(s) control on the legal arrangement through other means, or, as a last resort, hold the position of senior managing official(s). Article 2(28) of the AML Regulation defines it as "any natural person who ultimately owns or controls a legal entity or an express trust or similar legal arrangement". The Regulation also introduced Chapter IV with a specific focus on beneficial ownership transparency. In particular, Article 51 lays out the criteria to identify beneficial owners in various cases, such as for legal entities—through ownership interest (Article 52), control (Article 53) or a combination (Article 54)—, but also for legal arrangements or similar legal entities (Article 55), and for express trusts and similar arrangements (Articles 57–58).

[111] RBA-based exceptions are allowed—e.g., it can "be completed during the establishment of a business relationship if necessary so as not to interrupt the normal conduct of business and where there is little risk" (Article 23(2)).

[112] Article 20(1)(c) of Regulation (EU) 2024/1624.

[113] Article 20(1)(d) of Regulation (EU) 2024/1624.

[114] Article 20(1)(f) of Regulation (EU) 2024/1624.

[115] Financial Action Task Force (2020c), pp. 29–30. Annex I of AML Regulation includes as a higher risk variable "the extent to which the business relationship is conducted on a non-face-to-face basis".

[116] Recommendation 17. Financial Action Task Force (2012).

Other duties concern setting internal controls and procedures in compliance with the RBA (e.g., policies, screenings, training programs, independent audits), and the obligation to submit Suspicious Transaction Reports (STRs)—in some jurisdictions known also as Suspicious Activity Reports (SARs). Their submission is the core duty of the framework, to which the other ones are oriented. They are sent to FIUs (or sector-specific authorities) when the entity "suspects or has reasonable ground to suspect that funds are the proceeds of a criminal activity, or are related to terrorist financing".[117] Indeed, the goal is for authorities to be informed when an entity "knows, suspects or has reasonable grounds to suspect that funds or activities, regardless of the amount involved, are the proceeds of criminal activity or are related to terrorist financing or criminal activity".[118] As per Article 71(1), the transaction cannot be performed until the STR is sent and further instructions are complied with. However, if abstaining is impossible or is likely to frustrate efforts to pursue the beneficiaries of a suspected transaction [. . .], the obliged entity concerned shall inform the FIU immediately after performing it.[119]

5.2.4 *From the FATF Standards to Regulatory and Technical Standardisation*

The FATF Recommendations are global regulatory standards, instruments of soft law, and formulated accordingly—i.e., with 'should' language.[120] Some of the laid out requirements are to be implemented at national level by *law*, which means by "any legislation issued or approved through a Parliamentary process or other equivalent means provided for under the country's constitutional framework, which imposes mandatory requirements with sanctions for non-compliance",[121] others by *law or enforceable means*—i.e., "regulations, guidelines, instructions or other documents or mechanisms that set out enforceable AML/CFT requirements in mandatory language with sanctions for non-compliance, and which are issued or approved by a competent authority".[122] The regulatory activity of the FATF is not, however, the only ongoing effort to set standards in the crypto-asset space.

[117] Recommendation 20 about FIs. Recommendation 21 outlines the principles of 'tipping-off' (it is prohibited to disclose an STR was filed) and 'confidentiality' (protection from liability for breaches of disclosure restrictions).

[118] Article 69(1) of Regulation (EU) 2024/1624.

[119] Article 71(2) of Regulation (EU) 2024/1624.

[120] To assess compliance, however, 'should' is interpreted as 'must' (Financial Action Task Force, 2012, p. 128).

[121] Due to the framework's global nature and the involvement of various legal systems, the FATF Recommendations specify "the notion of law also encompasses judicial decisions that impose relevant requirements, and which are binding and authoritative in all parts of the country" (Financial Action Task Force, 2012, p. 115).

[122] Financial Action Task Force (2012), p. 115.

From a technical perspective, other initiatives have AML/CFT repercussions. In particular, standardisation efforts addressed blockchain technology and DLTs, where standards are an instrument to "accelerate the process of technology implementation, reduce transaction costs, level out regulatory risks, improve the interoperability of systems, and improve the quality of interaction between market participants, as well as it will increase the attractiveness of securing assets on a blockchain".[123] This landscape is populated by voluntary industry-driven initiatives, generating a fragmented scenario where the main focus is on terminology and security. A few international actions of technical standardisation are worth mentioning,[124] to introduce their relationship with regulatory standardisation, explored in Chap. 7.

First, the International Organisation for Standardisation (ISO) is the largest developer of voluntary standardisation, focusing on commercial, technical, and industrial standards. The ISO/TC 307 Technical Committee (TC) was created in 2016 for blockchain and DLT standardisation, to lay out a common language for safe and secure cryptocurrency use, including ISO/CD 22739:2020 on terminology, ISO/TR 23455:2019 on smart contracts, ISO/ TR 23244:2020 on privacy and data protection, ISO 23257:2022 on architecture, ISO/TS 23258:2021 on taxonomy and ontology, ISO/TR 23576:2020 on security management of digital asset custodians, ISO/TS 23635:2022 on governance. ISO/TC 68/SC 8 focused on reference data for financial services, where ISO 24165 introduced the Digital Token Identifier.[125]

Secondly, within the International Telecommunication Union (ITU), the Telecommunication Standardisation Sector (ITU-T) develops international standards (i.e., ITU-T Recommendations) to define infrastructural elements.[126] While the ITU-T Study Groups are technical groups that develop the Recommendations, Focus Groups are a flexible pre-standardisation exercise to respond to immediate needs.[127] The work of two Focus Groups is cited in this publication: the one on 'Application of DLT' and the one on 'Digital Currency including Digital Fiat Currency (DFC)', both active from 2017 to 2019. The Focus Group-DFC is a

---

[123] König et al. (2020), p. 1. World Economic Forum (2020). Standardisation initiatives include European Telecommunications Standards Institute (ETSI) Industry Specification Group on Permissioned DL, ITU-T Focus Group, working groups by ISO, IEEE, Worldwide Web Consortium (W3C), EU Agency for Cybersecurity, European Committee for Electrotechnical Standardisation (CENELEC), Internet Engineering Task Force. Further, NISTIR 8202 Blockchain Technology Overview published by National Institute of Standards and Technology (NIST), Distributed Ledger and Blockchain Technology Study Group by ANSI Accredited Standards Committee X9, specifications issued by the German Institute for Standardisation (DIN).

[124] In line with the literature and despite the value of the ERC Token standard, this work does not consider "company specific protocols or processes which are sometimes falsely called 'standard' [. . .] as such implementations are only relevant for individual solutions and not globally applicable standardisation that is independent from the chosen blockchain platform" (König et al., 2020, p. 4).

[125] Johnstone (2021b), p. 139. König et al. (2020), p. 6.

[126] ITU-T (2022a).

[127] ITU-T (2022c).

banking, fintech and telecom discussion forum, to share best practices, and develop deliverables, requirements for network infrastructure and CBDC standards.[128]

Third, the Cryptocurrency Security Standard (CCSS), introduced in 2014 and maintained by the CCSS Steering Committee and the Cryptocurrency Certification Consortium (C4), is a complementary open standard on cryptocurrency storage and usage—i.e., "a set of requirements for all information systems that make use of cryptocurrencies, including exchanges, web applications, and cryptocurrency storage solutions".[129] It covers only wallet management.[130]

Although technical standards often pursue compliance goals, they usually refer to existing regulatory frameworks and do not pursue the establishment of regulatory standards. The two categories of standardisation, however, feature common aspects that mostly relate to the interplay between regulatory agencies and the expertise held by the private sector. In both contexts the lines are easily blurred between standards set by regulatory agencies and self-regulatory initiatives, as the first ones often rely on the second ones. This is because standardisation is one of the ways to solve or mitigate the problem of information asymmetry, as those inside the industry typically know their industry better than regulators. Often, this asymmetry is tackled by involving experts in regulatory processes or by adopting standards as minimum safeguards. The methodologies may mirror different phases of the development of a sector. Usually, self-regulatory efforts arise when there is minimal or non-existent regulation and are introduced for the industry to survive and grow.[131] While in the early phases standards may be perceived as a hindrance, the evolution of the industry introduces a plethora of stakeholders with various objectives and incentives. At this point, the appeal of short-term advantages is often overridden by long-term interests, providing a fertile ground to introduce standards in the form of 'best practices'. Later, 'oversight regulation' is often driven by the shortcomings of self-regulatory initiatives.[132]

When a domain evolves quickly, regulators tend to rely on instruments that allow rapid responses, and they are often less formal. In these cases, standards are more about technical aspects than about distribution of powers.[133] Nonetheless, on a broader level financial regulators access industry expertise in many ways. Authorities often rely for technical advice and/or policy execution on self-regulatory organisations that are private sector authorities. The US SEC ordinarily draws from the monitoring and enforcement capabilities of the private sector,

---

[128] ITU-T (2022b).

[129] C4 (2022).

[130] Chapter 2 also mentioned other initiatives such as the ITC, the TTI, and the TTF.

[131] For instance, hacks can stimulate oversight and drive market participants to establish SROs (Tsuchiya and Hiramoto, 2021b, p. 3). Industry members have different position: some want to be free from any centralised control or only accept community-based oversight, others actively seek to be regulated—e.g., for the sake of legitimacy, to be accepted into commercial activities, as a competitive advantage (Johnstone, 2021a, p. 21).

[132] Johnstone (2021b), pp. 135–136.

[133] Brummer (2015a), p. 68.

and almost every major regulatory authority receives suggestions from consumer panels, stakeholder groups, interested private actors, in terms of preferred regulatory strategies. Nevertheless, the extent to which the private sector is formally involved in the decision-making process varies instead significantly. When self-regulatory organisations play a crucial role, such as in the US financial regulation and supervision, their involvement can go beyond self-regulation and private actors can take part in decision-making processes together with regulators.[134]

Despite usually pursued separately, regulatory (e.g., FATF) and technical (e.g., ISO, ITU-T) standardisation are not detached concepts. On the contrary, they may address similar issues, and share self-regulatory organisations and industry stakeholders as invaluable source of knowledge. The importance of their interplay is highlighted by the ongoing debates on the crypto travel rule, outlined below, and on CBDC interoperability (Chap. 6). As explored in Chap. 7, cross-disciplinarity embedded into (techno-)regulatory processes is at the heart of innovative regulatory methodologies today. From this perspective, cross-disciplinarity could be a step forward from cross-functionality (i.e., presence of members of various regulatory authorities with different experiences and responsibilities) that is currently praised in the FATF architecture, where there is a combination of financial authorities and officials from LEAs.[135]

5.3 The EU AML/CFT Regime for Crypto-Asset Transactions

A key part of the EU activity in the AML/CFT sphere consists of incorporating FATF Standards into Union law. Arguably, this alters their dynamics of diffusion: once a considerable number of jurisdictions legally endorse soft law, standards partially lose their nature of informal institutions, voluntary best practices, or products of private global governance. In the context of EU integration, EU law "acts as a legalisation mechanism that transforms soft law from informal transnational best practice into embedded rules".[136] The way standards are 'hardened' influences the institutionalisation of global financial regulation.[137] After all, "the boundaries between voluntary and mandatory regulations, state and nonstate regulations, private and public law, and hard and soft law cannot always be sharply drawn".[138] Against this backdrop, considering the dynamics of global financial regulation, in this work

[134] Brummer (2015d), pp. 18, 32.

[135] Brummer (2015d), p. 106.

[136] Newman and Bach (2014), pp. 430–432. The authors underlined the links between domestic law, global standards, soft law and private governance, while providing insights into the reasons for the resilience of some international standards vis-à-vis a frequent lack of global institutionalisation.

[137] Newman and Bach (2014), p. 433.

[138] Vogel (2008), p. 265.

the role of standards in the EU is explored from a state of the art (in this chapter) and from evolutionary angle (in Chap. 7).

Among other aspects, Article 5 of the Treaty on the European Union (TEU) requires EU actions to comply with the principles of subsidiarity and proportionality.[139] Arguably, it is not possible to achieve AML/CFT objectives in the Internal Market through regulatory actions at Member State level (principle of subsidiarity). Indeed, after three decades of activity in the area, the EC still underlines the detrimental effects of criminals exploiting the fragmentation among national regimes, and entities with cross-border activities having to comply with different approaches. From this perspective, Union action is required to ensure a level playing field when fighting inherently cross-border problems. The way in which EU initiatives do not go beyond what is necessary to achieve their goals (principle of proportionality) is underlined below (i.e., minimum harmonisation).

The EU AML/CFT action is not a stand-alone framework. Besides the link with standardisation initiatives, it interacts with other pieces of EU legislation, in the areas of financial services and criminal law. Chiefly, it connects to the rules on payments and transfer of funds—e.g., Directive 2009/110/EC, known as Electronic Money Directive 2 (EMD2), Directive (EU) 2015/2366, known as Payment Services Directive 2 (PSD2). Other ties concern CDD and identification—e.g., the Regulation (EU) 910/2014, the eIDAS Regulation, which lays out rules on electronic identification for electronic transactions, with the amendments introduced by Regulation (EU) 2024/1183, known as eIDAS 2.0, which laid out the European Digital Identity Framework. For a broader analysis of how these and other frameworks interact from an EU perspective, the reader is referred to Barbereau et al. (2024).[140] The relationship of the EU AML/CFT regime with the 2020 Digital Finance Package is underlined below.

5.3.1 The Involvement of EU Law: From Harmonisation to the 2021 AML Package

From 1991 onwards, the EU has drafted legislation to harmonise Member States' responses in the AML/CFT sphere. In terms of regulatory methodology, until 2024 EU actions took the form of Directives of minimum harmonisation, where Member States can adopt stricter provisions than those laid out by the European regulator and considerable discretion is left to national transposition.[141] The EC recently

[139] Treaty on the European Union (2012).

[140] While the EMD2 and the PSD2 offer complementary insights in terms of definitions, they do not provide innovative elements for what concerns mitigating the risks emerging from the socio-technical features of crypto-asset transactions. This is why, for the sake of consistency, they are not analysed comprehensively in this book.

[141] Article 5 of the AMLD: "Member States may adopt or retain in force stricter provisions in the field covered by this Directive to prevent money laundering and terrorist financing, within the limits of Union law".

confirmed the value of the approach, as the alternative of maximum harmonisation would be incompatible with the RBA.[142] Meanwhile, the evolution of EU measures to fight the misuse of the financial system mirrors the increasing socio-economic inter-connections at the global level and within the Single Market. This is not surprising, as integration provides opportunities to legitimate business, but also to criminals willing to launder illicit proceeds or fund criminal activities.

The preceding sections outlined the development of the scope of AML/CFT measures at the international level, from a limited framework to a comprehensive scheme. The EU harmonisation effort shows a similar process. The First AML Council Directive 91/308/EEC (1AMLD) had a narrow scope in line with the original 1990 FATF Recommendations. However, it laid out the foundations of a framework on which the Second and Third Directives continued to rely. It took ten years before the Second AML Directive 2001/97/EC (2AMLD) updated the 1AMLD to comply with the 'FATF 40 Recommendations', whose first version was adopted in 1996. Similarly, the Third Directive 2005/60/EC (3AMLD) is closely related to the tightening of FATF's Standards, as updated in 2003 and expanded to terrorist financing from 2001 onwards.[143]

Notwithstanding the ground-breaking character of early initiatives, the modern EU AML/CFT framework was established by the Fourth Directive (EU) 2015/849 (4AMLD), coupled with Regulation (EU) 2015/847 on information accompanying transfer of funds.[144] Three years later, a remarkable step forward was brought about by the Fifth AML Directive (EU) 2018/843 (5AMLD), whose provisions, outlined above, addressed the anonymity of VCs and providers of related services. The legal basis of the current EU AML/CFT regime is Article 114 of the TFEU.

Additionally, Directive (EU) 2018/1673 focused on combating money laundering by means of criminal law, mostly in terms of prompting efficiency in cross-border cooperation and building upon Council Framework Decision 2001/500/JHA with regard to the criminalisation of money laundering.[145] Meanwhile, Directive

---

[142] European Commission (2021a), p. 5. Among EU requirements laid out by directives, a directive of 'minimum harmonisation' sets minimum standards and Member States retain the right of setting stricter ones, while in the case of 'maximum harmonisation' they cannot introduce stricter rules.

[143] The political and economic context of the 3AMLD was the aftermath of 09/11 and other terrorist attacks such as the 2004 bombings in Madrid. The definition of 'serious crimes', the 'predicate offences', was aligned to 2001 Council Framework Decision 2001/500/JHA, whose Article 3(5)(f) includes as 'serious crimes' all offences "punishable by deprivation of liberty or a detention order for a maximum of more than one year or, as regards those States which have a minimum threshold for offences in their legal system, all offences punishable by deprivation of liberty or a detention order for a minimum of more than six months".

[144] In 2012, the FATF had extensively renovated its Recommendations, which still lie at the core of the new EU provisions.

[145] Reference is to the need of a sufficiently uniform definition of predicate offences and criminal treatment, including self-laundering (Recital 11: "Member States should ensure that certain types of money laundering activities are also punishable when committed by the perpetrator of the criminal activity that generated the property ('self-laundering') [...]") and to pay attention to new risks and challenges generated by VCs (Recitals 5 and 6).

(EU) 2017/1371 defined financial crimes affecting the financial interest of the EU, included in the predicate offences, while Directive (EU) 2017/541 introduced a common understanding of the terrorist financing crime. Lastly, Directive (EU) 2019/1153 aimed to facilitate information exchange between authorities.

The landscape of EU legislative activities on AML/CFT started evolving significantly in the past years. In July 2021 the EC put forward a set of legislative proposals—dubbed 'AML Package'—to implement its May 2020 Action Plan for a comprehensive Union policy on preventing money laundering and terrorist financing.[146] The goal was not to thoroughly transform the framework, but to overcome the fragmentation caused by the national transposition of a directive-based and principle-based regime, thus ensuring its effective and consistent implementation. Meanwhile, this narrowed the gap between AML/CFT actions and the Digital Finance Package adopted in September 2020. Reference is primarily to what was to become Regulation (EU) 2023/1114, the Regulation on Markets in Crypto-Assets (MiCA Regulation) and its definitions of crypto-assets (Article 3(1)(5)) and crypto-asset service provider (Article 3(1)(15)).

The AML Package is largely based on Regulations and consists of rule-based obligations binding for all (natural and legal) persons within the EU. This means the regime is applicable at domestic level in a direct and immediate way, without needing to be transposed into national legislation. Hence, the Union's approach to AML/CFT changes in terms of legal instrument for the sake of uniformity. The AML and the Digital Finance Packages adopt the same methodology of issuing their foundational norms through Regulations—in the AML Package all provisions that apply to regulated entities are laid out by Regulations, while organisational aspects of national regimes are governed by a Directive—, and in both cases the legal basis is Article 114 of the TFEU on the approximation of laws when necessary to the establishment and functioning of the Internal Market.[147] In the two packages, the choice of legal basis is justified, respectively, with the need to remove establishment obstacles and improve the functioning of the internal market for financial services, and the capacity of money laundering and terrorist financing to generate cross-border level economic losses, functional disruption, and reputational damage.[148]

The AML Package implements the 2020 Action Plan, which was drafted in response to a set of analyses of the effectiveness the regime.[149] It is based on six pillars and chiefly on the need for harmonised and directly applicable rules, which had emerged as a priority to deal with cross-border situations. Three out of the six pillars demanded legislative action, and led to three legislative acts adopted in May 2024, to establish an EU-wide AML/CFT single rulebook, EU-level supervision, as well as a support and co-operation system among FIUs.

[146] European Commission (2020).

[147] Treaty on the Functioning of the European Union (2012).

[148] Respectively, Regulation (EU) 2023/1114, p. 4, and European Commission (2021a), p. 4.

[149] European Commission (2019c).

5.3.2 *The EU-Wide Rulebook Under Regulation (EU) 2024/1624*

The single rulebook is established by Regulation (EU) 2024/1624 on the prevention of the use of the financial system for money laundering and terrorist financing purposes (AML Regulation), as well as by Regulation (EU) 2023/1113 that recast Regulation (EU) 2015/847 to expand traceability requirements to crypto-assets. The main points of the first act are the expansion of the list of 'obliged entities' to include CASPs, the clarification of the requirements on internal policies, controls and procedures, and the granularisation of CDD measures, the streamlining of beneficial ownership requirements,[150] the clarification of red flags,[151] and the strengthening of the measures to mitigate the misuse of bearer instruments, and the inclusion of a limit to the use of cash for large transactions.

From this last perspective, an EU-wide limit to cash payments of EUR 10,000 is set by Article 80, dubbed 'limits to large cash payments in exchange for goods or services'.[152] In this respect, the EC goes beyond FATF Standards, to tackle Union-level risks.[153] To this end, Article 80(1) prevents 'persons trading in goods or providing services' from accepting cash payments of over EUR 10,000 in a single transaction or several transactions which appear to be linked. Member States can adopt a lower limit and the EC will assess the impact of lowering the threshold in three years. The threshold does not apply to private operations between individuals not acting in a professional function, nor to transactions made at credit institutions, albeit in the last case the operation shall be reported.[154]

Article 80 belongs to Chapter VIII, dubbed "measures to mitigate risks deriving from anonymous instruments", which includes Article 79 on 'anonymous accounts and bearer shares and bearer share warrants'. Article 79(1) prohibits financial institutions and CASPs from keeping "anonymous bank and payment accounts, anonymous passbooks, anonymous safe-deposit boxes or anonymous crypto-asset accounts as well as any account otherwise allowing for the anonymisation of

[150] The AML Regulation sets rules to identify the beneficial owners of corporate and other legal entities, and a harmonised approach to beneficial ownership. It includes provisions to ensure consistent identification of beneficial owners of trusts and similar legal entities/arrangements. It sets disclosure requirements for nominee shareholders and directors and provides for mandatory beneficial ownership registration for non-EU entities doing business with an EU regulated entity or acquire real estate in the EU.

[151] The AML Regulation clarifies rules on transaction identification. Further, to ease compliance with reporting duties and improve the effectiveness of analytical and cooperation activities, the AMLA is entrusted to develop technical standards with a uniform common template for STRs (Recital 139 of Regulation (EU) 2024/1624).

[152] Article 2(1)(43) defines 'cash' as "cash as defined in Article 2(1), points (c) to (f) of Regulation (EU) 2018/1672", which includes currency, bearer-negotiable instruments, commodities used as highly-liquid stores of value, and prepaid cards.

[153] European Commission (2021a), p. 3.

[154] Article 80(4) of Regulation (EU) 2024/1624.

the customer account holder or the anonymisation or increased obfuscation of transactions, including through anonymity-enhancing coins".[155] Relatedly, Recital 160 clarifies how it is necessary to prohibit anonymous crypto-wallets. This is because crypto-assets' anonymity makes them vulnerable to criminal misuse, and anonymous crypto-wallets render transfers untraceable and hampers the identification of suspicious linked transactions and the application of adequate CDD.[156]

With reference to CDD measures, specifications are introduced on identification and identity verification, as well as the conditions to use means of electronic identification. In particular, regulated entities shall accept for CDD purposes electronic identification means if they meet the requirements of Regulation (EU) 910/2014 as per assurance levels 'substantial' or 'high' and relevant qualified trust services.[157] This pursues coherence with other Union policies on remote customer onboarding in compliance with the Digital Finance Strategy. The eIDAS Regulation, as amended by eIDAS 2.0, defines 'electronic identification' as "the process of using person identification data in electronic form uniquely representing either a natural or legal person, or a natural person representing another natural person or a legal person" (Article 3(1)(1)), and 'electronic identification means' as "a material and/or immaterial unit containing person identification data and which is used for authentication for an online service or, where appropriate, for an offline service" (Article 3(1)(2)).[158] As explored below, the new AML Authority would be in charge of providing details on simplified and enhanced CDD measures.

On an important side note, the original version of the proposal of the AML Regulation provided that financial institutions and CASPs had to apply CDD when initiating or executing an occasional transaction that consists of a transfer of funds or crypto-assets as per Regulation (EU) 2023/1113, exceeding EUR 1000. During the legislative process, however, the provision was modified to apply only to financial institutions. What is now Article 19(3) provides that CASPs shall apply CDD when carrying out an occasional transaction that amounts to a value of at least EUR 1000, but also that they shall apply at least CDD measures related to identification and verification of the identity of the customer when carrying out an occasional transaction where the value is below EUR 1000.

5.3.3 Regulation (EU) 2024/1620 and the New AML Authority

Besides a single rulebook, the Action Plan outlined the need for EU-level supervision. This urgency had been underlined for some time, and Regulation (EU)

---

[155] If the instrument exists, CDD measures are to be applied before it is used.

[156] Regulation (EU) 2024/1624, Recital 160. Furthermore, as per Article 79(3) companies are prohibited from issuing bearer shares and shall convert the existing ones, unless they are listed or their shares are issued as intermediated securities, while the issuance of bearer share warrants is only allowed in intermediated form.

[157] Article 22(5)(b) of Regulation (EU) 2024/1624.

[158] Regulation (EU) 910/2014; Regulation (EU) 2024/1183.

2019/2175 had already attributed to the EBA core competencies on the coordination and monitoring of the implementation of the AML/CFT framework.[159] This methodology, however, had not proven sufficient vis-à-vis the difficulties of competent authorities to cooperate effectively both domestically and cross-border, the existing divergences in the application of the RBA, also in terms of supervision, and the specificities of the EBA's governance model.[160] Accordingly, the AML Package put forward a proposal for a Regulation creating an EU Authority for AML/CFT,[161] a step that is seen as "crucial for ensuring the efficient and adequate supervision of obliged entities that pose a high risk [. . .] strengthening common supervisory approaches for all other obliged entities, and facilitating joint analyses and cooperation between FIUs".[162]

The resulting AMLA Regulation was adopted as Regulation (EU) 2024/1620, and the rules-based nature of the AML Regulation is expected to provide a consistent framework for the AMLA to supervise its application.[163] The seat of the AMLA was set in Frankfurt am Main, Germany.[164] The powers bestowed on AMLA pursue the objectives laid out by Article 1(3) of Regulation (EU) 2024/1620 and include (a) direct supervision on certain obliged entities in the financial sector, including CASPs—in particular, "high-risk cross-border credit institutions and financial institutions with activity in a significant number of Member States, selected periodically; and, in exceptional cases, any entity whose material breaches of applicable requirements are not sufficiently or in a timely manner addressed by its national supervisor",[165] (b) monitoring, analysis and exchange of information on money laundering and terrorist financing risks in the EU, (c) coordination and oversight of AML/CFT supervisors of both the financial sector and the non-financial sector, including self-regulatory bodies, and (d) coordination and support of FIUs.[166] In this sense, for what concerns the financial sector the AMLA has both direct and indirect supervisory competences. They are outlined in Sections 3 and 4 of Regulation (EU) 2024/1620, respectively.

One of the key tasks entrusted on the AMLA concern the development of risk-based specifications—in the form of draft regulatory technical standards (RTSs) and draft implementing technical standards (ITSs)—of compliance aspects as per Regulation (EU) 2023/1113, Regulation (EU) 2024/1624, and Directive (EU) 2024/1640, including targeted financial sanctions and supervisory methodology.[167] The AMLA is also expected to "establish a central AML/CFT database with

[159] Covolo (2020), p. 250.

[160] European Commission (2021b), p. 3. Recital 10 of Regulation (EU) 2024/1620.

[161] European Commission (2021b). European Parliamentary Research Service (2023).

[162] Recital 3 of Regulation (EU) 2024/1620.

[163] European Commission (2021a), p. 3.

[164] Recital 8 and Article 4 of Regulation (EU) 2024/1620. European Commission (2024).

[165] Recital 19 of Regulation (EU) 2024/1620.

[166] Recital 5 and Articles 5–6 of Regulation (EU) 2024/1620.

[167] Recitals 10–12 and Articles 49 and 53 of Regulation (EU) 2024/1620.

information collected from all supervisory authorities, and should make such information available to any supervisory authority and non-AML/CFT authority within the system where necessary, on a confidential and need-to-know basis".[168] Relatedly, as per Article 5(5)(i-j), the AMLA is expected to develop tools and services to enhance the analysis capabilities of FIUs, in combination with IT and AI services and tools for secure information sharing. It is also expected to develop expert knowledge on detection, analysis, and dissemination methods of suspicious transactions. This has a clear impact in the context of crypto-asset analytics as outlined in Chap. 4.

5.3.4 *EU Law, International Standards, and AMLA's RTSs*

AML/CFT measures adopted at the EU level are deeply intertwined with FATF Standards. Besides the prestige of the international framework, the cross-border nature of money laundering and terrorist financing would make siloed Union actions largely ineffective. For this reason, the AMLA pursues international coordination and the adoption of measures compatible with (or at least as stringent as) international ones.[169] The value of the tie is undisputed, but the formal relationship between EU law and international standards is a more complex and open-ended topic. It concerns the FATF's action but also BCBS's standards, in terms of implementation of the standards into EU law and legal basis for the participation of EU institutions in standard-setting processes. In line with the evolution of EU financial integration, the ECB, the EC and the EBA take part into the BCBS together with national authorities, the ECB also as a representative of the Single Supervisory Mechanism (SSM).[170] However, some areas tackled by the BCBS, such as AML/CFT, fall within the competences of national supervisory authority, not of the SSM.[171]

In this context, the relationship between EU law and BCBS standards was analysed under the lens of an increasing politicisation of a technocratic debate on financial regulation. In the wake of the 2008 crisis, an emerging distrust in technical knowledge reduced the perceived value of technocracy as a basis for authority.[172] In addition, although the participation of EU institutions in the BCBS standard-setting process causes problems of legal basis under EU law, the issue was largely ignored upon the establishment of the Banking Union. Against this backdrop, literature focused on the need to improve the credibility of technocratic authorities

[168] Recital 18 and Articles 5(1)(d) and 11 of Regulation (EU) 2024/1620.

[169] Recital 1 of Amsden et al. (2019).

[170] The EC and the EBA are observers; the ECB and SSM represent the Monetary and the Banking Union.

[171] Viterbo (2019), pp. 212–213, 223.

[172] Viterbo (2019), pp. 206, 227. The change of approach and perspective clearly emerges when comparing post-crisis literature with previous analyses of the success of the BCBS system—e.g., Kerwer (2005), pp. 619–220.

in terms of transparency, accountability, protection of social values and public policy goals, by involving non-technical players and the civil society in developing standards.[173] This is not surprising: "when global standards are effective, the question of how to subject them to democratic control often arises", notably in terms of the accountability of standard-setters.[174] In this sense, also crypto-asset regulation is affected by challenges arising from the relationship between FATF Standards, the mechanisms of EU law, and the dynamics between regulatory and technical standards.

From this perspective, one may consider how the AMLA is expected to draft RTSs and ITSs on key aspects of AML/CFT compliance. As per Article 49(1) of Regulation (EU) 2024/1620, the AMLA can draft RTSs within the limits set by Article 290 of the TFEU—i.e., a legislative act may delegate to the EC the adoption of non-legislative acts to supplement or amend non-essential elements. Objectives, content and scope are defined in the legislative acts. RTSs are technical, do not imply policy choices and their content is limited by the delegating act—their draft is submitted to the EC for adoption, which is by means of regulations or decisions.[175]

These instruments are not new to the EU financial services and banking domain, nor to the AML/CFT framework. Indeed, for instance, draft RTSs were published in 2021 by EBA on the AML/CFT central database,[176] and in 2017 by the ESAs on the implementation of group wide AML/CFT policies in third countries,[177] adopted by the EC in 2019,[178] and by the EBA on central contact points,[179] adopted by the EC in 2018.[180] A recent related example concerns the draft RTSs on supervisory colleges under the MiCA Regulation.[181]

Already the 5AMLD, in combination with the regime introduced by Article 9a of Regulation (EU) 2019/2175 on EBA's tasks related to AML/CFT—in particular, by amending Regulation (EU) 1093/2010, which established the EBA—, referred to RTSs in Article 45 (6–7, 10–11), and to guidelines in Articles 17, 18(4) and 48(10)—e.g., on risk factors to be considered when performing CDD. The AML Package, however, besides appointing a dedicated Authority, increased the array of matters to be covered by RTSs. The qualification grants the outcome of the AMLA's work, when adopted by the EC, with the status of Delegated Regulation and related binding effects. Indeed, they are to be adopted as a supplement to the AML Regulation. The AMLA is also mandated to adopt guidelines, recommendations and opinions on several topics, as per Articles 6 and 54 of Regulation (EU) 2024/1620.

---

173 Viterbo (2019), pp. 206, 228.

174 Kerwer (2005), p. 611.

175 Article 49(1–4) of Regulation (EU) 2024/1620.

176 European Banking Authority (2021).

177 European Banking Authority et al. (2017).

178 European Commission (2019b).

179 European Banking Authority (2017).

180 European Commission (2018a).

181 European Banking Authority (2024).

The difference between adopting draft RTSs and issuing guidelines emerges from Recital 10 of Regulation (EU) 2024/1620. On the one hand, "[c]ertain aspects of the methodology, which can incorporate harmonised quantitative benchmarks, such as approaches for classifying the risk profile of obliged entities, including their inherent and residual risk profiles, should be detailed in directly applicable binding regulatory measures [...] in order to ensure effective interaction between AML/CFT supervision and prudential supervision".[182] On the other hand, "[o]ther aspects of the methodology, which require wider supervisory discretion, such as approaches to assessing the internal controls of obliged entities, should be covered by non-binding guidelines, recommendations and opinions of the Authority".[183]

For instance, the AMLA is expected to issue guidelines on risk factors for regulated entities,[184] and on information necessary to perform standard, simplified and enhanced CDD.[185] In the development of the guidelines, findings of international organisations and standard setters are to be heeded. In particular, the most comprehensive drafting concerns the application of the RBA to CDD. As per Article 19(9) of the AML Regulation, the AMLA is tasked to specify: (a) entities, sectors and transactions with higher risk; (b) related thresholds for occasional transactions and business relationships; and (c) criteria to identify linked transactions. The standards must build on the inherent risk levels of business models and the EC's supranational risk assessment. The AMLA is also expected to develop RTSs setting out (i) minimum information (i.e., standard dataset) to be obtained when performing standard, simplified and enhanced CDD, depending on each customer's risk level, inherent risk of the service, transaction's nature, amount and recurrence, channels used); (ii) simplified CDD measures to be applied in lower risk situations; (iii) reliable and independent sources to perform identity verification of natural and legal persons; and (iv) a list of attributes for an eID scheme and relevant trust services (as set out by the eIDAS Regulation as amended by the mentioned eIDAS 2.0) to fulfil the requirements.[186]

The goal is to enable the private sector to develop secure innovative means to perform identity verification and CDD, also remotely.[187] Additionally, as per Article 69(5) of the AML Regulation, the AMLA is expected to provide draft RTSs outlining a common template for reporting suspicious transactions, to be used uniformly throughout the EU. The objective is to ease compliance and reporting but also to increase the effectiveness of analysis and cooperation among FIUs.[188]

---

[182] Recital 10 of Regulation (EU) 2024/1620.

[183] Recital 10 of Regulation (EU) 2024/1620.

[184] Article 19(9) of Regulation (EU) 2024/1624.

[185] Article 28 of Regulation (EU) 2024/1624.

[186] Article 22 of Regulation (EU) 2024/1624.

[187] Recital 74 of Regulation (EU) 2024/1624. Indeed, these RTSs "should provide sufficient clarity to allow market players to develop secure, accessible and innovative means of verifying customers' identity and performing customer due diligence, including remotely, while respecting the principle of technology neutrality" (Recital 74 of Regulation (EU) 2024/1624).

[188] Recital 139 of Regulation (EU) 2024/1624.

5.4 The Crypto Travel Rule and Active Cooperation

Over the years, the FATF's framework has expanded the scope of its measures to include (a part of) the crypto-asset space. However, the approach still relies on 'active cooperation' and there was arguably no alteration of the framework's fundamentals to tailor the regime to the specificities of the crypto-asset world. On the one hand, RBA-based procedures and policies were adapted to crypto-assets, and most jurisdiction made considerable progress in responding to emerging risks. On the other hand, these efforts are insufficient to address comprehensively the array of problems associated with crypto-assets and thrust on the industry burdens that may be counter-productive. One of the most topical examples is the technological difficulty encountered by service providers when it comes to ensuring originators and recipients of crypto-asset transactions are identifiable and not anonymous, to comply with the so-called 'crypto travel rule'.[189]

The crypto travel rule expands information sharing measures, previously applicable only to transfer of funds performed via wire transfers (the 'travel rule'), to the crypto-asset space. These rules require financial institutions to collect and share with their counterparties certain data to ensure traceability throughout the payment chain. Against the backdrop of the findings of the previous chapters, it is not surprising that an 'active cooperation'-based regime may generate friction when applied to crypto-assets. Indeed, although obligations such as the crypto travel rule may further integrate crypto-assets and the traditional financial system, they also pose substantial risks of displacing activities towards unsupervised areas—e.g., to DEXes, given their proximity to the inspiration underpinning the 'blockchain hype'.[190]

5.4.1 The Travel Rule: FATF Recommendation 16 and Regulation (EU) 2015/847

The goal of FATF Recommendation 16 on 'wire transfers' is to thwart the capacity of criminals to misuse the wire transfer system to move their funds. This is pursued by making sure to detect any attempt, trace the relevant transactions and collect the necessary information to hold them accountable. Hence, a duty is imposed on some regulated entities to collect, share and, in specific cases, make available to the competent authorities (e.g., FIUs and LEAs) certain information on originators

[189] Goforth (2021), p. 11. For further details: Pocher (2025).

[190] Johnstone (2021e), p. 76.

and beneficiaries of all wire transfers, both cross-border and domestic.[191] In other words, a set of data must accompany the funds throughout the payment chain.

Details on data to be collected and shared are laid out in the Interpretative Note to Recommendation 16, where a different regime concerns domestic and cross-border transfers.[192] In this context, diverse rules are imposed on financial institutions and MVTSs depending on whether they are (i) the ordering, (ii) the intermediary or (iii) the beneficiary entity. From the perspective of ordering financial institutions, cross-border wire transfers must include: (a) name of the originator, (b) originator account number—or, if not applicable, a unique transaction reference number; (c) originators' address, or national ID number, or customer ID number, or date/place of birth; (d) name of the beneficiary; (e) beneficiary account number—or, if not applicable, a unique transaction reference number.[193] For cross-border transfers, countries may adopt a minimum threshold no higher than EUR/USD 1000—whether in a single transaction or more transactions that appear to be linked—, below which they can apply the domestic regime. All data must be verified for accuracy and stored as per the record-keeping obligations. Accordingly, the ordering financial institution should not be allowed to execute the transfer if it does not comply with the requirements. Secondly, intermediary financial institutions must ensure originator and beneficiary information are retained with the cross-border transfer and take reasonable measures to identify cases where any data is lacking, which also means having procedures to reject or suspend the transfer and take follow-up actions.[194] Lastly, beneficiary financial institutions must take reasonable measures to identify cross-border transfers that lack some data, in terms of both real-time and post-event monitoring.

The FATF's travel rule was implemented in the EU in 2015. Although the AML Package marks a decisive change from a principles-based to a rules-based regime, the EU AML/CFT effort has never been a stranger to Regulations. Indeed, the 4AMLD was accompanied by Regulation (EU) 2015/847 on information accompanying transfers of funds (Fund Transfers Regulation (FTR)) sent or received by a PSP or an intermediary PSP established in the Union (Article 2(1)). Article

[191] As per FATF Recommendation 16, wire transfer is any electronic transaction on the originator's behalf through a financial institution to make funds available to a beneficiary at a beneficiary financial institution. Transfers where both originator and beneficiary are financial institutions acting on their behalf, are exempted from the travel rule. The originator is the "account holder who allows the wire transfer from that account, or where there is no account, the natural or legal person that places the order with the ordering financial institution to perform the wire transfer". The beneficiary is the "natural or legal person or legal arrangement who is identified by the originator as the receiver of the requested wire transfer" (FATF Recommendation 16).

[192] This distinction is relevant because crypto-asset transfers are deemed inherently cross-border.

[193] For domestic wire transfers if the ordering financial institution can make this data available within a specific timeframe, only the account number or unique transaction reference must be included with the transfer itself.

[194] Pursuant to the FATF's Glossary, reasonable measures are defined as "appropriate measures which are commensurate with the money laundering or terrorist financing risks".

2(4) excludes PSP-to-PSP fund transfers, and other cases, from the regime. In this case, 'funds' are defined as "banknotes and coins, scriptural money and electronic money",[195] and the concept of 'transfer of funds' refers to transactions performed, at least partially, by electronic means, including credit transfers, direct debits, money remittances and transfers via payment cards, e-money instruments, mobile phones or other digital/IT devices (Article 3(9)). As per the FTR, the transfer's domestic or cross-border nature is assessed in terms of intra-EU (all PSPs involved are EU-based) and extra-EU (Articles 5–6).

5.4.2 The Advent of the Crypto Travel Rule: Recent Evolutions

Before the Interpretative Note to Recommendation 15 on 'new technologies' was revised in 2018, the travel rule bore no mention to crypto funds, and at the EU level the FTR included no reference to the crypto-asset sphere. However, the revision of the Interpretative Note addressed a specification on the application of Recommendation 16 to VA transfers. Countries were asked to introduce new rules on financial institutions and VASPs, whereby (i) originators obtain and hold required and accurate originator information and required beneficiary information, submit it to the beneficiary (if any) timely and securely, and on request make it available to the authorities; and (ii) beneficiaries obtain and hold required originator information and required and accurate beneficiary information, and on request make it available to the authorities. The scope of application of other rules laid out by Recommendation 16 was extended accordingly—e.g., data monitoring, freezing actions, prohibiting transactions with designated persons/entities.

Consistently, the AML Package included a recast of the FTR to narrow the crypto travel rule gap and adjust the regime to specific crypto-asset features. The reform was adopted as Regulation (EU) 2023/1113.[196] The new rules target PSPs, CASPs and intermediary PSPs and introduce the obligation to collect and make accessible to the authorities specific data on originators and beneficiaries of crypto-asset transfers (Fig. 5.1). As outlined above, the reference is to MiCA's definition of 'crypto-assets', that corresponds to FATF's definition of 'virtual assets', since the definition of CASPs encompasses VASPs. In its Recital 8, the Regulation (EU) 2023/1113 explicitly targets crypto-asset-related anonymity, as "[t]heir global reach, the speed at which transactions can be carried out and the possible anonymity offered by their

[195] By reference to Article 4(15) Directive 2007/64/EC (PSD) replaced by Article 4(25) Directive (EU) 2015/2366 (PSD2). The definition of 'funds' refers to Directive 2009/110/EC (EMD2), where e-money is "electronically, including magnetically, stored monetary value as represented by a claim on the issuer which is issued on receipt of funds for the purpose of making payment transactions as defined in point 5 of Article 4 of Directive 2007/64/EC, and which is accepted by a natural or legal person other than the electronic money issuer" (Article 2(2)).

[196] For a broader analysis on the crypto travel rule and related challenges, please see Financial Action Task Force (2024a) and Pocher (2025).

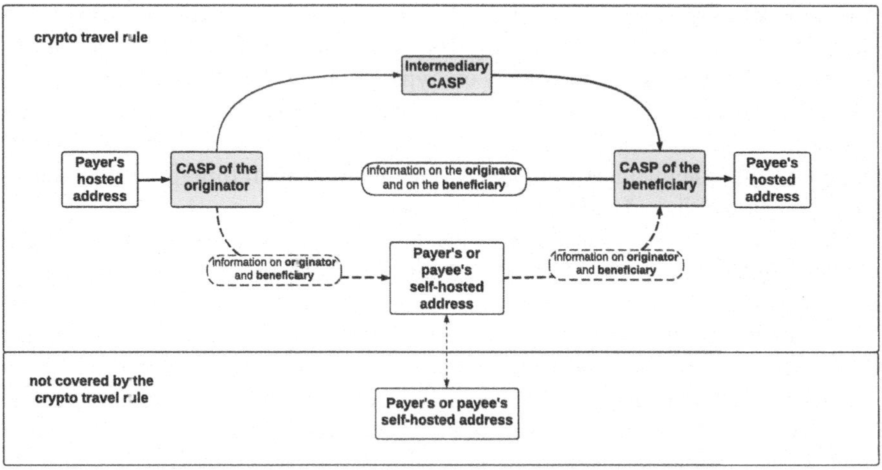

Fig. 5.1 Information exchange as per Regulation (EU) 1113/2023. Based on Pocher (2025)

transfer make virtual assets particularly susceptible to criminal misuse, including in cross-border situations".

The new regime applies to transfers of funds sent or received by a PSP or an intermediary PSP established in the EU, transfers of crypto-assets,[197] also including transfers of crypto-assets by crypto-ATMs, where the CASP of the originator or the beneficiary is established in the EU.[198] Taking into consideration the risks related to crypto-assets and their specificities, all related transfers are considered cross-border transfers rather than domestic, as required by the FATF's Interpretative Note to Recommendation 16. In particular, Recital 27 of the Regulation (EU) 2023/1113 outlines how "[d]ue to the inherent borderless nature and global reach of transfers of crypto-assets and of the provision of crypto-asset services, there are no objective reasons to distinguish the treatment of money laundering and terrorist financing risks of national transfers from that of cross-border transfers. In order to reflect those specific features, no exemption from the scope of this Regulation should be granted to domestic low-value transfers of crypto-assets, in line with the FATF requirement to treat all transfers of crypto-assets as cross-border."

In line with the RBA, the original version of the recast proposal distinguished between transfers (i) of more than EUR 1000—i.e., individual transfers exceeding the threshold or more transfers seemingly linked—and (ii) below this threshold,

[197] Crypto-asset transfers are defined as "any transaction with the aim of moving crypto-assets from one distributed ledger address, crypto-asset account or any other device allowing to store crypto-assets to another, carried out by at least one crypto-asset service provider acting on behalf of either an originator or a beneficiary, irrespective of whether the originator and the beneficiary are the same person and irrespective of whether the crypto-asset service provider of the originator and that of the beneficiary are one and the same" (Article 3(1)(10) of Regulation (EU) 2023/1113).

[198] Article 2(1) of Regulation (EU) 2023/1113.

where the latter were subject to a more lenient regime. This approach was rejected during the legislative process, arguing that the requirements should not depend on the amount because the pseudonymity of crypto-assets enables "large illicit transfers while circumventing traceability obligations and avoiding detection, by structuring a large transaction into smaller amounts", and most of these assets are "highly volatile and their value can fluctuate significantly within a very short time-frame that makes the calculation of linked transaction more uncertain".[199]

Hence, no matter the transferred value, according to Article 14(1–3) the CASP of the originator is required to: (a) obtain and hold for five years accurate—i.e., verified for accuracy—information on the originator: name, distributed ledger address and/or crypto-asset account number, address, official ID number, customer ID number or date and place of birth, current Legal Entity Identifier (LEI) or equivalent (if applicable);[200] (b) obtain and hold for five years certain accurate information on the beneficiary: name and distributed ledger address and/or crypto-asset account number, current LEI or equivalent (if applicable);[201] (c) securely submit all of the above to the beneficiary entity in advance of, simultaneously or concurrently with the transfer.[202]

The CASP of the beneficiary is required to: (i) monitor that the required data is included in the transfer or follows it; and (ii) before making the assets available to the payee, verify the accuracy of the data using reliable and independent sources.[203] Further, intermediary CASPs must ensure all data is relayed with the transfer, as well as comply with data retention obligations.[204] Upon request, all the information must be shared with the authorities.

Meanwhile, it is prohibited for originating CASPs to execute any transfer before they can ensure full compliance, and beneficiary CASPs must establish procedures to apply when the required data is lacking, to decide whether to execute, reject or suspend the transfer, and to determine follow-up actions.[205] Notably, if the beneficiary or intermediary CASP realises there is missing/incomplete information, it must "reject the transfer or ask for the required information on the originator and the beneficiary before or after making the crypto-assets available to the beneficiary,

[199] Recital 30 of Regulation (EU) 2023/1113.

[200] Article 14(1) of Regulation (EU) 2023/1113. Article 14(6–7) provides criteria for accuracy verification. The LEI is "a unique alphanumeric reference code based on ISO 17442 standard assigned to a legal entity" (Article 3(23)).

[201] Article 14(2) of Regulation (EU) 2023/1113.

[202] As provided by Article 14(4), the data as per Article 14(1–2) does not need to be directly included in the transfer. In addition, as per Article 15(1) in case of a batch file transfer from one originator, Article 14(1) shall not apply to the individual transfers, provided the batch file contains the information as per Article 14(1–3), verified as per Article 14(5–6), and the individual transfers contain the originator distributed ledger address, crypto-asset account number, or individual identifier.

[203] Article 16(1) and (3) of Regulation (EU) 2023/1113.

[204] Article 16(1) and (3) of Regulation (EU) 2023/1113.

[205] Article 17(1) of Regulation (EU) 2023/1113.

on a risk-sensitive basis".[206] If a CASP repeatedly fails to provide the required data, the beneficiary CASP must (a) take actions such as issuing warnings or setting deadlines, return the crypto-assets to the originator, or alternatively hold the crypto-assets so they are not made available to the beneficiary, pending review from the authorities; (b) report the failure and adopted measures to the authorities; (c) consider the missing/incomplete data when deciding on the suspiciousness of the transfer or related transactions to report them accordingly.[207] Intermediary CASPs that become aware of missing/incomplete information can decide whether to reject the transfer and return the assets or to ask for further data, and follow-up measures are to be taken if the counterparty fails to cooperate.[208]

5.4.3 *Regulation (EU) 2023/1113: Self-Hosted Addresses and Other Debates*

The Regulation (EU) 2023/1113 provides for the possibility that a 'distributed ledger address'—defined as "an alphanumeric code that identifies an address on a network using distributed ledger technology or similar technology where crypto-assets can be sent or received"—and/or a 'crypto-asset account number'—i.e., an account held by a CASP "in the name of one or more natural or legal persons which can be used for the execution of transfers of cryptoassets"—may not exist in some transfers.[209] Accordingly, in terms of data to collect, any reference to a 'distributed ledger address' is limited to cases in which the transfer is "registered on a network using distributed ledger technology or similar technology", and any reference to an 'account number' is limited to situations in which "such an account exists and is used to process the transaction".[210] When this is not the case, the CASP of the originator must ensure the transfer is accompanied by a 'unique transaction identifier' that allows traceability of the transfer back to the originator and the beneficiary (Fig. 5.1).[211]

Because the AML/CFT framework is intermediary-based, it is not surprising the regime does not apply to 'person-to-person transfers',[212] defined as "a transaction between natural person acting as consumers for purposes other than trade, business or profession. without the use or involvement of a CASP or other obliged entity".[213]

---

[206] Article 17(1) of Regulation (EU) 2023/1113.

[207] Articles 17(2), 18, 21 and 22(2) of Regulation (EU) 2023/1113.

[208] Article 20 of Regulation (EU) 2023/1113.

[209] Article 3(18) and (19) of Regulation (EU) 2023/1113.

[210] Article 14(1)(b) of Regulation (EU) 2023/1113.

[211] Articles 14(3) and 3(12) of Regulation (EU) 2023/1113.

[212] Article 2(4) of Regulation (EU) 2023/1113.

[213] Article 3(14) of Regulation (EU) 2023/1113. Similarly, the MiCA Regulation excludes hardware and software providers of non-custodial wallets from its scope of application (Recital 59 of Regulation (EU) 2023/1114 (2023)).

One of the key points of Regulation (EU) 2023/1113, however, explicitly covers the regime applicable to transfers involving self-hosted wallets, using the innovative label of 'self-hosted addresses', defined as distributed ledger addresses not linked to a CASP nor to a similar entity established outside the EU.[214] Indeed, the regime applies to crypto-asset transfers to or from a self-hosted address if a CASP is involved, although it acknowledges the complexity of this regulatory endeavour and provides for a further evaluation to be performed by the EC.[215]

In Regulation (EU) 2023/1113, transfers involving self-hosted addresses are provided with specifications in the context of the duties of originating and beneficiary CASPs. In particular, as per Articles 14(5) and 16(2), respectively, the CASP of the originator and of the beneficiary must obtain and hold the information mentioned above and ensure the transfer of crypto-assets can be individually identified. In addition, in case of a transfer exceeding EUR 1000 to a self-hosted address, the CASP of the originator must "take adequate measures to assess if such address is owned or controlled by the originator", and in case of a transfer exceeding EUR 1000 from self-hosted address the CASP of the beneficiary must take adequate measures to assess if the address is owned or controlled by the beneficiary. Indeed, upon transfers to/from self-hosted addresses, the CASP can usually collect information from the customer. In principle, the CASP is not required to verify data on the user of the self-hosted address. However, when the amount exceeds EUR 1000 and is sent/received by/from a CASP on behalf of a customer to/from a self-hosted address, the CASP must verify that the self-hosted address is owned or controlled by that customer.

While the regime for transfers involving self-hosted addresses generates one of the key controversies surrounding the FTR recast, another topical aspect concerns the interplay between the travel rule and data protection rules. Although the domain of privacy and data protection is not directly addressed by this work, in this scenario a few remarks are warranted. Indeed, the debate underlines the need to design the interplay between the AML/CFT sphere and privacy and data protection safeguards in the regulatory framework, which will be explored in Chap. 6 in terms of privacy-transparency trade-offs. Likewise, the specific crypto travel rule context (but the same could be argued outside the crypto-asset space) testifies to the need to design a regulatory framework whose compliance can be eased by technology—i.e., RegTech solutions. This topic is at the heart of Chap. 7.

As provided for by Article 25(1–2) of Regulation (EU) 2023/1113, the processing of personal data for its purposes is subject to the GDPR. Indeed, the data required by Article 14 must be submitted in compliance with the GDPR. Nonetheless, as outlined in Recital 34, crypto-assets exist in a 'borderless virtual reality', and many jurisdictions outside the EU have different data protection rules and/or enforcement measures. In this regard, Recital 19 argues the personal data transfer to

214 Article 20 of Regulation (EU) 2023/1113.

215 Recital 38 of Regulation (EU) 2023/1113. As per Recital 58, considering the high risks associated with self-hosted addresses and corresponding complexities (e.g., verification of ownership data), by 1 July 2026 the EC will assess the need of additional risk mitigation measures, including possible restrictions. The EC will assess effectiveness and proportionality of the mechanisms to verify the accuracy of the ownership information.

a third country must comply with the relevant GDPR regime. At the same time, however, service providers with branches or subsidiaries outside the EU should not be hampered from sharing data about suspicious transactions within the same organisation but must apply adequate safeguards. Because of this complex interplay, Regulation (EU) 2023/1113 mandates on the European Data Protection Board, in consultation with the EBA, the duty to issue guidelines on how to implement in practice data protection requirements when transferring personal data to third countries in the context of a crypto-asset transfer. The EBA is also mandated to issue guidelines on suitable procedures to be adopted to determine whether to execute, reject or suspend a transfer whenever, upon transferring personal data to third countries, it is not possible to ensure compliance with the relevant data protection requirements.[216]

5.4.4 Active Cooperation and the Challenge of Attribution vis-à-vis Disintermediation

While the international debate evolves towards extending the scope of the travel rule to crypto-asset transactions, the controversy comprises technical issues interwoven with policy decisions and business incentives, mirroring the tension between the evolution of crypto-assets and the needs of an AML/CFT regime that is intermediary based. At least three problems have emerged:

(i) the impact of the rule to self-hosted to hosted wallet transactions and the legitimacy of restrictions;
(ii) the challenge of linking crypto-asset-related activity to the respective actors, at least in terms of attribution to real-world identities to be identified as originators and beneficiaries;
(iii) the absence of global standards and technical solutions to underpin affordable compliance.

The first two issues could be phrased as a challenge of attribution of crypto-asset activities, under two perspectives: (a) who is to be (and can be) regulated under the AML/CFT scheme, and (b) who are the real-world identities involved in the transaction as payer and payee. In other words, both viewpoints relate to the issue of accountability frequently mentioned in this work, albeit in this research accountability is usually referred to end users (i.e., payer/payee). The problem sub (iii) is denounced by the industry, and it is an underlying issue that assumes a regulated entity is identified but lacks a RegTech solution to comply with the requirements.[217]

[216] Pocher (2025) elaborates further on these matters.

[217] de Koker and Goldbarsht (2022), p. 309. Recital 50 of Regulation (EU) 2023/1113: "[i]n order to ensure technology neutrality, this Regulation should not mandate for the use of a particular technology when crypto-asset service providers transfer transaction information. To ensure the

As the AML/CFT regime is traditionally based on the role of intermediaries in the detection of suspicious transactions, also Regulation (EU) 2023/1113 pivots on CASPs. When this approach is transposed to crypto-assets, however, it generates foundational problems. Arguably, this extension of preventive measures "fails to address the technological and structural peculiarities that distinguish cryptocurrencies from traditional banking and financial systems".[218] Although the previous chapters limited the value of the 'blockchain hype', showing how crypto-asset ecosystems are more intermediated than advertised, permissionless blockchains are inherently middlemen-free. In addition, individual freedom is at the core of the onset of DLT-based monetary applications and there are trends of enhanced disintermediation—e.g., self-hosted wallets significantly impact the efficacy of AML/CFT rules.

Notably, two scenarios generate a twofold regulatory issue. On the one hand, in case of self-hosted to self-hosted wallet transactions the fact that there is no regulated entity involved eludes the travel rule and cash-related restrictions. While this encouraged regulators to consider restrictions, in terms of bans or often threshold limits, the issue generated a heated debate. Questions of legitimacy have arisen, and advocacy groups argue it could give way to total surveillance—at odds with fundamental liberties such as privacy and autonomy, and with financial inclusion—and also possibly generate a displacement of a portion of activities towards unsupervised areas.[219] On the other hand, in case of self-hosted to hosted wallet transfers, when regulated entities receive a transfer they are required to obtain originator data but have no counterparty to interact with. Hence, self-hosted wallet holders could eventually be unable to transact with regulated PSPs, if unable or unwilling to provide the necessary information, or if the PSP adopts a de-risking approach and refuses to accept any transaction to/from self-hosted wallets in light of their (perceived) risk.

Hence, conflicting sentiments arise about the implementation of the crypto travel rule by the AML Package. While it is not easy to mitigate the risk of abuses without displacing illicit activities to P2P transfers, one wonders whether restricting self-hosted wallets unduly affects the freedom of economic activity, and/or whether the degree of enforceability of such limitations should bear any weight in the relevant policy-making.[220] Indeed, under the current regime it seems impossible to enforce restrictions outside the scope of regulatable entities,[221] while CASPs denounce

efficient implementation of requirements applicable to crypto-asset service providers under this Regulation, standard setting initiatives involving or led by the crypto-asset industry will be critical. Those protocols should be interoperable through the use of international or Union-wide standards in order to allow for a swift exchange of information".

[218] Covolo (2020).

[219] Whitehouse-Levine and Kelleher (2020).

[220] Pocher (2021a).

[221] Pocher (2021b).

the lack of affordable compliance tools, and experts outline the application of compliance requirements is over-burdening the industry.

Meanwhile, DeFi shows that even if the development of innovative services is influenced by regulation, part of the crypto-asset space is still leveraging technology to stay outside the border of compliance. These new schemes generate a challenge of attribution of activities to a regulatable entity. The crypto travel rule is a prime example of how AML/CFT regulation is still dependent to the model of CEXs and has not captured DEXes yet.[222] Relatedly, doubts have arisen about the nature of P2P trading platforms and DEXes, as strictly speaking these entities do not provide a service of exchange or conversion. Indeed, P2P exchanges provide users with a marketplace, handled by a software, that aids the connection between prospective buyers and sellers.[223] While the issue has been debated in the US, its scope narrows significantly when considering the understanding of CASP provided by MiCA, referenced by the AML Package. Indeed, Article 3(1)(16) and (18) of Regulation (EU) 2023/1114 include as 'crypto-asset service' the operation of a trading platform—where "multiple third-party purchasing and selling interests in crypto-assets, in the system and in accordance with its rules, in a way that results in a contract, either by exchanging crypto-assets for funds or by the exchange of crypto-assets for other crypto-assets"—,[224] the execution of orders on behalf of third parties, placing activities, order reception and transmission on behalf of third parties and the provision of related advice. But even when a P2P platform falls within the scope of a given AML/CFT framework, identifying the entity that can be the target of the compliance regime is problematic due to the non-centralised architecture. Indeed, usually a DEX project after its launch does not involve an organised group but is operated automatically by the protocol and governance tokens holders.[225]

In this context, not only the share of crypto-asset activity performed in contexts of enhanced disintermediation is not trivial, but the CEX-centric nature of compliance can generate a substantial shift of liquidity to DEXes. For the time being, the increase of DEX trading volume was linked to two drivers. Firstly, the total value locked in DeFi projects increased from USD 250 million in January 2019 to USD 1 billion in January 2020 to over USD 27 billion in January 2021 to almost USD 180 billion in November 2021. It then plummeted to USD 50 billion in the first half of 2023, in the aftermath of the so-called 'crypto winter'. During the first half of 2024, the total value locked in DeFi projects has steadily increased again up to over USD 100 billion.[226] Secondly, the fact that DEXes currently do not fall within the VASP definition may have displaced speculative and illegal activity towards parts of the markets more complex to reach by regulation.[227] While the definition of the

[222] Johnstone (2021d).

[223] Covolo (2020), pp. 235–236.

[224] Regulation (EU) 2023/1114, Article 3(1).

[225] Massari and Catalini (2021).

[226] DeFi LLama (2024); Chainalysis (2024).

[227] Johnstone (2021d), p. 125. Massari and Catalini (2021).

MiCA Regulation can mitigate the formal exclusion from the scope of the regime, it does not solve the qualification of 'full decentralisation',[228] as well as the technical conundrum that makes it impossible to thrust 'active cooperation' duties on them. This is highly problematic, especially given the increase of DeFi-related laundering misuse.[229]

5.5 Conclusions

This chapter investigated the AML/CFT regulatory context. Although the primary target of this book is EU law, Union-level initiatives are intertwined with the activity of the FATF in its prime function of global standard-setter. In this domain, most content of EU initiatives consists of implementing the FATF Recommendations. Indeed, besides the undisputable prestige of the framework, the cross-border nature of money laundering and terrorist financing challenges siloed regional or local actions. Against this backdrop, this chapter addressed the evolution of AML/CFT regimes and the impact of the concept of predicate offences on the scope of application of compliance regimes countering financial crime. Accordingly, it provided an overview on the perception of crypto-asset-related risks and the (purported) anonymous character of the sphere. To do so, it referred to scandals depicting cryptocurrencies as the currency of choice of darknet market-places on the dark web, accessed using anonymity-enhancing tools, while also reporting data on the likely overestimation of crypto-asset-related money laundering and terrorist financing.

Further, focus was on the FATF as a sector-specific player within the dynamics of global financial regulation. In doing so, it underlined how models and products of technocratic cooperation are influenced by their position within a hierarchical system and analysed FATF Recommendations as global standards and instruments of soft-law, as well as their evolution along with the ways to transmit value over the Internet. Meanwhile, this chapter outlined the main AML/CFT obligations, through the lens of their implementation at EU level. Notably, it underlined how the RBA underpins all duties imposed on regulated entities and specified details of CDD and STR compliance. Moreover, it analysed selected technical standardisation initiatives on crypto-assets, blockchain technologies or DLTs. It underlined how technical

[228] Zetzsche et al. (2023).

[229] Chainalysis (2022, 2024). The Spartan Protocol hack is a prime example of the use of DeFi for money laundering. After over USD 300 million-worth of cryptocurrency was stolen, the hackers converted the funds into anyETH and anyBTC (i.e., Ethereum and Bitcoin composites respectively built on separate blockchains to the originals), then swapped some anyBTC for Bitcoin. At this point two DeFi chain-hopping protocols were used to convert funds into ETH and renBTC, and the funds were sent to a DEX and swapped for new ETH and wrapped ETH. The use of these platforms makes investigations significantly more complex. Lastly, the funds were sent to Tornado Cash. The hack took place in May and the hackers continued to launder funds until October. Notably, the activity would have been less effective if they had used centralised services, also on the grounds of their capacity to freeze funds in the event of suspicions (Chainalysis, 2022, pp. 7, 12).

and regulatory standards entail different methodologies but share the interplay between regulatory agencies and private sector expertise. It expanded on the nature of the AML/CFT EU regulatory methodology as minimum harmonisation, while addressing the main initiatives included in the AML Package that pursues to overcome fragmentation. In doing so, it accounted for the impact of the process whereby standards are embedded into domestic law.

In this respect, this chapter focused on the different goals of the AML Package to establish an EU-wide AML/CFT Single Rulebook, a system of EU-level supervision, and a support and cooperation system among FIUs. Relatedly, it underlined the prospective limitation of large cash payments and the prohibition of anonymous crypto-asset wallets. At this point, it analysed the AMLA Regulation, placing the overview in the context of how an EU-based crypto-asset-oriented research on AML/CFT is affected by the relationship between FATF Standards, the technical nature of compliance in the crypto-asset space, the mechanisms of EU law, and the dynamics between regulatory and technical standards. Starting from the formal relationship between EU law and international standards, this chapter addressed the AMLA and its task of drafting RTSs.

The application of the intermediary-based approach to the crypto-asset space generates significant problems, exemplified by the difficulty to comply with the crypto travel rule and the related recast of the FTR at the EU level. The debate provides insights that go beyond its specifics and is an emblem of the tension between the nature of crypto-asset ecosystems and a framework of 'active cooperation'. In this context, a multifold challenge of attribution of crypto-asset activities emerges. The chapter focused on the impacts of the compliance regime on P2P or self-hosted to hosted wallet transfers and the legitimacy of possible consequent restrictions. Meanwhile, it heeds the challenge of linking transactions to the respective actors, at least in terms of attribution to real-world identities. Finally, it contextualised the shortcomings of the current approach vis-à-vis the revolution brought about by DeFi platforms and DEXes also in terms of laundering trends.

References

Adler, D. (2018). Silk road: The dark side of cryptocurrency. *Fordham Journal of Corporate & Financial Law Blog*. https://news.law.fordham.edu/jcfl/2018/02/21/silk-road-the-dark-side-of-cryptocurrency/

Amsden, Z., Arora, R., Bano, S., Baudet, M., Blackshear, S., Bothra, A., Cabrera, G., Catalini, C., Chalkias, K., Cheng, E., Ching, A., Chursin, A., Danezis, G., Di Giacomo, G., Dill, D. L., Ding, H., Doudchenko, N., Gao, V., Gao, Z., Garillot, F., et al. (2019). The libra blockchain - white paper. https://mitsloan.mit.edu/shared/ods/documents?PublicationDocumentID=5859

Barbereau, T., Weigl, L., & Pocher, N. (2024). Financial regulation, political context, and technology in the European union. In G. Fridgen, T. Guggenberger, J. Sedlmeir, & N. Urbach (Eds.), *Decentralization technologies*. Springer. https://doi.org/10.1007/978-3-031-66047-4_2

Brummer, C. (2015a). The architecture of international financial law. In *Soft law and the global financial system: Rule-making in the 21st century*. Cambridge University Press. https://doi.org/10.1017/CBO9781316423875.004

Brummer, C. (2015b). Introduction: The perils of global finance. In *Soft law and the global financial system: Rule-making in the 21st century*. Cambridge University Press. https://doi.org/10.1017/CBO9781316423875.002

Brummer, C. (2015c). *Soft law and the global financial system: Rule-making in the 21st century*. Cambridge University Press. https://doi.org/10.1017/CBO9781316423875

Brummer, C. (2015d). Territoriality and financial statecraft. In *Soft law and the global financial system: Rule-making in the 21st century*. Cambridge University Press. https://doi.org/10.1017/CBO9781316423875.003.

Burgess, A., Hamilton, R., & Leuprecht, C. (2024). Terror on the blockchain: The emergent crypto-crime-terror nexus. In D. Goldbarsht & L. de Koker (Eds.), *Financial crime, law and governance: Navigating challenges in different contexts. Ius gentium: Comparative perspectives on law and justice series* (vol. 116). Springer. https://doi.org/10.1007/978-3-031-59547-9_9

C4. (2022). Cryptocurrency security standard (CCSS). https://cryptoconsortium.github.io/CCSS/

Casanovas, P., de Koker, L., & Hashmi, M. (2022). Law, socio-legal governance, the internet of things, and industry 4.0: A middle-out/inside-out approach. *Multidisciplinary Scientific Journal, 5*, 64–91. https://doi.org/10.3390/j5010005

Chainalysis. (2022). The 2022 crypto crime report. Original data and research into cryptocurrency-based crime. https://go.chainalysis.com/2022-Crypto-Crime-Report.html

Chainalysis. (2024). The 2024 crypto crime report. The latest trends in ransomware, scams, hacking, and more. https://go.chainalysis.com/crypto-crime-2024.html

Council Directive 91/308/EEC. (1991). Council Directive 91/308/eec on prevention of the use of the financial system for the purpose of money laundering. http://data.europa.eu/eli/dir/1991/308/oj

Council of Europe. (1990). Council of Europe (1990) ETS no. 141 convention on laundering, search, seizure and confiscation of the proceeds from crime. https://rm.coe.int/168007bd23

Council of Europe. (2005). Council of Europe (2005) CETS no. 198 convention on laundering, search, seizure and confiscation of the proceeds from crime and on the financing of terrorism. https://rm.coe.int/168008371f

Covolo, V. (2020). The eu response to criminal misuse of cryptocurrencies: The young, already outdated 5th anti-money laundering directive. *European Journal of Crime, Criminal Law and Criminal Justice, 28*(3), 217–251. https://doi.org/10.1163/15718174-bja10003

de Koker, L., & Goldbarsht, D. (2022). Financial technologies and financial crime: Key developments and areas for future research. In D. Goldbarsht & L. de Koker (Eds.), *Financial technology and the law. Combating financial crime* (vol. 47, pp. 303–320). Springer. https://doi.org/10.1007/978-3-030-88036-1_13

de Koker, L., & Goldbarsht, D. (2024a). Fatf's risk-based approach: Has the pendulum swung too far? In D. Goldbarsht & L. de Koker (Eds.), *Financial crime and the law. Ius gentium: Comparative perspectives on law and justice series* (vol. 115). Springer. https://doi.org/10.1007/978-3-031-59543-1_10

de Koker, L., & Goldbarsht, D. (2024b). Towards a global approach to combating financial crime. In D. Goldbarsht & L. de Koker (Eds.), *Financial crime, law and governance: Navigating challenges in different contexts. Ius gentium: Comparative perspectives on law and justice series* (vol. 116). Springer. https://doi.org/10.1007/978-3-031-59547-9_1

de Rechtspraak. (2024). Developer of tornado cash gets jail sentence for laundering billions of dollars in cryptocurrency. https://www.rechtspraak.nl/Organisatie-en-contact/Organisatie/Rechtbanken/Rechtbank-Oost-Brabant/Nieuws/Paginas/Developer-of-Tornado-Cash-gets-jail-sentence-for-laundering-billions-of-dollars-in-cryptocurrency.aspx

DeFi LLama. (2024). Defi llama dashboard. https://defillama.com

Department of the Treasury FinCEN. (2013). Guidance on the application of fincen's regulations to persons administering, exchanging, or using virtual currencies. https://www.fincen.gov/resources/statutes-regulations/guidance/application-fincens-regulations-persons-administering

Department of the Treasury FinCEN. (2019). Guidance on the application of fincen's regulations to certain business models involving convertible virtual currencies. https://www.fincen.gov/sites/default/files/2019-05/FinCEN%20Guidance%20CVC%20FINAL%20508.pdf

Directive 2001/97/EC. (2001). Directive 2001/97/ec of the European Parliament and of the Council amending Council Directive 91/308/eec on prevention of the use of the financial system for the purpose of money laundering. http://data.europa.eu/eli/dir/2001/97/oj

Directive 2005/60/EC. (2005). Directive 2005/60/EC of the European Parliament and of the Council on the prevention of the use of the financial system for the purpose of money laundering and terrorist financing. http://data.europa.eu/eli/dir/2005/60/oj

Directive 2009/110/EC. (2009). Directive 2009/110/ec of the European Parliament and of the Council on the taking up, pursuit and prudential supervision of the business of electronic money institutions amending directives 2005/60/ec and 2006/48/ec and repealing directive 2000/46/ec. http://data.europa.eu/eli/dir/2009/110/oj

Directive (EU) 2015/2366. (2015). Directive (eu) 2015/2366 of the European parliament and of the council on payment services in the internal market, amending Directives 2002/65/ec, 2009/110/ec and 2013/36/eu and regulation (EU) no 1093/2010, and repealing Directive 2007/64/ec. http://data.europa.eu/eli/dir/2015/2366/oj

Directive (EU) 2015/849. (2015). Directive (EU) 2015/849 of the European parliament and of the council on the prevention of the use of the financial system for the purposes of money laundering or terrorist financing, amending regulation (EU) no 648/2012 of the European Parliament and of the Council, and repealing Directive 2005/60/ec of the European Parliament and of the Council and Commission Directive 2006/70/ec. http://data.europa.eu/eli/dir/2015/849/oj

Directive (EU) 2017/1371. (2017). Directive (EU) 2017/1371 of the European Parliament and of the Council on the fight against fraud to the union's financial interests by means of criminal law. http://data.europa.eu/eli/dir/2017/1371/oj

Directive (EU) 2017/541. (2017). Directive (EU) 2017/541 of the European parliament and of the council on combating terrorism and replacing council framework decision 2002/475/jha and amending council decision 2005/671/jha. http://data.europa.eu/eli/dir/2017/541/oj

Directive (EU) 2018/1673. (2018). Directive (EU) 2018/1673 of the European Parliament and the Council on combating money laundering by criminal law. http://data.europa.eu/eli/dir/2018/1673/oj

Directive (EU) 2018/843. (2018). Directive (eu) 2018/843 of the European Parliament and of the Council amending Directive (EU) 2015/849 on the prevention of the use of the financial system for the purposes of money laundering or terrorist financing, and amending directives 2009/138/ec and 2013/36/eu. http://data.europa.eu/eli/dir/2018/843/oj

Directive (EU) 2019/1153. (2019). Directive (EU) 2019/1153 of the European Parliament and the Council laying down rules facilitating the use of financial and other information for the prevention, detection, investigation or prosecution of certain criminal offences, and repealing council decision 2000/642/jha. http://data.europa.eu/eli/dir/2019/1153/oj

Directive (EU) 2024/1640. (2024). Directive (EU) 2024/1640 of the European Parliament and of the Council of 31 may 2024 on the mechanisms to be put in place by member states for the prevention of the use of the financial system for the purposes of money laundering or terrorist financing, amending Directive (EU) 2019/1937, and amending and repealing Directive (EU) 2015/849. http://data.europa.eu/eli/dir/2024/1640/oj

European Banking Authority. (2017). Final report on joint draft regulatory technical standards on the criteria for determining the circumstances in which the appointment of a central contact point pursuant to article 45(9) of Directive (EU) 2015/849 is appropriate and the functions of the central contact point. https://www.eba.europa.eu/sites/default/documents/files/documents/10180/1890699/dae7b11d-1c7c-4995-ae9d-b48bfb6e1048/Final%20Draft%20RTS%20on%20CCP%20to%20strengthen%20fight%20against%20financial%20crime%20%28JC%202017%2008%29.pdf

European Banking Authority. (2021). Final report on draft regulatory technical standards under article 9a (1) and (3) of regulation (EU) no 1093/2010 setting up an aml/cft central database and specifying the materiality of weaknesses, the type of information collected, the practical implementation of the information collection and the analysis and dissemination of the information contained therein. https://www.eba.europa.eu/sites/default/files/document_library/Publications/Draft

European Banking Authority. (2024). Final report. Draft regulatory technical standards on supervisory colleges under article 119(8) of regulation (EU) no 2023/1114 (MICAR). https://www.eba.europa.eu/sites/default/files/2024-06/a4ac65e2-fd2c-45a3-98d3-1f9aa5ac608b/Final20Report20on20RTS20on20colleges20under20MiCAR.pdf

European Banking Authority, European Insurance and Occupational Pensions Authority, and European Securities and Markets Authority. (2017). Final report on draft joint regulatory technical standards on the measures credit institutions and financial institutions shall take to mitigate the risk of money laundering and terrorist financing where a third country's law does not permit the application of group-wide policies and procedures. https://www.eba.europa.eu/sites/default/files/document_library/Publications/Draft20Technical20Standards/2017/JC20RTS20on20the20implementation20of20group20wide20AML-CFT20policies20in20third20countries20/1035746/Final20Report20on20Joint20RTS20on203rd20countries.pdf

European Commission. (2018a). Commission delegated regulation (EU) 2018/1108. Supplementing Directive (EU) 2015/849 of the European Parliament and of the Council with regulatory technical standards on the criteria for the appointment of central contact points for electronic money issuers and payment service providers and with rules on their functions. http://data.europa.eu/eli/reg_del/2018/1108/oj

European Commission. (2019b). Commission delegated regulation (EU) 2019/758. Supplementing Directive (EU) 2015/849 of the European Parliament and of the Council with regard to regulatory technical standards for the minimum action and the type of additional measures credit and financial institutions must take to mitigate money laundering and terrorist financing risk in certain third countries. http://data.europa.eu/eli/reg_del/2019/758/oj

European Commission. (2019c). Communication from the commission - towards better implementation of the eu's anti-money laundering and countering the financing of terrorism framework. https://eur-lex.europa.eu/legal-content/EN/TXT/?uri=CELEX%3A52019DC0360

European Commission. (2020). Communication from the commission on an action plan for a comprehensive union policy on preventing money laundering and terrorist financing. 2020/c 164/06. https://eur-lex.europa.eu/legal-content/EN/TXT/?uri=CELEX%3A52020DC0164

European Commission. (2021a). Proposal for a regulation of the European Parliament and of the Council on the prevention of the use of the financial system for the purposes of money laundering or terrorist financing. https://eur-lex.europa.eu/legal-content/EN/TXT/?uri=CELEX%3A52021PC0420

European Commission. (2021b). Proposal for a regulation of the European Parliament and of the Council establishing the authority for anti-money laundering and countering the financing of terrorism and amending regulations (EU) no 1093/2010, (EU) 1094/2010, (EU) 1095/2010. https://eur-lex.europa.eu/legal-content/EN/TXT/?uri=CELEX%3A52021PC0421

European Commission. (2024). Press release: Commission welcomes the selection of Frankfurt as the seat for the authority for anti-money laundering and countering the financing of terrorism. https://ec.europa.eu/commission/presscorner/detail/en/ip_24_972

European Court of Justice. (2001). Judgment (second chamber) of 2 september 2001. case c-790/19. parchetul de pe lângă tribunalul braşov v lg and mh. Request for a preliminary ruling from the curtea de apel braşov. Reference for a preliminary ruling—prevention of the use of the financial system for the purposes of money laundering and terrorist financing—Directive (EU) 2015/849—directive 2005/60/ec—offence of money laundering—laundering by the perpetrator of the predicate offence ("self-laundering"). https://eur-lex.europa.eu/legal-content/EN/TXT/?uri=CELEX%3A62019CJ0790

European Parliamentary Research Service. (2023). Anti-money laundering authority (AMLA). https://www.europarl.europa.eu/RegData/etudes/BRIE/2022/733645/EPRS_BRI(2022)733645_EN.pdf

Federal Bureau of Investigation. (2023). Tornado cash co-founders accused of helping cybercriminals launder stolen crypto. https://www.fbi.gov/news/stories/tornado-cash-co-founders-accused-of-helping-cybercriminals-launder-stolen-crypto

Financial Action Task Force. (2012). International standards on combating money laundering and the financing of terrorism & proliferation: The fatf recommendations. Retrieved January 2025 from https://www.fatf-gafi.org/publications/fatfrecommendations/documents/fatf-recommendations.html

Financial Action Task Force. (2014). Virtual currencies – key definitions and potential AML/CFT risks. https://www.fatf-gafi.org/media/fatf/documents/reports/Virtual-currency-key-definitions-and-potential-aml-cft-risks.pdf

Financial Action Task Force. (2015). Guidance for a risk-based approach: Virtual currencies. https://www.fatf-gafi.org/media/fatf/documents/reports/Guidance-RBA-Virtual-Currencies.pdf

Financial Action Task Force. (2019). Guidance for a risk-based approach: Virtual assets and virtual asset service providers. https://www.fatf-gafi.org/publications/fatfrecommendations/documents/guidance-rba-virtual-assets.html

Financial Action Task Force. (2020a). 12-month review of the revised fatf standards – virtual assets and virtual asset service providers. http://www.fatf-gafi.org/media/fatf/documents/recommendations/12-Month-Review-Revised-FATF-Standards-Virtual-Assets-VASPS.pdf

Financial Action Task Force. (2020b). Fatf report to the g20 finance ministers and central banks governors on so-called stablecoins. http://www.fatf-gafi.org/media/fatf/documents/recommendations/Virtual-Assets-FATF-Report-G20-So-Called-Stablecoins.pdf

Financial Action Task Force. (2020c). Guidance on digital id. http://www.fatf-gafi.org/media/fatf/documents/recommendations/Guidance-on-Digital-Identity.pdf

Financial Action Task Force. (2020d). Virtual assets red flag indicators of money laundering and terrorist financing. https://www.fatf-gafi.org/media/fatf/documents/recommendations/Virtual-Assets-Red-Flag-Indicators.pdf

Financial Action Task Force. (2021a). Second 12-month review of the revised fatf standards on virtual assets and virtual asset service providers. https://www.fatf-gafi.org/media/fatf/documents/recommendations/Second-12-Month-Review-Revised-FATF-Standards-Virtual-Assets-VASPS.pdf

Financial Action Task Force. (2021b). Virtual assets and virtual asset service providers - updated guidance for a risk-based approach. https://www.fatf-gafi.org/publications/fatfrecommendations/documents/guidance-rba-virtual-assets-2021.html

Financial Action Task Force. (2021c). Guidance on risk-based supervision. http://www.fatf-gafi.org/media/fatf/documents/Guidance-Risk-Based-Supervision.pdf

Financial Action Task Force. (2024a). Targeted update on implementation of the fatf standards on virtual assets and virtual assets service providers. https://www.fatf-gafi.org/content/dam/fatf-gafi/recommendations/2024-Targeted-Update-VA-VASP.pdf.coredownload.inline.pdf

Financial Action Task Force. (2024b). High-risk jurisdictions subject to a call for action. https://www.fatf-gafi.org/content/fatf-gafi/en/publications/High-risk-and-other-monitored-jurisdictions/Call-for-action-june-2024.html.

Financial Action Task Force. (2024c). Jurisdictions under increased monitoring. https://www.fatf-gafi.org/content/fatf-gafi/en/publications/High-risk-and-other-monitored-jurisdictions/increased-monitoring-june-2024.html

Financial Crimes Enforcement Network. (2024). AML/CFT notice of proposed rulemaking. https://www.govinfo.gov/content/pkg/FR-2024-07-03/pdf/2024-14414.pdf

Financial Crimes Enforcement Network, Board of Governors of the Federal Reserve System, Federal Deposit Insurance Corporation, National Credit Union Administration, and Office of the Comptroller of the Currency. (2024). Interagency statement on the issuance of the AML/CFT program notices of proposed rulemaking. https://www.fincen.gov/sites/default/files/shared/Interagency-Statement-on-the-Issuance-of-the-AML-CFT-Program-Notices-of-Proposed-Rulemaking-FINAL.pdf

Goforth, C. (2021). Crypto assets: A fintech forecast. *Banking & Finance Law Review, 37*, 5–24.

Goldbarsht, D. (2024). Dancing in the dark: Terrorist financing via the dark web. In D. Goldbarsht & L. de Koker (Eds.), *Financial crime and the law. Ius gentium: Comparative perspectives on law and justice series* (vol. 115). Springer. https://doi.org/10.1007/978-3-031-59543-1_7

Irwin, A. S. M., & Dawson, C. (2019). Following the cyber money trail: Global challenges when investigating ransomware attacks and how regulation can help. *Journal of Money Laundering Control, 22*(1), 110–131. https://doi.org/10.1108/JMLC-08-2017-0041

ITU-T. (2022a). ITU-T in brief. https://www.itu.int/en/ITU-T/about/Pages/default.aspx

ITU-T. (2022b). List of focus groups that have completed their activities. https://www.itu.int/en/ITU-T/focusgroups/Pages/concluded.aspx

ITU-T. (2022c). ITU-T groups. https://www.itu.int/en/ITU-T/groups/Pages/default.aspx

Jardine, E. (2021). Policing the cybercrime script of darknet drug markets: Methods of effective law enforcement intervention. *American Journal of Criminal Justice, 46*, 980–1005. https://doi.org/10.1007/s12103-021-09656-3

Johnstone, S. (2021a). Acquiring the tradition. In S. Johnstone (Ed.), *Rethinking the regulation of cryptoassets. Cryptographic consensus technology and the new prospect*. Edward Elgar. https://doi.org/10.4337/9781800886797.00010

Johnstone, S. (2021b). Complexities in a developing technology. In S. Johnstone (Ed.), *Rethinking the regulation of cryptoassets. Cryptographic consensus technology and the new prospect.* Edward Elgar. https://doi.org/10.4337/9781800886797.00016

Johnstone, S. (2021c). An emerging market. In S. Johnstone (Ed.), *Rethinking the regulation of cryptoassets. Cryptographic consensus technology and the new prospect*. Edward Elgar. https://doi.org/10.4337/9781800886797.00018

Johnstone, S. (2021d). Regulatory building blocks and other concerns. In S. Johnstone (Ed.), *Rethinking the regulation of cryptoassets. Cryptographic consensus technology and the new prospect*. Edward Elgar. https://doi.org/10.4337/9781800886797.00015

Johnstone, S. (2021e). Responses from the centre. In S. Johnstone (Ed.), *Rethinking the regulation of cryptoassets. Cryptographic consensus technology and the new prospect*. Edward Elgar. https://doi.org/10.4337/9781800886797.00012

Karasek-Wojciechowicz, I. (2021). Reconciliation of anti-money laundering instruments and European data protection requirements in permissionless blockchain spaces. *Journal of Cybersecurity, 7*, tyab004. https://doi.org/10.1093/cybsec/tyab004

Kavallieros, D., Myttas, D., Kermitsis, E., Lissaris, E., Giataganas, G., & Darra, E. (2021a). Understanding the dark web. In B. Akhgar, M. Gercke, S. Vrochidis, & H. Gibson (Eds.), *Dark web investigation*. Springer. https://doi.org/10.1007/978-3-030-55343-2_1

Kavallieros, D., Myttas, D., Kermitsis, E., Lissaris, E., Giataganas, G., & Darra, E. (2021b). Using the dark web. In B. Akhgar, M. Gercke, S. Vrochidis, & H. Gibson (Eds.), *Dark web investigation*. Springer. https://doi.org/10.1007/978-3-030-55343-2_2

Kermitsis, E., Kavallieros, D., Myttas, D., Lissaris, E., & Giataganas, G. (2021). Dark web markets. In B. Akhgar, M. Gercke, S. Vrochidis, & H. Gibson (Eds.), *Dark web investigation*. Springer. https://doi.org/10.1007/978-3-030-55343-2_4

Kerwer, D. (2005). Rules that many use: Standards and global regulation. *Governance: An International Journal of Policy, Administration, and Institutions, 18*(4), 611–632. https://doi.org/10.1111/j.1468-0491.2005.00294.x

König, L., Korobeinikova, Y., Tjoa, S., & Kieseberg, P. (2020). Comparing blockchain standards and recommendations. *Future Internet, 12*, 222. https://doi.org/10.3390/fi12120222

Marquardt, P., Rosenberg, G., & Schisa, W. (2022). Digital assets and sanctions compliance: Tornado cash and beyond. https://www.iflr.com/article/2at0k2n6ovj2j92nms64g/digital-assets-and-sanctions-compliance-tornado-cash-and-beyond

Massari, J., & Catalini, C. (2021). Defi, disintermediation, and the regulatory path ahead. https://www.theregreview.org/2021/05/10/massari-catalini-defi-disintermediation-regulatory-path-ahead/

Merchant, G. E., & Allenby, B. (2017). Soft law: New tools for governing emerging technologies. *Bulletin of the Atomic Scientists, 73*(2), 108–114. https://doi.org/10.1080/00963402.2017.1288447

Newman, A., & Bach, D. (2014). The European union as hardening agent: Soft law and the diffusion of global financial regulation. *Journal of European Public Policy, 21*(3), 430–452. https://doi.org/10.1080/13501763.2014.882968

Pocher, N. (2021a). Crypto-wallets and the new eu aml package: Where are the battle lines drawn? https://www.law.kuleuven.be/citip/blog/crypto-wallets-and-the-new-eu-aml-package/

Pocher, N. (2021b). Self-hosted wallets: The elephant in the crypto room? https://www.law.kuleuven.be/citip/blog/self-hosted-wallets/

Pocher, N. (2025). Traceability of crypto-asset transfers under the new eu AML/CFT regime: The crypto travel rule between challenges and open issues. In J. Lee & A. Darbellay (Eds.), *A research agenda for financial law and regulation* (pp. 197–220). Edward Elgar. https://doi.org/10.4337/9781803929996.00017

Regulation (EU) 1093/2010. (2010). Regulation (EU) 1093/2010 of the European Parliament and of the Council of 24 November 2010 establishing a European supervisory authority (European banking authority), amending decision no 716/2009/ec and repealing commission decision 2009/78/ec. http://data.europa.eu/eli/reg/2010/1093/oj

Regulation (EU) 2015/847. (2015). Regulation (EU) 2015/847 of the European Parliament and of the Council of 20 May 2015 on information accompanying transfers of funds and repealing regulation (EC) no 1781/2006. http://data.europa.eu/eli/reg/2015/847/oj

Regulation (EU) 2019/2175. (2019). Regulation (EU) 2019/2175 of the European Parliament and of the Council of 18 December 2019 amending regulation (EU) 1093/2010 establishing a European supervisory authority (European banking authority), regulation (EU) 1094/ 2010 establishing a European supervisory authority (European insurance and occupational pensions authority), regulation (EU) 1095/2010 establishing a European supervisory authority (European securities and markets authority), regulation (EU) 600/2014 on markets in financial instruments, regulation (EU) 2016/1011 on indices used as benchmarks in financial instruments and financial contracts or to measure the performance of investment funds, and regulation (EU) 2015/847 on information accompanying transfers of funds. http://data.europa.eu/eli/reg/2019/2175/oj

Regulation (EU) 2023/1113. (2023). Regulation (EU) 2023/1113 of the European Parliament and of the Council of 31 May 2023 on information accompanying transfers of funds and certain crypto-assets and amending Directive (EU) 2015/849 (recast). http://data.europa.eu/eli/reg/2023/1113/oj

Regulation (EU) 2023/1114. (2023). Regulation (EU) 2023/1114 of the European Parliament and of the Council of 31 May 2023 on markets in crypto-assets, and amending regulations (EU) no 1093/2010 and (EU) no 1095/2010 and Directives 2013/36/eu and (EU) 2019/1937. http://data.europa.eu/eli/reg/2023/1114/oj

Regulation (EU) 2024/1183. (2024). Regulation (EU) 2024/1183 of the European Parliament and of the Council of 11 April 2024 amending regulation (EU) no 910/2014 as regards establishing the European digital identity framework. http://data.europa.eu/eli/reg/2024/1183/oj

Regulation (EU) 2024/1620. (2024). Regulation (EU) 2024/1620 of the European Parliament and of the Council of 31 May 2024 establishing the authority for anti-money laundering and countering the financing of terrorism and amending regulations (EU) no 1093/2010, (EU) no 1094/2010 and (EU) no 1095/2010. http://data.europa.eu/eli/reg/2024/1620/oj

Regulation (EU) 2024/1624. (2024). Regulation (EU) 2024/1624 of the European Parliament and of the Council of 31 May 2024 on the prevention of the use of the financial system for the purposes of money laundering or terrorist financing. http://data.europa.eu/eli/reg/2024/1624/oj

Regulation (EU) 910/2014. (2014). Regulation (EU) 910/2014 of the European Parliament and of the Council of 23 July 2014 on electronic identification and trust services for electronic transactions in the internal market and repealing Directive 1999/93/ec. http://data.europa.eu/eli/reg/2014/910/oj

Treaty on the European Union. (2012). Consolidated version of the treaty on the European Union annexed to the final act of the intergovernmental conference which adopted the treaty of Lisbon, signed on 13 December 2007. http://data.europa.eu/eli/treaty/teu_2016/oj

Treaty on the Functioning of the European Union. (2012). Consolidated version of the treaty on the functioning of the European Union annexed to the final act of the intergovernmental conference which adopted the treaty of Lisbon, signed on 13 December 2007. http://data.europa.eu/eli/treaty/tfeu_2016/oj

Tsuchiya, Y., & Hiramoto, N. (2021a). Dark web in the dark: Investigating when transactions take place on cryptomarkets. *Forensic Science International: Digital Investigation, 36*, 301093. https://doi.org/10.1016/j.fsidi.2020.301093

Tsuchiya, Y., & Hiramoto, N. (2021b). How cryptocurrency is laundered: Case study of coincheck hacking incident. *Forensic Science International: Reports, 4*, 100241. https://doi.org/10.1016/j.fsir.2021.100241

UN General Assembly. (1988). Convention against illicit traffic in narcotic drugs and psychotropic substances. opened on 20 Dec. 1988, entered into force on 11 Nov. 1990. https://www.unodc.org/pdf/convention_1988_en.pdf

UN General Assembly. (1999). Convention for the suppression of the financing of terrorism. Opened on 9 Dec. 1999, entered into force on 10 Apr. 2002. https://treaties.un.org/doc/db/terrorism/english-18-11.pdf

UN General Assembly. (2000a). Convention against transnational organised crime. res. 55/25 of 15 Nov. 2000, into force on 29 Sep. 2003. https://www.unodc.org/documents/treaties/UNTOC/Publications/TOC%20Convention/TOCebook-e.pdf

UN General Assembly. (2000b). Protocol against the smuggling of migrants by land, sea and air, supplementing the united nations convention against transnational organized crime. https://www.unodc.org/documents/treaties/UNTOC/Publications/TOC%20Convention/TOCebook-e.pdf

UN General Assembly. (2000c). Protocol to prevent, suppress and punish trafficking in persons, especially women and children, supplementing the united nations convention against transnational organized crime. https://www.unodc.org/documents/treaties/UNTOC/Publications/TOC%20Convention/TOCebook-e.pdf

UN General Assembly. (2001). Protocol against the illicit manufacturing of and trafficking in firearms, their parts and components and ammunition, supplementing the united nations convention against transnational organized crime. res. 55/255 of 31 May 2001, into force on 3 Jul. 2005. https://www.unodc.org/documents/treaties/UNTOC/Publications/TOC%20Convention/TOCebook-e.pdf

UN General Assembly. (2003). Res. 58/4 of 31 October 2003. Convention against corruption. Opened on 9 Dec. 2003, entered into force on 14 Dec. 2003. https://www.unodc.org/documents/treaties/UNCAC/Publications/Convention/08-50026_E.pdf

U.S. Department of the Treasury. (2022). Press release. U.S. treasury sanctions notorious virtual currency mixer tornado cash. https://home.treasury.gov/news/press-releases/jy0916

Viterbo, A. (2019). The European Union in the transnational financial regulatory arena: The case of the Basel committee on banking supervision. *Journal of International Economic Law, 22*, 205–228. https://doi.org/10.1093/jiel/jgz013

Vogel, D. (2008). Private global business regulation. *Annual Review of Political Science, 11*, 261–82. https://doi.org/10.1146/annurev.polisci.11.053106.141706

Whitehouse-Levine, M., & Kelleher, L. (2020). *Self-hosted wallets and the future of free societies*. Blockchain Association. https://theblockchainassociation.org/wp-content/uploads/2020/11/Self-Hosted-Wallets-and-the-Future-of-Free-Societies.pdf

World Economic Forum. (2020). Global standards mapping initiative: An overview of blockchain technical standards. https://www3.weforum.org/docs/WEF_GSMI_Technical_Standards_2020.pdf

Zetzsche, D. A., Buckley, R. P., Arner, D. W., & van Ek, M. (20203). Remaining regulatory challenges in digital finance and crypto-assets after MiCA. Technical Report, Committee on Economic and Monetary Affairs (ECON), Policy Department for Economic, Scientific and Quality of Life Policies, European Parliament. https://www.europarl.europa.eu/thinktank/en/document/IPOL_STU(2023)740083

Chapter 6
Trade-Offs in Central Bank Digital Currencies

6.1 Introduction

The previous chapters explored how the promise of an electronic version of cash, possibly grounded on DLTs, has been electrifying the world over the past decade. This prospect of technological disruption spurred an excitement that reminds of the advent of the Internet in the 1990s.[1] As explained in Chaps. 2 and 3, the core premise of crypto-asset developments lies in the functioning of blockchain systems. Being secured by cryptography and economic incentives and governed (in principle, at least) by non-centralised consensus, they enable value transfers that transcend the need of a central authority. Against this backdrop, these setups showed the potential to replace legacy financial infrastructures, by eliminating layers of intermediation and informing a new 'hype' of direct participation in a new global economy.[2]

Chapters 3 and 4 elaborated on anonymity and disintermediation in crypto-asset ecosystems, and on the socio-technical issues of obfuscation and traceability. Considering the tension between private transactions and accountability, they investigated the trade-off between anonymity and transparency from an AML/CFT standpoint. Chapters 4 and 5 showcased the extent to which AML/CFT measures pivot on identification and identity verification, while anonymity is dependent on the observer and anonymous transactions are those that cannot be related to identifiable individuals. In line with the CBDC discourse, this chapter primarily addresses the trade-off between privacy and transparency—as outlined in Chap. 3, anonymity is one of the means to protect privacy. Indeed, not only privacy and transparency, but also confidentiality and auditability, are not a zero-sum game, and can be balanced

[1] Pocher and Veneris (2022a).

[2] Pocher and Veneris (2022a); Werbach (2020); Walch (2019); Casey et al. (2018).

N. Pocher, *Crypto-Asset Ecosystems and the EU Anti-Money Laundering Framework*, Law, Governance and Technology Series 76,
https://doi.org/10.1007/978-3-031-94698-1_6

in different ways.[3] Since technology can be leveraged to embed a specific balance, a crypto-asset scheme can be assessed using given technical features.

The idea of leveraging tokenisation to reach widespread adoption of digital money has unsettled both governments and the private sector. (Global) stablecoin projects reached the headlines but also run into significant challenges—e.g., Facebook/Meta's Libra/Diem (Chap. 2).[4] Amidst this quest for value interconnection, monetary institutions have been trying to innovate payments and transmission channels, but also to rethink the essence of cash.[5] A vast body of literature has addressed the drivers behind CBDC projects, including the possible disappearance of cash, which could deprive citizens of government-issued money, and in the pursuit of novel payment channels for monetary sovereignty and geopolitical purposes.[6] Although central banks' interest in digital currencies started in 2014, most initiatives stepped into the spotlight around 2019 and typically explore the deployment of blockchain technology. In 2021, with 86% of central banks reportedly exploring CBDC,[7] it became clear that if the full potential of this interconnection is fulfilled, it will affect many fields, including law and regulation at large.[8]

The relationship between CBDCs and regulation inherently differs from the one between crypto-assets and regulation. This is due to the regulated nature of the stakeholders involved in CBDC projects and to their goals, which for the most part diverge from those of crypto-assets.[9] Indeed, the choice to consider CBDCs within the scope of this work does not intend to convey the message that crypto-assets and digital fiat money are concepts that can be equated from a phenomenological or ideological perspective. While investigating CBDC projects, however, it becomes clear that their design provides most valuable insights into the features of crypto-asset ecosystems. Most importantly, CBDCs display in a clear fashion the traits of privacy, anonymity and transparency introduced by the previous chapters, as well as showcase their socio-technical aspects.

The multi-stakeholder interest in CBDCs offers the chance to dissect these models and understand the way their features are influenced by technical and social factors, which are in turn affected by regulation. In setting the design of a specific CBDC model—composed of many design choices that lead to embedding various properties—,[10] a balance (or trade-off) is chosen between privacy, anonymity, and transparency, which sheds a light on how these characteristics can be assessed in crypto-asset ecosystems as well. In Chap. 4, accountability emerged as ensured

[3] Pocher and Veneris (2022b); Michalopoulos et al. (2024).

[4] Amsden et al. (2019); Diem (2022).

[5] Allen et al. (2020a); Auer et al. (2020); Allen et al. (2020b); Pocher and Veneris (2022a).

[6] Sandner et al. (2020); European Central Bank (2020a); Bank for International Settlements (2021a); Swartz (2020); Pocher and Sedlmeir (2024).

[7] Boar and Wehrli (2021).

[8] Al-Fuqaha et al. (2015); Ahlgren et al. (2016); Pocher and Veneris (2022a).

[9] Pocher and Veneris (2022a).

[10] Pocher and Sedlmeir (2024).

by auditability, which assumes access to (certain) data is allowed in given circumstances without breaching confidentiality. In addition, the design of AML/CFT compliance in CBDCs and the question of setting cross-border standards inspires a broader discussion on the value of AML/CFT standardisation also when regulating crypto-asset ecosystems.

Against this backdrop, this chapter will (a) provide foundational notions on CBDCs and account for key events in their evolution, (b) focus on the value of interoperability and the need for standardisation, (c) summarise core aspects of CBDC design, (d) evaluate the impact of public and private stakeholders, (e) investigate the link between AML/CFT compliance in CBDCs and regulatory aspects of the use of cash vis-à-vis privacy and data protection concerns, (f) explore the privacy and transparency dimensions of CBDCs, showing the role of trade-offs and the dynamics of balancing confidentiality and auditability, (g) elaborate on how features such as PETs impact on the issue at hand, and (h) show how they can be used to evaluate specific models to create a preliminary classification.

6.2 Overview on Central Bank Digital Currencies

Payment transmission systems have significantly evolved in the past decades, in line with the overall digitalisation of the economy.[11] This had an impact on both the infrastructural advancements in the institutional domain—e.g., real-time gross settlement (RTGS), fast retail and instant payments—, and the FinTech private sector.[12] Today, from a technical and development perspective many efforts are pursued jointly, through mechanisms of public-private partnership (PPP).[13] In this context, central banks started entertaining the idea of creating digital sovereign money.[14]

One may find various definitions of 'sovereign currency', that in broad terms is understood as one "set as such by a sovereign law, issued by an authorised issuer, and whose value results from a statutory rule".[15] Central banks and monetary authorities traditionally issue two types of 'central bank money':

(i) *general purpose or fiat money*: the official currency also known as cash, consisting of coins and banknotes. It is legal tender—i.e., it is legally recognised as a means to satisfactorily meet financial obligations—, and available to the public; and

[11] Pocher and Veneris (2022a).

[12] Carstens (2021).

[13] Pocher and Veneris (2022a).

[14] Allen et al. (2020a); Barotini and Holden (2019); Opare and Kim (2020).

[15] ITU-T Focus Group on Digital Currency (2019).

(ii) *bank reserves or settlements accounts*: provided exclusively to authorised institutions participating in RTGS systems (e.g., commercial banks and non-bank PSPs), through the opening of reserves accounts.[16]

'Central bank money' is a liability of a central bank. By contrast, most money in circulation is 'commercial bank money' or 'electronic money (e-money)'. Because it is issued by financial institutions—e.g., commercial banks, non-bank PSPs and e-money institutions—, it is a liability of private entities to the public.[17]

6.2.1 CBDC Typology and Drivers

At the present day there are three types of investigations into CBDC schemes, developed in a parallel fashion and responding to different needs:

(i) *wholesale CBDC*: a settlement scheme between financial institutions, detached from the concept of cash flows. Various designs and technologies have been explored by the public sector, often in partnership with private entities, with the goal to update or complement existing solutions for central bank deposits and improve money transmission in terms of speed and security;
(ii) *retail CBDC*: a digital form of fiat money offered to the public as legal tender, for every-day use. It is the most transformative subset of CBDCs and, to different extents depending on the specific design, it expands the concept of 'central bank money'. It requires central banks to safeguard stability, efficiency and security when devising issuance and distribution mechanisms;
(iii) *cross-border CBDC*: as both retail and wholesale transactions have both a domestic and an international dimension,[18] cross-border CBDC projects focus on developing interconnections between various domestic CBDC schemes to integrate validity checks, while reducing transaction friction, latency, and fees.[19]

The CBDC concept draws from many disciplines such as economics, technology, law, finance, sociology, which challenges the pursuit of comprehensive definitions. A retail CBDC can be defined as "a credit-based currency in terms of value, a cryptocurrency from a technical perspective, an algorithm-based currency in terms of implementation, and a smart currency in application scenarios".[20] Since the early

[16] They are scriptural deposits recorded on a ledger held, settled and managed by the central bank.

[17] However, the end-user has a claim against a financial institution to redeem the value in 'central bank money'—i.e., cash—on demand (Allen et al., 2020a). For definitions and conceptual disambiguation: ITU-T Focus Group on Digital Currency (2019); Bank for International Settlements (2020); Brummer (2019); Geva (2018); Bossu et al. (2020).

[18] Themistocleous et al. (2023).

[19] Pocher and Sedlmeir (2024); Fanti and Pocher (2022).

[20] Yao (2018), p. 2.

days of their explorations, it was clear that the concept of CBDC was not well-defined, and it was used in various ways. In summary, however, it is mostly used to refer to a new form of central bank money that in principle can serve both as a medium of exchange and as a store of value.[21]

Although central banks and governments have motivated their interest in CBDCs in various ways, linking their growing interest to many drivers,[22] a few factors seem to have played a key role. First, the use of cash has been decreasing—especially in countries such as Sweden or Canada—, in favour of digital alternatives such as debit and credit card transactions and electronic transfers. Secondly, after private altcoins and tokenisation initiatives followed Bitcoin and Ethereum, up to DeFi,[23] the attempts to limit the volatility of these instruments led to the development of (global) stablecoins.[24] Thirdly, the development of digital money outside traditional financial networks challenges payment and monetary policy mechanisms, and pose the risk of currency substitution and of strong geopolitical impact.[25] In this sense, the investigation of digital fiat money pursues financial stability. Meanwhile, CBDC interest mirrors the effort to leverage digital cash technologies into a new functional form of money to serve a growing global economy, to shape a new interplay between citizens and monetary instruments.[26] Finally, CBDCs are investigated to provide payment efficiency, new monetary policy transmission channels, financial inclusion, safety/privacy and regulatory compliance.[27]

6.2.2 *History of Domestic and Cross-Border CBDC Projects*

Central bank interest in digital money for wholesale purposes started emerging in 2014, while most retail CBDC initiatives gained notoriety about five years later. As of today, central banks explore plans to issue digital sovereign currencies, and multi-stakeholder commentaries touch upon diverse aspects such as security, privacy, technology infrastructure, regulation, and cross-border challenges.[28]

---

[21] Committee on Payments and Market Infrastructures - Bank for International Settlements (2018), p. 3.

[22] Adrian and Mancini-Griffoli (2019); Allen et al. (2020b). CBDC policy goals include mitigating currency substitution, fostering safety, resilience, efficiency and competitiveness of payment systems, financial inclusion, as well as continuous access to central bank money (World Economic Forum, 2021a, p. 23. World Economic Forum, 2021d, p. 200).

[23] Amler et al. (2021).

[24] Amsden et al. (2019).

[25] Barotini and Holden (2019); Bank for International Settlements (2020).

[26] Rennie and Steele (2021).

[27] Opare and Kim (2020); Auer et al. (2022); Michalopoulos et al. (2024).

[28] Auer et al. (2020); European Central Bank (2020a); Khiaonarong and Humphrey (2019); Pocher and Sedlmeir (2024).

2015–2018 The first pilots in wholesale CBDCs, DLT-based settlement and cross-border transfers, emerged in 2015–2016 with the initiatives by Bank of Canada (Project Jasper), Bank of England (RSCoin),[29] Monetary Authority of Singapore (Project Ubin), ECB and Bank of Japan (Project Stella), Deutsche Bundesbank (Project Blockbaster), Banque de France (Project Madre), and Banco Central do Brasil (Project Salt). While the Monetary Authority of Hong Kong (HKMA) (Project LionRock) was still addressing interbank settlements, retail projects started focusing on the relation between digital fiat money and cash—e.g., Sveriges Riksbank (e-Krona Project). The 2017–2018 pilot initiatives are both retail—e.g., central banks of Finland (Project e-hryvnia), Turkey (Digital Lira), Ukraine, Cambodia (Project Bakong), Uruguay (Project e-Peso), Israel (Project e-Shekel), Venezuela (Project Petro), the Marshall Islands—and wholesale—e.g., Denmark, South Africa (Project Khokha), Switzerland (Project Helvetia), New Zealand, Norway, Thailand (Project Inthanon). They contribute to depicting CBDC concepts often very diverse.[30]

2019 In early 2019, around 70% of central banks declared to be engaging in CBDC activities.[31] Although only a few of them voiced plans to issue within the medium term, in 2019 CBDC research reached the headlines. A key moment was the announcement of the Libra project, rebranded to Diem in 2020 and abandoned in 2022.[32] After reports were published by the Bank of Korea and the Bank of Japan, the first cross-border settlement mechanism between DLT platforms was concluded by Bank of Canada and Monetary Authority of Singapore within Project Jasper/Ubin.

2020 At the beginning of 2020, central banks working on CBDCs had risen to 80%, nearly half of them at the Proof of Concept (PoC) phase and a few pilots.[33] In July, the Bank of Lithuania issued the first state-backed digital collector coin, LBCOIN. In the U.S., remarkably silent up to this point, in May the non-profit Digital Dollar Project released a whitepaper on the reasons for a digital USD, while the Federal Reserve Bank of Boston announced a collaboration with MIT's Media Lab. In October, the first CBDC, the Sand Dollar, was launched by the Central Bank of the Bahamas. Meanwhile, the Eastern Caribbean Central Bank launched DXCDCaribe, Brazil launched the PIX instant payment platform, the Bank of Russia unveiled

---

[29] Danezis and Meiklejohn (2016).

[30] Auer et al. (2020); Pocher and Veneris (2022a).

[31] Barotini and Holden (2019).

[32] Amsden et al. (2019). Along with the efforts to digitise fiat money, one cannot ignore the impact of private initiatives. In early 2020, Facebook/Meta renamed Libra to Diem, and unsuccessfully pursued a Swiss licence. In April 2021 the focus was limited to the U.S. as a stablecoin backed 1:1 with assets to the US dollar, and in January 2022 the Diem Association sold its assets to Silvergate (Diem, 2021; Bloomberg, 2022; Diem, 2022). In May 2021, Diem established a partnership with Silvergate which became the exclusive issuer of the stablecoin. The role played by Diem's regulatory hurdles in abandoning the project emerged from the sale announcement (Diem, 2021).

[33] Boar et al. (2020).

interest in a Digital Ruble, and the Reserve Bank of Australia started researching a wholesale CBDC. Meanwhile, in October the ECB issued a report on principles and configurations for a possible Digital Euro.[34]

2021 At the beginning of 2021, 86% of central banks were exploring CBDCs: 60% at the stage of doing advanced experiments and 14% at a pilot phase.[35] The EC and the ECB announced a cooperation on a Digital euro and launched the project,[36] while the e-CNY's testing was widened and launch was announced by early 2022. Retail initiatives were reportedly initiated in New Zealand, Vietnam, Kazakhstan (Digital Tenge) Madagascar (e-Ariary), Nigeria (e-Naira), Honduras, Guatemala (iQuetzal), Bhutan (Digital Ngultrum), Laos, Peru, Philippines, Palau, Brazil (Digital Real), Tanzania, Mexico, Namibia, Zimbabwe, Singapore (Project Orchid).[37] Concurrently, the Bank of Korea issued a competition for CBDC PoCs.

This era also shows the maturation of cross-border CBDC projects—e.g., the 2019–20 Project Aber by the Saudi Arabian Monetary Authority and the Central Bank of UAE, and Project Inthanon-LionRock by the HKMA and the Bank of Thailand. Indeed, starting from 2021, the BIS has explored the interactions between CBDC systems, both retail and wholesale,[38] sparking interest in academia as well.[39] In February, a major collaboration was announced by the HKMA, the Central Bank of UAE, the Bank of Thailand and the People's Bank of China, while other projects address the issue of cross-border CBDC schemes, such as Projects Dunbar and Jura.[40] In December, the Reserve Bank of Australia announced the end of Project Atom on a wholesale CBDC for tokenised syndicated loans.[41]

The operational burden of operating across various systems may be eased by developing and adhering to common technical standards (e.g., message formats, cryptographic techniques, data requirements and user interfaces), but also aligned regulatory and supervisory standards on KYC and transaction monitoring.[42] Indeed, both technical and regulatory standards are necessary to interoperability at different levels—e.g., messaging, privacy, AML/CFT, identity, DLT protocols.[43] In particular, there are three methods to set up a cross-border and cross-currency CBDC, with different consequences: (i) developing compatible standards, (ii) interlinking different systems, (iii) creating a single multi-currency system. Among these

[34] European Central Bank (2020a).

[35] Boar and Wehrli (2021).

[36] European Central Bank (2021a, 2021b).

[37] CBDC Tracker (2024).

[38] Auer et al. (2021a, 2021b). On cross-border CBDC research initiatives: Fanti and Pocher (2022).

[39] Kochergin and Dostov (2020); Jung and Jeong (2021), p. 133.

[40] Auer et al. (2021b); Bank for International Settlements (2021b).

[41] Reserve Bank of Australia (2021). A 'syndicated loan' is a loan that is offered by a group of lenders (the 'syndicate', composed of financial institutions and institutional investors) to a single borrower (usually a corporation, projects requiring a very large loan) to mitigate the risk.

[42] Auer et al. (2021b).

[43] World Economic Forum (2021c), p. 187.

options, only the last case leads to an integrated ‘payment system’, comprising a single set of participants, a single infrastructure, a single ledger, a single rulebook and a single governance. In the other cases, interoperability relies on ‘payment arrangements’.[44]

The BIS urged the inclusion of cross-border considerations in CBDC projects, and is expected to lead standardisation through its CPMI working group and Innovation Hubs.[45] The choice among different options exerts significant impacts on the resulting privacy-transparency trade-off of the given model.[46] This, in turn, requires careful planning and extensive techno-regulatory reflections.[47]

2022 The CBDC trend continued in 2022: wholesale CBDC research was disclosed in Denmark and retail initiatives in Jordan, Iraq, Nepal, Oman, Qatar, Saudi Arabia, Uganda, Yemen, Zambia, Rwanda, Taiwan, Trinidad and Tobago, Sudan, Malaysia, Iran. In January, the Federal Reserve published a paper to initiate public discussion about a U.S. CBDC,[48] and later the Federal Reserve Bank of Atlanta disclosed its Project Hamilton, while the BIS and the Federal Reserve Bank of New York announced a partnership to investigate a wholesale CBDC model.[49] In March, the U.S. President issued an executive order,[50] which mandates urgent CBDC exploration by the Government and the Federal Reserve. Meanwhile, the Bank of Korea completed a first phase of testing and the Bank of Russia concluded a pilot.[51] In January, 76% of Arab central banks were reportedly researching CBDCs, among which two central banks are expected to issue a CBDC within three years.[52] In March, the BIS concluded the mCBDC Project Dunbar,[53] explicitly drawing interoperability and competition best practices from the Pix project.[54] In October, the BIS Innovation Hub Hong Kong Centre published the outcomes of the collaboration with the HKMA and the Hong Kong Applied Science and Technology Research Institute, presenting a prototype developed within Project Aurum focusing on a combination between a wholesale and a retail CBDC model.[55] Towards the end of 2022, the ECB reported on the progress of the Digital euro project.[56]

---

[44] Auer et al. (2021b); Böhme and Auer (2020); Fanti and Pocher (2022).

[45] Duffie (2020); Auer et al. (2020); PYMNTS (2020); Bank for International Settlements (2021a).

[46] For an analysis of how privacy and transparency properties depend substantially on each specific technical design of the cross-border CBDC: Fanti and Pocher (2022), pp. 11–16.

[47] For an overview on technology and regulation in cross-border projects: Fanti and Pocher (2022).

[48] The Federal Reserve (2022).

[49] CBDC Tracker (2024).

[50] US Presidential Actions (2022).

[51] CBDC Tracker (2024).

[52] Arab Monetary Fund (2022). Arab central banks are those of Jordan, UAE, Bahrain, Tunisia, Algeria, Djibouti, Saudi Arabia, Sudan, Syria, Somalia, Iraq, Oman, Palestine, Qatar, Comoros, Kuwait, Lebanon, Libya, Egypt, Morocco, Mauritania, Yemen.

[53] With Corda-based and Quorum-based prototypes. Bank for International Settlements (2022a).

[54] Duarte et al. (2022).

[55] Bank for International Settlements (2022b).

[56] European Central Bank (2022a, 2022b).

2023 In 2023, many of the remaining countries voiced at least interest in pursuing research initiatives on CBDCs, in their retail or wholesale dimension. This is the case for Mauritania, Belarus, South Korea, Armenia, the Maldives, Colombia, Mauritius, Montenegro. Bank of Jamaica launched a retail CBDC known as JAM-DEX, and the Solomon Islands announced a PoC of their Bokolo Cash CBDC.[57] In June, Project Rosalind set out to develop prototypes for an API interface to distribute retail CBDCs. In September, Project Sela was concluded by the BIS and the central banks of Israel and Hong Kong, proving the possibility to design a retail CBDC ecosystem to combine accessibility, competition, cybersecurity, without losing key aspects of physical cash. In October, Project Mandala was launched between the BIS and the monetary authorities of Australia, South Korea, Malaysia, and Singapore, to explore compliance requirements for cross-border payments. From May to October, Project Polaris by the BIS released a series of reports on designing secure and resistent CBDC systems with focus on offline CBDC payments.[58] In June, the EC published a set of two legislative proposals to lay the groundwork for a possible issuance of a Eurosystem's CBDC.[59] In November, Project Tourbillon was concluded and proved the viability of a so-called cash-like anonymity for retail CBDCs.[60] Meanwhile, the ECB concluded the 'investigation phase' on a Digital euro and announced a subsequent two-year 'preparation phase'.[61]

2024 At the beginning of 2024, reportedly 134 countries/currency unions, representing 98% of global GDPR, are actively exploring a CBDC.[62] In March 2024, Project Aurum 2.0 was launched to explore privacy improvements for retail CBDC payments. This is the continuation of the collaboration between the Hub's Hong Kong Centre and the HKMA, building on the Aurum prototype. In June, the BIS launched Project Rialto to improve instant cross-border wholesale payments. Meanwhile, Project mBridge opens up to further international participation after reaching the stage of minimum viable product.[63] In June 2024, Qatar launched its PoC and Kyrgyzstan unveiled its research efforts for a Digital Som.[64] Meanwhile, the ECB published the first report of the mentioned 'investigation phase' into a Digital euro [65]

---

[57] CBDC Tracker (2024).

[58] Michalopoulos et al. (2024).

[59] European Commission (2023).

[60] BIS Innovation Hub and Swiss National Bank (2023).

[61] European Central Bank (2023).

[62] Atlantic Council (2024).

[63] BIS Innovation Hub (2024).

[64] CBDC Tracker (2024).

[65] European Central Bank (2024).

6.3 The Impacts of CBDC Design Choices

Retail CBDC models offer a rich variety of design options that span from access and distribution of the digital currency, to the management of the ledger and of payments, to the daily with end-users.[66] Some overarching characteristics have emerged as key to ensure sufficient safeguards: (i) need to balance end-user privacy and data protection with safeguards against financial integrity (e.g., AML/CFT, anti-fraud), (ii) universal and unrestricted accessibility, (iii) resilience, continuous operation online and offline, (iv) security, and (v) high performance, scalability for daily and cross-border use.[67] Although (retail) CBDCs are proposed as a solution to a wide range of policy challenges, no system can address in the best way all these goals. As technical design options can be leveraged to operationalise specific objectives, stakeholders are called to define their priorities and objectives and, accordingly, their designs.[68] In particular, most of these design choices are not binary, but placed on a spectrum.[69] Some policy options are crucial—e.g., the approach to privacy and individual rights, roles and responsibilities of the public and private sector—and translate into trade-offs to be defined, such as anonymity vs. centralised identity-based services, self-reliance vs. reliance on distributors, and centralised vs. distributed control.[70] The following sections elaborate on key components of the design of any retail CBDC system that impact on these type of trade-offs.

6.3.1 *What Type of Ledger and What Distribution Model?*

CBDC investigations have leaned towards the implementation of some form of DLT.[71] It is largely believed that, also in a CBDC context, a DLT-based architecture facilitates frictionless settlement, global interoperability, high levels of security, and low-latency, while also diminishing the role of intermediaries and the need for trust between the parties involved.[72] This happens often in the form of partnering with private FinTech companies, hence leveraging enterprise-grade permissioned blockchains that suit institutional use cases.[73] To date, the majority of CBDC projects assume a central authority and a permissioned system. The latter is

[66] Pocher and Sedlmeir (2024); Fanti and Pocher (2022); The White House (2022).

[67] Pocher and Veneris (2022a); Veneris et al. (2021); Michalopoulos et al. (2024).

[68] Mahari et al. (2022).

[69] Pocher and Sedlmeir (2024); Michalopoulos et al. (2024).

[70] Oliver Wayman Forum (2022), p. 12.

[71] Böhme and Auer (2020).

[72] Sethaput and Innet (2023); Pocher and Sedlmeir (2024).

[73] OMFIF and CCB (2023).

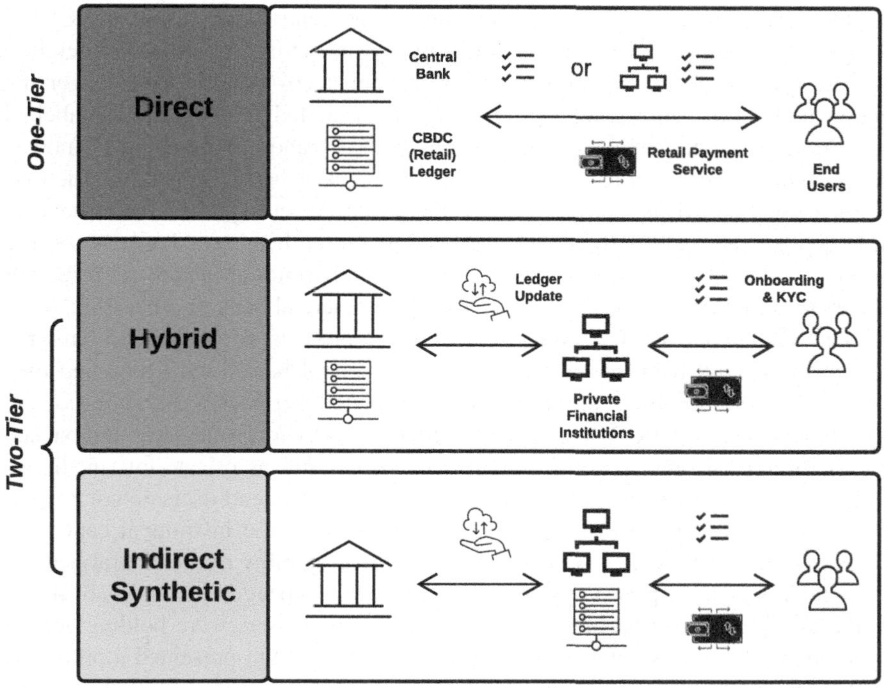

Fig. 6.1 Overarching types of retail CBDC architectures. Based on Pocher and Veneris (2022a)

managed by one or more trusted entities.[74] However, it was also argued how permissioned blockchains feature considerable shortcomings vis-à-vis centralised ledgers—e.g., in the areas of performance, deployment complexity, and access control.[75]

The core architecture and distribution model of a CBDC can be designed in various ways and may involve public and private actors.[76] Chiefly, they can be: (i) *one-tier*: the system is under sole management of the central bank (e.g., distribution, KYC, settlement); or (ii) *two-tier*: when financial institutions (e.g., commercial banks, PSPs) act as intermediaries for end-users. As shown in Fig. 6.1 above, CBDC architectures can be 'direct', 'hybrid', or 'indirect/synthetic'. The direct structure is described as unilateral,[77] as only the central bank is involved (e.g., it holds the CBDC ledger and handles user relationships) and the CBDC is a direct claim of the public against the central bank. On the contrary, 'hybrid' and 'indirect/synthetic'

[74] The White House (2022).

[75] Sedlmeir (2023); Pocher and Sedlmeir (2024).

[76] Adrian and Mancini-Griffoli (2019); Auer et al. (2020); Viñuela et al. (2020).

[77] Soderberg et al. (2022), p. 8.

CBDCs are two-tier.[78] In the 'hybrid' model, the central bank holds the CBDC ledger, but payment services are provided by private actors. A part of the literature provides for a further distinction: if the central bank keeps the full CBDC ledger, the model is 'hybrid', while if it keeps only the wholesale ledger, the design is labelled 'intermediated'. Nonetheless, both in the 'hybrid'' and 'intermediated' models the CBDC remains a direct claim against the central bank, even if transactions are managed by private actors.[79] In 'synthetic' CBDCs the private sector handles transactions and updates the ledger, held indirectly by the central bank by settling reserve accounts.[80] In this case, the CBDC is not a liability of the central bank, but the end-user holds a claim against the issuing commercial bank or other PSP.

The vast majority of ongoing retail CBDC projects adopt a hybrid model, where the central bank issues CBDCs to commercial banks and PSPs, and they distribute them to users providing account-related services.[81] By contrast, in synthetic schemes the CBDC is a stablecoin offered by a private actor and backed by its reserve account with the central bank, which means private intermediaries bear a responsibility to cover the relevant liability.[82] When end-users do not possess a direct claim on the central bank, some authors argue the instrument cannot be defined as a CBDC, which is assumed to be a direct liability of the central bank.[83] Nonetheless, other experts argue that if the stablecoin is pegged 1:1 to the sovereign currency by means of regulation, it is ostensibly as if users were holding central bank money.[84] In this context, for example, Project Aurum presented a prototype that envisions the issuance of two types of tokens within a two-tier CBDC system. The model foresees a wholesale CBDC issued to financial institutions, to be then distributed by them in a retail system. From the retail perspective, end-users would be offered two different types of tokens: (a) 'intermediated' CBDC or CBDC-token, a liability of the central bank, and (b) CBDC-backed stablecoins, issued by financial institutions.[85]

[78] Auer et al. (2021a, 2021b), p. 17.

[79] Bank for International Settlements (2022b), p. 4. Auer et al. (2021b).

[80] Adrian and Mancini-Griffoli (2019). In these cases, financial institutions hold reserve accounts with the central bank.

[81] Duffie and Economy (2022), p. 10. This is the foreseen case for the Digital euro, where "PSPs would distribute digital euro and be responsible for relationships with end users" (European Central Bank, 2023, p. 18).

[82] Bossu et al. (2020); Kriwoluzky and Kim (2019); Group of 30 (2020); Bossone (2020), p. 38. This resembles special-purpose licences granted to non-bank FinTech firms in jurisdictions such as India, Hong Kong, China, and Switzerland (Adrian & Mancini-Griffoli, 2019).

[83] Bossu et al. (2020).

[84] Kriwoluzky and Kim (2019); Soderberg et al. (2022), p. 8.

[85] Bank for International Settlements (2022b), pp. 3, 18.

6.3.2 *What Type of Wallet?*

CBDC architectures can deploy different types of wallets and their design, as explored in Chap. 7, can include a combination of more than one type of wallet. As with other digital wallets, also in CBDC systems wallets serve the function of authenticating the end-user and are the interface for performing transactions, storing private and public keys used to sign them.[86] On the one hand, access to a token-based means of payment relies on the validity of the traded object. In principle, it is an anonymous and bearer instrument grounded on cryptographic principles, while in an account-based CBDC access depends on the identification and identity verification of the account holder, reminiscent of traditional accounts requiring KYC.[87] Hence, in an account-based CBDCs the system comprises a ledger and a payment service, which refers to how payments are initiated, verified, cleared, and settled.[88] Yet, this classification is known to fall short in covering all potential CBDC designs.[89] It also presents key aspects of ambiguity, such as the fact that account updates can be represented as spending a token and receiving a new one.[90]

From another standpoint, a CBDC wallet can be hardware-based or software-based, which follows another distinction introduced in Chap. 2. The choice of a hardware-based wallet means, from a security perspective, relying on tamper-proof cryptographic chips, such as secure elements, that can protect cryptographic keys and ensure the correct processing of bilateral payments. This feature emerges as key in the context of offline CBDC payments.[91] Software-based wallets, instead, rely on cryptography and security protocols which may prove of more suitable application for large-scale deployment.[92] As explored below, hardware- and software-based functionalities can be combined in various ways.[93]

---

[86] As explored in Chap. 3, wallets can be custodial or non-custodial. If the wallet is custodial in a token-based system the custodian holds the private keys to sign a transaction, while in case of identity-based access it holds the link between identity and CBDC account necessary for authentication. If the wallet is non-custodial, in a token-based system end-users manage their own private keys, while in the case of identity-based access they must be able to prove ownership independently of any distributor—e.g., through a national ID system (Oliver Wayman Forum, 2022, p. 33).

[87] Allen et al. (2020a); Fanusie (2020); Kochergin and Dostov (2020). In other words, "in an account-based CBDC, ownership is tied to an identity, and transactions are authorised via identification. In a CBDC based on digital tokens, claims are honoured based solely on demonstrated knowledge, such as a digital signature" (Carstens, 2021, p. 17).

[88] Viñuela et al. (2020); Group of 30 (2020). The impact of account-based and token-based systems on the integration of CBDCs and IoT was addressed in Pocher and Zichichi (2022).

[89] Garratt et al. (2020).

[90] Gross et al. (2021).

[91] Michalopoulos et al. (2024).

[92] Pocher and Sedlmeir (2024).

[93] Michalopoulos et al. (2024); Pocher and Sedlmeir (2024); The White House (2022); Veneris et al. (2021).

6.3.3 How Can End-User Identity Be Managed?

'Identity management' refers to the decision on which data to collect on individuals and with whom to share it, and the literature provides guidelines related to CBDC systems.[94] In particular, one can find classifications of the possible relationships between the system and individual identities of end-users. This relationship can be: (i) *anonymous*: when the individual is not known to the central bank, distributors, other counterparties, and it is extremely difficult to determine real-world identities on the basis of the accessible data; (ii) *pseudonymous*: when, although real-world identities are not recorded, a unique identifier is linked to each transaction and authorised parties can determine real-world identities for purposes such as law enforcement and investigation; or (iii) *knowable*: when real-world identities are known to the central bank and/or to distributors and are linked to all accounts and transactions.[95]

It follows that the level of end-user privacy can range between complete anonymity—e.g., when a distributor assigns a system identifier not tied to the user's real-world identity and obscured from transactions, which is unlikely for KYC reasons—to fully centralised and identity-based services. Along this spectrum, three viable configurations emerge, where identity is (i) *pseudonymous* to all, (ii) *known* to the distributor but not the whole CBDC system, or (iii) *known* to both the central bank and the distributor. One can see how identity management have strong potential of influencing the level of individual privacy for end-users, from high individual privacy to high provision of centralised identity-based services.[96]

In this context, end-users' privacy can be assessed with reference to the central bank, if the system is centralised, or also in relation to the distributor(s). This is far from trivial: while in public surveys privacy protection always ranks as a top priority in payments, individuals do not only care about what data is collected, but also with whom it is shared and for what purpose. The participants in the CBDC system (e.g., central bank, distributors, PSPs) can be granted different levels of visibility into user data.[97] As argued above, multiple solutions can be adopted within the same CBDC scheme, and a regime of anonymity and pseudonymity can be provided for low-value transactions and low-balance wallets, possibly coupled with the limit to hold only one CBDC wallet, and in conjunction with an identity-compliant wallet, while 'step-up authentication' mechanisms can allow additional risk-based checks.[98]

[94] Oliver Wayman Forum (2022), pp. 25, 36.

[95] Oliver Wayman Forum (2022), pp. 25, 36. Pocher and Sedlmeir (2024).

[96] For instance, the existence of an independent (outside the central bank's perimeter) national ID system arguably allows for a centralised-based system that does not change a jurisdiction's privacy approach (Oliver Wayman Forum, 2022, pp. 21, 25, 37).

[97] Oliver Wayman Forum (2022), pp. 17–18, 36.

[98] Oliver Wayman Forum (2022), pp. 21, 39. Michalopoulos et al. (2024).

6.3.4 *Can the CBDC Be Transferred Offline?*

There is a worldwide consensus that a CBDC system should include an offline functionality.[99] To this end, central banks are exploring or piloting various designs.[100] In particular, the BIS defines three categories of offline CBDC transactions: fully offline, intermittently offline, and staged offline.[101] While a 'fully offline' CBDC system enables payments without the need for a direct ledger connection, the other two models require synchronisation to various degrees.[102] While the definition of 'offline' payment turns out to be quite nuanced, offline CBDCs align with several system goals, including (a) system resilience and accessibility (e.g., during connectivity or system disruptions, in regions with infrastructure deficiencies); (b) financial inclusion and accessibility (e.g., in underserved communities); (c) lower transaction costs (by reducing the load on the online ledger) & enhanced scalability; (d) end-user privacy, as the absence of a fully private digital alternative to cash generates concerns;[103] and (e) end-user experience and trust.[104]

Offline transactions can be implemented using hardware and software-based technologies.[105] On the one hand, Secure Elements (SEs) are tamper-resistant hardware platforms found in smart cards—e.g., chip-and-PIN, SIM cards, and biometric ID.[106] Alternatively, Trusted Execution Environments (TEEs) are secure areas of a microprocessor that offer increased integrity and confidentiality of the code executed and data stored or processed in them.[107] TEEs comprise a synergy of hardware and software components that isolate and protect it from the rest of the unsecured machine and the corresponding operating system.[108] From a software perspective, on the other hand, ZKPs provide, similarly to TEEs, computational integrity and confidentiality of the private input (with respect to the verifier).[109] Another approach is to issue debit-like cards, pre-loaded with a number of CBDCs from the end-user's wallet held on a smart device. The cards can be programmed with near-field communication and, when activated by a nearby radio-frequency

[99] Minwalla et al. (2023); Bank for International Settlements (2023); Kiff (2023).

[100] Armelius et al. (2021); Chu et al. (2022); Alper (2021); Brodsky et al. (2023).

[101] Bank for International Settlements (2023).

[102] Michalopoulos et al. (2024) elaborate on the various offline CBDC types and provide a description of a possible offline CBDC payment cycle.

[103] Bank for International Settlements (2023); Choi et al. (2023).

[104] Michalopoulos et al. (2024), p. 1. Soderberg et al. (2022), p. 13.

[105] Allen et al. (2020b); Veneris et al. (2021); Gang and Mount Union of Science and Technology (2019); Michalopoulos et al. (2024).

[106] GlobalPlatform (2018).

[107] Garrido Munilla et al. (2022).

[108] Sabt et al. (2015).

[109] Unlike SEs and TEEs, ZKPs do not provide confidentiality toward the prover, which can access all the data underlying the computation (Michalopoulos et al., 2024, p. 2; Garrido Munilla et al., 2022).

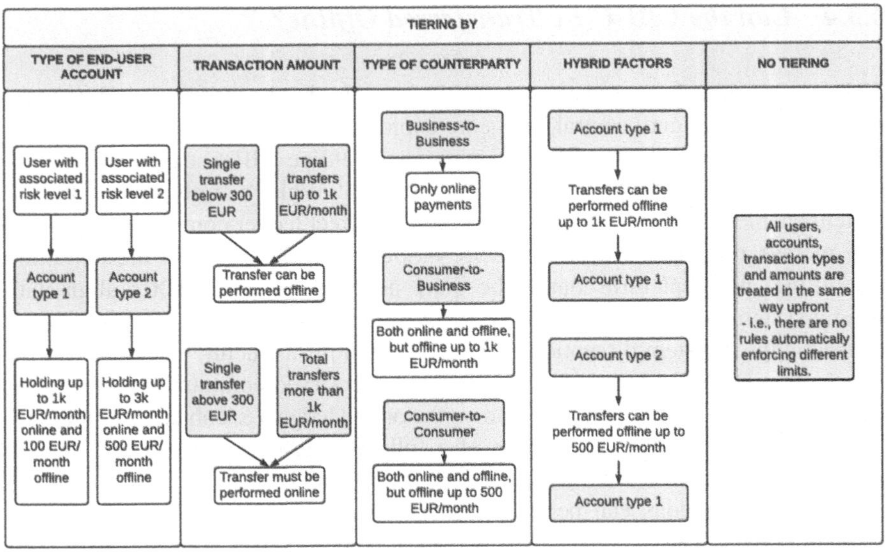

Fig. 6.2 Examples of transaction and account tiering in the context of integrating online and offline functionalities in a CBDC system. Based on Michalopoulos et al. (2024)

signal—e.g., a merchant's terminal—, they can transmit offline the required amount, as credit/debit cards.[110]

Offline payments may seem less problematic than from the perspective of their criminal misuse than their online/remote counterparts, because the need of the physical presence of the end-user can be seen as a liability for anyone wishing to misuse them for illicit activities. Nevertheless, it was reported that reliable proofs of proximity are hard to achieve,[111] which in brief means it is possible to mask remote payments as proximity payments, potentially to benefit from strict compliance rules foreseen for offline transactions. In turn, this requires for offline payment similar risk mitigation measures as online payments.[112]

6.3.5 *Are Transactions and/or Accounts Tiered?*

As described further below and in Chap. 7, the technical design of a (CBDC) system can be leveraged to embed compliance aspects.[113] Not all elements of compliance

110 Veneris et al. (2021); World Economic Forum (2021d).

111 Ranganathan and Capkun (2017).

112 Michalopoulos et al. (2024).

113 Pocher and Veneris (2022b).

can be integrated in the same way, neither do they require the same technical capabilities—e.g., computation power, storage. For instance, the integration of checks for financial sanctions is likely simpler than embedding AML/CFT checks (Chap. 5). This is primarily because, while sanctions compliance operates within a rules-based system for individual transactions, which is based on compiled lists,[114] AML/CFT compliance operates within a risk-based system, navigating nuanced scenarios affecting the collection of transactions, defining risk parameters, and balancing diverse requirements.[115]

In the CBDC context, the need to balance various regulatory requirements can lead to a multi-layered design that accommodates various options by integrating different trade-offs within the same system through 'access/transaction tiering'.[116] This means that the features offered by the system vary depending on the attributes of a given account or transaction.[117] This can be done for a variety of purposes, such as privacy, security, financial inclusion, and an AML/CFT risk-based approach.[118] In particular, tiering can be based on the user account—e.g., between two less risky accounts as per a level of CDD—, transaction amount thresholds—e.g., transfers can be facilitated below a certain amount—, counter-party types—e.g., business-to-business, business-to-consumer, and consumer-to-consumer—, and other hybrid factors—e.g., total turnover transacted between two accounts in a certain time window exceeds a certain amount).[119] Managing these trade-offs gives rise to a spectrum of (online and offline) design options for a CBDC system.[120] Figure 6.2 depicts examples of transaction tiering in the context of online and offline functionalities of the CBDC system.

6.3.6 The Public-Private Interplay

Different CBDC designs lead to diverging public-private monetary policy dynamics. The topic relates to a broader discussion on the preferable degree of competition between public (central banks, governments) and private (e.g., commercial banks, financial institutions, corporations) actors in digital currencies. In the CBDCs context, the main controversy is whether society can best reap this opportunity if central banks replace private financial institutions and FinTech firms or rather join forces with them.[121] While the first option is more straightforward but hardly

[114] Cipriani et al. (2023).

[115] Pocher and Veneris (2022a); Michalopoulos et al. (2024).

[116] Michalopoulos et al. (2024).

[117] The White House (2022).

[118] Michalopoulos et al. (2024).

[119] The White House (2022); Michalopoulos et al. (2024).

[120] Michalopoulos et al. (2024).

[121] Kriwoluzky and Kim (2019); Group of 30 (2020); Nabilou (2019); Brunnermeier and Niepelt (2019); Pocher and Veneris (2022a).

feasible at a large scale, two-layered approaches assume the central bank is willing to waive a portion of power.[122] Two-layered CBDCs, however, vary in terms of boundaries of the involvement of private actors in the value chain.[123] The collaboration between central banks and distributors does not translate into a binary decision, and a range of options sees control distributed at different degrees.[124] Most importantly, in hybrid structures central banks still hold the CBDC ledger and manage end-users accounts, while in both hybrid and synthetic cases payment services, relationships with end-users, and AML/CFT processes are managed by the private sector.

The idea of outsourcing CBDC activities to private actors has generated academic and political debate.[125] In PPPs, public sector's goals meet profit objectives of the private industry,[126] while public authorities benefit from private sector's expertise and flexibility.[127] In the CBDC arena, the main question is how to guarantee innovation, efficiency, fair competition and financial inclusion against monetary and financial stability risks, that are traditional objectives guaranteed by central banks themselves.[128] In a nutshell, PPPs seek to preserve comparative advantages: private actors interact with end-users, develop interface designs and innovate, while public institutions regulate, supervise and supply trust. Public-private scenarios may stimulate competition, foster innovation and inclusion, while reducing risks and costs for central banks. By contrast, they may pose financial stability and liquidity risks in case of synthetic CBDCs if the responsibility to maintain adequate asset backing rests on private actors.[129] Further issues are raised by collection, use and dissemination of the data and metadata of end-user payments. Additionally, CBDC private stakeholders may have different incentives than public entities and be in a different market position than ordinary private actors in PPPs, since FinTech companies already provide substantial hardware to central banks.[130] For instance, they may pursue profit maximisation at the cost of abusing of information advantage or conceal operational weaknesses, and the consequent loss of trust would generate instability.[131]

[122] Jagati (2020).

[123] Adrian (2020).

[124] Oliver Wayman Forum (2022), p. 23. Soderberg et al. (2022), p. 9.

[125] Conflicting PPP definitions exist. In brief, they are arrangements "between government and the private sector in which partially or traditionally public activities are performed by the private sector" (Savas, 2000, p. 4). Similarly, see Bexell and Moerth (2010), p. 6. Bevir (2009), p. 85.

[126] Vutsova and Ignatova (2014), p. 85. Ross and Yan (2015), p. 449.

[127] Linder (1999).

[128] Group of 30 (2020); Auer et al. (2022).

[129] Bank for International Settlements (2021a); Carstens (2021), p. 17. Kriwoluzky and Kim (2019); Nabilou (2019); Ojo (2021); Auer et al. (2020).

[130] Jagati (2020).

[131] Kriwoluzky and Kim (2019), p. 13.

Hence, foreseeably central banks would need either to manage complex infrastructures or set up advanced supervision schemes.[132] Establishing and taking part in a new retail payment model requires skills that are far from traditional for central banks, also in terms of technical expertise vis-à-vis the impacts of possible failures on the economy and financial stability. Reportedly, this remains true in all possible involvement scenarios of the central bank, be it as scheme leader, coordinator, participant, or supervisor, depending on the CBDC design. Although some concerns may be mitigated by partnering with FinTech firms, managing vendors and partners also requires new abilities. Alternatively, the private sector can be involved by adopting a hybrid model where distributors operate part of the system.[133]

6.4 AML/CFT Considerations in the CBDC Domain

When CBDCs started to emerge, it was clear that their innovative techno-legal character was accompanied by a certain degree of tradition in terms of the stakeholders involved—i.e., central banks and regulated intermediaries such as financial institutions and PSPs. From this perspective, CBDC issues are channelled into a familiar structure of regulated environments. Nonetheless, CBDCs bring about a few outstanding dilemmas, influenced by the specific design. A selection of these regulatory conundrums is addressed in this chapter, albeit with no attempt to offer a comprehensive account. Naturally, CBDCs raise many other regulatory issues, most of which belong to areas traditionally less harmonised across jurisdictions than AML/CFT—e.g., private and property law, contract law, tax law, insolvency law, private international law.[134]

As a preliminary issue, given the CBDC-hype, it is interesting that almost no jurisdiction would currently allow their issuance without amending domestic laws. A 2020 IMF study highlighted how CBDC issuance poses several risks for the central banking community, burdening it with legal, financial, and reputational questions.[135] Two public law domains, 'central bank law' and 'monetary law', are crucial to warrant CBDCs a sound legal basis, and experts concluded that while the first one could be addressed through reforms, the latter poses structural policy challenges of less straightforward solution. First, if a CBDC is to be a liability of the central bank (i.e., direct, hybrid and intermediated forms) its issuance must be regulated by 'central bank laws'.[136] This is necessary to warrant the CBDC a legal

[132] Auer et al. (2020).

[133] Oliver Wayman Forum (2022), pp. 14–15.

[134] Bossu et al. (2020); Brummer (2019).

[135] Bossu et al. (2020).

[136] 'Central banks laws' establish central banks, their decision-making bodies, autonomy, and their mandate: actions beyond it generate challenges vis-à-vis administrative law principles of 'attribution' and 'specialty' (Bossu et al., 2020, p. 13).

basis in compliance with the principle of attribution of powers and central bank mandate. Likewise, the qualification of a CBDC as 'currency' must be regulated under 'monetary law': if it is to be used as a means of payment to extinguish monetary obligations, 'monetary law' must treat is as such.[137] Overall, it was argued the legal treatment in both fields will largely depend on the technical and operational design, and reforms are required to ensure the soundness of the framework. Notably, controversies arise as to the lack of legal basis to issue token-based instruments, and account-based CBDCs to the public. Both aspects would require relevant amendments.[138]

Although their AML/CFT aspects are discussed extensively, CBDCs are not treated as crypto-assets, but as fiat currency.[139] Several studies outline how different architectures may lead to various AML/CFT repercussions, where key questions concern the allocation of compliance duties, account management, identity/transaction checks. The relevance of CBDC-related AML/CFT discussions emerges by the ongoing development of a new sensitivity to the interplay between technology, regulation, and technical standardisation. Indeed, in line with what was suggested in Chap. 5 and is explored in Chap. 7, CBCD or stablecoin interoperability requires AML/CFT technical standards, whose development is currently hindered because the framework has not been yet "collated into a standardised data format to allow for automation".[140] Interestingly, it was suggested that a given government or organisation establishes a (centralised) database to provide regulated entities in the digital currency space with transaction- or customer-related risk scores on illicit activity.[141]

6.4.1 CBDCs and Limits to the Flow of Cash

Chapter 4 outlined how altcoins have increasingly evolved toward higher cryptographic complexity. Accordingly, the FATF voiced growing concerns in terms of virtual-to-virtual layering,[142] pervasive obfuscation mechanisms were complemented by the advent of DEXes, unhosted wallets and cross-chain atomic swaps.[143] In this context, the FATF identified examples of anonymity as 'red flag indicators' of suspicious activities in the crypto-asset sphere.[144] As explored in Chap. 3,

[137] 'Monetary law' lays out the foundation for the use of monetary value. The basic principle is that it is up to a sovereign State to establish its currency system (Bossu et al., 2020, p. 27).

[138] Bossu et al. (2020).

[139] Allen et al. (2020a).

[140] World Economic Forum (2021c), p. 187.

[141] World Economic Forum (2021c), p. 187.

[142] Financial Action Task Force (2021).

[143] Pocher (2021a, 2021b).

[144] Financial Action Task Force (2020).

controversies on anonymity in financial transactions well preceded the advent of crypto-assets. Not only the debate on e-cash dates to the 1990s,[145] but the core issue originated with regard to physical cash. Indeed, cash is reportedly one of the preferred means of transfer for money laundering and terrorist financing purposes, and in Europe most STRs concern its use or its smuggling.[146] Even if cash is still the favourite means of payment also for the legal economy, it was estimated only one-third (at most) of circulating cash serves legitimate purposes, and several analyses correlate cash diffusion and illicit activities.[147]

The fight against financial crime has long faced the fact that the trait of anonymity is inherent to this means of payment—one of the purest examples of a fungible asset—, and it addressed it by leveraging identification and traceability. Indeed, (some form of) identification is arguably needed to safeguard the payment system, and AML/CFT and anti-fraud practices imply a trade-off between access to the means of payment and traceability. If CBDCs are designed to replicate cash-like anonymity, but at the same time overcome the physical limitations of coins and banknotes, significant concerns arise. The vulnerability of a fully anonymous CBDC system make some level of identification crucial in a CBDC design.[148]

Interestingly, cash being dangerous from an AML/CFT perspective was one of the drivers of e-money solutions, due to the degree of control they can enable through programmability.[149] Indeed, monitoring and/or limiting the use of cash is a widespread method to counter criminal activities and was one of the first measures to mitigate money laundering and terrorist financing risks, by establishing thresholds for its use and incentives for traceable means of payment. Three types of thresholds can limit the flow of cash, placed on (i) purchases (e.g., on all/certain goods, day/month/per person limit depending on the type of costumer, AML/CFT obligations on cash-intensive businesses), (ii) cross-border transfers (e.g., FATF's Recommendation 32 on 'cash couriers' and its Interpretative Note on 'declaration' or 'disclosure' systems), and (iii) banknote denomination.[150] Meanwhile, cash transactions above certain volumes may trigger compliance duties and other measures—e.g., Interpretative Note to FATF's Recommendation 29 suggests a reporting system for large cash transactions. Against this backdrop, it is pivotal to underline that although CBDCs are usually benchmarked to cash in terms of capacity to offer privacy and anonymity, this feature is far from limitless, and many jurisdictions have implemented transactional reporting thresholds and other limitations.[151]

---

[145] Chaum (1983); Chaum et al. (2021); Magnuson (2020).

[146] Riccardi and Levi (2018), p. 135.

[147] Riccardi and Levi (2018), pp. 139–141.

[148] Bank for International Settlements (2021a). Carstens (2021), p. 17. Michalopoulos et al. (2024).

[149] Allen et al. (2020b); Nabilou (2019).

[150] Riccardi and Levi (2018), pp. 147–148.

[151] World Economic Forum (2021b), p. 157.

As per cross-border transfers, Regulation (EU) 2018/1672 provides for a declaration obligation on natural person entering or leaving the Union carrying cash of a value of EUR 10,000 or more (Article 3(1)). Here, 'cash' comprises (i) currency, (ii) bearer-negotiable instruments, (iii) commodities used as highly-liquid stores of value, and (iv) prepaid cards (Article 2(1)(a)), where 'currency' means coins and banknotes circulating as a medium of exchange, the holders of 'bearer-negotiable instruments' can claim a financial amount without having to prove identity or entitlement (e.g., traveller's cheques, promissory notes), the definition of a 'commodity used as a highly-liquid store of value' refers to an annexed list of goods with a high value-volume ratio and easily convertible into currency (e.g., coins with gold content of at least 90%), and 'prepaid cards' are non-nominal, not linked to a bank account, and store (or provide access to) a monetary value that can be used for payments, to acquire goods or services and to redeem currency (Article 2(1)(c-f)).

Furthermore, as overviewed in Chap. 5, in the EU CDD obligations arise for financial institutions when customers perform transactions of EUR 15,000 or more. In Canada and in the U.S., regulated entities must report transactions of CAD/USD 10,000 or more within 24-hours.[152] In the past, the EU had unsuccessfully considered unified restrictions to payments in cash,[153] while some countries already limit cash use between private individuals and/or between consumers and businesses, and/or between businesses, if no regulated intermediary is involved in the transaction.[154] Bearer's instruments, such as bearer's checks and passbooks, are usually equated to cash. Illustratively, the following limits are in place: EUR 500 in Greece; EUR 1000 in France (only for residents, otherwise EUR 10,000), Spain (for a non-resident consumer the limit is EUR 10,000); EUR 3000 in Portugal (for residents, otherwise EUR 3000), in Poland (not applicable between private individuals), in Belgium (not applicable between consumers), Lithuania; EUR 5000 in Bulgaria, Italy, Slovenia (not applicable between consumers); EUR 7000 in Latvia; EUR 10,000 in the Czech Republic, Malta (for selected goods), Croatia (for business registered in Croatia); EUR 15,000 in Slovakia.[155] In these jurisdictions, transfers of higher values must be made through regulated intermediaries. Similar strategies are applied in Jamaica, Mexico, Uruguay and India.

As outlined in Chap. 5, however, the AML Regulation brought about an EU-wide cash-payment limit of EUR 10,000 for professional purposes.[156] As per Article 59(1) of the AML Regulation, "persons trading in goods or providing services may accept or make a payment in cash only up to an amount of EUR 10,000 or equivalent amount in national or foreign currency, whether the transaction is carried out in a single operation or in several operations which appear to be linked", where Article

[152] FINTRAC (2019). 31 U.S.C. Title 31.

[153] Ecorys and Centre for European Policy Studies (2017).

[154] Sands et al. (2017).

[155] European Consumer Centre France (2022); European Consumer Centre Germany (2024).

[156] Regulation (EU) 2024/1624.

59(4) specifies the limit does not apply to "(a) payments between natural persons who are not acting in a professional function; (b) payments or deposits made at the premises of credit institutions. In such cases, the credit institution shall report the payment or deposit above the limit to the FIU". While the 4AMLD had tried to mitigate cash-related risks by including among obliged entities 'persons trading in goods' when making/receiving cash payments amounting to more than EUR 10,000, the approach proved ineffective vis-à-vis the differences at Member State level. Hence, in conjunction with the Union-wide limit, 'persons trading in goods' would no longer be considered regulated entities.[157]

Indeed, the AML Regulation prevents traders in goods and services from accepting cash above EUR 10,000 for a single purchase, while it allows Member States to establish lower ceilings. In this respect, the EC is expected to assess costs, benefits and impacts of lowering the limit and its enforceability.[158] The approach towards cash-related risks also emerges in the FTR recast, Regulation (EU) 2023/1113, where simplified regimes for transfers below EUR 1,000 do not apply if originating PSPs receive the funds in cash, or if beneficiary PSPs pay out the funds in cash.[159]

6.4.2 The Privacy and Data Protection Conundrum

After the adoption of the GDPR, a wave of global-scale sensitivity to data protection concerns started to permeate the law and technology domain. At times, this seems at odds with AML/CFT, while blockchain-based environments raise specific questions. An extensive array of contributions addresses the interplay of blockchain, privacy and data protection,[160] where scholars focused on contrasts in permissionless blockchains,[161] PETs and de-anonymisation. The topic is most relevant to CBDCs and is at the heart of heated debates: public-private dynamics of CBDC designs originate diverging questions, as private actors may be made part of mechanisms of information exchange detrimental to the privacy of end-users.

A literature review shows how AML/CFT aspects are often discussed as opposed to privacy and data protection: the more data is (or can be) disclosed to regulated entities and LEAs, the more intrusive the consequences may be on financial aspects of end-users' lives.[162] By contrast, a system with full privacy ostensibly thwarts compliance regimes. These considerations are mirrored by the research on CBDC

---

157 Recital 18 of Regulation (EU) 2024/1624.

158 Recital 164 of Regulation (EU) 2024/1624.

159 Articles 5(3)(a), 6(2)(a) and 7(4) of Regulation (EU) 2023/1113.

160 Finck (2019); Karasek-Wojciechowicz (2021); Salmensuu (2018); Berberich and Steiner (2016); Goodell and Aste (2019).

161 Karasek-Wojciechowicz (2021).

162 Garratt and van Oordt (2019).

designs, with attempts to build anonymity-oriented pilots while avoiding drawbacks. Relatedly, experts put forward a CBDC architecture to combine privacy with oversight by holding CBDCs outside of custodial relationships.[163] This is based on the distinction between privacy and data protection, to be heeded when applying privacy by design. Indeed, although the latter is favoured for data protection, data protection concerns access and use of private information once it is collected (i.e., prevention of unauthorised use of data), while privacy means preventing individuals and businesses from revealing data on their habits and behaviours. It follows that privacy, as architectural property and fundamental design feature, cannot depend on authorities 'granting' or 'guaranteeing' it through data protection schemes.[164] In this sense, data should not be collected to begin with.

As mentioned above, the privacy and transparency properties of CBDC models depend on the technical design. Each technology stack embeds a choice pertaining to architecture (e.g., specifics of the ledger), that affect the roles and relationships between processes and software systems.[165] Evidently, the role played by private actors within a CBDC model influences the data flow and data protection dynamics. Remarks were provided on data access and accessibility depending on whether distributors (i.e., providers of CBDC gateway services) act as wholesale processors, in a system where each entity processes its transactions, processing agents, where distributors participate in the core system and access a broad range of data and meta-data (e.g., users' profiles and buying patterns) according to the chosen model for identity management and data storage, or custodians and gateways in a centralised model, where distributors perform limited functions and access little information.[166]

Although this debate is relevant to digital payments at large,[167] CBDCs are vulnerable to aid mass monitoring, profiling, surveillance, threaten data protection, security, and potentially safety.[168] Chiefly, concerns about data abuse arise from the combination of transaction, geolocation, social media and search data, and the protection of individual privacy against governments and commercial players was framed as a basic right. In this respect, the understanding of CBDC-related privacy is broad:[169] albeit often treated as a single concept, it concerns different stakeholders—e.g., central banks, settlement and payment providers, retailers. In this sense, experts focused on how to govern access to the system, to establish public-private roles in guarding identity and transaction data, but also under which

[163] Goodell et al. (2021).

[164] Goodell et al. (2021), pp. 3, 6.

[165] Fanti and Pocher (2022), p. 11.

[166] Oliver Wayman Forum (2022), pp. 49–54.

[167] Garratt and van Oordt (2019); Goodell et al. (2021).

[168] Tronnier et al. (2022).

[169] Rennie and Steele (2021), pp. 6–17. Bank for International Settlements (2021a).

conditions public entities can access data and metadata and if/how to share it with the private sector.[170]

Against this backdrop, public-private CBDCs generate pressing dilemmas. While significant concerns followed financial digitisation, PPPs may offer more secure solutions than other setups, easing the application of advanced cryptography to wallet architectures and transaction environments and speeding up the application of DLTs, thus protecting consumers, lowering costs and strengthening compliance. At the same time, specific technologies require adequate controls to protect personal data and, in the absence of safeguards, a CBDC based on a public (permissioned) blockchain could become the "most privacy-invading citizen surveillance tool we have ever seen".[171] Relatedly, data privacy preferences and regulatory frameworks vary across the globe and CBDC initiatives embody context-specific inclinations.[172]

6.4.3 The Competence for AML/CFT Compliance

If one of the CBDC drivers is the intention to mirror cash usability, it makes little sense for the whole set-up and corresponding procedures to resemble those of traditional bank accounts.[173] Hence, it is not a surprise that token-based CBDCs were argued to be more conducive to goals of financial inclusion and access to central bank money than account-based ones. Nonetheless, not only it was argued CBDC implementation offers the perfect opportunity to mitigate some of the new risks by embedding sophisticated AML/CFT detection and anti-fraud solutions,[174] but it is also clear that if a CBDC initiative underestimates AML/CFT compliance during the design phase it does not mean users and regulated entities will be allowed to operate beyond such principles. Instead, one can expect compliance burdens to be shifted to private entities offering CBDC product/services to the end-users. These observations lead to preferring either a two-layered structure or one where the CBDC itself offers strong anonymity, but regulators require PSPs converting CBDCs to other currencies to implement KYC on their customers.[175]

As mentioned above, CBDC architectures have different AML/CFT repercussions. A key question relates to the responsibility for compliance duties, KYC, account management, identity and transaction checks. While in a direct CBDC structure the central bank would need new resources and expertise,[176] two-layer

[170] Carstens (2021). Oliver Wayman Forum (2022), pp. 17–18. Gross et al. (2021); Tronnier et al. (2022).

[171] Jagati (2020).

[172] Carstens (2021).

[173] Michalopoulos et al. (2024).

[174] Oliver Wayman Forum (2022), p. 19.

[175] Pocher and Veneris (2022a).

[176] Bossu et al. (2020), p. 10.

models allow compliance to be outsourced to PSPs and commercial banks, to be either managed directly or delegated. As central banks do not traditionally interact with the general public and do not engage in activities such as customer onboarding, customer service, dispute resolution, technology maintenance, transaction monitoring and compliance,[177] two-tier structures appear as largely favoured.[178] This is the approach that emerges from the ongoing discussions regarding a Digital euro. In this context, a recent ECB report highlights how PSPs "would only have access to online digital euro transaction details to the extent necessary to ensure compliance with EU law, such as anti-money laundering rules",[179] which is also in line with the regulatory approach of the EC's Digital euro Package.[180]

6.5 Privacy vs. Transparency: The Topical Role of Trade-Offs

As argued in Chaps. 3 and 4, anonymity and privacy are not binary properties, but range within a spectrum. In this respect, the two concepts refer to two different abilities of the individual to exert control on which personal data is shared/when/with whom (privacy) and not to have their identity known (anonymity).[181] Meanwhile, crypto-asset anonymity has a socio-technical nature,[182] influenced on the on the one hand by specific tools, governance, and system architecture, and the other hand by the possibility of identification and traceability and the use of forensic techniques.[183] Undeniably, policy makers are caught between offering CBDC users the highest degree of anonymity, making identity data hardly accessible to the public and the private sector, and establishing identity-based services. In different jurisdictions, this tension is influenced by aspects that are not necessarily related only to CBDCs—e.g., the attitude towards data protection and digital ID management.[184]

Although a privacy-transparency tension is inherent to CBDCs, in line with the arguments of Chap. 4 the relationship emerges as a trade-off. To establish the desired one, it is possible to rely on technology (e.g., cryptographic techniques) and/or on regulation that sets data governance policies (e.g., usage or access limitations). While the first option seems more resilient and tamper-proof (e.g., independence from political changes, lack of compliance), policy measures are more flexible

[177] Zhang (2020); Sidorenko et al. (2021), p. 498. Böhme and Auer (2020).

[178] Michalopoulos et al. (2024).

[179] European Central Bank (2024), p. 3.

[180] European Commission (2023).

[181] Oliver Wayman Forum (2022), pp. 17–18.

[182] Rogaway (2016). Sardá et al. (2019), pp. 557–564.

[183] Pocher and Veneris (2022b).

[184] Oliver Wayman Forum (2022), p. 21.

and adapt to societal needs.[185] Against this backdrop, not only CBDCs can be designed to embed various privacy-transparency trade-offs, but DLTs themselves are conducive to balancing the individual right to privacy against AML/CFT public interests. While a fully transparent CBDC, with visible real-world identities, may violate human rights, if privacy is provided without limitation, and no information can be revealed, misuses for illicit purposes may not be averted.[186] Luckily, nuanced solutions are available, and most CBDCs offer some privacy to end-users and some visibility to authorities. These trade-offs can be addressed from the perspectives of confidentiality and auditability,[187] and designs can be classified accordingly and correlated with the AML/CFT understanding of anonymity.

The connection between technical and regulatory compliance suggests design-based regulatory techniques, explored in Chap. 7.[188] Indeed, the notion that compliance ought to be considered from the early stages of the design of a system is gaining momentum, and this forward-looking approach requires preliminary engineering and standard setting having regard to both the regulatory objectives to be pursued and the available technical options.

6.5.1 *The Role of Privacy-Enhancing Technologies*

Privacy by design was first formalised with regard to PETs, to exemplify how technology can pursue regulatory goals.[189] Indeed, PETs can be defined as "technologies or systems that incorporate technical processes, methods or knowledge to achieve specific privacy or data protection functionality, or that implement specific requirements of data protection laws and reduce the risks associated with processing personally identifiable information, such as the risk of data breaches".[190] As explored in the previous chapters, privacy and anonymity are twofold, and PETs can be implemented to protect individual privacy, but also to pursue enhanced anonymity and cripple the fight against illicit activities. This janiform use responds to different goals and is mirrored at the implementation level by specific combinations.

From an AML/CFT perspective, end-user privacy and data protection must be balanced with accountability—i.e., the "understanding of transaction information by the authorised third parties, or the degree to which a given environment allows an authorised entity to audit confidential transaction information by viewing and

[185] Oliver Wayman Forum (2022), pp. 17–18.

[186] Michalopoulos et al. (2024); Pocher and Veneris (2022b).

[187] Pocher and Veneris (2022b); European Central Bank and Bank of Japan (2020).

[188] Pocher and Veneris (2022b); Pocher and Zichichi (2022); Nabilou (2019); Zetzsche et al. (2020); Torra (2017); Yeung (2017); Hoess et al. (2024).

[189] Cavoukian (2011). Hustinx (2010), pp. 253–255. Tamò-Larrieux (2018), pp. 22–23.

[190] World Economic Forum (2021e), p. 12.

interpreting the information".[191] In a financial scenario, this typically means that third parties need to scrutinise transactions. Often, the deployment of PETs poses auditability challenges, but they can also offer compromises to tackle privacy and confidentiality issues generated by sharing data in a distributed environment by limiting data access to unauthorised parties. Reportedly, they are the best technology option to replicate the privacy feature of cash, where they can "maximise the potential of CBDC for achieving policy goals while providing privacy".[192]

While PETs support privacy and transparency in various ways, the balance is technically challenging. If they are applied concurrently "there could be a trade-off between enhancing confidentiality and effective auditability".[193] Hence, experts analysed the ways privacy can be coded into blockchain systems,[194] and the compatibility with regulation. For instance, not all PETs have the same impact on data retrieval, where the AML/CFT goal is not only proactive compliance (e.g., balance and payment limits),[195] but also retroactive (e.g., data retention, auditing and mandated disclosure). In this respect, the ECB and Bank of Japan 2020 delved into the impacts of different PETs on the balance between confidentiality and auditability when sharing payment and securities settlement data in a permissioned distributed network.[196] Indeed, when PETs are applied to transaction data to make it confidential—i.e., prevent unauthorised parties from viewing and interpreting it, where 'view' refers to the existence of visible transaction data and 'interpret' to the possibility to derive value and identities—,[197] they impact data auditability in different ways. Accordingly, PETs are systematised as segregating, hiding, and unlinking.[198]

The study shows how PETs exert different impacts on the auditability of confidential transaction data, where auditability is measured by assessing (i) accessibility to necessary data—i.e., the auditor can access the data it needs to perform the audit via alternative data sources, that exist by design or are credible parties implementing PETs—, (ii) reliability of the obtained data—i.e., the auditor can be certain the original data can be acquired using the obtained data—, and (iii)

[191] European Central Bank and Bank of Japan (2020), p. 1.

[192] World Economic Forum (2021b), p. 157.

[193] European Central Bank (2020b).

[194] Renwick and Gleasure (2020).

[195] Michalopoulos et al. (2024).

[196] The project was limited to transactions between participants of a wholesale system, thus excluding by its findings end-user data (European Central Bank and Bank of Japan, 2020, p. 3), the analysis provides insights into confidentiality and auditability levels in a crypto-asset scenario.

[197] European Central Bank and Bank of Japan (2020), p. 4.

[198] As reported by European Central Bank and Bank of Japan (2020), the function of *segregating PETs* is to share information on a 'need to know' basis, so that each participant's visibility is limited to a subset of transactions. Secondly, *hiding PETs* foster confidentiality at transaction level by implementing cryptography against unauthorised interpretation. Finally, *unlinking PETs* conceal the identities of the parties from the pseudonyms stored on the ledger, making it difficult to determine transaction relationships from ledger data.

efficiency of the auditing process, measured by resources' consumption. When all criteria are met, auditability is effective.[199] In other words, effective auditing is performed when the auditor receives the necessary data from trusted sources or from identifiable participants and can verify its correctness with what is recorded on the ledger, and the process does not require excessive resources.[200] Reportedly, effective auditability can take place after the application of segregating PETs, Quorum's private transaction, Perdersen commitment, and centralised mixing.[201]

As anticipated above, PETs may be combined to deliver the desired balance. For instance, ZKPs are key in financial applications, as they "enable auditability and prevention of fraudulent activity, even within the scope of private transaction data" and are "efficient enough to be used for verifying all the protocol rules in a blockchain-based financial system with auditing capabilities".[202] From this viewpoint, an accurate assessment of ZKP auditability reportedly depends for the most part on the given implementation. In case only transaction amounts are hidden, for instance, the evaluation on auditability resembles that of Pedersen commitment.[203]

6.5.2 Classifying Embedded Trade-Offs

The way regulatory requirements are embedded into CBDC designs reveals trade-offs between privacy and transparency, where different use cases showcase diverging policy choices. Meanwhile, the specific design of a DLT-based system, such as the implementation of specific PETs, unveils a balance between confidentiality and auditability. Hence, a CBDC scheme embeds a specific trade-off between privacy and transparency in the form of confidentiality and auditability. This way of thinking mirrors the methodology underpinning privacy by design, notably the notion of embedding privacy into the design, thus making it an "essential component of the core functionality being delivered".[204] Accordingly, CBDC schemes can be classified as per the trade-off between privacy/confidentiality and transparency/auditability they embed. Against this backdrop, this section highlights concrete examples of how technology can be leveraged to reach various objectives. To this end, Fig. 6.3 places several proposals for CBDC design across a spectrum of conceivable nuances. It is important to note that the classification considers the design as a whole—for this reason, the level of confidentiality of the whole design may diminish when it features different types of transactions with different features,

[199] European Central Bank and Bank of Japan (2020), pp. 15–17.

[200] European Central Bank and Bank of Japan (2020), p. 24.

[201] European Central Bank and Bank of Japan (2020).

[202] World Economic Forum (2021b), p. 162.

[203] European Central Bank and Bank of Japan (2020), pp. 20–21.

[204] Information & Privacy Commissioner of Ontario (2013).

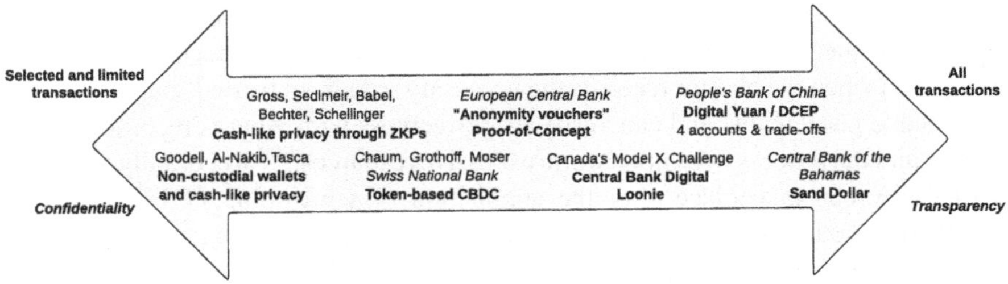

Fig. 6.3 Selected CBDC projects ranging from accountable anonymity to transparency. Elaborated based on Pocher and Veneris (2022a); Pocher (2023); Michalopoulos et al. (2024)

in comparison to one that only features anonymous transactions. This does not mean in any way that a 'mixed design' does not achieve a high level of 'cash-like privacy' for a specific subset. On the contrary, such designs are arguably the most compatible with the ultimate objective of balancing confidentiality with auditability in a flexible way.[205]

As explored in Chap. 4, studies on identity privacy have largely focused on eliminating identifiers, where a solution has not yet been found to make it impossible for attackers to gather information on the identity of senders/recipients if it is recorded on a ledger whose content is available publicly or selectively. Hence, reportedly, it may not be feasible for CBDCs to achieve cash-like anonymity if such data is recorded on the ledger. Meanwhile, experts focused on achieving transaction privacy without preventing validators from verifying consistency of transaction amounts with account balances and compliance with predefined requirements, often through ZKPs. Other solutions leverage secure multiparty computation, rotation of public keys and TEE hardware-enclaved computing.[206] From a CBDC perspective, a way to offer anonymity while reaching a desirable level of accountability is to provide tailored solutions for different types of transactions, setting up schemes that can be defined as 'mixed solutions'.[207] Indeed, in theory privacy can be tackled selectively, meaning certain low-value transactions could be undertaken without acquiring identity data. This type of CBDC model usually involves a token-based solution. Evidently, any trade-off will need to be identified at the beginning of the design cycle. Nevertheless, registration and identity verification can still take place when a user signs up.

Owner-Custodianship and Cash-Like Privacy As mentioned above, a CBDC can combine privacy and oversight by holding CBDCs outside of custodial relationships.[208] The proposal by Goodell and Aste (2019) is grounded on the distinction

[205] Michalopoulos et al. (2024); Pocher and Veneris (2022a).

[206] Allen et al. (2020b).

[207] Pocher and Veneris (2022b).

[208] Goodell et al. (2021). On self-custody see also Barresi and Zatti (2020).

between privacy and data protection, where privacy is a key design feature that cannot depend on data protection. Reportedly, "exceptional access mechanisms that allow authorities to trace the counterparties to every transaction and, therefore, do not achieve anonymity at all".[209] In other words, data on individuals and businesses should not be collected to begin with. In this respect, the proposal mirrors the core features of cash—i.e., privacy, owner-custodianship, fungibility, and accessibility. Accordingly, it relies on non-custodial wallets and envisions PETs to ensure transaction counterparties are not revealed, while ensuring compliance with regulation. Three options are considered: (i) stealth addresses, Pedersen commitments, ring signatures; (ii) ZKPs; and (iii) blind signatures or blind ring signatures.[210] The scheme is overseen by the public sector, operated by regulated private entities, and can be tuned to different needs.[211] As account-based systems cannot offer privacy if identifiers can lead to determine transaction parties, the system is token-based and non-custodial wallets do not carry unique identifiers or addresses that can be associated with other transactions, and do not reveal data that can identify bearers, owners, sources of funds (e.g., keys or addresses associated with other transactions).[212] The proposal pursues an anonymity defined as 'true but partial', where parties are anonymous but all transactions are controlled by a regulated entity. No one can unmask counterparties; even if authorities have all records some transactions involve non-custodial wallets, as it happens with cash. Hence, even if one knows all retail users and their transaction history, it is impossible to link non-custodial wallets to specific users.[213]

Cash-Like Privacy Through the Use of ZKPs Gross et al. (2021) put forward another 'mixed' CBDC solution. For what concerns the degree of privacy, their account-based model features three types of transactions, defined as 'fully private', 'semi-private', and 'fully transparent'.[214] The first option foresees 'cash-like' transfers performed within a 'privacy pool' inspired by Zcash, but replacing the UTXO-based model with an unspent account state model. In this case, zk-SNARKs are leveraged so that neither the identities of the parties nor the transaction amount are revealed to third parties, yet imposing by design balance, transfer and turnover limits for purposes of regulatory compliance.[215] Secondly, 'semi-private' transfers take place between accounts held in said 'privacy pool' and transparent CBDC accounts, which resemble commercial bank accounts. Thirdly, 'fully-transparent' transfers are performed between transparent CBDC accounts.

[209] Goodell et al. (2021), pp. 3, 6 and 12.

[210] Goodell et al. (2021), pp. 3, 7.

[211] For instance, prohibit certain businesses from accepting payments larger than a given amount without collecting additional data or impose on specific individuals a cap on withdrawals.

[212] Goodell et al. (2021), pp. 2, 5–7, 10.

[213] Goodell et al. (2021), pp. 12, 22.

[214] Gross et al. (2021), pp. 16–19, 23–25.

[215] Gross et al. (2021), pp. 21–23.

Token-Based Transaction Privacy Bearer-type token-based CBDCs may provide higher transaction anonymity, especially when the payment is hardware-based—e.g., prepaid cards storing tokens for offline use. In this respect, Chaum et al. (2021) argued token-based systems are the only avenue to reach a cash-like transaction privacy. At the same time, the hardware-based subset presents some features that may not suit a CBDC scenario, chiefly in terms of online transferability and AML/CFT compliance. In proposing a non-DLT-based CBDC that is a "true digital bearer instrument", it was claimed a token-based option is necessary for assets not to be associated with transaction history—contrary to what happens with account-based systems.[216] The proposed architecture is, however, software-based, for the sake of transparency and accountability. In this architecture, payers and payees interact only with commercial banks. Payers are identified when they withdraw CBDCs, and merchants upon receipt. Other than this, no identification is needed to perform the transaction, which means customers' and merchants' identities are not unveiled to the central bank. The withdrawn coins are subject to an encryption performed by the smartphone that 'blinds' the relevant number. When the merchant deposits the coins, the central bank can carry out anti-double spending checks without knowing which user withdrew it nor the total transactions amounts. Building on E-Cash, GNU Taler and Chaum's work,[217] the privacy of buyers is safeguarded by blind signatures, preventing commercial and central banks from linking transactions to buyers. Meanwhile, conversion limits may be imposed for AML/CFT purposes, and the GNU Taler key-exchange protocol aims to ensure income transparency and consumer privacy. Hence, KYC and authentication services are performed by commercial banks. Finally, the authors specify the possibility to implement jurisdiction-specific limits on withdrawals/payments.

Semi-anonymity and the EUROchain The European Central Bank (2019) explored the application of cash-like anonymity to a retail CBDC as part of the EUROchain network. The group conceived a DLT-based simplified PoC for a two-tier CBDC where a degree of privacy for low-value transactions is ensured with no detriment to AML/CFT controls for higher values. The PoC was developed on Corda with the goal to avoid that users' identities and transaction histories are seen by the central bank and intermediaries other than the one chosen by end-users. The latter are onboarded by an intermediary of their choice, and receive a pseudonymous identity that will be their CBDC network address.[218] On top of this, end-users are equipped with untransferable anonymity vouchers, to transfer a specific amount of CBDCs within a given timeframe with no oversight on transaction data. The thresholds are enforced at the intermediary level, with an authority issuing the vouchers and carrying out checks for large-value transactions. Features of enhanced privacy are based on Corda's confidential party mode, allowing states to be

[216] Chaum et al. (2021).

[217] Chaum (1983).

[218] European Central Bank (2019), p. 3.

assigned to end-users with one-time keys not revealing pseudonymous identities.[219] However, Corda's data segregation model does not solve the issue of intermediaries being able to build knowledge graphs based on past transaction data of CBDC units. Moreover, privacy could be enhanced with rotating public keys, ZKPs and hardware enclave computing.[220]

Canadian's Model X 'Mixed solutions' are strongly related to the objective of supporting offline transactions. A Canadian PoC developed by a team from the University of Toronto and York University provided a CBDC model in the context of a competition published by the Bank of Canada in April 2020.[221] The approach underpinning the proposed Central Bank-issued Digital Loonie (CBDL) is two-phased and account-based; the scheme is first centralised and later evolves towards decentralisation. In particular, users obtain wallet addresses, represented by quasi-anonymous identifiers, after undergoing an e-KYC performed by a third-party authenticator. Although the system is not built to identify and share users' identity or transaction-data to other system parties, the users do not remain anonymous if the encrypted process triggers compliance flags, or if there is any court order. It is proposed wallets have upper limits sufficient for typical cash-like transactions, and special provisions, such as reduced functionality or expiration dates, for visitors. For offline transactions, there is a CBDL-card, and a smart-device-based functionality that emulates it. For AML/CFT purposes offline transfers via CBDL-cards could be capped.[222]

China's e-CNY As highlighted above, the People's Bank of China 2021 is consistently expanding the scope of the e-CNY's pilot. The e-CNY is informed by the principle of 'anonymity for small value and traceable for high value' (concept known as 'controllable' or 'managed' anonymity) and is reported to offer four or five types of accounts/wallets. The decision on which account to assign to a given end-user depends on characteristics such as CBDC amounts, anticipated use, and other information provided by the same user during the registration procedure. Reportedly, the two most anonymous types of account (i.e., 'least privileged wallets') require few identifying pieces of information and notably they do not require to provide a real-world identity. In these cases, risks of money laundering and other criminal abuses are mitigated by strict balance and transaction limits—e.g., a daily transaction limit and a low balance limit. On the contrary, depending on the provided information, the least anonymous types of wallet must be opened at a counter and can be linked to a bank account or even used as one. Further, the restrictions (if any) vary, depending on the 'strength of customer personal information', with regard to the types of transactions that can be performed and to

[219] European Central Bank (2019), p. 7.

[220] European Central Bank (2019), pp. 9–10.

[221] Veneris et al. (2021).

[222] The report foresees the application of PETs in the advanced stages of the project, when the need may arise to obfuscate data (e.g., transactions) from private validators (Veneris et al., 2021).

the relevant amounts.[223] While the e-CNY reportedly achieves cash-like anonymity from the perspective of end-users and operating institutions because the latter are not able to see who is paying what to whom, the People's Bank of China can trace the flow because it can see the links between addresses and real-world identities. From this point of view, this CBDC system was argued to "exchange privacy for compliance".[224]

Transparency and the Sand Dollar If one proceeds along the anonymity to transparency spectrum, we find transparency-oriented solutions that comply with current regulatory frameworks for e-payments. Obviously, privacy and data protection requirements still need to be met, but transactions could be fully transparent to the entity operating the infrastructure. A high level of transparency is already offered by one of the few CBDC projects already operating, launched by the Central Bank of the Bahamas in late 2020. Its CBDC tokens represent a claim on the central bank and are recorded and transferred on a private DLT with all parties being identifiable.[225]

6.6 Conclusions

Research into crypto-assets dynamics requires a cross-disciplinary effort, and CBDC explorations provide a revolutionary insight into these interplays. This chapter provides an overview of key elements regarding digital fiat money, heeding a selection of debates elicited by publications by leading institutions, private actors, and monetary authorities. Although many central banks are not yet convinced that the benefits of issuing a CBDC outweigh risks and costs, they keep carrying out extensive research and PoCs. Along these lines, the chapter disambiguates the notion of 'central bank money' and underlines the difference between wholesale and retail CBDC use cases, as well as the main drivers underpinning the respective interest. It outlines the history of CBDC projects to value the various approaches and sketch the general trends, while addressing candidate designs and architectures (e.g., direct, hybrid, intermediated or synthetic models) for retail CBDCs. Meanwhile, it focuses on the impact of public-private interplays and cross-border CBDC models. Later, it explores a set of regulatory issues raised by CBDCs from an AML/CFT perspective and contextualises the debate within the broader anonymity problem generated by physical cash and the establishment of limits to cash transfers. Furthermore, it tackles privacy and data protection concerns and the competence for AML/CFT compliance in different public-private designs.

Building on the previous sections of this work, this chapter introduces the existence of trade-offs between anonymity and transparency in CBDCs, whose

[223] Working Group on E-CNY People's Bank of China (2021).

[224] Duffie and Economy (2022), p. 32ff.

[225] Boar et al. (2020).

designs can embed various balances between individual privacy and AML/CFT interests to have identity-based services. In this respect, the majority of the available CBDC proposals offer some privacy to end-users and some visibility to authorities and/or other participants of the CBDC system. Relatedly, it shows how trade-offs can be addressed from the perspectives of confidentiality and auditability and are correlated with AML/CFT anonymity. Further, the chapter overviews segregating, hiding and unlinking PETs, exemplifying how they generate different balances between privacy/confidentiality and accountability/auditability.

Finally, this chapter provides details on how examples of CBDC systems can be classified in terms of their embedded trade-off between privacy/confidentiality and transparency/auditability. It underlines the concept of 'mixed solutions' that provide for options tailored to given types of transactions and/or end-users—e.g., higher anonymity for low-value transactions and low-balance wallets. In this context, the large-scale interest in CBDCs provides almost unique insights into cross-disciplinary efforts. This highlights the interplay of technology, regulation, and technical standardisation, and provides preliminary benchmarks to think about anonymity and transparency in CBDCs in a way that enables the application of the methodologies addressed by Chap. 7. In doing so, the need for techno-regulatory standards emerged vis-à-vis the current lack of standardisation in a form that allows automation—e.g., for what concerns risk indicators and the implementation of machine-to-machine (M2M) payments, that are both topics explored as use cases in Chap. 7—, also in relation to risk scores related to transactions and customers.

References

Adrian, T. (2020). *Evolving to work better together: Public-private partnerships for digital payments*. https://www.imf.org/en/News/Articles/2020/07/22/sp072220-public-private-partnerships-for-digital-payments

Adrian, T., & Mancini-Griffoli, T. (2019). *The rise of digital money*. https://www.imf.org/en/Publications/fintech-notes/Issues/2019/07/12/The-Rise-of-Digital-Money-47097

Ahlgren, B., Hidell, M., & Ngai, E. C. H. (2016). Internet of things for smart cities: Interoperability and open data. *IEEE Internet Computing*, *20*(6), 52–56. https://doi.org/10.1109/MIC.2016.124

Al-Fuqaha, A., Guizani, M., Mohammadi, M., Aledhari, M., & Ayyash, M. (2015). Internet of things: A survey on enabling technologies, protocols, and applications. *IEEE Communications Surveys Tutorials*, *17*(4), 2347–2376. https://doi.org/10.1109/COMST.2015.2444095

Allen, J. G., Rauchs, M., Blandin, A., & Bear, K. (2020a). *Legal and regulatory considerations for digital assets*. https://www.jbs.cam.ac.uk/faculty-research/centres/alternative-finance/publications/legal-and-regulatory-considerations-for-digital-assets/

Allen, S., Capkun, S., Eyal, I., Fanti, G., Ford, B., Grimmelmann, J., Juels, A., Kostiainen, K., Meiklejohn, S., Miller, A., Prasad, E., Wuest, K., & Zhang, F. (2020b). *Design choices for central bank digital currency: Policy and technical considerations*. https://ftp.iza.org/dp13535.pdf

Alper, T. (2021). *Further details of 'offline' Chinese Digital Yuan 'hard wallet' emerge*. https://cryptonews.com/news/further-details-of-offline-chinese-digital-yuan-hard-wallet-8891.htm

Amler, H., Eckey, L., Faust, S., Kaiser, M., Sandner, P., & Schlosser, B. (2021). Defi-ning DeFi: Challenges & pathway. In *IEEE 3rd Conference on Blockchain Research & Applications for Innovative Networks and Services (BRAINS)*. https://doi.org/10.1109/BRAINS52497.2021.9569795

Amsden, Z., Arora, R., Bano, S., Baudet, M., Blackshear, S., Bothra, A., Cabrera, G., Catalini, C., Chalkias, K., Cheng, E., Ching, A., Chursin, A., Danezis, G., Di Giacomo, G., Dill, D. L., Ding, H., Doudchenko, N., Gao, V., Gao, Z., . . . Zhou, R. (2019). *The libra blockchain - White paper*. https://mitsloan.mit.edu/shared/ods/documents?PublicationDocumentID=5859

Arab Monetary Fund. (2022). *Arab monetary fund releases a study on "trends of issuing CBDCs in the arab region"*. https://www.amf.org.ae/en/content/arab-monetary-fund-releases-study-trends-issuing-central-bank-digital-currencies-cbdcs-arab

Armelius, H., Claussen, C. A, & Hull, I. (2021). *On the possibility of a cash-like CBDC*. https://ideas.repec.org//p/zbw/esprep/231485.html

Atlantic Council. (2024). *Central bank digital currency tracker*. https://www.atlanticcouncil.org/cbdctracker/

Auer, R., Cornelli, G., & Frost, J. (2020). *Rise of the central bank digital currencies: Drivers, approaches and technologies*. https://www.bis.org/publ/work880.htm

Auer, R., Boar, C., Cornelli, G., Frost, J., Holden, H., & Wehrli, A. (2021a). *CBDCs beyond borders: Results from a survey of central banks*. https://www.bis.org/publ/bppdf/bispap116.htm

Auer, R., Haene, P., & Holden, H. (2021b). Multi-CBDC arrangements and the future of cross-border payments. https://www.bis.org/publ/bppdf/bispap115.htm

Auer, R., Banka, H., Boakye-Adjei, N. Y., Faragallah, A., Frost, J., Natarajan, H., & Prenio, J. (2022). *Central bank digital currencies: A new tool in the financial inclusion toolkit?* https://www.bis.org/fsi/publ/insights41.htm

Bank for International Settlements. (2020). *Central bank digital currencies: Foundational principles and core features*. https://www.bis.org/publ/othp33.htm

Bank for International Settlements. (2021a). *CBDCs: An opportunity for the monetary system*. https://www.bis.org/publ/arpdf/ar2021e3.pdf

Bank for International Settlements. (2021b). *Inthanon-lionrock to mbridge: Building a multi CBDC platform for international payments*. https://www.bis.org/publ/othp40.htm

Bank for International Settlements. (2022a). *Project dunbar: International settlements using multi-CBDCs*. https://www.bis.org/publ/othp47.pdf

Bank for International Settlements. (2022b). *Project aurum: A prototype for two-tier central bank digital currency (CBDC)*. https://www.bis.org/publ/othp57.pdf

Bank for International Settlements. (2023). *Project Polaris: Handbook for offline payments with CBDC*. https://www.bis.org/publ/othp64.htm

Barotini, C., & Holden, H. (2019). *Proceeding with caution. A survey on central bank digital currency*. https://www.bis.org/publ/bppdf/bispap101.htm

Barresi, R. G., & Zatti, F. (2020). *The importance of where central bank digital currencies are custodied: Exploring the need of a universal access device*. https://doi.org/10.2139/ssrn.3691263

Berberich, M., & Steiner, M. (2016). Blockchain technology and the GDPR - How to reconcile privacy and distributed ledgers? Technical core features and use cases of the blockchain technology. *European Data Protection Law Review*, 2(3), 422–426. https://doi.org/10.21552/EDPL/2016/3/21

Bevir, M. (2009). *Key concepts in governance*. SAGE Publishing. https://doi.org/10.4135/9781446214817

Bexell, M., & Moerth, U. (2010). Introduction: Partnerships, democracy, and governance. In M. Bexell & U. Moerth (Eds.), *Democracy and public-private partnerships in global governance*. Palgrave Macmillan. https://doi.org/10.1057/9780230283237_1

BIS Innovation Hub. (2024). *BIS innovation hub projects*. https://www.bis.org/about/bisih/projects.htm

BIS Innovation Hub and Swiss National Bank. (2023). *Project Tourbillon. exploring privacy, security and scalability for CBDCs*. Final report. https://www.bis.org/publ/othp80.pdf

Bloomberg. (2022, January 31). *Silvergate purchases blockchain payment network assets from Diem*. https://www.bloomberg.com/press-releases/2022-01-31/silvergate-purchases-blockchain-payment-network-assets-from-diem

Boar, C., & Wehrli, A. (2021). *Ready, steady, go? – Results of the third BIS survey on central bank digital currency*. https://www.bis.org/publ/bppdf/bispap114.pdf

Boar, C., Holden, H., & Wadsworth, A. (2020). *Impending arrival - A sequel to the survey on central bank digital currency*. https://www.bis.org/publ/bppdf/bispap107.htm

Böhme, R., & Auer, R. (2020). *CBDC architectures, the financial system, and the central bank of the future*. https://voxeu.org/article/cbdc-architectures-financial-system-and-central-bank-future

Bossone, B. (2020). Money and customer funds in the world of digital finance: Who really owns what? *Journal of Payments Strategy & Systems, 15*(1). https://ideas.repec.org/a/aza/jpss00/y2021v15i1p37-53.html

Bossu, W., Itatani, M., Margulis, C., Rossi, A. D. P., Weenink, H., & Yoshinaga, A. (2020). *Legal aspects of central bank digital currency: Central bank and monetary law*. https://www.imf.org/en/Publications/WP/Issues/2020/11/20/Legal-Aspects-of-Central-Bank-Digital-Currency-Central-Bank-and-Monetary-Law-Considerations-49827

Brodsky, B., Dubey, A., & Tercero Lucas, D. (2023). *Enabling offline payments in an online world. A practical guide to offline payment design*. https://www.lipisadvisors.com/whitepapers

Brummer, C. (2019). *Cryptoassets: Legal, regulatory, and monetary perspectives*. Oxford University Press. https://doi.org/10.1093/oso/9780190077310.001.0001

Brunnermeier, M. K., & Niepelt, D. (2019). On the equivalence of private and public money. *Journal of Monetary Economics, 106*, 27–41. https://doi.org/10.1016/j.jmoneco.2019.07.004

Carstens, A. (2021). *Digital currencies and the future monetary system*. https://www.bis.org/speeches/sp210127.pdf

Casey, M., Crane, J., Gensler, G., Johnson, S., & Narula, N. (2018). *The impact of blockchain technology on finance: A catalyst for change*. https://cepr.org/publications/books-and-reports/geneva-21-impact-blockchain-technology-finance-catalyst-change

Cavoukian, A. (2011). *Privacy by design*. Office of the Information and Privacy Commissioner.

CBDC Tracker. (2024). *Today's central bank digital currencies status*. https://cbdctracker.org/timeline. Last accessed: July 19, 2024.

Chaum, D. (1983). *Blind signatures for untraceable payments*. http://www.hit.bme.hu/~buttyan/courses/BMEVIHIM219/2009/Chaum.BlindSigForPayment.1982.PDF

Chaum, D., Grothoff, C., & Moser, T. (2021). *How to issue a central bank digital currency*. https://www.snb.ch/en/mmr/papers/id/working_paper_2021_03

Choi, S., Kim, B., Kim, Y.-S., & Kwon, O. (2023). *Central bank digital currency and privacy: A randomized survey experiment*. https://www.bis.org/publ/work1147.htm

Chu, Y., Lee, J., Kim, S., Kim, H., Yoon, Y., & Chung, H. (2022). Review of offline payment function of CBDC considering security requirements. *Applied Sciences, 12*. https://doi.org/10.3390/app12094488

Cipriani, M., Goldberg, L. S., & La Spada, G. (2023). Financial sanctions, SWIFT, and the architecture of the international payment system. *Journal of Economic Perspectives, 37*(1), 31–52. https://doi.org/10.1257/jep.37.1.31

Committee on Payments and Market Infrastructures - Bank for International Settlements. (2018). *Central bank digital currencies*. https://www.bis.org/cpmi/publ/d174.pdf

Danezis, G., & Meiklejohn, S. (2016). Centrally banked cryptocurrencies. In *Proceedings of the Network and Distributed Systems Security Symposium*. https://doi.org/10.14722/ndss.2016.23187

Diem. (2021). *Diem announces partnership with silvergate and strategic shift to the united states*. https://www.diem.com/en-us/updates/diem-silvergate-partnership/. May 12, 2021.

Diem. (2022). *Statement by diem CEO Stuart Levey on the sale of the Diem group's assets to silvergate*. https://www.diem.com/en-us/updates/stuart-levey-statement-diem-asset-sale/. January 31, 2022.

Duarte, A., Frost, J., Gambacorta, L., Koo Wilkens, P., Song Shin, H. (2022). *Central banks, the monetary system and public payment infrastructures: Lessons from Brazil's Pix.* https://www.bis.org/publ/bisbull52.pdf

Duffie, D. (2020). Interoperable payment systems and the role of central bank digital currencies. In *Stanford University Graduate School of Business Research Paper.* 10.2139/ssrn.3604665.

Duffie, D., & Economy, E. (2022). *Digital currencies. The US, China, and the world at a crossroads.* https://www.hoover.org/research/digital-currencies-us-china-and-world-crossroads

Ecorys and Centre for European Policy Studies. (2017). *Study on an EU initiative for a restriction on payments in cash.* https://ec.europa.eu/info/sites/default/files/economy-finance/final_report_study_on_an_eu_initative_ecorys_180206.pdf

European Central Bank. (2019). *Exploring anonymity in Central bank digital currencies.* https://www.ecb.europa.eu/paym/intro/publications/pdf/ecb.mipinfocus191217.en.pdf

European Central Bank. (2020a). *Report on a digital euro.* https://www.ecb.europa.eu/pub/pdf/other/Report_on_a_digital_euro~4d7268b458.en.pdf

European Central Bank. (2020b). *Tiered CBDC and the financial system.* https://www.ecb.europa.eu/pub/pdf/scpwps/ecb.wp2351~c8c18bbd60.en.pdf

European Central Bank. (2021a). *Press release 14 July 2021. Eurosystem launches digital euro project.* https://www.ecb.europa.eu/press/pr/date/2021/html/ecb.pr210714~d99198ea23.en.html

European Central Bank. (2021b). *Eurosystem report on the public consultation on a digital euro.* https://www.ecb.europa.eu/pub/pdf/other/Eurosystem_report_on_the_public_consultation_on_a_digital_euro~539fa8cd8d.en.pdf

European Central Bank. (2022a). *Progress on the investigation phase of a digital euro.* https://www.ecb.europa.eu/paym/digital_euro/investigation/governance/shared/files/ecb.degov220929.en.pdf?8eec0678b57e98372a7ae6b59047604b

European Central Bank. (2022b). *Progress on the investigation phase of a digital euro – Second report.* https://www.ecb.europa.eu/paym/digital_euro/investigation/governance/shared/files/ecb.degov221221_Progress.en.pdf?f91e0b8ff8cbd6654d7e6b071a8f7071

European Central Bank. (2023). *A stocktake on the digital euro. Summary report on the investigation phase and outlook on the next phase.* https://www.ecb.europa.eu/euro/digital_euro/timeline/profuse/shared/pdf//ecb.dedocs231018.en.pdf

European Central Bank. (2024). *Progress on the preparation phase of a digital euro. First progress report.* https://www.ecb.europa.eu/euro/digital_euro/progress/shared/pdf/ecb.deprp202406.en.pdf

European Central Bank and Bank of Japan. (2020). *Balancing confidentiality and auditability in a distributed ledger environment.* https://www.ecb.europa.eu/paym/intro/publications/pdf/ecb.miptopical200212.en.pdf

European Commission. (2023). *Digital euro package.* https://finance.ec.europa.eu/publications/digital-euro-package_en

European Consumer Centre France. (2022). *Cash payments limitations.* https://www.europe-consommateurs.eu/en/shopping-internet/cash-payment-limitations.html

European Consumer Centre Germany. (2024). *Cash payment: Cash limits in Europe.* https://www.evz.de/en/shopping-internet/cash-payment-limitations.html

Fanti, G., & Pocher, N. (2022). *Privacy in cross-border digital currency: A transatlantic perspective.* https://www.atlanticcouncil.org/in-depth-research-reports/issue-brief/privacy-in-cross-border-digital-currency-a-transatlantic-approach/

Fanusie, Y. J. (2020). Central bank digital currencies: The threat from money launderers and how to stop them. In *The Digital Social Contract: A Lawfare Paper Series* (pp. 1–23). https://www.lawfaremedia.org/article/central-bank-digital-currencies-threat-money-launderers-and-how-stop-them

Financial Action Task Force. (2020). *Virtual assets red flag indicators of money laundering and terrorist financing.* https://www.fatf-gafi.org/media/fatf/documents/recommendations/Virtual-Assets-Red-Flag-Indicators.pdf

Financial Action Task Force. (2021). *Virtual assets and virtual asset service providers - Updated guidance for a risk-based approach.* https://www.fatf-gafi.org/publications/fatfrecommendations/documents/guidance-rba-virtual-assets-2021.html

Finck, M. (2019). *Blockchain regulation and governance in Europe.* Cambridge University Press. https://doi.org/10.1017/9781108609708

FINTRAC. (2019). *Canada's legislation: The proceeds of crime (money laundering) and terrorist financing act. 31 U.S.C. title 31 - Money and finance, subtitle IV - Money, chapter 53 – Monetary transactions, subchapter II - Records and reports on monetary instruments trans, sec. 5331 - Reports relating to coins and currency received in nonfinancial trade or business.* https://laws-lois.justice.gc.ca/eng/acts/P-24.501/FullText.html

Gang, X., & Mount Union of Science and Technology. (2019). *Analysis of the central bank's digital currency DC/EP dual offline payment scenarios and solutions.* https://www.mpaypass.com.cn/news/201912/06094420.html

Garratt, R. J., & van Oordt, M. R. C. (2019). *Privacy as a public good: A cash for electronic cash.* https://www.bankofcanada.ca/wp-content/uploads/2019/07/swp2019-24.pdf

Garratt, R. J., Lee, M. J., Malone, B., & Martin, A. (2020). *Token-or account-based? A digital currency can be both.* https://ideas.repec.org/p/fip/fednls/88550.html

Garrido Munilla, G., Sedlmeir, J., Uludağ, Ö., Alaoui, I. S., Luckow, A., & Matthes, F. (2022). Revealing the landscape of privacy-enhancing technologies in the context of data markets for the IoT: A systematic literature review. *Journal of Network and Computer Applications, 207*, 103465. https://doi.org/10.1016/j.jnca.2022.103465

Geva, B. (2018). Banking in the digital age – Who is afraid of payment disintermediation? In *European Banking Institute Working Paper Series.* https://digitalcommons.osgoode.yorku.ca/cgi/viewcontent.cgi?article=1329&context=all_papers

GlobalPlatform. (2018). *Introduction to secure elements.* https://globalplatform.wpengine.com/resource-publication/introduction-to-secure-elements/

Goodell, G., & Aste, T. (2019). Can cryptocurrencies preserve privacy and comply with regulations? *Frontiers in Blockchain, 2*(4). https://doi.org/10.3389/fbloc.2019.00004

Goodell, G., Al-Nakib, H. D., & Tasca, P. (2021). A digital currency architecture for privacy and owner-custodianship. *Future Internet, 13.* https://doi.org/10.3390/fi13050130

Gross, J., Sedlmeir, J., Babel, M., Bechtel, A., & Schellinger, B. (2021). Designing a central bank digital currency with support for cash-like privacy. *SSRN Electronic Journal.* https://doi.org/10.2139/ssrn.3891121

Group of 30. (2020). *Digital currencies and stablecoins: Risks, opportunities, and challenges ahead.* https://group30.org/images/uploads/publications/G30_Digital_Currencies.pdf

Hoess, A., Pocher, N., Roth, T., & Fridgen, G. (2024). Towards a design science research process for legal compliance by design. In *Proceedings of the Pacific Asia Conference on Information Systems (PACIS).* https://aisel.aisnet.org/pacis2024/track04_dessci/track04_dessci/3

Hustinx, P. (2010). Privacy by design: Delivering the promises. *Identity in the Information Society, 3*(2). https://doi.org/10.1007/s12394-010-0061-z

Information & Privacy Commissioner of Ontario. (2013). *Privacy by design.* https://www.ipc.on.ca/wp-content/uploads/2013/09/pbd-primer.pdf

ITU-T Focus Group on Digital Currency. (2019). *Taxonomy and definition of terms for digital fiat currency.* https://www.itu.int/en/ITU-T/focusgroups/dlt/Documents/FGDLT-D2.1.pdf

Jagati, S. (2020). *CBDCs with a twist: The public-private solutions needed for adoption.* https://cointelegraph.com/news/cbdcs-with-a-twist-the-public-private-solutions-needed-for-adoption

Jung, H., & Jeong, D. (2021). Blockchain implementation method for interoperability between CBDCs. *Future Internet, 13*(5). https://doi.org/10.3390/fi13050133

Karasek-Wojciechowicz, I. (2021). Reconciliation of anti-money laundering instruments and European Data protection requirements in permissionless blockchain spaces. *Journal of Cybersecurity*, 1–28. https://doi.org/10.1093/cybsec/tyab004

Khiaonarong, T., & Humphrey, D. (2019). Cash use across countries and the demand for CBDC. In *International Monetary Fund Working Papers.* https://www.imf.org/en/Publications/WP/

Issues/2019/03/01/Cash-Use-Across-Countries-and-the-Demand-for-Central-Bank-Digital-Currency-46617

Kiff, J. (2023). Taking digital currencies offline. In *International Monetary Fund – Finance & Development Magazine*. https://www.imf.org/en/Publications/fandd/issues/2022/09/kiff-taking-digital-currencies-offline

Kochergin, D., & Dostov, V. (2020). Central banks digital currency: Issuing and integration scenarios in the monetary and payment system. In *Proceedings of the Business Information Systems Workshops* (Vol. 394, pp. 111–119). https://doi.org/10.1007/978-3-030-61146-0_9

Kriwoluzky, A., & Kim, C. H. (2019). Public or private? the future of money. In *Monetary Dialogue Papers – European Parliament*. https://www.europarl.europa.eu/thinktank/en/document/IPOL_IDA(2019)642356

Linder, S. (1999). Coming to terms with the public-private partnerships: A grammar of multiple meanings. *American Behavioural Scientist, 43*(1), 35–51. https://doi.org/10.1177/00027649921955146

Magnuson, W. (2020). *Blockchain democracy: Technology, law and the rule of the crowd.* Cambridge University Press. https://doi.org/10.1017/9781108687294

Mahari, R., Hardjono, T., & Pentland, A. (2022). AML by design: Designing a central bank digital currency to stifle money laundering. *MIT Science Policy Review*. https://doi.org/10.38105/spr.j0hildxtyi

Michalopoulos, P., Olowookere, O., Pocher, N., Sedlmeir, J., Veneris, A., & Puri, P. (2024). Compliance design options for offline CBDCs: Balancing privacy and AML/CFT. In *Proceedings of the IEEE International Conference on Blockchain and Cryptocurrency (ICBC)*. https://doi.org/10.1109/ICBC59979.2024.10634398

Minwalla, C., Miedema, J., Hernandez, S., & Sutton-Lalani, A. (2023). A central bank digital currency for offline payments. In *Bank of Canada Working Paper 2023-2*. https://www.bankofcanada.ca/2023/02/staff-analytical-note-2023-2/

Nabilou, H. (2019). Testing the waters of the rubicon: The European Central Bank and central bank digital currencies. *Journal of Banking Regulation, 21*(4), 299–314. https://doi.org/10.1057/s41261-019-00112-1

Ojo, M. (2021). Balancing public-private partnerships in a digital age: CBDCs, central banks and technology firms. *Munich Personal RePEc Archive*. https://mpra.ub.uni-muenchen.de/107716/

Oliver Wayman Forum. (2022). *Retail central bank digital currency: From vision to design. A framework to align policy objectives and technology design choices*. https://www.oliverwymanforum.com/content/dam/oliver-wyman/ow-forum/future-of-money/Retail-Central-Bank-Digital-Currency-From-Vision-to-Design.pdf

OMFIF and CCB. (2023). *The role of blockchain in banking. Future prospects for cross-border payments*. https://www.omfif.org/blockchainbanking/

Opare, E. A., & Kim, K. (2020). A compendium of practices for central bank digital currencies for multinational financial infrastructures. *IEEE Access, 8*, 810–847. https://doi.org/10.1109/ACCESS.2020.3001970

Pocher, N. (2021a). *Crypto-wallets and the new EU AML package: Where are the battle lines drawn?* https://www.law.kuleuven.be/citip/blog/crypto-wallets-and-the-new-eu-aml-package/

Pocher, N. (2021b). *Self-hosted wallets: The elephant in the crypto room?* https://www.law.kuleuven.be/citip/blog/self-hosted-wallets/

Pocher, N. (2023). *Distributed ledger technologies between anonymity and transparency: AML/CFT regulation of cryptocurrency ecosystems in the EU*. PhD thesis, Alma Mater Studiorum Università di Bologna, KU Leuven, Universitat Autònoma de Barcelona. 10.48676/unibo/amsdottorato/10659

Pocher, N., & Sedlmeir, J. (2024). Decentralization beyond disintermediation: The case of central bank digital currencies. In G. Fridgen, T. Guggenberger, J. Sedlmeir, & N. Urbach (Eds.), *Decentralization technologies*. Springer Cham. https://doi.org/10.1007/978-3-031-66047-4_12

Pocher, N., & Veneris, A. (2022a). Central Bank digital currencies. In D. A. Tran, M. T. Thai, & B. Krishnamachari (Eds.), *Handbook on blockchain*. Springer. https://doi.org/10.1007/978-3-031-07535-3_15

Pocher, N., & Veneris, A. (2022b). Privacy and transparency in CBDCs: A regulation-by-design AML/CFT scheme. *IEEE Transactions on Network and Service Management*, *19*(2), 1776–1788. https://doi.org/10.1109/TNSM.2021.3136984

Pocher, N., & Zichichi, M. (2022). Towards CBDC-based machine-to-machine payments in consumer IoT. In *Proceedings of the 37th ACM/SIGAPP Symposium on Applied Computing*. https://doi.org/10.1145/3477314.3507078

PYMNTS. (2020). *BIS to open four new innovation hubs over next two years*. https://www.pymnts.com/news/banking/2020/bis-to-open-four-new-innovation-hubs-over-next-two-years/

Ranganathan, A., & Capkun, S. (2017). Are we really close? Verifying proximity in wireless systems. *IEEE Security & Privacy*, *15*(3), 52–58. https://doi.org/10.1109/MSP.2017.56

Regulation (EU) 2018/1672. (2018). Regulation (EU) 2018/1672 of the European Parliament and of the Council of 23 October 2018 on controls on cash entering or leaving the union and repealing Regulation (EC) no 1889/2005. http://data.europa.eu/eli/reg/2018/1672/oj

Regulation (EU) 2023/1113. (2023). Regulation (EU) 2023/1113 of the European Parliament and of the Council of 31 May 2023 on information accompanying transfers of funds and certain crypto-assets and amending Directive (EU) 2015/849 (recast). http://data.europa.eu/eli/reg/2023/1113/oj

Regulation (EU) 2024/1624. (2024). Regulation (EU) 2024/1624 of the European Parliament and of the Council of 31 May 2024 on the prevention of the use of the financial system for the purposes of money laundering or terrorist financing. http://data.europa.eu/eli/reg/2024/1624/oj

Rennie, E., & Steele, S. (2021). Privacy and emergency payments in a pandemic: How to think about privacy and a central bank digital currency. *Law, Technology and Humans*, *3*(1). 10.5204/lthj.1745

Renwick, R., & Gleasure, R. (2020). Those who control the code control the rules: How different perspectives of privacy are being written into the code of blockchain systems. *Journal of Information Technology*, *36*(1). https://doi.org/10.1177/0268396220944406

Reserve Bank of Australia. (2021). *Project atom. exploring a wholesale CBDC for syndicated lending*. https://www.rba.gov.au/payments-and-infrastructure/central-bank-digital-currency/pdf/project-atom-report_2021-12.pdf

Riccardi, M., & Levi, M. (2018). Cash, crime and anti-money laundering. In C. King, C. Walker, & J. Gurulé (Eds.), *The Palgrave handbook of criminal and terrorism financing law*. Palgrave Macmillan. https://doi.org/10.1007/978-3-319-64498-1_7

Rogaway, P. (2016). *The moral character of cryptographic work*. https://web.cs.ucdavis.edu/~rogaway/papers/moral-fn.pdf

Ross, T. W., & Yan, J. (2015). Comparing public–private partnerships and traditional public procurement: Efficiency vs. flexibility. *Journal of Comparative Policy Analysis: Research and Practice*, *17*(5), 448–466. https://doi.org/10.1080/13876988.2015.1029333

Sabt, M., Achemlal, M., & Bouabdallah, A. (2015). Trusted execution environment: What it is, and what it is not. In *Proceedings of the International Conference on Trust, Security and Privacy in Computing and Communications*. IEEE. https://doi.org/10.1109/trustcom.2015.357

Salmensuu, C. (2018). *The general data protection regulation and blockchains*. https://ssrn.com/abstract=3143992

Sandner, P., Gross, J., Grale, L., & Schulden, P. (2020). *The digital programmable euro, libra and CBDC: Implications for European banks*. 10.2139/ssrn.3663142

Sands, P., Campbell, H., Keatinge, T., & Weisman, B. (2017). *Limiting the use of cash for big purchases: Assessing the case for uniform cash thresholds*. https://www.hks.harvard.edu/sites/default/files/centers/mrcbg/files/80_limiting.cash.pdf

Sardá, T., Natale, S., Sotirakopoulos, N., & Monaghan, M. (2019). Understanding online anonymity. *Media, Culture and Society*, *41*(4), 557–64. https://doi.org/10.1177/0163443719842074

Savas, E. S. (2000). *Privatisation and public-private partnerships*. Chatham House.

Sedlmeir, J. (2023). *Blockchain adoption in organizations: Technical barriers and potential solutions*. PhD thesis, University of Bayreuth. 10.15495/EPub_UBT_00007183

Sethaput, V., & Innet, S. (2023). Blockchain application for central bank digital currencies (CBDC). *Cluster Computing, 26*(4), 2183–2197. https://doi.org/10.1007/s10586-022-03962-z

Sidorenko, E. L., Sheveleva, S. V., & Lykov, A. A. (2021). Legal and economic implications of central bank digital currencies (CBDC). In S. I. Ashmarina, J. Horák, J. Vrbka, & P. Šuleř (Eds.), *Economic systems in the new era: Stable systems in an unstable world*. Springer Cham. https://doi.org/10.1007/978-3-030-60929-0_63

Soderberg, G., Bechara, M., Bossu, W., Che, N. X., Davidovic, S., Kiff, J., Lujonga, I., Mancini-Griffoli, T., Sun, T., & Yoshinaga, A. (2022). *Behind the scenes of central bank digital currency. emerging trends, insights, and policy lessons*. https://www.imf.org/en/Publications/fintech-notes/Issues/2022/02/07/Behind-the-Scenes-of-Central-Bank-Digital-Currency-512174

Swartz, L. (2020). *New money: How payment became social media*. Yale University Press. https://doi.org/10.2307/j.ctv10sm94k

Tamò-Larrieux, A. (2018). *Designing for privacy and its legal framework: Data protection by design and default for the Internet of Things*. Springer. https://doi.org/10.1007/978-3-319-98624-1

The Federal Reserve. (2022). *Money and payments: The US dollar in the age of digital transformation*. https://www.federalreserve.gov/publications/files/money-and-payments-20220120.pdf

The White House. (2022). *Technical design choices for a U.S. Central Bank digital currency system*. https://www.whitehouse.gov/wp-content/uploads/2022/09/09-2022-Technical-Design-Choices-US-CBDC-System.pdf

Themistocleous, M., Rupino da Cunha, P., Tabakis, E., & Papadaki, M. (2023). Towards cross-border CBDC interoperability: Insights from a multivocal literature review. *Journal of Enterprise Information Management, 36*(5), 1296–1318. https://doi.org/10.1108/JEIM-11-2022-0411

Torra, V. (2017). *Data privacy: Foundations, new developments and the big data challenge*. Springer Cham. https://doi.org/10.1007/978-3-319-57358-8

Tronnier, F., Harborth, D., & Hamm, P. (2022). Investigating privacy concerns and trust in the digital Euro in Germany. *Electronic Commerce Research and Applications, 53*, 101158. https://doi.org/10.1016/j.elerap.2022.101158

US Presidential Actions. (2022). *Executive order on ensuring responsible development of digital assets*. https://www.whitehouse.gov/briefing-room/presidential-actions/2022/03/09/executive-order-on-ensuring-responsible-development-of-digital-assets

Veneris, A., Park, A., Long, F., & Puri, P. (2021). Central bank Digital Loonie: Canadian cash for a new global economy. In *Osgoode Legal Studies Research Paper*. https://ssrn.com/abstract=3770024

Viñuela, C., Sapena, J., & Wandosell, G. (2020). The future of money and the central bank digital currency dilemma. *Sustainability, 12*(22). https://doi.org/10.3390/su12229697

Vutsova, A., & Ignatova, O. (2014). The role of public-private partnership for effective technology transfer. *Applied Technologies and Innovations, 10*(3), 83–90. https://doi.org/10.15208/ati.2014.14

Walch, A. (2019). Regulating blockchain: Techno-social and legal challenges. chapter In *Code(Rs) we trust: Software developers as fiduciaries in public blockchains*. Oxford University Press. https://doi.org/10.1093/oso/9780198842187.003.0004

Werbach, K. (2020). The siren song: Algorithmic governance by blockchain. In K. Werbach (Ed.), *After the digital tornado: Networks, algorithms, humanity*. Cambridge University Press. https://doi.org/https://doi.org/10.1017/9781108610018

Working Group on E-CNY People's Bank of China. (2021). Progress of research development of e-CNY in China. http://www.pbc.gov.cn/en/3688110/3688172/4157443/4293696/2021071614584691871.pdf

World Economic Forum. (2021a). *The role of the public sector and public-private cooperation in the era of digital currency growth*. https://www3.weforum.org/docs/WEF_Digital_Currency_Governance_Consortium_White_Paper_Series_2021.pdf

World Economic Forum. (2021b). *Privacy and confidentiality options for central bank digital currency*. https://www3.weforum.org/docs/WEF_Digital_Currency_Governance_Consortium_White_Paper_Series_2021.pdf

World Economic Forum. (2021c). *Defining interoperability*. https://www3.weforum.org/docs/WEF_Digital_Currency_Governance_Consortium_White_Paper_Series_2021.pdf

World Economic Forum. (2021d). CBDC technology considerations. https://www3.weforum.org/docs/WEF_Digital_Currency_Governance_Consortium_White_Paper_Series_2021.pdf

World Economic Forum. (2021e). *Glossary*. https://www3.weforum.org/docs/WEF_Digital_Currency_Governance_Consortium_White_Paper_Series_2021.pdf

Yao, Q. (2018). A systematic framework to understand central bank digital currency. *Science China Information Sciences*, *61*(3). https://doi.org/10.1007/s11432-017-9294-5

Yeung, K. (2017). Hypernudge: Big data as a mode of regulation by design. *Information, Communication & Society*, *20*(1), 118–136. https://doi.org/10.1080/1369118X.2016.1186713

Zetzsche, D. A., Arner, D. W., & Buckley, R. P. (2020). Decentralized finance. *Journal of Financial Regulation*, *6*(2). https://doi.org/10.1093/jfr/fjaa010

Zhang, T. (2020). Deputy managing director Tao Zhang's keynote address on CBDC. https://www.imf.org/en/News/Articles/2020/03/19/sp031920-deputy-managing-director-tao-zhangs-keynote-address-on-central-bank-digital-currency

Chapter 7
Techno-Regulatory Standards and 'Through Design' Approaches

7.1 Introduction

The increasing complexity of crypto-assets and the diffusion of DLT-based use cases in the financial sector has drawn significant attention from law and policymakers. As a wide range of stakeholders explore these technologies on a global scale, risks and uncertainties arise with regard to regulatory approaches, both within the AML/CFT context and beyond it. While this is hardly unusual when it comes to innovation, in this field the urgency stems from the extensive reach and industry-altering impact of the combination of P2P mechanisms and tokenisation. Drawing on the elements outlined in the previous chapters, the difficulty in applying regulation to the crypto-asset space is arguably due to the concurrent presence of (i) assets, such as the different types of tokens outlined in Chap. 2; (ii) a set of technologies that can be used to different ends (e.g., P2P technologies, distributed systems, tokenisation); (iii) innovative actors (e.g., developers, miners, exchanges, FinTech companies, P2P platforms); (iv) traditional actors, such as traditional financial institutions; and (v) different scopes of application of the technologies, at times overlapping or concurring (e.g., financial applications, supply chain, self-sovereign identity, certification). The combination of these elements shapes the crypto-asset sphere and mirrors its nature of an ecosystem of socio-technical ecosystems, as argued in Chap. 4.

In addition, these categories are under constant development. The primary challenge lies in grasping the internal mechanisms of each socio-technical environment, often non-centralised, to understand the factors at play to devise appropriate rules and enforcement approaches. Against this backdrop, the relationship between the law, crypto-asset ecosystems, technologies and entities—i.e., assets and actors, respectively—is complicated. Reportedly, different approaches are possible when the law meets new technologies. Regulators may decide to (i) do nothing, an attitude described as a permissive 'wait and see' approach, (ii) introduce tight restrictions,

N. Pocher, *Crypto-Asset Ecosystems and the EU Anti-Money Laundering Framework*, Law, Governance and Technology Series 76,
https://doi.org/10.1007/978-3-031-94698-1_7

such as outlawing certain activities or the provision and/or acquisition of certain products or services, (iii) issue flexible 'case by case' permissions, (iv) set up structured and restricted regulatory experiments such as 'regulatory sandboxes', or (v) devise new regulatory frameworks.[1] Evidently, these approaches and their possible combinations exert both positive and negative impacts on the targeted domains, and come with strings attached. Hence, a regulatory strategy should suit the given phase of the evolution of a technology. For instance, while a 'wait and see' approach can be beneficial in the early days, over time it proves insufficient to handle the arising regulatory questions, which generates 'case-by-case' decisions.[2]

As emerged in the previous chapters, the relationship between crypto-assets and AML/CFT rules is multi-faceted. In some ways, this mirrors usual issues generated by innovation, but the debate also entails more peculiar angles. In particular, the implementation of DLT-based solutions, tokenisation, and encryption, enables direct collaboration between individuals, but also creates obfuscation opportunities that challenge existing frameworks through novel types of service providers. In summary, it is not surprising the combination between (a) the lower degree of access control of (some) crypto-asset ecosystems, (b) the anonymity levels of some of them, and (c) their cross-border character, originated the regulatory willingness to mitigate their vulnerability to endanger the financial system. As outlined in Chap. 5, international and domestic frameworks were established to fight the abuse of crypto-assets for illicit purposes and extended to a new domain the traditional approach to the prevention of criminal exploitation of institutions, solutions or technologies to cleanse ill-gotten money or fund illicit activities. Accordingly, frameworks leaned on gateway points resembling traditional intermediaries. As emerged from Chaps. 3 and 4, however, the concept of disintermediation challenges this traditional methodology, especially from an evolutionary perspective.

7.1.1 Technology- vs. Individual Case-Based AML/CFT Regulation

Chapters 4 and 6 highlighted how crypto-asset ecosystems can enshrine different degrees of anonymity and accountability. Likewise, they outlined how red flag indicators point to specific risks generated by AECs and the implementation of given technologies. Evidently, not all crypto-assets and providers of related services pose the same challenges to the AML/CFT regime. Once again, the differences may

[1] Zetzsche et al. (2017), p. 5. Regulatory approaches to DLTs were classified as follows: (i) adoption of a 'wait and see' approach, (ii) application of existing frameworks, (iii) issuing guidance, (iv) establishment of sandboxes, (v) regulatory cooperation, (v) adoption of new legislation (Finck 2019, pp. 153ff). These methodologies are explored by Magnuson (2020), pp. 177–190. More recently, Buckley et al. (2023), pp. 27–42, provided a technology-agnostic overview of these approaches in the context of 'smart regulation'.

[2] Finck (2019), p. 155.

pertain to all the components of these socio-technical ecosystems—e.g., technologies implemented at application or platform level, by the actors involved, practices deployed by users, strategies developed by LEAs and analytics companies. Hence, a suitable regulatory methodology should necessarily account for the different levels of risk, in compliance with the RBA, and appropriately distinguish between use cases.

From this perspective, literature provides different types of regulatory approaches to new technologies, where rules target either the implementation of a technology (e.g., DLT-based applications) or to a specific application (e.g., crypto-assets, DLT-based or not). The first case is termed technology-based regulation, where the targeted applications are pinpointed based on the implemented technology, usually because the latter has an impact the regulator wants to address (e.g., all DLT-based applications, targeting the effects exerted by some trait of DLTs). In the second case, efforts target the function of specific tools, in a use case-based fashion.[3] Use case-based regulation allows to consider specificities of concrete cases—e.g., crypto-assets, a subtype, even just one of them. Focusing on individual cases is beneficial when a technology can originate diverse impacts. Besides these two categories, there are mixed situations where a regulatory regime is tailored to a set of use cases implementing a specific technology—e.g., crypto-assets embedding a given PET.

As explored below, all these methods feature, to different extents, an inherent risk of over-fitting (Chap. 1). This is because the technological dynamism of crypto-assets generates an undeniable risk rules may be already outdated when they enter into force, or shortly after. Arguably, the goal should not be to avoid the risk altogether, but to establish frameworks that prove useful despite the changes.

7.1.2 Categorising Impacts and the Sandbox Model

In the early stages of crypto-assets, scholars identified three types of interplay DLT-based applications can have with regulatory frameworks. The reasoning appears still relevant today despite the increased complexity, and can be extended to crypto-assets. According to said analysis, a first set of instruments, usually implemented by regulated actors and overall compatible with existing frameworks, are placed in a 'recycle box'. This is the case of blockchain-based interbank settlement systems (e.g., the Ripple network, wholesale CBDCs) and blockchain-banking.[4] A second set of use cases pursues objectives straightforwardly illegal, thus placed in a 'dark

[3] Technological neutrality does not correspond to use case-based regulation. Strictly speaking, the latter does not require a neutral approach towards the implemented technology, nor that the goal is to set broadly applicable principles. However, the two concepts share the idea that regulation should not be drafted in technological silos.

[4] Maupin (2017).

box'. For instance, AECs arguably seek a level of unaccountability that clashes with AML/CFT and provisions grounded on the transparency of value exchanges. As a middle category, the 'sandbox' collects innovations whose essence, despite not inherently illegal, involves risks that call for specific regulatory action. Illustratively, implementations that bypass regulated entities (e.g., some DEXes).

The use cases falling in the 'recycle box' often require some adaptation of existing rules, but usually do not challenge the basic structure of the measures. In principle, they do not require new policy trade-offs. For instance, wholesale CBDCs may rely on the anonymity-transparency trade-off deemed appropriate by the international financial system. Hence, unless they put forward products and services with different societal spillovers, recycle box initiatives do not raise specific anonymity-transparency issues. The situation is similar, albeit opposite, for the 'dark box group'. Even when these use cases stimulate a re-evaluation of what is illegal—i.e., they can generate a shift in the societal attitude towards some activities, which may lead to reconsider their qualification—, said re-evaluation lies in policy-making choices rather than in the relationship between new instruments and existing frameworks—i.e., it is still possible to apply existing frameworks to them. For instance, even if we argue crypto-assets changed the perception of the amount of transaction privacy society is willing to give up for the sake of regulatory oversight, DLTs are 'just' the technology that prompted this change in perception towards anonymous transactions. Hence, if the current regulatory framework is applied, use cases that make it impossible to complete KYC or that purposefully hinder transaction monitoring are breaching AML/CFT measures. These are the use cases positioned towards the anonymity end of the anonymity-transparency spectrum.

On the contrary, the last category offers insights into how different types of crypto-assets challenge AML/CFT schemes under the anonymity-transparency lens. Not complying with existing frameworks, albeit without thwarting their rationale, is a frequent occurrence for blockchain-based applications, chiefly due to the interplay of new and traditional stakeholders. To confront these cases, especially in the domain of financial services, regimes of 'regulatory sandbox' were established, where businesses are free to test their products and services without immediate regulatory repercussions, in agreement with the authorities and implementing a set of safeguards.[5] The idea is to encourage innovation while allowing regulators to cooperate with the industry in understanding the specificities of new products and services.

In this respect, over time other regulatory solutions were developed to suit the blockchain space as a context of governance through software code—i.e., safe harbours, modular contracts, information fiduciaries.[6] These regimes of 'struc-

[5] Zetzsche et al. (2017), p. 13. Regulation (EU) 2022/858.

[6] Weber et al. (2019), pp. 204ff. A safe harbor regime "excludes certain activities from legal obligations. When firms can take sufficient steps to police themselves, a safe harbour incentivises them to do so" (Weber et al. 2019, p. 204). Modular contracts make contract-drafting resemble coding, representing contractual clauses as components of a digital document via a markup language, while templates establish agreements on common scenarios (Weber et al. 2019, p. 206).

tured experimentalism' may replace reactive approaches.[7] With regard to DLT applications, four traits of an efficient sandbox were identified in global reach, cross-sectoral flexibility, start-up friendly structure, and use of case-tailored parameter-setting practices.[8] Although the sandbox approach has gained momentum in many jurisdictions (e.g., EU Digital Finance Package),[9] significant drawbacks suggest a shift towards more inclusive strategies.[10] Indeed, these regimes feature a few overarching frailties. For example, effective implementation requires a creative regulatory solution to be designed for all new cases, gathering the authorities of all sectors the innovation may impact on.[11] If the geographical scope is insufficient, the sandboxed activity would prove unfit in cross-border scenarios because the service, albeit regulated, is not standardised.[12] Additionally, given the wide application of DLTs, the different parameters of the sandbox should be tailored to "the underlying constellation of regulatory concerns raised in each case".[13] Evidently, this is not easy.

The efforts to regulate crypto-assets mirror their multi-layered structure and different regulatory standpoints. In addition, the debate confronts innovations of increasing complexity, whose collocation within existing schemes is often unclear. The early scope limitation of regulatory initiatives grew into a more mature approach of specialised expertise, informed by a sensitivity to standardisation needs. In some cases, this turned into token-based frameworks, introduced in Chap. 2, where the concept of token becomes a benchmark for regulation. On the contrary, technology-based approaches may not fully fit the fluidity of crypto-assets.

The previous chapters explored the presence of a multi-layered AML/CFT framework (e.g., global standards, EU law), technical and regulatory standardisation initiatives on DLTs and crypto-assets, the socio-technical nature of crypto-asset ecosystems, including their anonymity and transparency levels, and the possibility to anchor specific regulatory considerations (e.g., auditability, confidentiality) to given socio-technical factors (e.g., PETs, wallet types, public-private models), and finally to apply the same reasoning in designing applications to reach regulatory goals.

The application of information fiduciaries arose from noticing how entities are often exposed to liability, and the challenge worsens the more the entity is decentralised and autonomous. Hence, fiduciary duties may develop for public blockchains, aligning "the locus of legal responsibility with the locus of code on blockchain networks" (Weber et al. 2019, pp. 208–211).

[7] Zetzsche et al. (2017), p. 1.

[8] Maupin (2017).

[9] Regulation (EU) 2022/858.

[10] The effectiveness and efficiency of sandboxes (i) depend on the expertise of regulators, (ii) may not be sufficient to guarantee success, (iii) may not provide sufficient societal safeguards and transparency levels, (iv) is influenced by the quality of the regulatory text, (v) may be challenged by concerns about the legitimacy of the regulatory interventions (Zetzsche et al. 2017, p. 40).

[11] Maupin (2017), p. 11.

[12] Zetzsche et al. (2017), p. 40.

[13] Maupin (2017), p. 12.

When considering these concepts through the lens of the mentioned regulatory methodologies, one can pinpoint a set of recommendations for future AML/CFT regulation to account for the array of trade-offs between anonymity and transparency in crypto-asset ecosystems. Thus, this chapter outlines the value of (a) deploying design-based compliance and regulatory techniques, (b) shifting from the concept of 'code is law' to the compound notion of 'regulation-enabled compliance through design', exploring its essence and components, (c) establishing techno-regulatory standards adopted through polycentric co-regulatory models. Against this backdrop, this chapter provides (d) an example of application the proposed approach of techno-regulatory integration, and (e) suggestions on methodological elements for the intervention of EU law, chiefly in terms of legitimacy and effectiveness.

7.2 A Regulatory Methodology for the Crypto-Asset Space

From a comparative and diachronic standpoint, crypto-assets have been targeted by various regulatory methodologies. While the earliest frameworks emerged in 2016–2017 in the U.S., and major hustles occurred in 2018–2019, only from 2020 regulatory actions have started mirroring a higher level of awareness of the complexities and specificities of this sphere. Notwithstanding specific exceptions,[14] early initiatives targeted securities and addressed ICOs to provide safeguards to investors.[15] Generally, lawmakers intervened upon identifying risks that could thwart financial integrity, and AML/CFT regulation was a key tool to mitigate the side effects of the 'blockchain hype' in the financial domain. This is an example of reactive regulation, which responds to perceived threats, instead of addressing them proactively.

In recent times, a twofold scenario emerged: the understanding of expert communities increased significantly, and crypto-asset ecosystems kept developing. Hence, scholars and regulators started grasping the value of proactive initiatives to help all stakeholders (e.g., authorities, LEAs, financial institutions, PSPs) navigate the field. A proactive regulatory approach requires a detailed understanding of the field and assumes its development can be positively influenced through regulation. This seems even more crucial in a socio-technical context, where the characteristics of crypto-assets are linked to the stakeholders involved. From this perspective, the participation of a large array of actors in regulatory processes may provide a substantial insight into the nuances between the risks the regulator wants to mitigate.

The previous chapters underlined how confused definitions affect regulation in its drafting, application, and enforcement. From a first perspective, a framework is

[14] Such as the amendments to the Delaware General Corporation Law to record shares' ownership and issuance on DLTs.

[15] Hacker et al. (2019), p. 1.

based on normative considerations on the target to regulate: AML/CFT rules place duties on specific entities because they are deemed to be in a valuable position to mitigate a set of risks. Because anonymity is one of these risks, defining what it means in crypto-assets is pivotal to understand what the AML/CFT framework seeks to prevent. The need to define an acceptable degree of anonymity (if any) arose from the illegal consequences of allowing transactions between unknown parties. Anonymity is related to opaqueness vis-à-vis the difficulty to retrieve information on the origin of funds, reasons for operations and beneficial owners' identity,[16] while the possibility to transact anonymously and reduce transparency facilitates laundering.

Against this backdrop, a regulatory methodology that can account for the anonymity-transparency trade-offs in crypto-asset ecosystems should be tailored to their specificities, in terms of mirroring the nature of the target to be regulated. Accordingly, it should not only involve as many stakeholders as possible, but also heed variables bound to influence the anonymity risk or the concept of transparency useful for AML/CFT, i.e., auditability. From this perspective, crypto-assets call for a multi-stakeholder regulatory process that communicates with the industry. Meanwhile, it should heed the social factors, together with their influence on the anonymity level of a specific scenario—e.g., the combination between a given currency (or combinations thereof in case of cross-currency transactions), the platforms and the actors involved, also in terms of forensic strategies and user best practices that can be deployed vis-à-vis implemented technology. Accordingly, this section selects regulatory strategies highlighting suitable solutions.

7.2.1 *(Lack of) Accountability and the Teleological Approach*

Anonymous transactions are tainted by the unaccountability of those performing them. The socio-technical nature of crypto-assets exerts impacts in this respect: crypto-asset transactions are a multi-layered bundle of features, which spills into anonymity and transparency. Chapter 3 argued the two traits can be reconciled by pinpointing trade-offs and applying a teleological methodology. In this regard, an AML/CFT-specific approach to anonymity and transparency is key, and the literature shows a teleological reasoning when linking the notion of transparency to the retrievability of data on funds' origin and identity of clients and intermediaries. As outlined in Chap. 3, (some) blockchains are incompatible with financial transparency, as the transparency of non-centralised systems is not the one useful for oversight.[17] This is another reason to apply a teleological approach focused on a definition's context.

---

[16] These aspects relate to AML/CFT obligations, and their specificities are outlined in Chap. 5.

[17] Quiniou (2019), p. 20.

Chapter 3 reported how identification (i.e., establishing the real-world identity) and identity verification (i.e., verifying its authenticity) are crucial in CDD. The threshold for identification is set by the framework, and identifiability depends on the entity trying to achieve identification. The goal is not public retrievability of data, which would infringe confidentiality. On the contrary, this notion of identifiability is subjective; in crypto-assets some actors try to achieve identification and others to avert it. Thus, since anonymous data is not related to identifiable individuals,[18] for AML/CFT purposes an anonymous transaction is one that the entity trying to reach identification cannot (or finds significantly hard to) relate to an identifiable individual—i.e., CDD cannot be performed successfully, due to socio-technical aspects.[19]

In this respect, AML/CFT rules do not distinguish between anonymisation and strong pseudonymisation, including both the impossibility and the significant difficulty of linking data to (an) identified person(s). Operationally, the service may not be identity-based (e.g., a distributor assigns an identifier not tied to the user's real-world identity), or the user can opt not to have the real-world identity known. From a teleological perspective, anonymous transactions were linked to those that are untraceable and performed between a sender and a receiver without third parties being able to identify the actors involved.[20] Said transaction is not effectively auditable, thus anonymity is dependent on the observer (Chap. 3).

New technologies provide new pathways to accountability but also to disrupt data retrievability. Although the simple fact that a crypto-asset scheme is not immune to forensics does not make it AML/CFT compliant, it shows that not all anonymity-oriented crypto-assets are equally anonymous. As highlighted in Chap. 6, these schemes can be classified according to the impact of a given set of technologies on the anonymity risk and degree of accountability. Indeed, various PETs (and combinations thereof) generate different trade-offs between confidentiality and auditability.[21] The analysis of CBDC designs (Chap. 6) displayed how anonymity and transparency do not only ordinarily coexist, but also embody internal ambivalences. Transparency is used to generate or bypass trust but also generates loopholes that can aid deanonymisation. Online transparency embodies a dichotomy between enabling accountability and also surveillance.[22] The issue mirrors a general feature of the Internet, which has a twofold impact on anonymous communication by providing ways to undermine anonymity but also enhanced techniques to anonymise activities.[23]

The long-established debate between financial privacy and transparency shows how innovation only heightened a pre-existent complexity generated by opposing

---

[18] Information Commissioner's Office (2021).

[19] Karasek-Wojciechowicz (2021), p. 3.

[20] Edmunds (2020).

[21] European Central Bank and Bank of Japan (2020); Michalopoulos et al. (2024).

[22] Herian (2019), p. 77.

[23] Nicoll et al. (2003), p. v. Article 19 (2015).

interests. Although the urgency to set balances between anonymity and transparency does not originate from DLTs, crypto-assets made it more pressing by unlocking new opportunities both for lawlessness and accountability. Thus, the interplay of the principles informing online communication, coupled with the non-binary nature of these principles, requires setting balances policy-wise also when 'information' has a financial content. It follows that the only way to overcome clashes between anonymity and transparency traits is to agree on a desirable trade-off.

7.2.2 *Managing the Risk of Overfitting: Rules- and Principles-Based Approaches*

Literature on crypto-assets regulation shows increasing attempts of cooperation between computer scientists, lawyers, economists, ethicists and sociologists. Different knowledge domains often develop in silos, and they work together only when collaboration is perceived as a solution to a pressing risk. In this way, regulatory teamwork stems from urgency, which rarely prompts future-proof solutions. Likewise, reactive regulation is vulnerable to perceptive distortions and ideology-powered arguments, and the consequent regulatory process may not adequately consider phenomenological differences. Current-day approaches should consider the diversity within the crypto-asset space and its ever-evolving character, to avoid establishing overfitting regimes structured in such an over-tailored fashion that there is no room for them to evolve if not by breaking the boundaries of the same framework. Differently put, especially in finance, "crisis-inspired rules should not become a dogma", and even if a sandbox provides interesting insights, it cannot replace regulatory reforms.[24]

The overall evolution of crypto-asset regulation reflects the difficulties in fully grasping the deployed technologies and their socio-economic and legal impacts. It is complex to distinguish what is brought about by digital innovation and which disruptions are tied specifically to DLTs, just as it is not always easy to differentiate between the legal impacts of a DLT-based instrument and those of a similar one from a functional perspective but based on a different technology. The attention to taxonomy initiatives stemmed from leveraging the concept of token to bridge cross-disciplinary gaps. Although this could aid techno-legal communication through common references, the potential of cross-disciplinary initiatives is not (and should not be) limited to taxonomies. Growing attention is paid to the possibility to cooperate not only to define crypto-assets, but also to guide their development. In this context, expert techno-legal communities can have a proactive role in designing tools compatible with jointly agreed-upon values. Generally, this idea falls under the definition of 'regulation by design', explored below.[25] The major

[24] Zetzsche et al. (2017), p. 52.

[25] Hacker et al. (2019), p. 2.

opportunity offered by the token-based approach is the creation of a scheme for new ontological categories of assets, and ecosystems for their exchange, not limited to given domains. Appropriate structures must be devised for token creation and transfer, and they do not always correspond to (and/or are not considered) monetary and financial instruments.[26]

The issue of multiple regulatory approaches to crypto-assets is set within the broader context of different methodologies to mitigate risks and encourage innovation. A relevant distinction—well-known to the area of financial services regulation, albeit relatively new—is the one between rules-based and principles-based frameworks and compliance.[27] A rules-based regulatory style outlines detailed prescriptive provisions, while principles-based approaches focus on standards and rules stated broadly and oriented to the outcomes.[28] One could draw a parallel with the difference between Regulations and Directives under EU law. Nonetheless, even if the latter set goals that Member States choose how to reach, from a substantial perspective they often encompass detailed provisions as well. In real-world situations, frameworks usually feature a mix between the two approaches, and this is the case of the AMLD. Principles-based rules allow flexibility and are suitable when detailed schemes can generate a vicious cycle where gaps lead to new rules, which generate new gaps, prompting new rules, and so on.[29] This risk is rather a certainty when it comes to new technologies, and it is known as the risk of overfitting, where rules become technologically outdated soon after their entry into force or even before.[30] Hence, the idea of paying attention to the purpose behind a framework, rather than tailoring regulatory approaches to specific instances, could fit crypto-assets.

When considering the various and ever-evolving degrees of anonymity in crypto-assets, it seems unlikely a thoroughly rules-based scheme can be safe against the risk of overfitting. Measures to combat money laundering and terrorist financing need to confront a variety of instruments and may only be unified by focusing on the objective the framework pursues (e.g., forbid anonymous value exchanges by means of crypto-assets above a certain threshold, while crypto-assets feature different levels of anonymity). Nonetheless, it seems crucial to complement this methodology with more detailed and contextualised behavioural standards (e.g., predefined ways to avert anonymity) to avoid loopholes and guarantee the accountability of the actors involved.[31] Against this backdrop, a combination of rules-based and principles-based methodologies may arguably prove conducive to meet the crypto-asset space both where it is now and where it will be in the upcoming years.

[26] It is well-known that the widest types of information can be stored on DLTs (e.g., value transactions, land titles, intellectual property rights) and this is to some extent matched by the token categories explored in Chap. 2.

[27] Carter and Marchant (2011), pp. 157–165.

[28] Black et al. (2007), p. 191.

[29] Black et al. (2007), p. 193.

[30] Hacker et al. (2019), p. 17.

[31] Black et al. (2007), pp. 200–201.

In this respect, one of the goals of establishing cross-disciplinary collaboration mechanisms is to bridge the gap between the dynamism of innovative technologies and stringent rules-based approaches. Designing an efficient interplay of rules-based and principle-based reasoning, in fact, presents its shares of complexities. For instance, when regulators are asked to focus on their broader mandate, instead of deploying an 'overly rule-based approach' that can hinder innovation and 'overly stretch regulatory resources',[32] they are asked to develop a deep understanding of the process enabled by the given technology, which needs access to different types of expertise. Hence, while to foster harmonisation and limit overfitting one solution could be to adopt a mixed rules-based and principles-based methodology, this requires significant cross-disciplinary efforts to tie the framework to an actual understanding of the dynamics at hand.

7.2.3 The Impacts of Disintermediation on Regulatory Methodology

Chapters 3 and 4 argued in favour a teleological analysis of the anonymity of crypto-assets, noting that in an intermediary-based AML/CFT sphere this cannot overlook the notions of accountability and auditability. Although crypto-assets embody the idea of 'democratising' value exchanges, it has evolved into DeFi and techniques enabling enhanced disintermediation (e.g., self-hosted wallets, DEXes). While DeFi is a non-technical term depicting an ecosystem of DLTs, smart contracts, disintermediation and open banking,[33] its applications pursue transparent and trustless financial services, without involving intermediaries.[34] Not surprisingly, DeFi and enhanced disintermediation disrupt traditional regulation, as decentralisation potentially "undermine[s] traditional forms of accountability and erode[s] the effectiveness of traditional financial regulation and enforcement".[35] Indeed, while regulated intermediaries are (arguably) "positioned so as to be able to prevent wrongdoing by withholding necessary cooperation or consent",[36] in P2P transfers no third-party cooperation or consent is needed. Thus, even without assuming these initiatives pursue illegal goals, they ostensibly do not fall within the recycle box, but rather within the sandbox category,[37] and sandboxes were set up in various jurisdictions.

In this respect, the nature of DEXes spurred regulatory suggestions that shift the methodology from CEX-based to more innovation-friendly scenarios. In DEXes

[32] Zetzsche et al. (2017), p. 54.

[33] Zetzsche et al. (2020), p. 173.

[34] BitKom (2020), referenced by Zetzsche et al. (2020), p. 173.

[35] Zetzsche et al. (2020), p. 172.

[36] Gurrea-Martínez and Remolina (2019), p. 384 (note 16).

[37] Maupin (2017).

software is no longer 'used' to run the exchange, but rather 'is' the exchange. DEX platforms consist of general-purpose open-source software and resemble more online service providers (OSPs) than CEXes. Since software sets prices and transfers assets between buyers and sellers, the system can be (mis)used as users wish: what happens on the protocol depends on the users. From this perspective, the question arises on how to counteract harmful effects, also in terms of tracking and fighting illicit activity.[38] To avoid the use of regulation designed for centralised financial institutions, it was suggested to apply the 'safe harbour' approach of the DMCA's,[39] whereby under some conditions OSPs are not liable for the actions of users interacting on their platforms.[40] Likewise, the 'notice and takedown' methodology could be used for illegal content listed on DEXes, instead of stimulating developers to avoid self-regulation out of fear of being classified as exchanges. Decentralised protocols should be shielded from liability to allow them to delist blacklisted DeFi tokens when they are reported.[41]

Here, self-regulation is a component of a 'regulation designed for DEXes'. Reportedly, CEX-based AML/CFT regimes waste resources over problems solved by technology, while driving traceable activities towards untraceable worlds.[42] Accordingly, 'direct legal regulation' could be used to ensure regulated entities deploy monitoring systems that, as outlined in Chaps. 4 and 5, are provided by private companies. The regulatory goal is to establish a reporting and surveillance system, and the primary tool for regulating DEX protocols is 'code', while the law supplements it when the architecture falls short. Indeed, while it is not possible for code alone to hinder the (mis)use of DEXes, the use of RegTech solutions can be ensured by regulators contracting directly with service providers. Hence, the role of regulators is to ensure technology is used and reports are filed when needed.[43]

Nonetheless, this work previously argued how disintermediation in the crypto-asset space is not as clearcut as it may seem. The sphere is populated by both traditional and novel intermediaries, even if the latter are not always within the reach of regulatory efforts either by regulatory decision (e.g., crypto-to-crypto exchanges in the 5AMLD) or forced by the circumstances such as (perceived or actual) lack of enforceability (e.g., DEXes). Moreover, while a certain bewilderment is warranted by (some of) the enhanced disintermediation applications, arguably when benchmarks have already been set in the AML/CFT domain, even when

[38] Altschuler (2022), pp. 92–94, 99.

[39] Digital Millennium Copyright Act: 17 U.S.C. §512. The 'safe harbor' regime offers immunity from claims of copyright infringement if OSPs block access to infringing materials when notified. See also Zimmerman (2017).

[40] Altschuler (2022), p. 99. See also Barbereau and Bodó (2023).

[41] Altschuler (2022), p. 102, which refers to Antonopoulos (2021).

[42] Altschuler (2022), p. 107.

[43] Altschuler (2022), pp. 110, 112–113.

disintermediation clashes with active cooperation there might be no reason to overlook long-established principles.[44]

Illustratively, if the application of the RBA leads to limit volume-wise transactions involving anonymous instruments, such as cash or bearer shares, the same reasoning can be applied to crypto-asset transfers. A teleological approach—i.e., focused on what risks the framework tries to mitigate—leads to establishing equivalences. An example of this concept can be found in the text of the MiCA Regulation, stating "Union legislation on financial services should be guided by the principles of 'same activities, same risks, same rules' and of technology neutrality".[45] Indeed, in the EU regulation of financial markets, the principle 'same activity, same risks, same regulation' is typically accepted to minimise regulatory arbitrage.[46] Arguably, similar considerations inform FATF's position on non-custodial wallets and P2P transfers and the related unacceptably high risks in case of mass-adoption. Accordingly, national legislators may decide to ban or deny licenses to platforms operating with self-hosted wallets, or to set transactional/volume thresholds for P2P transfers, or also to mandate the involvement of a VASP or financial institution.[47] Another possible equivalence concerns EU provisions on 'e-money'. Against the background of anonymity being a risk factor, the approach is to ease CDD for cases of low risk—i.e., "[t]he anonymity associated with certain electronic money products exposes them to money laundering and terrorist financing risks. There are however significant differences across the sector, and not all electronic money products bear the same level of risk. For example, certain low value electronic money products, such as prepaid gift cards or prepaid vouchers, might present low risks [. . .]".[48] Article 19(7) of the AML Regulation provides conditions to simplify or even waive CDD duties for e-money based on the proven low risk posed by the nature of the product. This happens when, at the same time, the instrument (a) is not reloadable, and the amount stored does not exceed EUR 150, (b) is used exclusively to purchase goods or services provided by the issuer, (c) is not linked to a payment account and it does not allow exchanges for cash or for crypto-assets, and (d) the issuer monitors sufficiently the transactions or business relationship to detect suspicions activities.[49] The application of similar rules to crypto-asset activity may reduce gaps between value exchanges.

Meanwhile, despite its overall decentralised layout, DeFi features power reconcentration in parts of its value chain, albeit less regulated and transparent.[50] Regulation may evolve according to phenomenological developments, and effective

[44] This may be different from a policy-making perspective, as different choices are always possible.

[45] Recital 9 of Regulation (EU) 2023/1114.

[46] Katona (2021), p. 94.

[47] Financial Action Task Force (2020a), p. 15.

[48] Recital 58 of Regulation (EU) 2024/1624.

[49] Article 19(7) of Regulation (EU) 2024/1624.

[50] Zetzsche et al. (2020), p. 172. Indeed, among DeFi projects "the degree of decentralisation varies from protocol to protocol" (Zunzunegui 2022, p. 9).

oversight and risk control would be provided if regulation were to target the part of the value chain that is reconcentrated.[51] While the context is not equal to that of crypto-assets, this reasoning is arguably relevant to the latter as well.

7.2.4 Identifying the Risks: Rules-Based Indicators

As emerged in Chap. 5, the RBA is at the core of AML/CFT measures. Its flexibility allows compliance strategies to be devised that are proportionate to the specificities of regulated entities, but thrusts on the latter cumbersome evaluations. To guide efforts and aid compliance, as addressed in Chap. 4 various layers of risk assessments and anomaly indicators are issued to clarify benchmarks. Chiefly, they provide instructions on the application of enhanced CDD measures in specific circumstances. These indicators are published by different stakeholders, such as international and supranational institutions (e.g., FATF, EC, EBA), national legislators and regulators, supervisory, investigative and enforcement authorities (e.g., FIUs). Building on the interpretation of these indicators, each regulated entity retains the obligation to apply RBA-based measures from a concrete perspective.

In crypto-assets, just as in the traditional financial system, not all entities, tools, and stakeholders embody the same level of risk. According to the RBA, this consideration shall inform the design of regulatory and compliance responses not only from the standpoint of regulated entities. Indeed, the regulatory treatment must be tailored to the different degrees of danger to the integrity of the financial system, in line with the principle of proportionality. Chapters 4 and 5 contextualised red flag indicators as an integral part of the RBA. In this respect, it is common practice for regulated entities to deploy RegTech solutions to screen their operations and detect anomalous activities in an automated way. Mandatory transaction monitoring procedures are often grounded on these tools, that in turn heed the red flags of regulators. For crypto-asset-related operations, these software solutions are offered by blockchain analytics companies. Based on the alerts provided by these systems, the entity investigates the activities to decide whether to activate internal escalation procedures so that the competent person—usually, the Money Laundering Reporting Officer (MLRO)—can determine whether to submit an STR under the conditions outlined in Chap. 5. In this respect, RegTech applications perform the process of anomaly detection outlined in Chap. 4, to single out rare or suspicious events in terms of them being significantly different from the datasets.[52]

Red flag indicators are usually provided in rules-based format, which means they are phrased as templates of sequences of actions that suggest a suspicion, and are drafted in a way that is self-explainable, as required for auditing purposes. They are the basis of transaction monitoring solutions, whose alerts and hits are

[51] Zetzsche et al. (2020), p. 172.

[52] Kamišalić et al. (2021); Li et al. (2022); Shayegan et al. (2022).

generated through a process of rule-matching—i.e., they are produced when the system matches a given occurrence with one of the 'rules' identified as suspicious. For instance, a rule may be set in a RegTech application to flag all transfers of an amount that exceeds by 30% the average amount of the previous transactions performed by the same customer. Thus, if a situation of the sort arises, the system would match the occurrence with the rule, and flag the transfer accordingly.

Indeed, transaction monitoring solutions were defined as "predominantly rules-based thresholding protocols tuned for volume and velocity of transactions with tiered escalation procedures".[53] Hence, the preliminary review of a flagged transfer usually relies on 'suspiciousness heuristics'—e.g., political exposure, geographical dynamics, round numbers, transaction type and properties, behavioural logic—,[54] as enshrined by the indicators. Chief reference is to those outlined in Chaps. 4 and 5, issued by the FATF in 2020 with regard to VAs. The indicators were developed from an analysis of more than 100 case studies dated from 2017 to 2020 and include a section of anonymity that depicts vulnerabilities related to the technologies embedded in the crypto-asset or service provider, or to the ecosystem itself.

The debate on the respective merits of rules-based and principles-based standards is heated for accounting and auditing standards, where it was argued there is insufficient acknowledgment that the format of the standards affects their content. This is because the more effort is required, the more complex it is to comply without guidance and exceptions.[55] Likewise, rules-based auditing generates audit processes that are relatively uniform, unscalable and significantly redundant, while in principles-based audit efforts can be targeted to higher risks.[56] The debate chiefly concerns accounting standards and pivots on the difference between those issued by the FASB (more rules-based) and those issued by the IASB (more principles-based). In this context, rules-based standards are criticised because they encourage 'check-box' thinking—i.e., formal compliance with detailed criteria instead of substantial compliance, unsuitable to the complexity of the financial environment. On the other hand, the vagueness of principles-based standards requires expertise, leaving room for misinterpretation and inconsistencies.[57]

Against this backdrop, also in the AML/CFT field the regulatory methodology and the style used to draft risk indicators are key elements. The following are two examples of rules-based red flags: (i) with regard to transaction patterns: "incoming transactions from many unrelated wallets in relatively small amounts (accumulation of funds) with subsequent transfer to another wallet or full exchange for fiat currency"; (ii) with regard to anonymity: "moving a VA that operates on a

[53] Weber et al. (2018), p. 3.

[54] Weber et al. (2018), p. 3.

[55] Benson et al. (2006), p. 185.

[56] Sin et al. (2015), p. 282.

[57] Sin et al. (2015), p. 283. In any case, the prescriptiveness of auditing standards was argued to be highly influential on the audit's procedure and results.

public, transparent blockchain, such as Bitcoin, to a centralised exchange and then immediately trading it for an AEC or privacy coin".[58]

Red flag indicators, drafted by experts and reflecting their opinions, operate as empirical measures of AML/CFT risk. Likewise, they aim to provide a structure to think about these risks. In principle, they should provide clear benchmarks and their structure should be able to accommodate the development of new indicators as the sphere evolves. Nonetheless, the content of rules-based indicators is often less straightforward and more ambiguous than what it seems. Moreover, depending on the link with empirical findings (i.e., the phenomenological aspect highlighted in Chap. 2.) they may feature little normative content, and be for the most part descriptive. In addition, there can be considerable gaps between the indicators and best practices deployed in the industry (e.g., crypto travel rule debate).[59] In this respect, the creation of a 'transposition model' between red flag indicators and techno-regulatory standards could help clarify their meaning and streamline their application at the regulated entity-level. This could happen in the framework of the role of the AMLA. Their implementation could ostensibly be eased by developing the standards with the private entities offering crypto-asset-related analytics services and sharing them in an open-source format.

In practice, a considerable amount of time and human resources are needed to review the alerts generated by the rule-matching process. Tiered escalation procedures involve multiple layers of analysts deciding whether to escalate the item up to the MLRO. Because an alert can be a true or a false positive, rules-based systems have the advantage of interpretability, but their simplicity produces many false positives, estimated at around 95–98%.[60] Indeed, the discovery of patterns is demanding, and transaction datasets are massive, dynamic, high dimensional, complex from a combinatorial perspective, non-linear, as well as often fragmented, inaccurate, incomplete, or inconsistent, while the difficulty to automate the synthesis of information from different data streams leaves the task up to human analysts. Hence, a vicious circle stimulates over-reporting due to the cost asymmetry between false positives and false negatives.[61] The insufficiency of rules-based systems suggested the automation of an increasing array of processes, where machine learning-based methodologies are deployed and investigated in conjunction with forensic approaches.[62] Notably, as explored in Chap. 4 the combination between transaction graph analytics and machine learning is increasingly deployed in the AML/ CFT domain for transaction classification purposes. Indeed, the supervised activities involve transaction flow relationships between entities, which creates a

[58] Financial Action Task Force (2020d).

[59] In this regard, they share features with rules-based indicators in governance: Kaufmann and Kraay (2008).

[60] Eddin et al. (2021).

[61] Weber et al. (2018).

[62] Oad et al. (2021).

graph structure helpful for classification and to which specific algorithms can be applied (Pocher et al. 2023b).

7.2.5 Ranking the Risks: The Value of Taxonomies

The evolution of crypto-assets calls for increasingly complex RegTech solutions due to the great quantity and complexity of transaction data to be processed. Considering the enhanced disintermediation trend, regulated entities and LEAs need to analyse a growing number of transactions vis-à-vis sophisticated obfuscation techniques and without the assistance of regulated counterparties.[63] In this context, it is important to devise tools to aid compliance and reduce over-reporting.[64] Building on the need to provide future-proof benchmarks to enable communication between regulation and technology, and possibly automatic application and enforcement, a method worth exploring is a taxonomy that provides yardsticks to evaluate different levels of anonymity risk posed by different crypto-assets and/or ecosystems.

Although it may seem odd for a taxonomy to be future-proof and mitigate the risk of over-fitting, its design could merge principles-based and rules-based methodologies. This instrument comes to mind because of the use made for tokens, overviewed in Chap. 2, where the taxonomy instrument showed its capacity to merge flexibility with precision. Indeed, the token is used as a benchmark to bridge cross-disciplinary gaps and merge different understandings to reduce regulatory uncertainty. One of the most compelling aspects of such a framework is to provide experts with different backgrounds with a common frame of reference to work on and build a body of knowledge. A taxonomy that categorises crypto-assets and ecosystems according to their level of anonymity-related risk would prove useful. Nonetheless, because the concept of anonymity is socio-technical, it remains to be explored whether all—or a significant number of—these risks can be effectively modelled in a taxonomy fashion.

As outlined throughout this work, in crypto-assets the anonymity-transparency interplay pertains to different dimensions, and several ambivalences stem from the background against which crypto-asset have developed (e.g., online communication, financial sphere). The multi-layered complexity of crypto-asset socio-technical ecosystems suggests the adoption of a teleological approach to develop a conceptual understanding of both their nature and their regulatory consequences. Accordingly, a valuable approach arguably entails: (i) conceptualising the different trade-offs between, on one side of the spectrum, anonymity and privacy and, on the other side, transparency and auditability, that exist in the crypto-asset space; (ii) leveraging the RBA to develop an understanding of the AML/CFT risk featured by various

[63] Such as in the context of CDD or investigations on transactions originating from or destined to unhosted wallets or processed by DEXes.

[64] Pocher et al. (2023b).

use cases; (iii) designing a taxonomy-based framework to classify crypto-asset ecosystems according to this risk, in combination with techno-legal reasons that ground the classification (i.e., parameterised criteria); and (iv) leveraging the findings to establish a regime of techno-regulatory standards featuring a 'regulation-enabled compliance through design' approach. The next two sections explore the last element.

7.3 From 'Code is Law' to 'Through Design' Approaches

As outlined in Chap. 5, the AML/CFT approach to crypto-assets remains moulded on the gatekeeper-based model even after the advent of cases of enhanced dis-intermediation. Meanwhile, the implementation of the crypto travel rule raises multi-dimensional issues, and the industry declares to be lacking the technology to comply. In other words, despite the efforts of analytics companies, the sector has yet to develop an adequate RegTech solution. In this context, a key challenge is posed by transactions involving self-hosted wallets.

The idea that information on originators and beneficiaries must be collected and accompany crypto-asset transfers—as it ordinarily happens for wire transfers—explicitly aims to avert anonymity. In this situation, a technology-powered solution (crypto-asset transfers) is (purportedly) unable to comply with a piece of regulation (FATF's travel rule), because of a techno-logical gap (no effective tool). This gap, however, stems from a (partial) misalignment between regulatory provisions and the phenomenology of the targeted domain. Evidently, other factors hinder the application of the crypto travel rule. Not only VASPs/financial institutions may not possess, or have adequate procedures to collect, the identity-related information to be submitted to the counter-party, but some of this data may not exist or it may not be possible to collect it.

But how can the growing cases of non-centralisation and disintermediation be addressed by AML/CFT? As outlined in the previous chapters, not only is the crypto-asset space permeated by methods to obfuscate flows, but intermediary-based regulatory efforts are hindered when transactions do not involve regulatable entities—e.g., in a transfer between two self-hosted wallets what stands between the parties is just technology. In this context, the challenges in implementing the crypto travel rule shed a thought-provoking light on the interplay between technology and regulation. The effectiveness of active cooperation is vulnerable to criticism, and the value of tech-sensitive regulation was underlined.[65] Regulators shall develop ways to consider the features of these ecosystems and deploy a proactive, rather than reactive, model. One may consider a regulatory and compliance approach that is not new but modified to fit the crypto-asset sphere.

[65] De Filippi and Wright (2018). Zetzsche et al. (2020), p. 180.

7.3.1 *When the 'Law' Meets 'Code', Perhaps on a Blockchain*

The starting point is the widely known, and criticised, 'code is law' maxim, put forward in 1999 by Lessig to depict the regulatory impact of 'code' in the cyberspace as part of the founding arguments of the New Chicago School.[66] In his words, "the software and hardware (i.e., the 'code' of cyberspace) that make cyberspace what it is also regulate cyberspace as it is".[67] The concept was framed by Reidenberg under the label of 'lex informatica', and soon extended into 'law is code'.[68] Accordingly, 'code' complements law in its regulatory action, which leads to focus on how predefined regulatory elements can be built into technology.[69] This does not imply code 'replaces' or 'displaces' law, but that it exerts a 'normative influence' on individual behaviours—e.g., impact of software on user behaviour.[70] It does so in combination with other three factors: market dynamics, law itself, social norms.[71] The concept of regulation comes to include these four aspects.[72] In Lessig's words, it is possible to build the cyberspace to protect values deemed fundamental, or to design it not to uphold them. The issue is unavoidable as any choice includes "some kind of building. Code is never found; it is only ever made, and only ever made by us",[73] thus it is crucial to decide which values to embed.[74]

In this context, the idea of 'code is law' developed towards the 'law is code' argument that "law itself can be codified and defined as technological code".[75] The notion that code can control cyberspace behaviour ex ante or a priori (i.e., before the fact) gave birth to notions such as 'lex cryptographica' and 'cryptolaw',[76]

[66] Lessig (1998, 1999, 2006).

[67] Lessig (2006), pp. 4–5.

[68] Reidenberg (1998). For an overview of related research: Werbach (2019), pp. 149–173.

[69] Hassan and de Filippi (2017).

[70] In this context, regulation was defined by Black as "the intentional use of authority to affect behaviour of a different party according to set standards, involving instruments of information-gathering and behaviour modification" (Black 2002, p. 1, referenced by Finck 2019, p. 145).

[71] Lessig (1998, 1999). Finck (2019), p. 39. Lessig "did not say 'Code always disrupts law' or 'Code is superior to law.' His point was that software code and legal enactments are both mechanisms that can govern human behavior. Code is a form of law . . .and not necessarily the best one" (Werbach 2019, p. 153). Indeed, "one of the most important lessons from Lessig's analysis was that law and code are not binary alternatives" (Werbach 2019, p. 156).

[72] Lessig (1999). This generates the theory of the 'pathetic dot' (De Filippi and Wright 2018, p. 173).

[73] Lessig (2006), p. 6.

[74] Brown and Marsden (2013), p. 303, referenced by Finck (2019), p. 39. Accordingly, technology should be studied as a regulatory modality coexisting with the others (Werbach 2019, p. 153). Following this reasoning, the role of the law expands, regulating behaviour both directly and indirectly (and modern regulation is a mix), by regulating other modalities of regulation (Lessig 1998, p. 666).

[75] Möslein (2019), p. 277, referring to De Filippi and Hassan (2016).

[76] Differences emerged among these notions. 'Lex cryptographica' distances itself from Lessig's 'code is law' and other code-based regimes because it inherently operates on an autonomous basis,

and originated a series of debates that evolved into the controversial 'code as law'.[77] Indeed, 'regulation by code' was argued to allow the formalisation of contractual agreements into self-executing and self-enforcing predetermined code-based rules,[78] and blockchain technology, mostly through smart contracts, was seen as an enabler of an 'order without law' built on private (self-)regulatory frameworks.[79]

It was argued 'law' and 'code' are in a synergic relationship of extraordinary complexity, where code can implement self-regulation and reinforce or undermine public regulation, while law can subvert or strengthen code. It is interesting to focus on the intertwined and mutual relation between regulation and code,[80] as it perfectly exemplifies the way in which technology can interact, communicate, and evolve with regulation, as well as be designed accordingly. Evidently, negative impacts can be produced as well, and code can be leveraged to escape regulatory constraints, which reminds of cyberlibertarians. The argument pivots around the dynamic between code and regulation, and it allows me to argue in favour of the joint development of these two crucial building blocks of today's world, thus mitigating the risk of their siloed development. By no means this supports equating the concepts of code and law.[81] Indeed, what is relevant to this research is that, starting from 'law is code' arguments, design-based techniques were devised to pursue socio-legal outcomes through embedding legal principles and values into technology, thus fostering cross-disciplinarity. Accordingly, even if hyperbolic statements such as 'code is/as law' are not to be interpreted literally, the inter-relationship between 'law' and 'code' has laid the conceptual groundwork for valuable notions such as embedded regulation and embedded supervision, still explored to this day.[82]

Ostensibly, code—as a primary component of the broader concept of the 'design' of a given application—enables regulation and compliance to be approached in a proactive way, replacing 'command and control' techniques with a design-based methodology where compliance is embeddable.[83] Building on RegTech tools, these techniques require preliminary standard setting. Hence, the assumption is

independently from centralised authorities (De Filippi and Wright 2018, p. 207). 'Cryptolaw' is a new type of accessory legislation and jurisprudence emerged when DLTs implement and deliver law (Reyes 2017, p. 399). Crepaldi (2019).

[77] Hacker et al. (2019), pp. 22–23. Wright and De Filippi (2015). Yeung (2019).

[78] Hassan and de Filippi (2017), pp. 88–90.

[79] In using these concepts, this work acknowledges the interplay between 'rules', 'code' and 'law' generated considerable controversy, and that the legal and ethical challenges of 'regulation by code' were widely explored with regard to blockchain and machine learning. These elements, however, fall outside the scope of this work.

[80] Finck (2019), p. 39.

[81] "The equation between code and law (and of law and Code) is debatable at best" (Möslein 2019, p. 275).

[82] Auer (2022); Zetzsche et al. (2020); Buckley et al. (2023).

[83] Nabilou (2019); Pocher and Veneris (2022b); Yeung (2017).

that regulators can convert obligations—and, as outlined in detail below, also the way and methods to achieve compliance with them—into code that can be used for a given application to comply by design.[84] The idea that compliance can be streamlined into a design process developed from the concept of privacy by design put forward in 2011, later evolved into compliance 'by' or 'through' design explored below.[85] Albeit with a few important limitations, embedding compliance appears as a fitting methodology in a situation of enhanced disintermediation.[86]

Meanwhile, the possibility to exert impacts on these systems through technology relies on stakeholders to develop ways to do it effectively vis-à-vis the power dynamics between the actors involved. In CBDCs, as highlighted in Chap. 6, a method is PPPs, where public entities cooperate with the industry that owns the skills to develop technological tools. CBDCs, however, are obviously not an example of enhanced disintermediation, which means any equation must be approached with care. In this sense, the value of effective technology-based tools to comply with regulation emerges as most noteworthy. It is seemingly a power of technology spilling into the regulatory world. This power, however, can pursue regulatory objectives through predefined procedures and an adequate understanding of the techno-legal context.

7.3.2 *Placing the Debate Within the Crypto-Asset Domain*

Lessig argues that governance and commerce are shaping the cyberspace in ways very distant from its original architecture, allowing control and efficient regulation, thus challenging essential liberties.[87] In this sense, the argument is related to crypto-assets evolution, where the hype over time left room to (re)centralisation tendencies. In this respect, the DeFi space provides insights on how to extend regulatory safeguards to crypto-assets. A few methodologies appear disruptive because of their proactiveness in terms of interplay with technologies. In the early phase of the exploration, reference was to supervisory mechanisms, in the form of embedded supervision—i.e., "an automated form of compliance, monitoring, and supervision, using the system itself to implement, monitor, and enforce compliance requirements".[88] Going beyond supervision, the reasoning spilled into embedded regulation, and DeFi offers the chance to design regulation in a new way, where "regulatory approaches could be built into the design of DeFi, thus

---

84 Schrepel (2021a), pp. 44–45. Pocher and Veneris (2022b).

85 Casanovas et al. (2017); Cavoukian (2011); Torra (2017); Auer (2022).

86 See below for an analysis of the interplay between embedded regulation and embedded compliance, as well between regulation by design and compliance by design.

87 Lessig (2006), pp. 4–5.

88 Zetzsche et al. (2020), p. 202. Auer (2022).

potentially decentralising both finance and its regulation, in the ultimate expression of RegTech".[89] This methodology appears helpful in non-centralised systems.

Embedded regulation appears even more valuable when considering AML/CFT RegTech solutions,[90] where the use of technology is well-established, and developments are promising. To fully reap the benefits of these efforts, regulators, partnering with the industry, could develop technology-based systems and embed regulatory objectives through ad hoc compliance strategies. The technology-based trait of a regulatory approach can refer to a type of regulation that either (i) uses a specific technology as benchmark (i.e., it targets all implementations of a specific technology), or (ii) targets technology as regulatory tool (e.g., regulation by design). The term is here used as sub (ii), which means the use does not necessarily herald the use of DLTs as benchmarks without a complementary focus on other cases.

The way through this process is not straightforward, but a pivotal aspect is building on existing initiatives to capitalise on efforts to bridge gaps and discrepancies between terminologies and knowledge sets. Evidently, proactive regulation needs a dialogue with the industry that is hands-on developing projects based on these technologies, as well as with stakeholders that are already offering RegTech applications that leverage their extensive crypto-asset-related datasets. Cross-disciplinary communication to set up common frameworks (e.g., taxonomies, definitions of core concepts) and benchmarks (e.g., tokens) can thus lead the way to approaching the regulation of technological evolution not only ex post. This type of collaboration is viable when communication between different stakeholders is feasible—e.g., it is hard to picture a co-operation between AML/CFT regulators, forensic companies, and AEC developer communities. Nonetheless, the establishment of common languages may lead to a techno-legal mutual awareness of the impacts of a specific implementation (e.g., dark box, recycle box, sandbox), thus possibly informing more inclusive regulation and policy making.

7.3.3 Toward a Flexible Understanding of 'Code Is/As Law'

As mentioned above, experts elaborated on the 'code is law' and 'law is code' paradigms and developed the concepts of 'code as law' and 'law as code'. Accordingly, governments tried to transpose regulation into smart contracts or embed it directly into information systems, to generate automated enforcement that does not need constant monitoring.[91] Indeed, it was suggested to shift the

[89] Zetzsche et al. (2020), p. 172.

[90] E.g., Lootsma (2017); Yeung (2019); Arner et al. (2019b).

[91] The 'rules as code' movement took place from 2018 in Australia, Canada and France. It leverages computer languages to aid legal drafting and implementation. Other movements are 'better rules' and 'legislation as code' (Casanovas et al. 2022, p. 66, Goldbarsht and de Koker 2022, p. 7).

regulatory focus from 'code is law', where code is used to implement rules, to 'code as law', that relies only on technology to define and implement law. Reportedly, this approach could ensure compliance by embodying requirements into code-based systems, through a mechanism that enables a transaction only if it satisfies the logic embedded into code.[92] Although the strategy could seem efficient, from a conceptual standpoint it is difficult to agree with a strict equation between 'law' and 'code' to promote interventions on code itself to reach technical accountability. As noted in the literature, the code-based approach is tainted by lack of flexibility, and the regulatory action of code is useful only for objectively verified rules that can be defined in the code itself, while the formality of translating legal rules into code-based rules can enable people to bypass regulation exploiting the rigidity of the system.[93] It is for this reason, it is better to refer more broadly to 'design', although in the domain at hand design models usually include coding as a key component.

In this sense, among the manifold challenges posed by the combination of legal and technical trust in blockchain governance, the chief difference between cryptography and law stems from the distinction between human-to-human expression and computer programming. It is impossible to reduce the law to objective rules, but only portions of it. Reportedly, "hard-edged, cryptographically secured code can never fully encompass human intentions".[94] Indeed, law is dynamic and does not only consist of reading predefined codes, while DLTs' cryptography is inherently expressed in finite systems.[95] From this perspective, "the world is often too complex to be put into code", and the value of automation lies more in simplifying a contract's execution than in trying to automate all complexities.[96]

Nonetheless, successful crypto-asset regulation requires a combination between the law and the mechanisms underlying technologies.[97] In the crypto-asset space, architecture shapes behaviour or grants the power to shape it, which means "poorly designed code can be as harmful as poorly designed law".[98] Hence, code plays a role worth exploring within design models, but there is no need to even try to pursue an equation with the regulatory role of the law. While the concept of embedding compliance with rules is to be praised, and so is the value of devising rules that can be complied with through embedded mechanisms, the focus of this

---

[92] De Filippi and Wright (2018), pp. 196–199.

[93] De Filippi and Wright (2018), p. 200.

[94] Werbach (2019), pp. 221–222. In this context, "some rules and regulations are particularly suitable for formalisation into the language of code. This is particularly true with laws containing rules that are both straightforward and unambiguous [. . .]" (De Filippi and Wright 2018, pp. 195–196).

[95] Werbach (2019), p. 222.

[96] Auer (2022), p. 19.

[97] Werbach (2019), p. 203, argues that the fact that smart contracts do not require legal enforcement (if this is the case) does not render the law irrelevant, rather calls developers to study the law to understand where code and cryptographic solutions can match the functions of legal practice. Both 'governance by code' and 'law' have their own flaws; there is a need to draw from both.

[98] Werbach (2019), p. 233.

argument is on the communication and mutual influence between technology and regulation, and less on their respective regulatory traits. The relationship between the two has been explored in many ways. The 'ex-ante law is code' approach—based on converting legal rules into code to have users comply by design—is risky because it affects smart contracts directly. Thus, the less intrusive 'ex-post law is code' was suggested, while ways are investigated to make 'law more code-like' and 'code more law-like'.[99] Indeed, "the simplest way to make blockchain-based systems more consistent with legal enforcement is literally to connect the two".[100]

In this sense, a valuable reference can be made to Ricardian Contracts, that proposed to "identify and describe issues of financial instruments as contracts".[101] They are text files readable by people and parsable by programs and define a type of value for its issuance over the Internet, by identifying issuer/signatory, terms and clauses.[102] Their background is that smart contracts are used "to translate certain legal contractual terms and conditions of services they offer into safe-to-execute code".[103] However, the specificities of legal contracts and the multi-layered (e.g., domestic, supranational, international) and cross-disciplinary (e.g., civil, criminal, administrative) set of regulations they have to comply with challenges their deployment as such. Indeed, 'contract' is a specific notion in the legal world, specified by the different legal systems and jurisdictions, and legal wording references implicitly and explicitly to elements of the broader legal framework(s). On the contrary, a smart contract consists of software executed automatically when programmed conditions are met, translating "fragments of the legal prose of a contract into an executable piece of code".[104] Although the extensive literature on the legal status of smart contracts and their regulatory impact falls outside the scope of this work,[105] the role of standardisation in the establishment of a common techno-regulatory methodology emerges from analysing how the intelligibility of the legal wording must be safeguarded not to incur claims of the contract being void or voidable.[106]

A Ricardian Contract has three components: (i) legal code, a human-readable text of the contract, (ii) computer code, the executable smart contract, and (iii) parameters/variables affecting its execution. To properly link legal and computer code the cryptographic hash of the computer code is included into the legal code,

---

[99] Schrepel (2021a), pp. 44–45. 2019, pp. 203–223.

[100] Werbach (2019), p. 212.

[101] Werbach (2019), p. 212. The author refers to Werbach and Cornell (2017), pp. 101–170. Grigg (2004). The concept was introduced by Grigg (2000).

[102] Grigg (2004). Parsable means that machines can convert it into internal forms to search for name-value pairs.

[103] Cervone et al. (2020), p. 1. Murphy and Cooper (2016).

[104] Cervone et al. (2020), p. 1782.

[105] Some jurisdictions provide them with a clear legal status. They can be enforced internationally if compliant with UNCITRAL's condition (Cervone et al. 2020, p. 1782).

[106] The issue of the unequivocal and free willingness to accept the terms of smart contracts shows the value of intelligibility and readability by humans and machines (Cervone et al. 2020, p. 1782).

and that of the legal text is included into the computer code.[107] Weaknesses of Ricardian Contracts were addressed by initiatives such as the 'Smart Contracts Templates' and the 'Intelligible Contract', where the latter maps into the operational code the whole text of the legal contract.[108] Relatedly, Schrepel (2021b) analyses the challenges of smart contracts under the lens of their deployment in the EU and impacts on the Digital Single Market. It puts forward the 'Law + Technology' methodology to encourage their development, and it can be useful to handle crypto-assets challenges, dynamics and value exchanges.

In this field, a branch of legal informatics known as 'computational law' ('Complaw') focuses on bridging the gap between legal knowledge/reasoning, natural language, and machine-readable formats (e.g., through formal semantic representation).[109] Its primary focus is compliance management, which aims to develop computer systems that can assess, facilitate, or enforce, compliance. Overall, Complaw pursues to apply regulations without additional human input.[110] In particular, experts focused on trying to solve the problem of using standard technologies for the implementation of the mentioned Intelligible Contract leveraging solutions already exploited in the legal domain—e.g., the Akoma Ntoso standard, an XML OASIS standard for modelling legal resources, and the LegalRuleML standard, an OASIS standard that consists of an interchange language for legal rules both human- and machine-readable.[111]

7.3.4 Regulation-Enabled Compliance Through Design

A literature review of design-based methodologies shows a dichotomy between 'regulation by design' and 'compliance by design'. Indeed, the notions refer to two distinct perspectives. On the one hand, 'regulation by design' focuses on shaping regulation starting from a design-based perspective. On the other hand, 'compliance

[107] Werbach (2019), p. 212. The author refers to Werbach and Cornell (2017). Grigg (2004).

[108] Cervone et al. (2020). An Intelligible Contract is "a unique collection of linked machine-readable resources describing a legal contract, its legal prose, its legal context, and information on which parts of it can be automatically processed and how to do it". Mandatory components are (i) identification and referencing, (ii) document, (iii) context, (iv) process. Legal documents must be structured to preserve the logical and semantic structure of the text, serialised through standard technologies and linkable to other resources (Cervone et al. 2020, p. 1784).

[109] Athan et al. (2016); Cervone et al. (2020); Genesereth (2015); Surden (2012).

[110] Genesereth (2021).

[111] AkomaNtoso was applied in legal and non-legal contexts (e.g., modelling laws, legal changes, documents). It comprises an XML vocabulary to structure legal documents and a naming convention to identify legal resources; it supplies an informal ontology to identify entities and link them to portions of the legal text. The LegalRuleML standard allows to re-express legal prose and connect business rules to automatic legal reasoners. Cervone et al. (2020), p. 1785. The authors cite: Palmirani and Vitali (2011); Palmirani (2011); Peroni et al. (2017); Dimyadi et al. (2017); Palmirani et al. (2018); Vitali et al. (2019, 2018); Palmirani et al. (2017); Athan et al. (2014).

by design' refers to a compliance process grounded on embedding compliance into the design of a given tool.[112] Hence, the wording 'regulation by design' is imprecise when used to refer to compliance measures and not to the regulatory process at the roots of compliance. Therefore, in certain cases embedded regulation may be more correctly rephrased as embedded compliance, when it pinpoints the elements embedded into the given application as a set of tools that aid, and aim to ensure by design, compliance with the regulation.

Nonetheless, regulation can be drafted (or reformed) considering the need to comply with it through embedded procedures, as well as existing rules can be equipped with implementing acts that aid the embedding process. Hence, despite the overarching conceptual value of distinguishing the two phases (i.e., design of the regulatory framework and subsequent implementation through compliance measures) in practice they are two sides of the same coin. It is for this reason that, while they are distinct concepts, this works focuses on conceiving a regulatory approach that can aid its implementation by means of 'compliance by design' methods. In this book this joint analysis is termed 'regulation-enabled compliance by design'.

From a parallel perspective, in addition to 'by design' methodologies the concept of 'compliance through design' was put forward.[113] Indeed, 'compliance by design' has been extending its scope of application, and different approaches, meanings and fields of applications have been reviewed—i.e., 'regulatory compliance', 'compliance by detection', 'compliance by design', 'legal compliance by design'. Relatedly, four concepts were identified: (i) 'compliance by design', referring to formalised rules heeded in the design phase of a business or regulatory process;[114] (ii) 'legal compliance by design', focused on the legality of the whole process, encompassing approaches based on business processes and legal knowledge (i.e., properties of normative and legal systems);[115] (iii) 'compliance through design', including social and institutional aspects not (explicitly) included in the traditional approach;[116] and (iv) 'legal compliance through design'. The latter recognises a broader array of social, political, economic aspects, as well as governance and ethical elements, crucial to the design of legal compliance. In principle, compliance encompasses

---

[112] In broad terms, compliance is the "conformity in fulfilling requirements, or demonstrating conformity with regulatory constraints", which denotes a set of requirements are previously selected—e.g., laws, regulations, standards, best practices (Casanovas et al., 2017, p. 34). From this perspective, compliance is a granular concept not fully translatable into binary requirements (Hashmi et al., 2018, pp. 60–61), and is increasingly automated to optimise the use of resources (Casanovas et al., 2017, p. 34). It was argued the advantages of 'compliance by design' include the flexibility of the approach, that can adjust to additions or changes in the rules.

[113] Casanovas et al. (2017); Hashmi et al. (2018). Goldbarsht and de Koker (2022), p. 7.

[114] Hashmi et al. (2018), pp. 60–61. In compliance by design a set of rules is assessed and compliance is embedded into business practice (Casanovas et al. 2017, p. 34).

[115] Casanovas et al. (2017), p. 35. Hashmi et al. (2018), pp. 60–61.

[116] These are defined as interpretation processes, institutionalisation, modelling-coordination interface, citizens-law relation (Casanovas et al., 2017, p. 35).

technical, practical, and theoretical elements, and the 'through design' approach acknowledges the relation between different meta-models, and the impossibility to comprehensively automate it by normative and linguistic tools.[117] Although it seems possible to formalise aspects of legal compliance, this requires regulatory models that can bridge machine and human interfaces, as well as professional and institutional experiences.[118] Indeed, (semi-)automation does not only refer to compliance with a text. Whenever there are contrasting or contending rights, obligations and policies, a compliance strategy does not only respond to regulatory requirements but also to a broader set of variables.[119]

While the referenced literature is most thought-provoking, the specific features of the field of research at hand warrant the choice to refer jointly to 'by design' and 'through design' approaches. Indeed, several aspects—i.e., (i) the AML/CFT framework, (ii) its compliance impacts, (iii) the socio-technical features of crypto-asset ecosystems, (iv) the dynamics between the regulatory field and crypto-asset phenomenology—exemplify the crucial role of social, political, economic, governance and ethical elements whose importance led to formulating 'through design' methodologies. It also shows the importance of the design process in guaranteeing 'by design' outcomes—i.e., the 'by design' typically requires a 'through design'.[120] It follows the two perspectives can be merged into a joint compound concept—i.e., 'through design', that includes the 'by'. Hence, this work focuses on 'regulation-enabled compliance through design'.

7.4 'Through Design' Techno-Regulatory Standards

As argued in Chap. 5, FATF's Recommendations are instruments of soft law. Despite giving rise to powerful expectations within the international community, they are not directly binding. This remains true even if participating jurisdictions committed to transposing them into domestic law and enforcement measures are imposed in case of non-compliance. Soft law and standardisation are fundamental in the global financial domain, where the regulatory framework consists of a compound mix of

[117] Casanovas et al. (2017), pp. 45–46. Hashmi et al. (2018), pp. 60–61, 63, 68–70. The notion grounds models to represent and (semi-)automate compliance. The authors addressed differences/similarities between 'legal compliance by design' and 'regulatory compliance', and factors hindering (semi-)automation. A later publication describes it as intermediate, semi-automated, hybrid, modular, adaptive and scalable, partial, flexible (Casanovas et al., 2017, p. 80).

[118] Hashmi et al. (2018), pp. 68–70. For instance, the KYC practices deployed by a regulated entity can either foster or hinder a financial inclusion policy, depending on whether the latter is considered when responding to its AML/CFT duties (Casanovas et al., 2017, pp. 46–47).

[119] Casanovas et al. (2017), pp. 46–47. Casanovas et al. (2022), p. 71. Outside the Law and Technology literature, Butler et al. (2023) similarly addresses the concept of 'regulation through information technology'.

[120] On the role of information systems (IS) research in this context: Hoess et al. (2024).

rules, standards, and best practices, and are increasingly important as regulatory instruments.[121] Because there is a tendency to turn to domestic implementations to protect national sovereignty, an important goal of global standards has been to avoid or mitigate the so-called 'forum shopping' or 'jurisdiction shopping'.

In addition, Chap. 5 overviewed the extent to which technical standardisation has addressed DLTs beyond the specific AML/CFT action of the FATF. When analysing these initiatives, one can notice how technical standards usually do not refer to existing regulatory frameworks and do not pursue the establishment of regulatory standards, even when they are seen as drivers for mitigation of regulatory risks.[122] Nonetheless, technical and regulatory standardisation features common aspects, chiefly pertaining to the interplay between regulatory agencies and the expertise held by the private sector. The lines are easily blurred between standards set by regulatory agencies and self-regulatory initiatives, and standardisation is often used to mitigate problems of information asymmetry between the industry and regulators. This asymmetry can be tackled by involving experts in regulatory processes or by adopting standards that can act as minimum safeguards.

7.4.1 'Embedded Compliance' Between (Dis)intermediation and Institutional Adoption

The value of embedded compliance in a sphere such as that of crypto-assets, with its cases of enhanced disintermediation, appears relatively straightforward. Given the array of stakeholders and platforms (perceived as) difficult or impossible to control, the idea of doing so 'by design' can be tempting. This reasoning, however, may give rise to misunderstandings. In the same way it is difficult or impossible to enforce regulation on and within non-centralised ecosystems, it can be difficult or impossible to ensure they embed compliance into their design (e.g., by adopting a specific RegTech tool) and monitor their compliance strategies. Hence, this approach is far from straightforward. As argued above, it may not be always possible or easy to reach the internal dynamics of the relevant ecosystems to the point of exerting an influence on the protocol. Indeed, a certain degree of (re)centralisation may be needed for players to actually embed compliance measures into a given technological solution.

Nonetheless, conceptually this argument should not be seen as a hindrance to advocating for a 'regulation-enabled compliance through design' approach. On the one hand, part of the crypto-asset space responds to socio-technical queries other than those of traditional market dynamics; on the other hand, a portion of these ecosystems will continue to lie outside the scope of regulation. Embedded compliance provides a key to unlock new opportunities, to be welcomed by players

[121] Casanovas et al. (2022), p. 78.

[122] König et al. (2020), p. 1. World Economic Forum (2020b).

pursuing recognition within regulated environments, while it is not feasible to define measures that will be implemented by every crypto-asset platform, tool or service provider. Meanwhile, as repeatedly argued, for now the crypto-asset sphere remains more centralised and intermediary-based than advertised, and the 'decentralised label' is elusive.[123]

In this context, crypto-asset intermediaries are exponentially offering their services not only to retail clients but also to institutional players such as investment funds. From a methodological perspective, this requires cross-sectoral and forward-looking regulation and supervision. From a substantive perspective, arguably they should be subject to the same type of regulation and oversight as intermediaries operating with traditional and economically (i.e., functionally) equivalent assets, also in terms of consumer/investor protection and AML/CFT.[124]

Relatedly a growing connection can be witnessed between crypto-asset ecosystems (and relevant platforms and stakeholders) and the mainstream financial system. The growth of the crypto-asset space and related activity performed by conventional intermediaries are factors that are increasingly interlinking traditional intermediaries (e.g., banks, PSPs, institutional investors) with nodes of crypto-asset ecosystems (e.g., exchanges, trading platforms). Hence, conventional intermediaries may be exposed to an unregulated 'shadow' financial system, either directly or indirectly.[125] Illustratively, from a direct perspective there are instances of regulated entities that started interacting with the market of DeFi services to offer this type of products.[126] Givén the amount of "lightly regulated shadow crypto" entities, the need arises for technology-neutral rules.[127] Indeed, the (purported) decentralised nature of crypto-assets does not eliminate the need to safeguard public policy objectives, and technology can be leveraged to enforce AML/CFT standards. In this context, the concept of embedded supervision was put forward to enhance data quality for supervisors and reduce compliance costs for firms.[128] The term 'regulatory automata' depicts a framework that enables automated supervision, where monitoring systems can use decentralised trust-creating mechanisms.[129]

---

[123] Auer (2022), p. 2.

[124] Auer et al. (2022b), pp. iii, 3, 16. For an insightful analysis of the benefits of applying the notions of functional equivalence and regulatory equivalence to the blockchain context, please see De Filippi et al. (2022), p. 368.

[125] For this reason, the need arises to apply a comprehensive risk assessment and risk mitigation approach (Auer et al. 2022b, pp. 3–4).

[126] Katona (2021), p. 93.

[127] Auer (2022), p. 2.

[128] Auer et al. (2022b), pp iii, 3, 16. Embedded supervision "is distinct from other forms of 'suptech' or 'regtech', which aim to use machine learning or artificial intelligence to more efficiently monitor the financial industry. The key principle of embedded supervision is to rely on the trust-creating mechanism of decentralised markets for regulatory purposes too" (Auer et al. 2022b, p. 19).

[129] Embedded supervisory systems could automatically verify compliance with Basel III standards of an entity holding asset-backed tokens. They could be designed for supervisors to access

However, these mechanisms need an effective underpinning legal system and supporting institutions. For instance, DLTs provide evidence of a transfer of an asset-backed token, but the legal system must guarantee the link between the asset and the digital token,[130] and frameworks must be developed to deal with the responsibility for financial crime. In this way, DLTs can improve the quality of compliance and lower the costs, improving the current situation that sees stakeholders lobbying for lighter regimes and supervisors struggling to apply AML/CFT standards to crypto-assets. While one operational aspect of embedded supervision is for regulators/supervisors to contribute to the design of the market (e.g., standardisation to ensure interoperability), another important element is the development of an open source set of monitoring tools to clarify the application of regulatory requirements.[131]

7.4.2 From 'Regulated Self-Regulation' to 'Polycentric Co-Regulation'

As outlined in Chap. 5, the global regulation of finance heavily relies on 'voluntary compliance', with low institutionalisation,[132] and its standardisation mirrors the evolution of the industry. Usually, self-regulation arises in a situation of minimal regulation, and it is introduced out of necessity: industry members self-regulate for the sake of growth and survival.[133] In this context, self-regulation may guide technological change, especially in the form of standardisation.[134] In a second phase, oversight regulation is generally driven by flaws of self-regulation,[135] whose notion is debated, notably regarding the relationship between 'regulation' and 'governance', and 'self-regulation' and 'co-regulation'.[136]

Even if regulation is often equated with governance,[137] one distinctive trait of the former is the involvement of public institutions. Hence, governing actions

---

all transaction-level data or selected parts, while firms would define access rights instead of collecting/delivering data (Auer 2022, pp. 2–3, 9).

[130] It is crucial 'asset tokenisation' is validated by the legal system. Likewise, additional institutions could be required to guarantee the accuracy of external elements relevant to smart contracts' payoffs (Auer 2022, p. 4).

[131] Auer (2022), pp. 6, 19–20.

[132] Newman and Bach (2014), p. 432. Chap. 4 provides details on dynamics and actors.

[133] E.g., hacks can drive market actors to establish self-regulatory schemes (Tsuchiya and Hiramoto 2021a, p. 3).

[134] Standardisation may even replace law in some domains (Finck 2019, p. 169).

[135] Johnstone (2021a), p. 136.

[136] While a deep analysis of the topic falls outside the scope of this work, an overview provides context to the deployed methodology. For context-specific analyses: Pagallo et al. (2019); Borrás and Edler (2020); Trubek and Trubek (2007); Hofmann et al. (2017).

[137] This is Black's position, referenced by Hofmann et al. (2017), p. 1411, Finck (2019), p. 145.

within market regulatory systems—e.g., corporate governance or industry standards/practices, if agnostically viewed by the law—are excluded.[138] Counterintuitively, these instances of self-regulation may not be labelled as regulation;[139] in this sense, self-regulation consists of "non-binding norms of action, process, and behaviour, for whom sanctions of the formal regulatory type play no part".[140] By contrast, if there is a formal institutional involvement there is co-regulation, featuring interactions between general legislation and a self-regulatory entity.[141] In these instances, self-regulatory efforts of the private sector are granted legitimacy by being framed within legislative/governmental regulation. The interactions between regulatory forces may occur with higher or lower intensity: institutional intervention may be indirect—e.g., sanctions for failures to adopt standards/codes of practice (i.e., enforced self-regulation).[142] The legislator may also lay out principles to be implemented by private actors, which are best positioned to give them practical application—e.g., principles-based regulation, of which both the AML/CFT regime (so far) and the GDPR are prominent examples.[143]

Moving to the crypto-asset domain, 'top-down' legislation could appear a natural approach. However, in line with the previous chapters, the literature accounts for four problems: (i) the information asymmetry generated by technological evolution stimulates ill-advised fact-selection and the adoption of ill-suited terminology; (ii) a framework can be onerous to enforce when there are misunderstandings on the technology and its limitations; (iii) specific rules run the risk of adding excessive burdens; and (iv) 'command-and-control' methods tend to be rigid and lack flexibility.[144] Hence, also in the crypto-asset sphere there are attempts to apply AML/CFT methodologies informed by approaches other than 'command and control', 'hard law' and 'top-down' methods. These approaches are focused on dialogue, principles, and incentives.[145] Yet, these initiatives have been rare.

From a first perspective, certain stakeholders have engaged in self-regulatory efforts. Notably, cases were reported of voluntary application of CDD measures to acquire commercial and competition advantages, responding to market dynamics. To the same end, some intermediaries have opted out of accepting AECs.[146] The diversity among crypto-asset stakeholders emerges once again as a relevant aspect, with some actors cherishing freedom from any centralised control and others

[138] Marsden (2011).

[139] 'Regulation' and 'self-regulation' may be difficult to differentiate: Bennett and Raab (2020), p. 454.

[140] Marsden (2011), p. 118.

[141] Marsden (2011), p. 1. Pagallo et al. (2019), p. 2.

[142] Terminological choices vary: 'enforced self-regulation' was labelled as 'meta-regulation' in Black (2012).

[143] Regarding the GDPR: Bennett and Raab (2020), p. 453.

[144] Finck (2019), pp. 166–167.

[145] Finck (2019), pp. 144–145.

[146] Houben (2019).

actively seeking to regulate themselves to legitimise their activities and be perceived by the market as legitimate players. In other words, the second group pursues to be accepted into commercial activities, to drive the industry's applications towards social benefit, but other stakeholders may also view regulatory compliance as a competitive advantage over those that cannot handle the attached burdens.[147]

Meanwhile, the concept of 'scheme governance authority' was put forward in 2014,[148] in the early days of the regulation of crypto-assets. This can be a described as a 'self-governance' initiative, but because it is mandated it becomes a form of direct regulation—namely, of 'regulated self-regulation', often equated to 'co-regulation'.[149] In this respect, a twofold argument was raised. If there is no voluntary centralised scheme it is difficult to apply these rules, since the mandatory set up is feasible for centralised schemes only.[150] Nonetheless, such establishment could ensure accountability to regulators and supervisors and could lay out the conditions to interact with regulated financial services.[151] Around the same time, the EC mentioned the option of a central database to register users' identities and crypto-asset addresses, coupled with a system of user registration. Experts have voiced doubts as to its efficacy when it comes to users engaging in illicit activities.[152]

These approaches were not successful, and more recent initiatives bear no mention to them. This is not to say innovative methodologies are to be ruled out, and indeed 'regulation-enabled compliance through design' may change the paradigm. However, the need arises to decide on a regulatory methodology to implement it. To assess the possible means of application of such a regime, its establishment can be imagined in a self-regulatory fashion. In these scenarios, as underlined by Finck (2019), isolated instances of self-regulation lack the transparency to safeguard diverse public and private interests, and fail to consider the positions of external actors, while it is necessary to handle information asymmetry. Accordingly, pure self-regulation is inappropriate, while co-regulation may combine flexibility with public policy goals. In other words, there is no single best regulatory technique, and a combination between designs was praised.[153]

Co-regulation emerges particularly interesting in designing an AML/CFT regime that is suitable to the specifics of crypto-assets. In EU law, in co-regulation the objectives are defined by the legislator and their attainment is conferred to specific parties such as economic operators, social partners, NGOs.[154] Co-regulation reflects

[147] Johnstone (2021a), p. 21.

[148] European Banking Authority (2014), p. 14. It was an entity accountable to the regulator, to be established internally by a crypto-asset scheme.

[149] Finck (2019), p. 686.

[150] Nabilou (2019), pp. 272–274.

[151] European Banking Authority (2014), pp 39–40.

[152] Houben (2019).

[153] Finck (2019), pp. 170–171.

[154] European Commission (2003), replaced by European Commission (2016), referenced by Finck (2019), pp. 172–173.

innovative governance traits, including a shared exercise of power, the possibility to experiment and create knowledge through various insights into the application of standards.[155] Indeed, co-regulation shows considerable advantages, as (i) it mirrors the need to involve private actors in a regulatory process while guaranteeing public oversight; (ii) it ensures the initiative's reflexiveness;[156] (iii) its flexibility enables 'regulatory experimentalism'; (iv) it identifies best practices; (v) it allows early intervention, and for regulators and regulated entities to engage in early dialogue and develop technology in a way that is compatible with public policy objectives.[157]

In the domain at hand, co-regulation reconciles the centralising and decentralising forces of the blockchain, that is inherently both local (node-wise) and global (network-wise), and possibly decentralised at the infrastructure level and centralised at the governance level. Co-regulation mirrors the fact that governance is influenced by legal, social, technical, economic standards. The approach is process-oriented and can involve many stakeholders (i.e., more than authorities and firms).[158] Thus, 'polycentric co-regulation' was put forward by Finck (2019) as an enhanced version of co-regulation, involving a wide array of stakeholders (polycentric) and tailored to technology (it can rely on code). In particular, authorities involve a diverse set of actors in drafting, implementing, and enforcing regulation, relying on the potential of code. This collaboration heeds technological requirements without unduly delegating regulatory authority or abandoning public policy objectives.[159] The benefits of code emerge in different phases, such as in (i) law making, where technology fosters polycentric participation and deliberation,[160] (ii) implementation,[161] and (iii) enforcement of regulatory constraints.[162]

---

[155] Finck (2019), pp. 172–173. These elements were identified in new governance by Scott and Trubek (2002).

[156] I.e., for it to be understood by the regulated autonomous social systems.

[157] Finck (2019), pp. 174–175. Ranchordás (2015).

[158] Finck (2019), pp. 175–176.

[159] Finck (2019), pp. 144–145, 165.

[160] Technology can support polycentricity with new ways to influence specific laws, while aiding disorganised groups to exert political influence (Wu 2003, referenced by Finck 2019, pp. 178–180). However, online participation raises issues of legitimacy, effectiveness, accountability (Finck 2019, referring to Brown and Marsden 2013, p. 3).

[161] For implementation, the model of 'endogenous regulation' was suggested, similar to co-regulation, for regulators to leverage collaboration with core developers to incorporate regulation into the DLT and applications running on top of it. Reyes (2016), p. 195, referenced by Finck (2019), pp. 178–180.

[162] Reference was made to the methodologies introduced by Reidenberg (1998) and Lessig (1996), referenced by Finck (2019), pp. 178–180, and to the fact that new techniques can provide real-time feedback and allow regulators to react swiftly (Kaal and Vermeulen 2017, referenced by Finck 2019, pp. 178–180).

7.4.3 From 'Law + Technology' to Techno-Regulatory Standards

An interesting take on the way to have a cross-disciplinary evolution of technology at the EU level was provided by Schrepel (2021b), who termed the 'law + technology' approach and contextualised it in relation to smart contracts. Within this framework, law and technology interact in a cooperative and complementary fashion, pursuing a preservation of their spheres of influence while building on their strengths. The approach respects the features of a technology (in this case, blockchain), as this is viewed as a key element to ensure the survival of the ecosystem, but allows enforcement. Accordingly, the characteristics of smart contracts and their environment are analysed through the 'law + technology' lens to detect influential aspects and understand how to safeguard the evolution of the Digital Single Market.[163]

The need to combine the two perspectives originates from the fact that a blockchain application has both legal and technical aspects, and if they do not cooperate "one would have to succeed before the other takes over", which generates unbalanced development of the applications.[164] Accordingly, it is pivotal to establish a stable line of communication between law and technology, the latter mostly in terms of stakeholders holding knowledge and influence on the given domain. As argued in Chap. 5, regulators access industry expertise in different ways. In some cases, they rely on private sector authorities (self-regulatory organisations) for technical advice and/or policy execution, and major regulatory authorities receive suggestions on regulatory strategies from stakeholder groups and private actors. However, the extent to which the private sector is formally involved in the decision-making process varies significantly. When self-regulatory organisations play a crucial role, their involvement can go beyond self-regulation.[165] This type of involvement is the one in 'polycentric co-regulation'.

As argued in Chap. 5, regulatory and technical standardisation are not detached. Two topical examples are (i) the ongoing debates on the crypto travel rule and on CBDC interoperability, explored in Chap. 6, and (ii) from a conceptual standpoint, the notion of 'polycentric co-regulation', exemplifying how embedded processes are at the heart of valuable methodologies today. From this perspective, cross-disciplinarity could be a step forward from cross-functionality—i.e., presence of

[163] The methodology opposes 'technical fundamentalism'". The latter "consists of designing technology without relying on legal rules, and sometimes is a way of avoiding it" and leads to 'temporary autonomous zones'' where law is not enforced. It threatens the survival of the technology, as outside the 'temporary autonomous zone' the application of the law can lead to its extinction. 'Technical fundamentalism' also includes the attitude of rejecting "any technical modification under the pretext that it contradicts some founding principles, such as those extolled by Satoshi Nakamoto" (Schrepel 2021b, p. 14).

[164] Schrepel (2021b), p. 14.

[165] Brummer (2015a), pp. 18, 32.

members with different experiences and responsibilities—currently praised in the FATF's architecture.[166] In this context, an interesting reflection is sparked by the parts of the AML Regulation, Regulation (EU) 2024/1624, that entrust to the AMLA the crafting of RTSs, ITSs, guidelines, recommendations for regulated entities, supervisors or FIUs, to improve clarity of the rules, ensure consistency with standards, promote supervisory convergence (Chap. 5).

RTSs and ITSs are delegated instruments adopted by the EC to ensure consistency in the application of the AML Regulation. They are technical by nature, do not imply strategic decisions or policy choices. Their content is limited by the delegating act, as provided for by Article 290 of the TFEU. As reported in Chap. 5, they are not a new concept. In the AML Package, RTSs are chiefly targeted to enhancing the application of an RBA-based CDD, and namely they shall:

(i) specify: (a) entities, sectors and transactions with higher money laundering and terrorist financing risk; (b) related thresholds for occasional transactions; (c) criteria to identify linked transactions. The RTSs must build on the inherent risk levels of business models and the EC's SRA.[167]
(ii) set out (i) minimum data to collect in standard, simplified and enhanced CDD, depending on the customer's risk level, (ii) simplified measures applicable to lower risk situations; (iii) reliable and independent sources to perform identity verification; (iv) list of attributes for an eID scheme and relevant trust services to fulfil the requirements.[168]
(iii) specify the minimum requirements of group-wide procedures and policies.[169]

In addition, the AMLA is expected to issue ITSs to provide a common EU template for reporting suspicious transactions, to ease compliance but boost the effectiveness of FIUs' analyses and cooperation.[170]

The rules-based nature of the AML Regulation is expected to provide a consistent framework for the AMLA to supervise its application. If multi-stakeholder participation is ensured in decision-making, for instance as provided by the model of 'polycentric co-regulation', this type of regulatory forum—and the underlying regulatory methodology—could fit the need for an innovative AML/CFT approach to the crypto-asset sphere.

7.5 Use Case: CBCD-Based Machine-to-Machine Payments

This section describes a preliminary model of application of a methodology along the lines of 'regulation-enabled compliance through design'. The use case concerns the interaction between the worlds of Consumer Internet of Things (CIoT), machine-

[166] That is, the combination of financial authorities and LEAs (Brummer 2015a, p. 106).
[167] Article 19(9) of Regulation (EU) 2024/1624.
[168] Article 28(1) of Regulation (EU) 2024/1624.
[169] Article 16(4) of Regulation (EU) 2024/1624.
[170] Article 69(3) of Regulation (EU) 2024/1624.

to-machine (M2M) communication, and retail CBDCs.[171] While the integration of digital fiat money into M2M dynamics may unlock a novel layer of socio-economic synergy, it also generates complex regulatory questions mirrored by trade-offs. This section portrays the inter-play between technological features and regulatory options, showcasing an embryonic example of cross-disciplinary dialogue. The background of the analysis consists of two pillars. On the one hand, the last decade has brought into our life smart objects that leverage connectivity to provide innovative services. CIoT is a subset of these items: an interconnected system of ubiquitous digital devices used by consumers on a personal basis—e.g., wearable watches, home assistants, smart vehicles.[172] On the other hand, as explored in Chap. 6 central banks are increasingly investigating retail CBDCs for public use.[173]

Since interactive e-devices can communicate in the M2M fashion, a future was foreseen where smart machines can (inter)act autonomously also from an economic perspective.[174] This concept gives birth to a 'M2M economy', that is decentralised and grounded on the autonomy of its participants (i.e., (C)IoT devices). The literature underlines the benefits of integrating DLTs into (C)IoT projects, where they are conducive to improvements in scalability and smart contracts increase communication efficiency and security by predefining conditions for transfers of data and assets.[175] Accordingly, DLTs and programmability could reportedly contribute in a substantial way to the 'M2M economy' reaching its full potential. Among the challenges arising from enabling smart devices to exchange data and services without (or with limited) human intervention, however, the need emerges for them to handle payments.[176] In this sense, M2M payments consist of integrating payment processes into an automated processing of business transactions. Without M2M payments, (C)IoT runs the risk of remaining a siloed fragment of the bigger picture. Integration needs to rely on information exchanges performed without interruptions dependent on human actions such as manual confirmation.[177]

7.5.1 *Applying 'Trade-Offs Through Design'*

The deployment of CBDCs in a (C)IoT scenario generates regulatory hurdles, including the current lack of a normative framework for device-to-device transactions, adequate standardisation measures, frameworks of machine identities to

---

171 Pocher and Zichichi (2022).

172 Mercan et al. (2021). The acronym (C)IoT signals the argument is deemed applicable to the broader complex of IoT devices.

173 Auer et al. (2021a); Pocher and Veneris (2022b).

174 Prasad and Rohokale (2020); Schweizer et al. (2020).

175 Barbosa et al. (2018); Pocher and Zichichi (2022).

176 Schweizer et al. (2020); Mercan et al. (2021).

177 PPI AG (2020); Pocher and Zichichi (2022).

support the legal effects of the activities they perform, and the need to re-design transaction safeguards that may hinder a true M2M scenario.[178] In this context, the large-scale interest in CBDCs can provide the opportunity to define normative goals at the beginning of the design process, tackling technical and legal aspects jointly. This is in line with the 'regulation-enabled compliance through design' approach. Against this backdrop, it was argued that the automation featured by (C)IoT solutions requires a payment system that is compliant by design.[179]

If one assumes, within the limits outlined above, that design and code can become regulatory instruments, a crucial role is played by the analysis of the specific features to be tuned. This applies also to the integration between (C)IoT and CBDCs. Since (C)IoT devices are used in large economic sectors and their core functionalities consist of sensing and collecting data, surveillance issues arise when privacy and data protection are not adequately safeguarded.[180] When financial transactions are placed into the equation, risks increase consistently, and a chief trade-off concerns the concurrent presence of privacy and transparency requirements—e.g., data protection and AML/CFT.[181] While, as argued in Chap. 3 and investigated in Chap. 6, the privacy-transparency tension is found in all means of payments, programmability generates new forms of control and disclosure of sensitive information,[182] and the added value of CBDCs is to embed from the start a specific trade-off. The main examples reviewed in Chap. 6 are (i) full transparency; (ii) unlimited privacy; (iii) nuanced solutions. The last option is deployed by the majority of CBDCs projects, offering some privacy to consumers, in the form of confidentiality, and some visibility to authorities, in terms of auditability.[183]

Relatedly, a CBDC scheme can deploy different types of (combinations of) wallets. Digital wallets store private and public keys used to sign transactions digitally, and their features influence the autonomy of (C)IoT devices and the non-centralisation of M2M communications. There are at least five wallet design options that can be highlighted:[184]

(i) In an M2M scenario, an account-based wallet limits the device's access to the payment process because human authentication is required. However, there could be a main account-based wallet and several token-based wallets for devices.[185]
(ii) With regard to hardware-based vs. software-based wallets, the choice will likely depend on the operation scenario of the device and on the required

[178] E.g., two-factor authentication. Forster et al. (2021).

[179] Pocher and Zichichi (2022).

[180] Ahlgren et al. (2016); Mercan et al. (2021); Jabbar et al. (2021).

[181] Pocher and Zichichi (2022).

[182] Allen et al. (2020b).

[183] Pocher and Veneris (2022b).

[184] Pocher and Zichichi (2022), pp. 7–8.

[185] For the limitations inherent to the distinction between account-based and token-based wallets, please see Chap. 6.

degree of security—e.g., the implementation of hardware-based solutions may be feasible for some CIoT devices, and more complex in other scenarios.

(iii) While token-based CBDCs can be held by custodians on behalf of end-users, account-based CBDCs are intrinsically based on the relationship with a custodian.[186] Hence, non-custodial wallets are suitable for CIoT devices and resonate better with distributed structures. It is possible to combine the two types to suit different needs within the same ecosystem.

(iv) The distinction between parent wallets and sub-wallets may provide a fruitful combination in a M2M scenario.[187] It is possible for the (human) holder to have a main wallet as parent wallet and open several sub-wallets, controlled by the parent wallet, to set payment limits or conditions. A device could use this type of sub-wallet to make autonomous payments.

(v) As mentioned in Chap. 6, one of the requirements for a CBDC model is to provide for (a certain degree of) offline usability. Some CIoT devices are likely to run into this situation on a frequent basis—e.g., a smart vehicle needing to pay at a tollbooth, but no connection is available when passing through the gates. Chapter 6 explored related hardware- and software-based design options.

In terms of embedded privacy-transparency trade-off, as outlined in Chap. 6 CBDC research is heeding 'mixed solutions' to offer certain anonymity and a desirable level of privacy.[188] These models provide multiple wallet options tailored to different types of transactions and users—e.g., higher degrees of anonymity for transactions of low value. To do so, they may offer anonymity-oriented wallets but only to perform selected types of transactions. Ostensibly, albeit not necessarily, an anonymity-oriented CBDC is usually token-based. In this respect, it was argued users should be able to hold their CBDC tokens in a non-custodial fashion in compliance with the principle of 'privacy by design'.[189] This, combined with the mentioned limits in terms of amounts and types of transactions, appears suitable to smart devices. However, the model below shows this argument can also be nuanced, without being disregarded, within a scheme of tiered wallets with a main account-based wallet controlling token-based sub-wallets, thus implementing a different trade-off.[190]

---

[186] Goodell et al. (2021).

[187] The distinction concerns authorisation. A main parent wallet can be compared to a generic bank account for the use of fiat currency, while sub-wallets are comparable to prepaid cards linked to the account and with a limited amount of fiat.

[188] Pocher and Veneris (2022b).

[189] Goodell et al. (2021).

[190] Pocher and Zichichi (2022).

7.5.2 A Preliminary Model of Techno-Regulatory Integration

As anticipated, the deployment of DLTs in a scenario populated by billions of economically autonomous smart devices was deemed conducive to handle the necessary techno-regulatory requirements.[191] Seemingly, DLT-based means of payment are suitable to integrate payments into the CIoT, thus avoiding human involvement, manual confirmations and/or the need for exchanges between tokens. Nonetheless, beside the value of DLTs, it is the nature of retail CBDCs as fiat money that plays a key role in merging the physical and digital worlds in a seamless fashion, grounding the possible model for a two-tier retail CBDC system based on a DLT.[192]

The integration between a two-tier retail CBDC and CIoT is multi-layered, and a set of structural options must be tailored to the needs and constraints of smart devices. A preliminary model is displayed in Fig. 7.1. Smart machines are equipped with non-custodial token-based sub-wallets loaded with a given budget to pay automatically and independently, while (human) end-users hold custodial account-based parent wallets that rely on authentication and control the devices' wallets. The combination of the two wallet types safeguards privacy and allows trade-offs to be designed in a more flexible way.[193] As argued in Chap. 6, the integration between retail CBDCs, M2M payments and CIoT also requires multi-stakeholder-based standardisation, and CBDC projects seem to provide an invaluable opportunity to

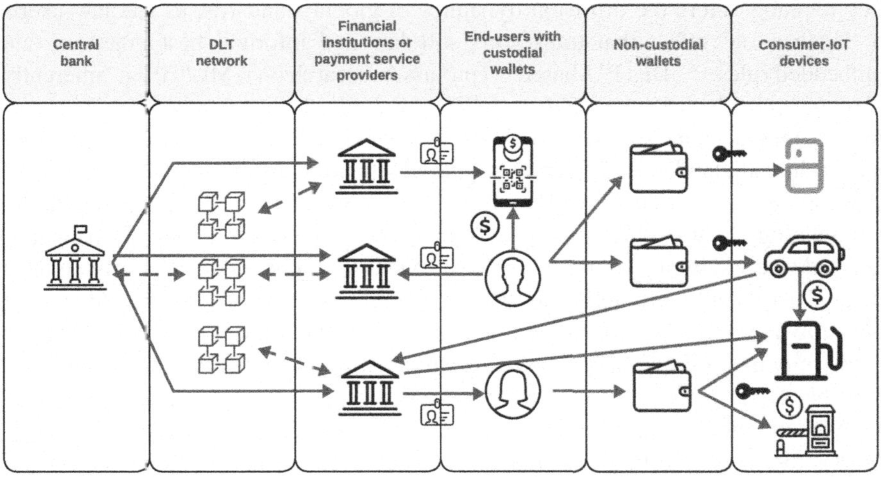

Fig. 7.1 Preliminary model of techno-regulatory integration in the field of Consumer IoT. Based on Pocher and Zichichi (2022)

---

[191] Schweizer et al. (2020); Forster et al. (2021); Pocher and Zichichi (2022).

[192] Pocher and Zichichi (2022).

[193] Pocher and Zichichi (2022).

develop it. Accordingly, the relevance emerges of applying 'by design' techniques to address regulatory concerns, especially when they generate seemingly opposing requirements. In this context, the deployment of DLTs in a CBDC design is conducive to reaching and embedding desired trade-offs.

7.6 The Intervention of EU Law: Notes on Legitimacy and Effectiveness

As outlined in Chap. 5, a considerable portion of the EU activity in the AML/CFT domain consists of transposing FATF Standards. Accordingly, the measures adopted at the EU level are closely intertwined with the Recommendations, also because the increasingly cross-border and international nature of money laundering and terrorist financing would make siloed Union actions largely ineffective. Hence the value of international coordination and cooperation and of adopting rules compatible with, or at least as stringent as, international ones.[194] This consideration underpins this work when addressing the AML/CFT regulation of crypto-asset ecosystems starting from international standardisation, which links the methodology to the broader sphere of global financial regulation as a compound of rules, standards, best-practices.

Although the concrete value of the tie between EU and international measures is undisputed, their formal relationship is more complex. Transposition into EU law arguably alters the diffusion dynamics of global standards, as EU law exerts a 'legalisation' effect that transforms soft law and informal best practices into embedded rules.[195] This EU-based crypto-asset research on AML/CFT is inherently challenged by the interplay between FATF Standards, the technical nature of crypto-asset compliance, the mechanisms of EU law, and the dynamics between regulatory and technical standards. Evidently, crypto-assets are constantly evolving and will develop in ways difficult to foretell. These circumstances call for a regulatory methodology that is 'flexible by design'—i.e., applicable to new instruments, networks, ecosystems, as they emerge. This is a major value of establishing a cross-disciplinary working group. Indeed, the process of laying out benchmarks to construe a crypto-asset taxonomy that accounts for the relevant trade-offs between anonymity and transparency should be conducted in a way that is as future-proof as possible.

As mentioned above, a valuable regulatory approach to the AML/CFT challenges of crypto-assets entails the design of a taxonomy framework to classify crypto-asset ecosystems from a functional perspective (i.e., according to their risk), in combination with the techno-legal reasons that ground the classification (i.e., parameterised criteria). The taxonomy instrument has already showcased its capacity of combining flexibility with precision in cross-disciplinary endeavours (Chap. 2).

[194] Recital 4 of Regulation (EU) 2024/1624.

[195] Newman and Bach (2014), pp. 430–432.

An interdisciplinary body of knowledge can then be leveraged to establish a regime of techno-regulatory standardisation as per a 'regulation-enabled compliance through design' methodology. Likewise, to create a future-proof instrument the taxonomy design should embody a combination of principles-based and rules-based approaches.

The final objective is to develop regulatory and compliance decisions that draw from the findings of the taxonomy—e.g., use its benchmarks as criteria on which to ground decisions—to shape a framework to apply AML/CFT to crypto-assets. Illustratively, when a given use case is at the extreme end of the anonymity scale, the given transactions—in the given crypto-asset or processed by a given entity—could be outlawed or limited if risks are deemed too high to be addressed by regulated entities. Limitations pertaining to e-money testify that trade-offs have already been established in the sphere of digital payments, thus there is no reason to use different standards for crypto-assets. Concurrently, the cross-disciplinary collaboration and development of common references (e.g., the taxonomy) could give rise to 'regulation-enabled compliance through design' mechanisms. The parameterisation of the risk levels could spur an application of these criteria to ensure compliance of a specific tool with the framework.

7.6.1 Legitimacy and the Need for Uniformity

The overarching role of global financial regulation, and notably the activity of the FATF, and the inherent cross-border nature of crypto-asset ecosystems, may challenge the EU involvement in crypto-asset regulation also in the AML/CFT domain. However, the mentioned complexities and the integration of the (Digital) Single Market warrant the involvement of EU law as the prime means to address the type of regulation foreseen in this work. As outlined in Chap. 5, AML/CFT measures are not a standalone framework in the EU, rather they interact with other areas such as payments and transfer of funds, financial services, criminal law, the eIDAS/eIDAS 2.0 regime. To a varying degree of intensity, depending on the specificity of the regimes, managing AML/CFT regulatory issues at the EU level also safeguards their interplays with other frameworks. In this context, EU-level integration can provide a powerful playing field to the regulatable portion of the crypto-asset space, while the considerable literature, policy and regulatory documents pertaining to AML/CFT harmonisation arguably provides an extensive array of arguments defending the role of EU law.

Since the application of DLT-based solutions to the financial sphere (later encompassing solutions not necessarily DLT-based) emerged as a disruptive techno-economic phenomenon, the latter calls for EU institutions to adopt an innovation-friendly approach combined with a critical analysis of relevant developments, to design sensible regulatory responses that can safeguard public policy objectives.[196]

[196] Decisions to be made go way beyond banning or allowing a use case. Sensible frameworks that balance innovation with public policy are needed and require a deep understanding of the technology (Finck 2019, p. 144).

To this end, "the cooperation of law and technology requires a uniform approach across the European space".[197] Indeed, the cross-border nature of (public permissionless) blockchain applications makes it difficult for developers and users to decide to comply only with the regulation of a given jurisdiction. For this reason, the effects of a national regime would not necessarily be limited to it, and a strong 'Brussels effect' was foreseen.[198] It is for this reason that 'law + technology' methodologies argue EU members could coordinate their actions and subsequent implementation strategies, especially when targeting the 'layer 1' of blockchains, thus influencing the architecture of the given blockchain, its core software.[199]

From this perspective, 'polycentric co-regulation' allows a technology-enabled expansion of the actors involved in the regulatory process. This could play a role in meeting the needs of consistency with values of democracy, participation, representation, and pluralism, and of decentralisation and experimentation required by crypto-assets. Accordingly, provided transparency is ensured within the co-regulation procedures, the approach could mitigate the accusations of democratic and legitimacy deficits currently tainting the activities of EU institutions.[200]

Evidently, controversies could arise in terms of legitimacy and legal basis regarding specificities of the taxonomy-based 'regulation-enabled compliance through design' approach.[201] This may depend significantly on the results of the taxonomy effort, which could suggest addressing them at a later stage. In any case, as explored in Chap. 5, one can witness an increasing opening of EU law towards the adoption of regulation-based regimes not only in the AML/CFT domain. From the perspective of regulatory methodology, one may focus on the legal instrument's shift in recent EU actions from the long-established directive-based approach of minimum harmonisation, to a regulation-based that aims to achieve uniformity for the foundational aspects of the regulatory frameworks. As outlined in Chap. 5, the methodology underpinned both the AML and the Digital Finance Packages, based on Article 114 of the TFEU on the approximation of laws, as it is necessary to the functioning of the internal market. The choice of legal basis was justified, respectively, to remove establishment obstacles and improve the functioning of the internal market for financial services,[202] and because money laundering and

[197] Schrepel (2021b).

[198] I.e., the type of unilateral regulatory globalisation by the hands of which rules originally adopted in a jurisdiction expand to the economic life of the marketplace at a global level.

[199] Schrepel (2021b), p. 15. 'Layer 2', instead, includes the technology and the applications that are deployed on top of the blockchain protocol (e.g., it is the layer where smart contracts work).

[200] Verbruggen (2009). Finck (2019), pp. 177–178. "Indeed, while the Union never regulates in isolation and is influenced by industry views even outside co-regulatory contexts, the latter technique can make such engagement explicit and add transparency." (Finck 2019, pp. 177–178).

[201] For an account of the existing controversies regarding regulation and risk assessments, the interested reader may refer to Yeung and Ranchordás (2024), pp. 41–77.

[202] European Commission (2020b), p. 4.

terrorist financing can generate cross-border economic losses, functional disruption, reputational damage.[203]

7.6.2 *Effectiveness: Standards and Flexibility 'Through Design'*

The concrete ways to move from the process of devising a taxonomy, which can subsequently inform a 'regulation-enabled compliance through design' regime, to embedding measures into technology are yet to be explored. Similarly, the specific method to combine the application of rules-bases and principles-based methodologies in the building stage of the taxonomy entails specific complexities that are to be addressed, especially since the link between the two frames of reference is not as clear as one could hope. In this respect, the AML/CFT regime offers an interesting field of experimentation because its measures are inherently shaped by the RBA—thus, their application is by nature tailored to the principle of proportionality, which demands a preliminary assessment of the levels of risk—and the RBA is in turn moulded on a multi-level variety of risk indicators that contribute to shaping final compliance outputs. Hence, a taxonomy-based 'regulation-enabled compliance through design' approach, within the meaning argued above, is inherently consistent with an RBA-based regime, and provides a degree of flexibility that can attempt to mitigate the mentioned risk of overfitting.

In this context, an important role is played by red flag indicators and the possibility to transpose them, leveraging a 'transposition model' to be devised, into techno-regulatory standards to clarify and benchmark their meaning and streamline their application. Notably, this 'regulatory experimentation' could take place within the framework of the responsibilities and competences thrust on the AMLA. Their implementation could be eased by developing the standards directly with the private sector offering crypto-asset analytics services and sharing them in an open-source format. Among indicators, anonymity risks are among the most relevant given their role as drivers of the regulation of the crypto-asset space.

In terms of effectiveness of this regulatory methodology, at least two other problems emerge. On the one hand, embedded regulation still needs an opening into (i.e., access to) these ecosystems. Considering the increasing tendencies of crypto-assets towards disintermediation, one cannot forget that this type of access is remarkably difficult to obtain (or even impossible to achieve) when there is no centralisation of power of any kind at the socio-technical level. On the other hand, the enforcement of any regulatory provision in the crypto-asset space is susceptible to generating controversies related to the origin and ideological roots of this sphere, as well as to the privacy and data protection elements outlined throughout this work.

---

[203] European Commission (2021a), p. 4.

Foreseeably, a fruitful cross-disciplinary and cross-industry cooperation, also in the form of PPPs, could aid the establishment of a fit-for-purpose enforcement strategy.

7.6.3 The Role of the EU in Setting Techno-Regulatory Standards

As mentioned above and explored in Chap. 5, the EU AML Package not only introduced a new domain-specific and EU-wide supervisory authority, the AMLA, but also entrusted it with a comprehensive drafting of operational specifications. The latter are addressed to a wide array of stakeholders, and cover the foundational aspects of the AML/CFT regime from a compliance perspective. Indeed, among its manifold competences, the AMLA is expected to adopt RTSs, ITSs, guidelines and recommendations for regulated entities, supervisors and/or FIUs, to improve the degree of clarity of AML/CFT rules, to ensure the consistency of EU measures with international standards, and to promote supervisory convergence.[204]

In this context, the AMLA framework could provide a suitable institutional and procedural background against which to implement regulatory solutions that blend the need for flexibility with that of ensuring an EU-wide common approach to the combination between law and technology. From a content perspective, however, these RTSs could be shaped in a more innovative fashion also in terms of drafting style. This would mirror in a more detailed way the dynamics between technical and regulatory provisions in a way that goes beyond what was done so far in the available examples of RTSs. To this end, the AMLA regime and its links with the procedures to adopt RTSs' proposals could be explored further, in combination with the impacts on EU law legitimacy. In broad terms, large-scale stakeholder involvement may mitigate most concerns.

Relatedly, Finck (2019) highlighted the risk of intra-EU fragmentation due to different national regimes, and an even more worrisome risk of 'race to the bottom'. In this regard, the usual EU response—i.e., issuance of a supranational framework—may not be viable in the crypto-asset space because of the insufficient capability of performing comprehensive assessments on the legal implications of blockchain technology and related innovation capacities.[205] Although from an AML/CFT perspective a supranational framework has already been introduced (Chap. 5.), these considerations can be applied to its specifications and implementing measures—e.g., RTSs and ITSs. Indeed, AML/CFT rules affect socio-economic and legal areas perceived as sensitive to the sovereignty of the Member States.

Going back to the reasoning by Finck (2019), for complex technology-related matters even when there is consensus on the appropriateness of a regulatory reform, there may be no certainty as to the principles to include and no political consensus

[204] Articles 1, 5 and 6 of Regulation (EU) 2024/1620.

[205] Finck (2019), pp. 180–181.

on overhauling (supra)national values. For this reason, she mentions the possibility to devise a '28th regime', that consists of an EU-framework that is alternative to national rules but does not replace them.[206] An example could be, in the case at hand, a set of techno-regulatory standards the industry can comply with on a voluntary basis. The goal would be to give an additional opportunity to stakeholders active in a cross-border fashion, fight the 'race to the bottom', and possibly lead to the adoption of standard secondary legislation.[207]

However, a 28th regime instead of regulatory uniformity through an institutionalised techno-regulatory model would not be a suitable methodology to adequately address the specifics of the AML/CFT sphere and crypto-asset ecosystems. This is largely due to the nature of the AML/CFT framework, in terms of protected values and interests, in the realm of financial system integrity, especially taking into consideration the inherently cross-border dynamics explored throughout this work for what concerns crypto-asset-related activities. Indeed, without a uniform approach the framework would still suffer from the significant fragmentation that drove the drafting of the AML Package, and in a broader sense also that of the Digital Finance Package. Moreover, the procedural specificities of 'polycentric co-regulation' and its combination with the taxonomy-based and 'regulation-enabled compliance through design' methodologies are elements that precisely aim to solve, or at least mitigate, some of the issues that usually arise when establishing a supranational regime that is perceived as too intrusive at a national level.

7.7 Conclusions

Against the backdrop of the increasing complexity of crypto-asset-related regulation, this chapter explored key aspects of a possible methodology to be applied at the EU level in the AML/CFT sphere. The chapter considered (i) the concurrent and ever-evolving presence of multiple assets, technologies, innovative and traditional stakeholders in the socio-technical ecosystems that compose the crypto-asset space; (ii) the diverse approaches put forward over recent years with respect to the regulation of new technologies; (iii) their interplay with the elements that, as outlined in the previous chapters, inform the AML/CFT regime. The analysis set out by overviewing the impacts of technology-based and individual-based regulation, as well as of mixed solutions, on the domain at hand. Accordingly, it underlined how, instead of aiming to eliminate crypto-asset-related risks once and for all, the goal can be to establish flexible and teleologically oriented frameworks that evolve

[206] The '28th regime' is a concept put forward by Monti (2010), referenced by Finck (2019), pp 180–181. A key example of this approach, also known as 'optional instrument', is the regime of the Societas Europaea introduced by Council Regulation (EC) No 2157/2001.

[207] In the meantime, the approach could help reflect on the process to adapt regulation to technological innovation, to serve both private and public interests (Finck 2019, pp. 180–181).

with technology. Relatedly, this chapter outlined the types of interplay DLT-based applications can have with regulatory frameworks and focused on the proactive instances of 'structured experimentalism' (e.g., regulatory sandboxes) that could replace reactive regulatory approaches.

Furthermore, it provided an overview of a set of methodological features of AML/CFT regulation, tailoring the analysis to anonymity-transparency trade-offs. Accordingly, it proposed the creation of a taxonomy to evaluate the levels of anonymity risk posed by crypto-assets and/or ecosystems, possibly leveraging a combination between principles-based and rules-based methods, claiming the participation of a large array of actors in regulatory processes may provide a substantial insight into the risks to be mitigated. Meanwhile, it suggested the creation of a 'transposition model' between red flag indicators (e.g., the ones of the FATF) and techno-regulatory standards, and explored the effects of enhanced disintermediation. The third section of the chapter investigated the possible shift from the widely known and criticised 'code is law' to a compound concept of 'regulation-enabled compliance through design', focusing on the communication level between technology and regulation, while it overviewed the underlying concepts of embedded regulation and embedded compliance, as well as related evolutions. It underlined the importance of tech-sensitive regulation and how the effectiveness of 'active cooperation' is vulnerable to criticism, while a proactive approach is needed. It underlined the importance of focusing on the mutual relation between regulation and code, without the need to equate or compare the two concepts. In this context, a key aspect is building on existing cross-disciplinary initiatives and furthering multi-stakeholder dialogue.

In the following, the chapter elaborated on the value of techno-regulatory standards and of placing their adoption within a polycentricity-based model of co-regulation. Accordingly, it assessed the role of techno-regulatory standards and elements of a possible methodology, exploring the differences between 'self-regulation', 'co-regulation' and the concept of 'law + technology'. Later, it provided an embryonic use case of the proposed approach, to exemplify the content of a model of techno-regulatory integration as an example of the type of communication to be institutionalised. Finally, it reviewed methodological elements for the intervention of EU law in the AML/CFT regulation of crypto-asset ecosystems in terms of legitimacy and effectiveness, overviewing the role of EU institutions in the design and implementation of such an innovative methodology. It considered the relationship of EU law with FATF Standards and global financial regulation, and the substantial and procedural value of establishing cross-disciplinary frameworks in line with the 'polycentric co-regulation' model. In particular, it suggested exploring the implementation of the regime within the competences of the AMLA—i.e., AMLA's role in drafting RTSs—, albeit possibly considering innovative drafting styles, to go beyond what was achieved by past instances of these instruments.

References

Ahlgren, B., Hidell, M., & Ngai, E. C.-H. (2016). Internet of things for smart cities: Interoperability and open data. *IEEE Internet Computing, 20*(6), 52–56. https://doi.org/10.1109/MIC.2016.124

Allen, S., Capkun, S., Eyal, I., Fanti, G., Ford, B., Grimmelmann, J., Juels, A., Kostiainen, K., Meiklejohn, S., Miller, A., Prasad, E., Wuest, K., & Zhang, F. (2020a). Design choices for central bank digital currency: Policy and technical considerations. https://ftp.iza.org/dp13535.pdf

Altschuler, S. (2022). Should centralized exchange regulations apply to cryptocurrency protocols. *Stanford Journal of Blockchain Law & Policy, 5*(1), 92–113.

Antonopoulos, A. M. (2021). Keynote address at the harvard law school blockchain and fintech initiative third annual conference: The rise of decentralized finance.

Arner, D. W., Zetzsche, D. A., Buckley, R. P., & Barberis, J. N. (2019). The identity challenge in finance: From analogue identity to digitized identification to digital KYC utilities. *European Business Organisation Law Review, 20*(1), 55–80. https://doi.org/10.1007/s40804-019-00135-1

Article 19. (2015). Right to online anonymity - policy brief. https://www.article19.org/data/files/medialibrary/38006/Anonymity_and_encryption_report_A5_final-web.pdf

Athan, T., Governatori, G., Palmirani, M., Paschke, A., & Wyner, A. (2014). Legal interpretations in legalruleml. In *Proceedings of SW4LAW+ DC@ JURIX*. https://ceur-ws.org/Vol-1296/paper2.pdf

Athan, T., Governatori, G., Palmirani, M., Paschke, A., & Wyner, A. (2016). Legalruleml: Design principles and foundations. In W. Faber & A. Paschke (Eds.), *Proceedings of the Reasoning Web International Summer School. Lecture notes in computer science* (pp. 151–188). Springer. https://doi.org/10.1007/978-3-319-21768-0_6

Auer, R. (2022). Embedded supervision: How to build regulation into decentralised finance. https://www.bis.org/publ/work811.pdf

Auer, R, Boar, C., Cornelli, G., Frost, J., Holden, H., & Wehrli, A. (2021). CBDCs beyond borders: Results from a survey of central banks. https://www.bis.org/publ/bppdf/bispap116.htm

Auer, R., Farag, M., Lewrick, U., Orazem, L., & Zoss, M. (2022). Banking in the shadow of bitcoin? The institutional adoption of cryptocurrencies. https://www.bis.org/publ/work1013.htm

Barbereau, T., & Bodó, B. (2023). Beyond financial regulation of crypto-asset wallet software: In search of secondary liability. *Computer Law & Security Review, 49*, 105829. https://doi.org/10.1016/j.clsr.2023.105829

Barbosa, A. C., Oliveira, T. A., & Coelho, V. N. (2018). Cryptocurrencies for smart territories: An exploratory study. In *Proceedings of the International Joint Conference on Neural Networks (IJCNN)* (pp. 1–8). https://doi.org/10.1109/IJCNN.2018.8489299

Bennett, C. J., & Raab, C. D. (2020). Revisiting the governance of privacy: Contemporary policy instruments in global perspective. *Regulation and Governance, 14*(3), 447–464. https://doi.org/10.1111/rego.12222

Benson, G. J., Bromwich, M., & Wagenhofer, A. (2006). Principles-versus rules-based accounting standards: The fasb's standard setting strategy. *ABACUS – A Journal of Accounting, Finance and Business Studies, 42*(2). https://doi.org/10.1111/j.1467-6281.2006.00196.x

BitKom. (2020). Decentralized finance (DEFI)—A new fintech revolution? The blockchain trend explained. https://www.bitkom.org/sites/default/files/2020-07/200729_whitepaper_decentralized-finance.pdf

Black, J. (2002). Critical reflections on regulation. *Australian Journal of Legal Philosophy, 27*, 1–35.

Black, J. (2012). Paradoxes and failures: 'New governance' techniques and the financial crisis. *Modern Law Review, 75*(6), 1037–1063. https://doi.org/10.1111/j.1468-2230.2012.00936.x

Black, J., Hopper, M., & Band, C. (2007). Making a success of principles-based regulation. *Law and Financial Markets Review, 1*, 191–206. https://doi.org/10.1080/17521440.2007.11427879

Borrás, S., & Edler, J. (2020). The roles of the state in the governance of socio-technical systems' transformation. *Research Policy, 49*(5), 103971. https://doi.org/10.1016/j.respol.2020.103971

Brown, I., & Marsden, C. (2013). *Regulating code*. MIT Press.

Brummer, C. (2015). The architecture of international financial law. In *Soft law and the global financial system: Rule-making in the 21st century*. Cambridge University Press. https://doi.org/10.1017/CBO9781316423875.004

Buckley, R. P., Arner, D. W., & Zetzsche, D. A. (2023). *FinTech: Finance, technology and regulation*. Cambridge University Press. https://doi.org/10.1017/9781009086943

Butler, T., Gozman, D., & Lyytinen, K. (2023). The regulation of and through information technology: Towards a conceptual ontology for IS research. *Journal of Information Technology, 38*(2), 86–107. ISSN 0268-3962, 1466-4437. https://doi.org/10.1177/02683962231181147

Carter, R. B., & Marchant, G. E. (2011). Principles-based regulation and emerging technology. In G. E. Marchant, B. R. Allenby, & J. R. Herkert (Eds.), *The growing gap between emerging technologies and legal-ethical oversight*. Springer. https://doi.org/10.1007/978-94-007-1356-7_10

Casanovas, P., de Koker, L., & Hashmi, M. (2022). Law, socio-legal governance, the internet of things, and industry 4.0: A middle-out/inside-out approach. *Multidisciplinary Scientific Journal, 5*, 64–91. https://doi.org/10.3390/j5010005

Casanovas, P., González-Conejero, J., & de Koker, L. (2017). Legal compliance by design (LCBD) and through design (LCTD): Preliminary survey. In *Proceedings of the 1st Workshop on Technologies for Regulatory Compliance at the 30th International Conference on Legal Knowledge and Information Systems (JURIX)*. https://ceur-ws.org/Vol-2049/05paper.pdf

Cavoukian, A. (2011). *Privacy by design*. Office of the Information and Privacy Commissioner.

Cervone, L., Palmirani, M., & Vitali, F. (2020). The intelligible contract. In *Proceedings of the 53rd Hawaii International Conference on System Science*. http://hdl.handle.net/10125/63959

Council Regulation (EC) No 2157/2001. (2001). Council regulation (EC) no 2157/2001 on the statute for a European company (SE). http://data.europa.eu/eli/reg/2001/2157/oj

Crepaldi, M. (2019). *The Authority of Distributed Consensus Systems: Trust, Governance, and Normative Perspectives on Distributed Ledgers*. Ph.D. Thesis, University of Bologna. 10.6092/unibo/amsdottorato/9432

De Filippi, P., & Hassan, S. (2016). Blockchain technology as a regulatory technology: From code is law to law is code. *First Monday, 21*. https://doi.org/10.5210/fm.v21i12.7113

De Filippi, P., Mannan, M., & Reijers, W. (2022). The alegality of blockchain technology. *Policy and Society, 41*(3), 358–372. https://doi.org/10.1093/polsoc/puac006

De Filippi, P., & Wright, A. (2018). *Blockchain and the law: The rule of code*. Harvard University Press. https://doi.org/10.2307/j.ctv2867sp

Dimyadi, J., Governatori, G., & Amor, R. (2017). Evaluating legaldocml and legalruleml as a standard for sharing normative information in the AEC/FM domain. In *Proceedings of the Lean and Computing in Construction Congress*. https://doi.org/10.24928/JC3-2017/0012

Eddin, A. N., Bono, J., Aparício, D., Polido, D., Ascensão, J. T., Bizarro, P., & Ribeiro, P. (2021). Anti-money laundering alert optimisation using machine learning with graphs. https://arxiv.org/abs/2112.07508

Edmunds, J. C. (2020). *Rogue money and the underground economy: An encyclopedia of alternative and cryptocurrencies*. ABC-CLIO.

European Banking Authority. (2014). Eba opinion on 'virtual currencies'. https://www.eba.europa.eu/sites/default/files/documents/10180/657547/81409b94-4222-45d7-ba3b-7deb5863ab57/EBA-Op-2014-08

European Central Bank and Bank of Japan. (2020). Balancing confidentiality and auditability in a distributed ledger environment. https://www.ecb.europa.eu/paym/intro/publications/pdf/ecb.miptopical200212.en.pdf

European Commission. (2003). Interinstitutional agreement on better law-making. https://eur-lex.europa.eu/legal-content/EN/TXT/?uri=CELEX%3A32003Y0724(01)

European Commission. (2016). Interinstitutional agreement between the european parliament, the council of the European union and the European commission on better law-making. https://eur-lex.europa.eu/legal-content/EN/TXT/?uri=CELEX%3A32016Y1021(01)

European Commission. (2020). Proposal for a regulation of the european parliament and of the council on markets in crypto-assets, and amending Directive (EU) 2019/1937.https://eur-lex.europa.eu/legal-content/EN/TXT/?uri=CELEX%3A52020PC0593

European Commission. (2021). Proposal for a regulation of the European parliament and of the council on the prevention of the use of the financial system for the purposes of money laundering or terrorist financing. https://eur-lex.europa.eu/legal-content/EN/TXT/?uri=CELEX%3A52021PC0420

Financial Action Task Force. (2020). 12-month review of the revised fatf standards – virtual assets and virtual asset service providers. http://www.fatf-gafi.org/media/fatf/documents/recommendations/12-Month-Review-Revised-FATF-Standards-Virtual-Assets-VASPS.pdf

Financial Action Task Force. (2020). Virtual assets red flag indicators of money laundering and terrorist financing. https://www.fatf-gafi.org/media/fatf/documents/recommendations/Virtual-Assets-Red-Flag-Indicators.pdf

Finck, M. (2019). *Blockchain regulation and governance in Europe*. Cambridge University Press. https://doi.org/10.1017/9781108609708

Forster, M., Gross, J., Kamping, A. K., Katilmis, S., Reichel, M., Sandner, P., & Schröder, P. (2021). The future of payments: Programmable payments in the IoT sector. https://jonasgross.medium.com/the-future-of-payments-programmable-payments-for-the-internet-of-things-iot-46460c74cef1

Genesereth, M. (2015). Computational law: The cop in the backseat. https://law.stanford.edu/publications/computational-law-the-cop-in-the-backseat/

Genesereth, M. (2021). What is computational law? https://law.stanford.edu/2021/03/10/what-is-computational-law/

Goldbarsht, D., & de Koker, L. (2022). From paper money to digital assets: Financial technology and the risks of criminal abuse. In D. Goldbarsht & L. de Koker (Eds.), *Financial technology and the law. Combating financial crime* (vol. 47, pp. 1–15). Springer. https://doi.org/10.1007/978-3-030-88036-1_1

Goodell, G., Al-Nakib, H. D., & Tasca, P. (2021). A digital currency architecture for privacy and owner-custodianship. *Future Internet, 13*. https://doi.org/10.3390/fi13050130

Grigg, I. (2000). Financial cryptography in 7 layers. In *Proceedings of the Financial Cryptography Fourth International Conference*. https://doi.org/10.1007/3-540-45472-1_23

Grigg, I. (2004). The ricardian contract. In *Proceedings of the First IEEE International Workshop on Electronic Contracting*. https://doi.org/10.1109/WEC.2004.1319505

Gurrea-Martínez, A., & Remolina, N. (2019). The law and finance of initial coin offerings. In *Cryptoassets: Legal, regulatory, and monetary perspectives*. Oxford University Press. https://doi.org/10.1093/oso/9780190077310.003.0006

Hacker, P., Lianos, I., Dimitropoulos, G., & Eich, S. (2019). *Regulating blockchain: Techno-social and legal challenges*. Oxford University Press. https://doi.org/10.1093/oso/9780198842187.001.0001

Hashmi, M., Casanovas, P., & de Koker, L. (2018). Legal compliance through design: Preliminary results of a literature survey. In *Proceedings of the 2nd Workshop on Technologies for Regulatory Compliance (TERECOM) Co-located with the 31st International Conference on Legal Knowledge and Information Systems (JURIX)*. https://ceur-ws.org/Vol-2309/06.pdf

Hassan, S., & de Filippi, P. (2017). The expansion of algorithmic governance: From code is law to law is code. *Field Actions Science Reports, 17*, 88–90. https://journals.openedition.org/factsreports/4518

Herian, R. (2019). *Regulating blockchain: Critical perspectives in law and technology*. Routledge. https://doi.org/10.4324/9780429489815

Hoess, A., Pocher, N., Roth, T., & Fridgen, G. (2024). Towards a design science research process for legal compliance by design. In *Proceedings of the Pacific Asia Conference on Information Systems (PACIS)*. https://aisel.aisnet.org/pacis2024/track04_dessci/track04_dessci/3

Hofmann, J., Katzenbach, C., & Gollatz, K. (2017). Between coordination and regulation: Finding the governance in internet governance. *New Media and Society, 19*(9), 1406–1423. https://doi.org/10.1177/1461444816639975

Houben, R. (2019). Cryptocurrencies from a money laundering and tax evasion perspective. *International Company and Commercial Law Review, 30*(5), 261–71.

Information Commissioner's Office. (2021). Introduction to anonymisation. https://ico.org.uk/media/about-the-ico/consultations/2619862/anonymisation-intro-and-first-chapter.pdf

Jabbar, R., Fetais, N., Kharbeche, M., Krichen, M., Barkaoui, K., & Shinoy, M. (2021). Blockchain for the internet of vehicles: How to use blockchain to secure vehicle-to-everything (V2X) communication and payment? *IEEE Sensors Journal, 21*(14), 15807–15823. https://doi.org/10.1109/JSEN.2021.3062219

Johnstone, S. (2021). Acquiring the tradition. In S. Johnstone (Ed.), *Rethinking the regulation of cryptoassets. Cryptographic consensus technology and the new prospect*. Edward Elgar. https://doi.org/10.4337/9781800886797.00010

Kaal, W. A., & Vermeulen, E. P. M. (2017). How to regulate disruptive innovation – from facts to data. *Jurimetrics, 57*, 43pp. https://doi.org/10.2139/ssrn.2808044

Kamišalić, A., Kramberger, R., & Fister, I., Jr. (2021). Synergy of blockchain technology and data mining techniques for anomaly detection. *Applied Sciences, 11*(17), 7987. https://doi.org/10.3390/app11177987

Karasek-Wojciechowicz, I. (2021). Reconciliation of anti-money laundering instruments and European data protection requirements in permissionless blockchain spaces. *Journal of Cybersecurity, 7*, tyab004. https://doi.org/10.1093/cybsec/tyab004

Katona, T. (2021). Decentralized finance: The possibilities of a blockchain 'money lego' system. *Financial and Economic Review, 20*(1), 74–102. https://doi.org/10.33893/FER.20.1.74102

Kaufmann, D., & Kraay, A. (2008). Governance indicators: Where are we, where should we be going? *The World Bank Research Observer, 23*(1). https://hdl.handle.net/10986/7588

König, L., Korobeinikova, Y., Tjoa, S., & Kieseberg, P. (2020). Comparing blockchain standards and recommendations. *Future Internet, 12*, 222. https://doi.org/10.3390/fi12120222

Lessig, L. (1996). The zones of cyberspace. *Stanford Law Review, 48*, 1403, 1408. https://doi.org/10.2307/1229391

Lessig, L. (1998). The new chicago school. *Journal of Legal Studies, 27*(S2), 661–691. https://doi.org/10.1086/468039

Lessig, L. (1999). *Code and other laws of cyberspace*. Basic Books. https://lessig.org/images/resources/1999-Code.pdf

Lessig, L. (2006). *Code v. 2.0*. Basic Books. https://archive.org/details/Code2.0

Li, Z., Xiang, Z., Gong, W., & Wang, H. (2022). Unified model for collective and point anomaly detection using stacked temporal convolution networks. *Applied Intelligence, 52*(3), 3118–3131. https://doi.org/10.1007/s10489-021-02559-0

Lootsma, Y. (2017). Blockchain as the newest regtech application - the opportunity to reduce the burden of KYC for financial institutions. *Banking & Financial Services Policy Report, 36*(8), 16–21.

Magnuson, W. (2020). *Blockchain democracy: Technology, law and the rule of the crowd*. Cambridge University Press. https://doi.org/10.1017/9781108687294

Marsden, C. (2011). Internet co-regulation and constitutionalism: Towards a more nuanced view. 10.2139/ssrn.1973328

Maupin, J. (2017). Mapping the global legal landscape of blockchain technologies. *CIGI Papers*. https://www.cigionline.org/sites/default/files/documents/Paper

Mercan, S., Kurt, A., Akkaya, K., & Erdin, E. (2021). Cryptocurrency solutions to enable micropayments in consumer IoT. *IEEE Consumer Electronics Magazine, 11*, 97–103. https://doi.org/10.1109/MCE.2021.3060720

Michalopoulos, P., Olowookere, O., Pocher, N., Sedlmeir, J., Veneris, A., & Puri, P. (2024). Compliance design options for offline cbdcs: Balancing privacy and AML/CFT. In *Proceedings of the IEEE International Conference on Blockchain and Cryptocurrency (ICBC)*. https://doi.org/10.1109/ICBC59979.2024.10634398

Monti, M. (2010). A new strategy for the single market - at the service of Europe's economy and society. https://www.europarl.europa.eu/document/activities/cont/201005/20100527ATT75093/20100527ATT75093EN.pdf

Möslein, F. (2019). Conflicts of laws and codes. Defining the boundaries of digital jurisdictions. In P. Hacker, I. Lianos, G. Dimitropoulos, & S. Eich (Eds.), *Regulating blockchain: Techno-social and legal challenges*. Oxford University Press.

Murphy, S., & Cooper, C. (2016). Can smart contracts be legally binding contracts? https://www.nortonrosefulbright.com/-/media/files/nrf/nrfweb/imported/norton-rose-fulbright--r3-smart-contracts-white-paper-key-findings-nov-2016.pdf

Nabilou, H. (2019). Testing the waters of the rubicon: The European Central Bank and Central Bank digital currencies. *Journal of Banking Regulation, 21*(4), 299–314. https://doi.org/10.1057/s41261-019-00112-1

Newman, A., & Bach, D. (2014). The European Union as hardening agent: Soft law and the diffusion of global financial regulation. *Journal of European Public Policy, 21*(3), 430–452. https://doi.org/10.1080/13501763.2014.882968

Nicoll, C., Prins, C. J. E. J., & van Dellen, M. J. M. (2003). *Digital anonymity and the law: Tensions and dimensions*. T.M.C. Asser Press.

Oad, A., Razaque, A., Tolemyssov, A., Alotaibi, M., Alotaibi, B., & Zhao, C. (2021). Blockchain-enabled transaction scanning method for money laundering detection. *Electronics, 10*(15), 1766. https://doi.org/10.3390/electronics10151766

Pagallo, U., Casanovas, P., & Madelin, R. (2019). The middle-out approach: Assessing models of legal governance in data protection, artificial intelligence, and the web of data. *Theory and Practice of Legislation, 7*(1), 1–25. https://doi.org/10.1080/20508840.2019.1664543

Palmirani, M. (2011). Legislative change management with Akoma-Ntoso. In G. Sartor, M. Palmirani, E. Francesconi, & M. A. Biasiotti (Eds.), *Legislative XML for the semantic web* (pp. 101–130). Springer. https://doi.org/10.1007/978-94-007-1887-6_7

Palmirani, M., Governatori, G., Athan, T., Boley, H., Paschke, A., & Wyner, A. (2017). Legalruleml core specification version 1.0. https://docs.oasis-open.org/legalruleml/legalruleml-core-spec/v1.0/legalruleml-core-spec-v1.0.html

Palmirani, M., Sperberg, R., Vergottini, G., & Vitali, F. (2018). Akoma ntoso version 1.0 part 1: XML vocabulary. http://docs.oasis-open.org/legaldocml/akn-core/v1.0/akn-core-v1.0-part1-vocabulary.html

Palmirani, M., & Vitali, F. (2011). Akoma-Ntoso for legal documents. In G. Sartor, M. Palmirani, E. Francesconi, & M. A. Biasiotti (Eds.), *Legislative XML for the semantic web* (pp. 75–100). Springer. https://doi.org/10.1007/978-94-007-1887-6_6

Peroni, S., Palmirani, M., & Vitali, F. (2017). Undo: The united nations system document ontology. In *Proceedings of The Semantic Web – ISWC 2017: 16th International Semantic Web Conference* (pp. 175–183). Springer. https://doi.org/10.1007/978-3-319-68204-4_18

Pocher, N., & Veneris, A. (2022). Privacy and transparency in CBDCS: A regulation-by-design AML/CFT scheme. *IEEE Transactions on Network and Service Management, 19*(2), 1776–88. https://doi.org/10.1109/TNSM.2021.3136984

Pocher, N., & Zichichi, M. (2022). Towards CBDC-based machine-to-machine payments in consumer IoT. In *Proceedings of the 37th ACM/SIGAPP Symposium on Applied Computing*. https://doi.org/10.1145/3477314.3507078

Pocher, N., Zichichi, M., Merizzi, F., Shafiq, M. Z., & Ferretti, S. (2023). Detecting anomalous cryptocurrency transactions: An AML/CFT application of machine learning-based forensics. *Electronic Markets, 33*(1), 37. https://doi.org/10.1007/s12525-023-00654-3

PPI AG. (2020). Internet of payments. https://www.ppi.de/en/payments/next-generation-payments/study-internet-of-payments-iop/

Prasad, R., & Rohokale, V. (2020). Internet of things (IoT) and machine to machine (M2M) communication. In *Cyber security: The lifeline of information and communication technology* (pp. 125–141). Springer. https://doi.org/10.1007/978-3-030-31703-4_9

Quiniou, M. (2019). *Blockchain: The advent of disintermediation*. Wiley.

Ranchordás, S. (2015). Innovation experimentalism in the age of the sharing economy. *Lewis & Clark Law Review, 19*, 871. https://law.lclark.edu/live/files/21702-lcb194art1ranchordaspdf

Regulation (EU) 2022/858. (2022). Regulation EU 2022/858 of the European Parliament and of the Council of 30 May 2022 on a pilot regime for market infrastructures based on distributed ledger technology, and amending Regulations EU No 600/2014 and EU No 909/2014 and Directive 2014/65/EU. http://data.europa.eu/eli/reg/2022/858/oj

Regulation (EU) 2023/1114. (2023). Regulation (EU) 2023/1114 of the European Parliament and of the Council of 31 May 2023 on markets in crypto-assets, and amending regulations (EU) no 1093/2010 and (EU) no 1095/2010 and directives 2013/36/eu and (EU) 2019/1937. http://data.europa.eu/eli/reg/2023/1114/oj

Regulation (EU) 2024/1620. (2024). Regulation (EU) 2024/1620 of the European Parliament and of the Council of 31 May 2024 establishing the authority for anti-money laundering and countering the financing of terrorism and amending regulations (EU) no 1093/2010, (EU) no 1094/2010 and (EU) no 1095/2010. http://data.europa.eu/eli/reg/2024/1620/oj

Regulation (EU) 2024/1624. (2024). Regulation (EU) 2024/1624 of the European Parliament and of the Council of 31 May 2024 on the prevention of the use of the financial system for the purposes of money laundering or terrorist financing. http://data.europa.eu/eli/reg/2024/1624/oj

Reidenberg, J. R. (1998). Lex informatica: The formulation of information policy rules through technology. *Texas Law Review, 76*(3), 552, 556. https://ir.lawnet.fordham.edu/faculty_scholarship/42

Reyes, C. L. (2016). Moving beyond bitcoin to an endogenous theory of decentralized ledger technology regulation: An initial proposal. *Villanova Law Review, 61*. https://digitalcommons.law.villanova.edu/vlr/vol61/iss1/5

Reyes, C. L. (2017). Conceptualising cryptolaw. *Nebraska Law Review, 2*, 384–445. https://digitalcommons.unl.edu/nlr/vol96/iss2/8

Schrepel, T. (2021a). *Blockchain + antitrust: The decentralisation formula*. Edward Elgar. https://doi.org/10.4337/9781800885530

Schrepel, T. (2021b). Smart contracts and the digital single market through the lens of a "law + technology" approach. https://op.europa.eu/en/publication-detail/-/publication/224da7da-1c18-11ec-b4fe-01aa75ed71a1/language-en

Schweizer, A., Knoll, P., Urbach, N., von der Gracht, H. A., & Hardjono, T. (2020). To what extent will blockchain drive the machine economy? Perspectives from a prospective study. *IEEE Transactions on Engineering Management, 67*(4), 1169–1183. https://doi.org/10.1109/TEM.2020.2979286

Scott, J., & Trubek, D. M. (2002). Mind the gap: Law and new approaches to governance in the European union. *European Law Journal, 8*(1), 4–6. https://doi.org/10.1111/1468-0386.00139

Shayegan, M. J., Sabor, H. R., Uddin, M., & Chen, C.-L. (2022). A collective anomaly detection technique to detect crypto wallet frauds on the bitcoin network. *Symmetry, 14*(2), 328. https://doi.org/10.3390/sym14020328

Sin, F. Y., Moroney, R. A., & Strydom, M. (2015). Principles-based versus rules-based auditing standards: The effect of the transition from AS2 to AS5. *International Journal of Auditing, 19*, 282–294. https://doi.org/10.1111/ijau.12045

Surden, H. (2012). Computable contracts. *University of California Davis Law Review*, 46–629. https://scholar.law.colorado.edu/faculty-articles/148

Torra, V. (2017). *Data privacy: Foundations, new developments and the big data challenge*. Springer. https://doi.org/10.1007/978-3-319-57358-8

Trubek, D. M., & Trubek, L. G. (2007). New governance & legal regulation: Complementarity, rivalry, and transformation. *Columbia Journal of European Law, 13*(3), 539–564. https://cjel.law.columbia.edu/print/2016/new-governance-legal-regulation-complementarity-rivalry-and-transformation/

Tsuchiya, Y., & Hiramoto, N. (2021). Dark web in the dark: Investigating when transactions take place on cryptomarkets. *Forensic Science International: Digital Investigation, 36*. https://doi.org/10.1016/j.fsidi.2020.301093

Verbruggen, P. (2009). Does co-regulation strengthen EU legitimacy? *European Law Journal, 15*, 425. https://doi.org/10.1111/j.1468-0386.2009.00471.x

Vitali, F., Palmirani, M., & Parisse, V. (2019). Akoma Ntoso naming convention version 1.0. https://docs.oasis-open.org/legaldocml/akn-nc/v1.0/akn-nc-v1.0.html

Vitali, F., Palmirani, M., Sperberg, R., & Parisse, V. (2018). Akoma Ntoso version 1.0. Part 2: Specifications. http://docs.oasis-open.org/legaldocml/akn-core/v1.0/akn-core-v1.0-part2-specs.html

Weber, M., Chen, J., Suzumura, T., Pareja, A., Ma, T., Kanezashi, H., Kaler, T., Leiserson, C. E., & Schardl, T. B. (2018). Scalable graph learning for anti-money laundering: A first look. https://arxiv.org/abs/1812.00076

Weber, M., Domeniconi, G., Chen, J., Weidele, D. K. I., Bellei, C., Robinson, T., & Leiserson, C. E. (2019). Anti-money laundering in bitcoin: Experimenting with graph convolutional networks for financial forensics. In *Proceedings of the Conference on Knowledge Discovery and Data Mining, Workshop on Anomaly Detection in Finance*. ACM. https://arxiv.org/abs/1908.02591

Werbach, K. (2019). *The blockchain and the new architecture of trust*. The MIT Press. https://doi.org/10.7551/mitpress/11449.001.0001

Werbach, K., & Cornell, N. (2017). Contracts ex machina. *Duke Law Journal, 67*, 101–170. https://scholarship.law.duke.edu/dlj/vol67/iss2/2

World Economic Forum. (2020). Crypto, what is it good for? An overview of cryptocurrency use cases. https://www3.weforum.org/docs/WEF_Cryptocurrency_Uses_Cases_2020.pdf

Wright, A., & De Filippi, P. (2015). Decentralized blockchain technology and the rise of lex cryptographia. 10.2139/ssrn.2580664

Wu, T. (2003). When code isn't law. *Virginia Law Review, 89*, 103–106. https://scholarship.law.columbia.edu/faculty_scholarship/844

Yeung, K. (2017). Hypernudge: Big data as a mode of regulation by design. *Information, Communication & Society, 20*(1), 118–136. https://doi.org/10.1080/1369118X.2016.1186713

Yeung, K. (2019). Regulation by blockchain: The emerging battle for supremacy between the code of law and code as law. *Modern Law Review, 82*(2), 207–239. https://doi.org/10.1111/1468-2230.12399

Yeung, K., & Ranchordás, S. (2024). *An introduction to law and regulation: Text and materials* (2nd edn.). University Press. https://doi.org/10.1017/9781009379007

Zetzsche, D. A., Arner, D. W., & Buckley, R. P. (2020). Decentralized finance. *Journal of Financial Regulation, 6*(2), 172–203. https://doi.org/10.1093/jfr/fjaa010

Zetzsche, D. A., Buckley, R. P., Arner, D. W., & Barberis, J. N. (2017). Regulating a revolution: From regulatory sandboxes to smart regulation. https://ir.lawnet.fordham.edu/jcfl/vol23/iss1/2/

Zimmerman, M. (2017). Your DMCA safe harbor questions answered. https://assets.fenwick.com/legacy/FenwickDocuments/DMCA-QA.pdf

Zunzunegui, F. (2022). How to regulate digital financial platforms: A research agenda. *Journal of International Banking Law and Regulation, 3*, 25pp. https://doi.org/10.2139/ssrn.4262693

Chapter 8
Concluding Remarks

8.1 Anonymity and an Unwarranted Double Standard

From a general perspective, two opposing elements emerged from this investigation into the interplay between the AML/CFT regime and crypto-asset ecosystems. On the one hand, the complexity of the underlying technologies has over time generated ambiguities concerning the specifics of relevant platforms and stakeholders. Preliminarily, the phenomenological picture of these ecosystems appears blurry regarding the degree of disintermediation and non-centralisation featured in different cases. Clearly, this goes to the detriment of any idea of accountability one may wish to establish. On the other hand, the 'blockchain hype' informed an overall perception that everything about crypto-assets is disruption, and that any regulatory framework—AML/CFT measures in particular, given their intermediary-based nature—is unravelled by the innovations brought about in this sphere. Often, disintermediation and non-centralisation are (mis)interpreted not only in terms of whether they are indeed featured by a given scenario, but also in terms of their consequences. Illustratively, on the one hand CEXes are treated like traditional financial intermediaries, and on the other one DEXes are portrayed as an unreachable underworld, often without considering key differences among them.

This does not mean these positions are completely unfounded. As explored in this work, it is challenging to grasp the traits that can be featured by a crypto-asset ecosystem or even by only one of its many stakeholders and components. At times it may be even impossible, before enough information is released about a specific project—e.g., in the relevant whitepaper or CBDC design report. Likewise, many of the concepts that underpin the enhanced disintermediation evolution are indeed disrupting the centralisation paradigm that is at the heart of traditional intermediary-based accountability mechanisms. Nonetheless, the twofold reasoning above can be challenged, insofar as it gives rise to a very odd outcome: although crypto-assets are not understood in full, and there is often a lack of clarity when discussing the

N. Pocher, *Crypto-Asset Ecosystems and the EU Anti-Money Laundering Framework*, Law, Governance and Technology Series 76,
https://doi.org/10.1007/978-3-031-94698-1_8

activities taking place within these ecosystems—e.g., in terms of identifying entities to be entrusted with regulatory duties—, there is somehow a sense of certainty that traditional regulatory principles and approaches must be changed entirely to address them. In this sense, one may argue there is a widespread confusion between the need to find the appropriate approach for handling regulatory issues of crypto-assets and the need to re-evaluate previous regulatory policy decisions because of the advent of crypto-assets. This does not mean policy decisions should not be changed or updated, but that adjusting the regulatory approach does not entail per se changing any determination concerning the values to protect and the objectives of the given framework. In other words, these elements are obviously related but should remain separate and treated accordingly when regulating new spheres.

Anonymity in crypto-assets is a perfect example of this tendency to use a double standard when it comes to crypto-assets. For instance, as explored in Chap. 7 the prohibition of anonymous bearer shares or prepaid cards seems to originate fewer controversies than the regulatory treatment of self-hosted wallets or privacy coins. The same is true for the trait of disintermediation and its interplay with the enforcement phase—e.g., different types of limits are placed on cash transactions, even if it is still possible to pass on a bag full of cash in a dark alley. The point is making this occurrence more difficult, by hindering any exploitation of financial operators in the endeavour to fill the bag of cash and/or make use of its content by disguising its origin, and to make it easier to detect these situations. By contrast, we debate on whether the (supposed) impossibility of enforcement of limitations on self-hosted wallets or DEXes should restrain any proposals for limitations.

Arguably, this double standard stems from the fact that in recent years crypto-assets, in combination with the increasing amount of personal data collected every day and the possibility to exploit it very efficiently for a vast array of purposes, created a heightened sensitivity to the importance of privacy and data protection. This, in turn, had an impact on the public perception as to the acceptable trade-off between anonymity and transparency, between privacy and the risks of surveillance, also in terms of financial transactions. Despite the importance of these considerations, this issue should not be confused or merged with the impossibility of implementing current regulatory frameworks in innovative spheres.

The crypto-asset space is complex, but its dynamics are not impossible to understand. Since the endeavour requires a less traditional form of interdisciplinary knowledge, it is likely that legal experts cannot sufficiently understand it with their own background. This means they must engage in cross-disciplinary endeavours and establish new forms of collaborations to grasp and address the challenges at stake. At the same time, the simple fact that a new scenario alters dynamics and benchmarks does not necessarily unravel regulation, and the need for new approaches does not mean that nothing can be saved. It does, however, require phenomenological analyses on which to structure new regulatory methodologies and processes.

Against this backdrop, these conclusions pivot on four pillars, addressed by the following sections. These pillars mirror the multi-layered approach deployed throughout this work and pertain to different levels of reasoning. The final output of this book consists of their combination. In particular, the remainder of these concluding remarks outlines findings concerning: (a) the anonymity-transparency trade-offs featured by crypto-asset socio-technical ecosystems, (b) the application of a holistic approach to drafting a risk-based taxonomy, (c) the value of establishing a polycentric techno-regulatory standardisation model in the EU, methodologically grounded on (d) 'regulation-enabled compliance through design'.

8.2 Anonymity-Transparency Trade-Offs in Crypto-Asset Socio-Technical Ecosystems

This work explored the interplay between crypto-assets and AML/CFT regulation from the viewpoint of anonymity risks vis-à-vis the transparent nature featured by some DLT implementations. Anonymity and transparency are pivotal notions in the world of DLTs and are considered inherent features of crypto-assets. In the development of the latter, encryption and ledger transparency played a key role. Anonymity and transparency are also key notions in the AML/CFT sphere, where anonymity generates risks of misuse of financial systems, while transparency aids compliance, supervision, investigation, and enforcement. This twofold perspective has long populated online communication and financial transactions, where anonymity is double-edged: it fosters illegality, but its absence violates human rights, posing at the same time AML/CFT and privacy concerns. Crypto-assets are a prime example of this dynamic.

While disambiguating the notions of anonymity and transparency, this work argued in favour of a teleological methodology. In other words, the analysis was informed by the specifics of the context, composed of crypto-assets and the AML/CFT framework. The latter is anchored to a domain-specific vision of mitigating risks generated by transactions that fall outside regulatory accountability mechanisms. The consequent understanding of anonymity, albeit not clearly defined, is tied to the intermediary-based nature of the regime. When applied to crypto-assets, this approach generates problems showcased by challenges such as the crypto travel rule, transfers involving self-hosted wallets, and difficulties in linking transactions to real-world identities.

The complexity that informs crypto-assets as ecosystems of socio-technical ecosystems is another element that warrants the adoption of a teleological approach to the definitions of anonymity and transparency. This helps develop a conceptual understanding of both their nature and their regulatory impacts. Indeed, the socio-technical essence of the crypto-asset space generates a granularisation of the concepts of anonymity and transparency. Since the characteristics of an ecosystem depend on technical and social elements, and on their interaction, crypto-asset features are inevitably multi-layered and can vary significantly. Transactions take place within and/or across ecosystems populated by many stakeholders, services, technical layers, where the concept of anonymity comes into play in different forms.

Accordingly, a 'dynamic' approach is needed. On the basis of the traits identified in this work, chiefly at the core of Chaps. 3 and 4, when specifics of crypto-assets meet the AML/CFT regime the concept of anonymity displays the features listed below.

- *Conceptually granular*: Anonymity is composed of different features. Their individual importance depends on the given perspective. Several elements are used as benchmarks to evaluate the anonymity of a crypto-asset scheme—e.g., they encompass notions of traceability, linkability, identifiability, pseudonymity, confidentiality, and privacy. These terms are often used imprecisely, also equated with anonymity, and their definitions are not always consistent—e.g., studies may anchor their assessments to the same metrics, but rely on different interpretations of them, thus giving different meanings to the same benchmarks.
- *Context specific*: Anonymity is a context-specific notion, which means its definition is bound to vary depending on the context. In the AML/CFT sphere, an anonymous transaction is one that cannot be related to an identified or identifiable individual. Relatedly, a subject is identifiable for a specific purpose when the entity in charge of the identification process can access the required data. Thus, anonymity can be evaluated only with respect to specific requirements against which to determine if identification has been reached.
- *Observer dependent*: Anonymity can be assessed only with respect to a specific actor trying to reach identification. A subject is identifiable if the entity in charge of identification can access the required data. A subject is identifiable or non-identifiable only with reference to a specific actor.
- *Broader understanding than other frameworks*: In AML/CFT, anonymity has a broader meaning than in other frameworks (e.g., data protection). It does not distinguish between anonymisation and strong pseudonymisation. It encompasses both the impossibility to link data to an identified person, and cases where the link is (only) significantly hampered. It follows that the same data can qualify as pseudonymous for data protection purposes and anonymous for AML/CFT ones.
- *Different from privacy*: Anonymity (better, anonymisation) is only one of the available techniques for enhancing privacy. In particular, anonymity requires the absence of identifiers. If there are identifiers, there is pseudonymity. Hence, both anonymity and pseudonymity relate to identity. Privacy is a broader concept and can be safeguarded in ways other than anonymity, and to different extents. Thus, techniques to enhance privacy do not necessarily exert impacts on identification.
- *Ranging on a spectrum*: Anonymity and transparency are not a zero-sum game. There is no perfect dichotomy between irresponsible anonymity and accountable identification. Along a spectrum ranging from complete anonymity to full transparency, at any given point the two features coexist in a specific balance. A subject/item is not identified or anonymous: these traits are combined into a specific trade-off.
- *Linked to disintermediation and obfuscation*: Crypto-asset ecosystems are more intermediated than expected, but trends of enhanced disintermediation pose substantial anonymity risks. Meanwhile, anonymity can be linked to cases of

transaction obfuscation and opaqueness of financial flows. These can be tied to traits of untraceability, unidentifiability and unlinkability, depending on the specifics.

- *Influenced by the interplay between forensics and anonymity enhancements*: Anonymity is influenced by the interplay of forensics and anonymity enhancements. Since they benchmark the level of traceability, forensic techniques operate as a trait d'union between pseudonymity and (un)accountability. Their role is defining the possibility and likelihood of linking a real-world identity to a (set of) crypto-asset transaction(s). This depends on their efficacy vis-à-vis privacy-enhancing methods. At the same time, the quality and efficacy of forensics influence anonymity enhancements, by prompting new means of obfuscation.
- *Mirroring unaccountability*: Cyber-libertarians advocate for a cyberspace where everyone operates anonymously and outside any accountability mechanism. Technology can be leveraged to reach opposing goals, and crypto-assets are a prime example of how it can generate pathways to accountability (e.g., forensics) but also to unaccountability (e.g., anonymity-enhancing methods). Anonymous transactions are tainted by the unaccountability of those performing them, while enhanced disintermediation and obfuscation are tied with (and at times pursue as a direct or indirect goal) unaccountability.

Meanwhile, the understanding of transparency relevant to this work required a twofold analysis, as exemplified below, between the notions of ledger transparency and financial transparency. The analysis is tightly tied to the concepts of auditability and accountability.

- *Ledger transparency*: The goal of many public blockchains is to combine user anonymity (better, pseudonymity) with transparency of operations. The ledger is transparent, and the complete transaction history is available to everyone. Network participants, however, are not related to their real-world identities, but to addresses that act as pseudonyms. Transparency of operations is a type of transparency that does not ensure accountability and differs from financial transparency. The type of transparency offered by public blockchains is a type of transparency useful for user interaction, not for oversight bodies.
- *Financial transparency*: Financial transparency is grounded on the connection to real-world identities—i.e., it relies on identifiability. From a regulatory perspective the notion of transparency is the one that aims to fight money laundering and terrorist financing, and this understanding is focused on the information on the origin of funds and on the identification of clients and intermediaries.
- *Auditability*: Financial transparency is tied to the concept of allowing auditability. While auditability assumes that access to a certain type of information is allowed in certain circumstances and by specific actors, it does not breach confidentiality of crypto-asset transactions.
- *Mirroring accountability*: The quest for transparency to ensure accountability is a common-place goal not only in the financial context, but also in information networks. The goal of ensuring auditability is to hold users accountable for their activities. Accountability is ensured by auditability.

Against this backdrop, the alleged paradox of public blockchains featuring both anonymity and transparency traits can be reframed as a combination of features whose interplay can be measured and reconciled by using benchmarked trade-offs and a teleological methodology. From the perspective of this research, the goal is the identification of specific benchmarks to differentiate between the various degrees of anonymity enshrined by crypto-asset ecosystems. The approach of this work starts from conceptualising the existing trade-offs between, on the one hand, anonymity and privacy and, on the other hand, transparency and auditability.

As highlighted in Chap. 6, the current large-scale interest in CBDCs offers an invaluable chance to understand the way their features are influenced by technical and social factors. When devising the design of a CBDC model, a trade-off is chosen between privacy, anonymity, and transparency, which sheds a light on how these characteristics play out in crypto-asset ecosystems as well. Most CBDC proposals offer some privacy to end-users and some visibility to authorities and/or other participants of the system. These 'mixed solutions' provide options tailored to given types of transactions and/or users (e.g., higher anonymity for low-value transactions and low-balance wallets). These trade-offs can be addressed from the perspectives of confidentiality and auditability, with direct impact on AML/CFT accountability. Relevant schemes can be classified as per these embedded trade-offs.

In this context, accountability emerges as a key conceptual link. Both obfuscation and disintermediation, hampering traceability, generate a situation where users are not accountable for their activities (e.g., transactions). While some stakeholders are trying to avoid regulatory constraints and surveillance, others are trying to re-establish it by applying different techniques, thus engaging in a never-ending race. On the ground of the socio-technical nature of crypto-asset ecosystems, the activities performed by this plethora of actors influence the overall character of the domain. Against this backdrop, the added challenge brought by crypto-assets when addressing the trade-offs between anonymity and transparency is not the presence of this interplay, but rather its peculiar and ever-evolving socio-technical composition.

8.3 A Holistic Approach to a Risk-Based Taxonomy Effort

A methodological outcome of this work concerns the value of taxonomies to enable cross-disciplinary cooperation, as introduced in Chap. 2. The approach has already proven conducive to balancing flexibility with precision in the realm of tokens. Provided it leverages both principle-based and rules-based methodologies, it can mitigate the risk of overfitting. Taxonomising allows the levels of anonymity risk posed by different crypto-assets and/or ecosystems to be evaluated and categorised accordingly. This can be done after having pinpointed the benchmarks of AML/CFT anonymity risk—emerged as chiefly linked to enhanced intermediation and obfuscation—and requires that the assessments be accompanied by details justifying the classification—e.g., criteria should be parameterised.

Such a taxonomy effort mirrors an interrelation exercise between empirical phenomena and theoretical schemes, which is grounded on selecting yardsticks on which to ground techno-regulatory reasoning. This approach is deployed in the preliminary taxonomy of CBDC designs provided in Chap. 6. The model is based on embedded privacy-transparency trade-offs, grounded on the possibility to link regulatory considerations (e.g., auditability, confidentiality) to socio-technical factors (e.g., PETs, wallet types, public-private models). However, since concepts of anonymity and transparency are socio-technical, it remains to be explored whether all AML/CFT risks can be effectively modelled in a taxonomy fashion and, if not, scope limitations and complementary approaches must be provided.

From a regulatory perspective, the value of deploying a 'system approach' lies in embracing the elements at play when devising a strategy to approach these ecosystems, thus avoiding reaching conclusions that are refuted by phenomenology. In this respect, this work argued that the difficulty in applying regulation to crypto-assets stems from the concurrent presence of (i) assets, such as the different types of tokens, (ii) a set of technologies deployable to different ends (e.g., P2P technologies, distributed systems, tokenisation); (iii) innovative actors (e.g., developers, miners, exchanges, FinTech companies, P2P platforms); (iv) traditional actors, such as traditional financial institutions; (v) different scopes of application of the technologies, at times overlapping or concurring (e.g., financial applications, supply chain, self-sovereign identity, and certification). The combination of these elements shapes crypto-assets and mirrors its nature of an ecosystem of socio-technical ecosystems.

Accordingly, the socio-technical nature of crypto-asset ecosystems requires that the modelling of anonymity and transparency deploys a methodology that is both suitable to measure AML/CFT risk and able to encompass a holistic perspective. Indeed, crypto-asset ecosystems feature a given anonymity-transparency trade-off for multiple reasons, including the way the systems generating and exchanging payment tokens are construed and governed. Hence, it is necessary to focus on the landscape in which crypto-assets are transferred through an accountability-based approach. This entails focusing on the evolution of non-centralisation and disintermediation scenarios, and on the interplay between the different socio-technical dimensions—e.g., interplay between forensics and anonymity enhancements.

In particular, as explored in Chaps. 4 and 5 the AML/CFT domain makes use of 'red flag indicators' where empirical elements suggesting suspicious activities are described to guide compliance responses and supervision. Chief reference is to the indicators published by the FATF, which substantially inform national and institutional guidance. These indicators are a key feature of RBA-based frameworks, and are usually provided in rules-based format, phrased as templates of sequences of actions that suggest a suspicion. A pivotal aspect concerns the methodology and style used to draft risk indicators to help detecting anomalous activities.

Red flag indicators operate as empirical measures of risks, and they provide a structure to think about them. In principle, they should provide clear benchmarks and their structure should be able to accommodate new indicators as the sphere evolves. The content of rules-based indicators, however, is often less straightforward

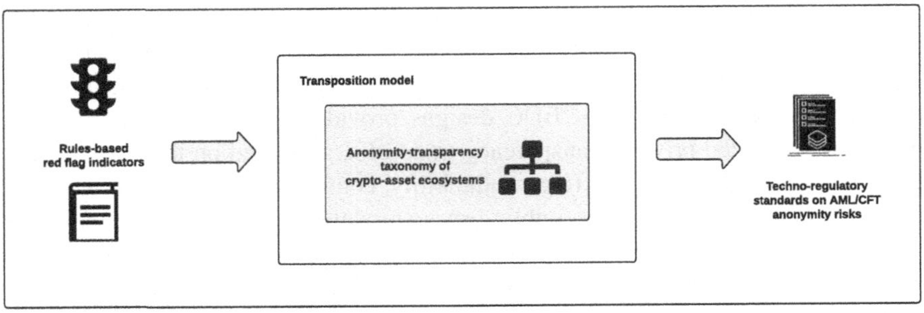

Fig. 8.1 Interplay between the proposed taxonomy and the proposed transposition model between red flag indicators and techno-regulatory standards. Based on Pocher (2023)

than desired. Moreover, depending on the link with empirical findings—i.e., the phenomenological aspects highlighted in Chap. 2—they may feature little normative content, and be for the most part descriptive. Furthermore, there can be considerable gaps between the indicators and industry best practices (e.g., crypto travel rule debate). Lastly, although rules-based systems have the advantage of interpretability, their simplicity produces an outstanding number of false positives—i.e., reportedly, more than 95% of the alerts generated from rule-matching are false positives.

While RegTech tools embedding machine learning are innovating this sphere, other initiatives may aid and support the development of more effective and efficient applications. In this respect, this work argued in favour of the creation of a 'transposition model' between red flag indicators and techno-regulatory standards. This model could help clarify the meaning of the indicators, streamline compliance at the regulated entity-level and would enshrine the holistic approach outlined above with regard to anonymity-transparency trade-offs. Indeed, as exemplified in Fig. 8.1 above, the model would draw directly from the mentioned taxonomy. Ideally, the findings included in the taxonomy could allow it to be used directly as a source of risk indicators, and the transposition process could happen in the framework of the competences entrusted to the AMLA. In particular, both their drafting and their implementation could be eased by developing standards with the private entities offering analytics services and sharing them in an open-source format.

8.4 Polycentric Techno-Regulatory Standardisation in the EU

The mentioned taxonomy should be grounded on the establishment of an institutionalised regime of techno-regulatory standards featuring the participation of a large array of actors in the regulatory process. This approach may provide a substantial insight into the risks to be mitigated and would leverage inputs from both AML/CFT efforts and technical standardisation on DLTs and crypto-assets.

Indeed, crypto-asset-related technical and regulatory standardisation is currently siloed, and in the AML/CFT domain there is a lack of the type of standardisation that allows automation of the compliance process for what concerns risk indicators. In this context, the design of AML/CFT compliance in CBDC systems can inspire a broader discussion on the value of standardisation in the crypto-asset space.

One of the goals of establishing cross-disciplinary collaboration is to bridge the gap between the dynamism of technologies and stringent rules-based regulatory approaches. Indeed, embedding cross-disciplinarity into regulatory processes is at the heart of innovative methodologies (Chap. 7). Designing an efficient interplay of rules-based and principle-based reasoning, however, requires significant cross-disciplinary efforts. To this end, Chap. 7 suggested how an EU-level institutionalised model of techno-regulatory standardisation could provide for a legitimate and effective response. The model could be established as a multi-stakeholder scheme of co-regulation, bearing in mind the impact of global financial regulation and the technical nature of compliance in crypto-assets. In other words, this work suggests devising techno-regulatory standards through polycentric co-regulation.

In particular, this regime could be implemented within the competences of the AMLA. The AMLA is expected to draft RTSs related to almost all parts of AML/CFT compliance. These RTSs are to be drafted as per Article 290 of the TFEU, which means they are submitted to the EC for adoption, they are technical, do not imply strategic or policy choices. If multi-stakeholder participation is ensured in decision-making following the model of 'polycentric co-regulation', this type of regulatory forum could fit the crypto-asset sphere. The AMLA framework could provide a suitable scenario to blend the need for flexibility with that of ensuring an EU-wide approach. However, the content of RTSs could be shaped as to blend technical and regulatory provisions in a way that goes beyond what has been done so far. The regime and its links with the procedures to adopt RTS proposal could be explored further, in combination with the impacts on EU law legitimacy. In broad terms, large-scale stakeholder involvement may mitigate most concerns.

In this context, AML/CFT is a valuable field for proactive regulatory experimentation because its measures are inherently shaped by the RBA. This means that their application is by nature tailored to the principle of proportionality, which demands a preliminary assessment of risk levels. Meanwhile, the RBA requires consideration of a multi-level variety of risk indicators that must contribute to shaping final compliance outputs. Hence, a taxonomy-based approach, within the meaning detailed above, is consistent with an RBA-based regime, and provides a degree of flexibility that mitigates the risk of overfitting.

8.5 A 'Regulation-Enabled Compliance Through Design' Regime

The first three pillars of these conclusions enshrine an underlying proactive approach to the management of techno-regulatory dynamics. Indeed, the way they elaborate on the interlink between technical and regulatory compliance assumes the latter can be embedded into technology. This concept is at the root of design-based techniques, in contrast to traditional command and control approaches. In particular, the suggestions outlined above are informed by a methodology labelled 'regulation-enabled compliance through design', as contextualised in Chap. 7. This approach entails a shift from the controversial concepts of 'code is/as law' and 'law is/as code' to a more comprehensive and flexible notion, focused on the mutual relationship between regulation and technology, without the need to equate or even compare the two.

The notion is anchored to the need of leveraging existing cross-disciplinary initiatives to further multi-stakeholder dialogue in a way that suits the dynamics of the target to regulate. In particular, the list below outlines the different components of 'regulation-enabled compliance through design'. The order of the concepts follows the arguments presented in Chap. 7.

- **Design**: The possibility to evaluate and taxonomise anonymity-transparency trade-offs inspires the establishment of AML/CFT techno-regulatory standards. The same reasoning can be applied to design from the start applications that embed given socio-technical aspects to reach regulatory and compliance goals. Indeed, in the same way a crypto-asset scheme can be assessed in terms of its embedded anonymity-transparency trade-off by referring to specific benchmarks (e.g., implementation of certain PETs, presence in the system of both private and public actors), technology can be leveraged to embed by design a specific balance into a given application. Implementing design options often includes coding, but 'code' is only one element of 'design'.
- **Regulation and compliance**: A proactive approach to managing the interplay between technology, compliance and regulation is enshrined by design-based techniques—i.e., compliance by design, regulation by design. Operationally, they are labelled embedded compliance and embedded regulation, at times used interchangeably in an imprecise fashion. In principle, regulation by design focuses on shaping regulation starting from a design perspective, while compliance by design refers to a process grounded on embedding compliance into the design of a tool. Despite the importance of distinguishing the two phases (i.e., design of the framework, compliance measures), in practice they are two sides of the same (crypto-)coin. Indeed, this work focused on how to conceive a regulatory approach to aid compliance by design. To include the two aspects, this approach is termed 'regulation-enabled compliance by design'.
- **By and Through**: The concept of compliance through design includes social, political, institutional, governance and ethical aspects not (explicitly) included in

Table 8.1 Dynamics of regulation-enabled compliance through design

Benchmarking anonymity and transparency to socio-technical elements, to evaluate risks posed by crypto-asset ecosystems and categorise these risks accordingly, thus linking regulatory considerations to socio-technical factors	**Anonymity-transparency taxonomy of crypto-asset ecosystems in terms of money laundering and terrorist financing risks**
'Translating' (often rules-based) regulatory provisions to describe empirical phenomena, into embeddable technical specifics with regulatory content	**Transposition model between the risk indicators and techno-regulatory standards**
Drafting regulation starting from the assumption that it will be complied with through design, hence providing techno-regulatory benchmarks to comply with it through design	**Techno-regulatory standardisation**

by design approaches. In the addressed research domain, there is a concurrent presence of several elements: (i) AML/CFT framework, (ii) compliance impacts, (iii) socio-technical features of crypto-asset ecosystems, (iv) dynamics between the regulatory field and crypto-asset phenomenology. This interplay shows similarities to the reasoning underlying the formulation of 'through design' methodologies. Because of the importance of the design process in guaranteeing 'by design' outcomes, however, in this work the two perspectives are merged into the compound concept of 'through design', which includes 'by design'.

As interpreted in this work, the notion of 'regulation-enabled compliance through design' underpins (at least) three specific operational scenarios (Table 8.1). These different aspects are mutually reinforcing and are included in the transposition dynamics outlined in Fig. 8.1. Indeed, the underlying concept is the same, albeit interpreted and analysed from different viewpoints. In broad terms, the notion concerns the way to address the mutual interplay between regulation and technology.

To exemplify the approach from an operational perspective, Chap. 7 provided a use case that addresses the interplay of M2M dynamics and retail CBDCs. In doing so, it displayed a preliminary process of modelling techno-regulatory integration, as an embryonic example of the type of cross-disciplinary communication and reasoning to be institutionalised.

8.6 Final Remarks

While the substantial components of these conclusions were outlined above, two more general remarks arose from this investigation. Indeed, the interplay between the crypto-assets and AML/CFT measures, interpreted through the lens of anonymity and transparency, provides valuable insights into the relationship between law and technology. In particular, one may focus on two examples concerning the value of standardisation as well as the importance of flexibility when addressing how crypto-assets are altering traditional dynamics.

On the one hand, the value of standardisation is increasingly pivotal when regulating new technologies. This is because this type of normative structure aids the establishment of regulatory mechanisms that foster cross-disciplinarity. Indeed, it provides stakeholders with different expertise with a common playing field and common references to start building new frameworks. In particular, standardisation is key in the domain of financial regulation, as it is almost inherently composed of a mix of rules, standards, and best practices. Because the importance of standards as regulatory instruments is constantly increasing, in the upcoming years it will be crucial to make sure the relevant processes feature an actual multi-disciplinary approach. Meanwhile, the interplay between the nature of standardisation initiatives as instruments of soft law and the consequences of their transposition into hard law should be carefully addressed. Despite the value of soft law, efforts should be exerted towards the implementation of cross-disciplinary standardisation models into hard law systems. This is what is suggested by the EU model of techno-regulatory standardisation proposed in this work.

On the other hand, the understanding and the interpretation of the crypto-asset space have so far been informed by an excessive rigidity. To face the challenges posed by the socio-technical specifics of this domain, we should deploy a more flexible reasoning. Crypto-assets, but the same could be relevant to other fields of new technologies, is a notion that encompasses different scenarios. It features growing connections with the mainstream financial system, where traditional intermediaries (e.g., banks, institutional investors) are interlinked with nodes of crypto-asset ecosystems (e.g., exchanges), but also displays thriving cases of enhanced disintermediation. Some of the latter end up having more ties with the traditional system than expected, giving rise to a process that tends to look more like a cycle than a spectrum. From a methodological perspective, this requires cross-sectoral and forward-looking regulation and supervision. From a substantive perspective, it requires diversified regulatory approaches, and possible equations between certain crypto-asset activities and those involving equivalent traditional assets, to avoid exposing the regulated world to unregulated risks, either directly or indirectly.

Against this backdrop, it is important to think dynamically about this domain, without placing it into a specific category, but rather acknowledging existing differences between various instances and applications. In the years to come, the crypto-asset space is bound to house an ever-growing number of nuances between anonymity and transparency, privacy and surveillance, centralisation and non-centralisation, disintermediation and control. This is because crypto-assets, when interpreted as an ecosystem of socio-technical ecosystems, emerge as a new sphere of activities, not as a single concept. Understanding the impacts of this consideration is crucial in the endeavour to regulate this space in the most effective and legitimate way, trying to balance regulatory safeguards with the desire to foster advanced innovation and development.

Reference

Pocher, N. (2023). *Distributed Ledger Technologies Between Anonymity and Transparency: AML/CFT Regulation of Cryptocurrency Ecosystems in the EU*. Ph.D. Thesis, Alma Mater Studiorum Università di Bologna, KU Leuven, Universitat Autònoma de Barcelona. 10.48676/unibo/amsdottorato/10659

The manufacturer's authorised representative in the EU is Springer Nature Customer Service Centre GmbH, Europaplatz 3, 69115 Heidelberg, Germany. If you have any concerns regarding our products, please contact ProductSafety@springernature.com

Printed and bound by CPI Group (UK) Ltd, Croydon, CR0 4YY
30/09/2026
02225239-0011